Serena Connolly
Wisdom from Rome

Trends in Classics – Pathways of Reception

General Editors
Franco Montanari and Antonios Rengakos

Editorial Board
Lorna Hardwick, Craig Kallendorf, Fiona Macintosh, Miltos Pechlivanos

Associate Editors
Anastasia Bakogianni and Rosanna Lauriola

Volume 8

Serena Connolly
Wisdom from Rome

Reading Roman Society and European Education in the Distichs of Cato

DE GRUYTER

ISBN 978-3-11-153639-2
e-ISBN (PDF) 978-3-11-078949-2
e-ISBN (EPUB) 978-3-11-078961-4
ISSN 2629-2556

Library of Congress Control Number: 2022937149

Bibliographic information published by the Deutsche Nationalbibliothek
The Deutsche Nationalbibliothek lists this publication in the Deutsche Nationalbibliografie; detailed bibliographic data are available on the Internet at http://dnb.dnb.de.

© 2024 Walter de Gruyter GmbH, Berlin/Boston
This volume is text- and page-identical with the hardback published in 2022.
Cover image: Paul Klee, Hauptweg und Nebenwege

www.degruyter.com

Acknowledgements

It has taken a long time for this book to reach print, and I have incurred many debts along the way. The Institute for Advanced Study provided me a stimulating environment in which to work, and I benefited from many fruitful conversations, especially with Alan Bowen. I am grateful to the Mellon Foundation for supporting my year there. I also benefited from the generous feedback of audiences at Indiana University, the International Congress on Medieval Studies at Kalamazoo, New York University, and Ohio Wesleyan University.

The anonymous readers of the press offered feedback that was incisive, thorough, and enormously helpful, and I thank them for their time and care. I am grateful to Carlo Vessella, Anne Hiller, the ever-patient Katerina Zianna, and everyone at De Gruyter for shepherding this project through the publication process swiftly and efficiently. My thanks also go to Michael Hendry, who compiled the indexes.

The staff at the Bibliothèque nationale, British Library, Vatican Library, and Biblioteca Capitolare, Verona, were patient, helpful, and generous with their time. The librarians at Rutgers University Library have been indefatigable, especially during 2020 and 2021, when they worked in the most difficult circumstances. The Classics Department at Rutgers provides a warm and supportive atmosphere in which to work; thank you to my colleagues and students for your encouragement and companionship.

Finally, I owe an enormous debt to my family for putting up with me as I have spent many hours sitting at a computer—to Oliver, Roger and Hazel, and Judith and Erik. And most of all to Paul, for everything, always.

Contents

Acknowledgements — V
List of Figures — XI
Introduction — XIII

Part I: The *Distichs* and Paraenesis

1   The *Distichs* — 3
The Text — 4
  Epistula — 4
  Breves Sententiae — 5
  Maxims — 7
Title — 15
Transmission — 16
Authorship — 19
Date — 23
Audience — 36

2   Ancient Wisdom — 40
Ancient paraenesis — 40
Form — 43
Universality — 48

3   Style — 53
Syntax — 57
  Instructions — 57
  Statements of wisdom — 61
Lexical Choice — 63
  Verbs — 64
  Nouns — 65
  Adjectives and adverbs — 66
  Lexical density — 67
Stylistics — 68
Proverbial language — 68
  Negatives — 71
  Binarism — 72

Part II: Content and Context

4   Friendship —— 77
Reciprocity —— 78
Friendship's benefits —— 88
How to be a friend —— 95
Problematic friends —— 96
Fables, *gnomai*, and proverbs —— 101

5   Money —— 108
Saving and spending —— 110
Want —— 118
Wealth —— 129
Reputation —— 133

Part III: Reception

6   *Legere et intelligere*: Editions and Commentaries for Schools and Homes —— 141
Using the *Distichs* —— 142
   Medieval Period —— 142
   Renaissance —— 149
   Early Modern Period —— 151
   Modern Period —— 152
Editions —— 153
Commentaries —— 158

7   Translations and Transformations —— 168
Translations —— 169
   Medieval —— 169
   Early Modern Period —— 179
   Modern Period —— 183
Transformations —— 185

Conclusion —— 190

Appendix: Selected Translations of DC 3.24 —— 193

Works Cited —— 203
Index of Subjects —— 227
Index Locorum —— 237

List of Figures

Fig. 1: Boas' stemma of the *Disticha Catonis*. —— 19
Fig. 2: Lexical density of select poetic texts and collections. —— 68
Fig. 3: Erasmus' commentary on *DC* 3.24. Bayerische Staatsbibliothek München, 4 L.impr.c.n.mss. 108, fol. 14r, urn:nbn:de:bvb:12-bsb00011397-1. *Catonis p[rae]cepta moralia: recognita atq[ue] interpretata ab Erasmo Roterodamo. Mimi Publiani. Septem sapientu[m] illustres sententi[a]e. Institutio homi[ni]s christiani uersib. hexametris. per Erasm. Roterodamum Isocratis Par[a]enesis ad Demonicum Rudolpho Agricola interprete, recognita per Martinum Dropium*, printed 1515. Image courtesy of Bayerische Staatsbibliothek, München. —— 156
Fig. 4: Select text and commentary on *DC* 3.24[25] from Arntzenius' edition. General Collection. Beinecke Rare Book and Manuscript Library, Yale University, Gnc36 735B, p. 240. *Dionysii Catonis Disticha de moribus ad filium. Cum notis integris Scaligeri, Barthii, Daumii; scholiis atque animadversionibus selectis Erasmi, Opitii, Wachii; et metaphrasi graeca Planudis et Scaligeri. Quibus accedunt Boxhornii dissertatio, et Henrici Cannegieteri rescripta Boxhornio de Catone; nec non Joan. Hild. Withofii dissertationes binae de distichorum auctore et vera illorum lectione. Recensuit, suasque adnotationes addidit Otto Arntzenius*, published 1754. Image courtesy of Beinecke Rare Book and Manuscript Library, Yale University. —— 157

Introduction

> *Rem, tibi quam noscis aptam, dimittere noli;*
> *Fronte capillata, post haec occasio calva.*
>
> Don't let slip away what you know is right for you:
> Opportunity has hair at the front, but is bald in the back.¹
> *Distichs of Cato* 2.26

> "Let's take the instant by the forward top."
> *All's Well*, V.iii.39.

The image is striking: Opportunity (or Occasion) personified as a figure with long hair in front, but bald in the back. It is easy to visualize and to remember.² Shakespeare's knowledge of the figure most likely came from the *Distichs of Cato*,³ and indeed he was so taken with it that he used it in three plays: *Much Ado about Nothing* ("he meant to take the present time by the top" I.ii.15–16), *Othello* (where Emilia reports that Othello said "To take the saf'st occasion by the front", III.i.52), and *All's Well* (see above). The figure was so well known in the sixteenth century that it was even used as a printer's mark.⁴ That a figure from the *Distichs* should have been this familiar is unsurprising: they were the first Latin text encountered by every student of Latin for over 1000 years.

Students remembered and knew them well. There are allusions to and quotations from the *Distichs* from our earliest medieval texts: already in Columba-

---

1 Unless otherwise stated, all translations in this book are my own. Wherever there is significant discussion of one of the *Distichs*, a Latin text is supplied, along with an English rendering. In aiming primarily to convey the wisdom of the *Distichs*, the translation privileges fluency and readability over strict fidelity to the original.
2 The image has a long pedigree: it must have been well known even before the fourth century BCE, when the sculptor Lysippus used it in his Turin Relief and the Trogir Fragment. Thinking of a copy of one of them, Posidippus (*Anth. Gr.* 16.275.7–10) explains the image: Ἡ δὲ κόμη τί κατ' ὄψιν; —Ὑπαντιάσαντι λαβέσθαι, νὴ Δία. —Τάξόπιθεν πρὸς τί φαλακρὰ πέλει; —Τὸν γὰρ ἅπαξ πτηνοῖσι παραθρέξαντά με ποσσὶν οὔτις ἔθ' ἱμείρων δράξεται ἐξόπιθεν ("Q: Why does it have hair at the front? A: So that someone who comes up against it can grab it, by Jove. Q: And why is it bald in the back? A: Because no one who was once overtaken by me on my winged feet will now seize me from behind, even though he wants to.") On depictions of Opportunity through the ages, see especially Rüdiger 1966.
3 Another possible source is Phaedr. *Fab.* 5.8 (= Perry 530 = Gibbs 536), though the use of the *Distichs* as a first Latin reader—Phaedrus usually came after them in curricula—makes it the more obvious choice.
4 On the printer's mark, see Boas 1931.

nus of Saint-Trod and Eugenius of Toledo in the seventh century, in Alcuin's *Praecepta vivendi* in the eighth, and in many, many others in the centuries that followed. Indeed, according to Richard Hazelton, "It would be pointless to cite the references to Cato that appear after the twelfth century; they are to be found literally everywhere"—and his point can stand for earlier centuries too.[5]

The work of "Cato" was highly regarded through the medieval period: a panegyric of Charlemagne compared the king and emperor to Cicero and Homer, but its highest compliment was that "he outdid the renowned sayings of Cato" (*inclita ... superat ... dicta Catonis*).[6] Indeed the *Distichs* were a yardstick for measuring eloquence and intelligence: in Chaucer, among the many references to the collection, a carpenter is disparaged with the words "He knew nat Catoun for his wit was rude."[7] They were also a measure of wisdom and forethought: in *Piers Plowman*, Reason's horse-servant is called "Catoun." It is unclear whether Langland meant the name to stand for Cato, the author of the *Distichs*, or for the text itself, and the ambiguity demonstrates nicely that the Cato-type was the embodiment of the *Distichs*' lessons.[8] Indeed, the new Catotype began to take on a life of his own. For example, the *Catwg Ddoeth*, a collec-

---

[5] Hazelton 1957, 159, n. 5. The task was taken up by Manitius 1892, 164–171, whose hundreds of references cover to the end of the thirteenth century. For another list, see Pietsch 1902, 6–10. Columban of Bangor is not to be confused with Columbanus of Saint-Trod, to whom the poems previously considered the work of Columban are now attributed: see Howlett 1995, 216–223. Eugenius of Toledo's *Carmen* 38, a hexameter poem, was sometimes thought to be the fifth book of the *Distichs* and was presented in manuscripts as such. The poem is moralizing and improving like the maxims, but different in form—it is not in couplets—and no one now doubts its attribution to Eugenius. According to Nève 1926, 9, Raymond de Beziers' fourteenth-century translation of the Hindu *Kalila and Dimna* quotes many times from the *Distichs*, and he even opens his work with *Cum animadverterem quamplurimum...*, the opening words of the *Epistula*, on which see the next chapter. There is a text of his translation in Hervieux 1899, 378–775.

[6] *Carmina Angilberti* 6.72. The panegyric, attributed to the Abbot of St. Riquier, is found in Duemmler 1881, 368. Charlemagne himself was to cite *DC* 2.31 in his protest against the Nicaean Synod, *Opus Caroli contra Synodum* III.26, ll. 9–12, which is available in Freeman 1998, 463. Boas 1952, 142, does not transmit the quotation accurately: Charlemagne uses the second person throughout.

[7] *Miller's Tale* A3227. Other references to the *Distichs*, which come from Brunner 1965, are found in the *Nun's Priest's Tale* B4130–4131, 4161–4167; *Tale of Melibee* B2370, B2415, B2495–6, B2678–9, B2873, B2791–3, B2794; *Merchant's Tale* E1377–8; *Canon's Yeoman's Prologue* G688–9. On Chaucer's use of the *Distichs*, see Hazelton 1956, xxiii-xxxvii, Holton 2008, and Connolly (forthcoming).

[8] Reason's Horse appears in C.4.17. The ambiguity of the reference is mentioned by Burrow 1990, 141, n. 9. Brunner 1965, 2: a quotation in Latin from *DC* 1.21 appears after C.8.336. On Langland's use of the *Distichs*, see also Hazelton 1956, xxxvii–xliv, and Breen 2010, 195.

tion of Welsh sayings, arose from the similarity of the name *Catwg*, a native wisdom figure, with that of Cato.[9] For centuries, the *Distichs* were considered the work of the wise "Cato", a characterization that led to and was reinforced by the conflation in the medieval period and later of Cato Censorius (or Elder) and Cato Uticensis (or Younger) into one Cato-type, a paragon of wisdom and virtue.[10]

Chaucer was not alone in assuming that every (educated) person had read the *Distichs*. *Carmina Burana* 19, which opens "*Si legisse memoras / ethicam Catonis*" ("If you recall reading the wisdom of Cato") and quotes from the collection, makes clear the assumption. The fact that the *Distichs* and their author were "pagan"—a fact that Langland seems to have recognized in his otherwise Christian poem—makes the assumption all the more surprising.[11] Yet the *Distichs* were so entrenched in the essential reading material of the medieval and early modern periods that in Spanish, for example, "primer" or "reader" was rendered "catón," a term also used for political readers through the nineteenth century, such as Alonso Rodríguez' *Catón Político Christiano*.[12]

With the emergence of vernacular European languages, the *Distichs* provided inspiration, most notably for the form and content of European works of wisdom, including the medieval *Proverbs of Alfred*.[13] And with the rise of Hu-

---

9 Constantine 2008, 120.
10 The connection was not made universally: the Medieval *Accessus ad auctores*, which included an introduction to the text, did not firmly attribute the *Distichs* to either of the two historical Catos, but instead acknowledged that while some attributed it to the Elder Cato, others named it for its "wise" (*catus*) material. See Wheeler 2015, 129–134. On the development of the Cato-type, see Carron 2009.
11 Galloway 1987 notes Langland's ability to blend Cato with the wider Christianity of the poem, though Breen 2010, 25, observes that the blending was not always successful.
12 On the political catón, see Delgado 1990, 372–373.
13 On the *Proverbs of Alfred*, see Arngart 1952. Other texts influenced by the *Distichs* include, in the English tradition, the Anglo-Saxon *Fæder Lārcwidas*, "How the Wise man tauȝt his Son," *Instructions to his Son* by Peter Idley, *Ratis Raving* and its companion piece "How the Good Wijf tauȝte Hir Douȝtir," and Heywood's sixteenth-century *Dialogue of Proverbs*. The list comes from Habenicht 1963, 4–6. The *Llibre de bons amonestements* was also inspired by the earlier Italian *Dottrina del Schiavo de Bari*, on which see Glaser 1954, 93, and Aguiló i Fuster 1951. In Spain, the *Distichs*' influence is felt in the works of the Arcipreste de Talavera (see Díaz de Bustamente 1999, 22–23) and in vv. 1015–1095 of the Catalan troubadour Guylem de Cervera's long poem of the thirteenth century (Thomas 1886, 97–108, and Bizzarri 2002, 127–148). Fray Anselmo Turmeda's *Llibre de bons amonestements*, which was the most popular first reader for Catalans from the fifteenth to the nineteenth centuries, was heavily influenced by the *Distichs*; likewise the *Libro maistrevole* of Giovanni Antonio Tagliente (1524), a teaching manual of elementary Italian for adults, on which see Grendler 1989, 158–159, and Jacobson Schutte 1986. Finally, on

manism, the *Disticha* became an inspiration—despite their wholly hexameter form—for epigrammatists, including Constable, More, and Jonson in England, and even inspired the Calvinist Theodore Beza to produce his own *Cato Censorius Christianus*, a collection of verses that, like the *Disticha*, criticized sloth, greed, and intoxication, among other vices.[14]

In the early modern period, the influence of the collection was felt widely and in multiple genres, including drama, *Hamlet* providing a nice example.[15] Indeed, the *Disticha* were so well known and their influence so widespread, that it becomes hard to know whether a writer was inspired directly or indirectly by the maxims, a fact that Cervantes reflects upon (*Don Quixote* 2.33): "Todo cuanto aquí ha dicho el buen Sancho—dijo la duquesa—son sentencias catonianas, o, por lo menos, sacadas de las mesmas entrañas del mismo Micael Verino" ("'Everything that the good Sancho has said here,' said the duchess, 'is Catonian maxims, or at the least taken from the very soul of Micael Verino'").[16] Verino, a short-lived Florentine poet, had produced well regarded distichs modeled on the *Disticha*. Cervantes' use of and obvious familiarity with the collection was such that he was even believed—erroneously—to have produced an edition of it.[17]

Around this time, the fame of "Cato" and his *Disticha* were spreading to the New World. In Peru, the Andean lord Guaman Poma de Ayala, author of a 1615 Andean history that equates the Incas and Romans temporally and culturally, mentions that in his culture's past, "boys and children were instructed and taught with chastisement as Cato of Rome did, who provided good examples and taught his children, so they were well brought up." We know that hundreds of copies of the *Disticha* were crossing the Atlantic in the seventeenth century, and Guaman Poma probably read the collection himself, maybe even as a child.[18] Copies of the *Disticha* were heading not just to the Spanish colonies, but also the fledgling United States, where just over a century later, Benjamin Franklin would be inspired by the *Disticha* as he compiled his *Poor Richard's*

---

the popularity in medieval France of precepts, a genre influenced by the *Disticha*, see Roussel 1994.

14 On the *Disticha*' influence on later epigram, see Crane 1986, especially 165–169, 180, and 185–186. On Beza's *Cato Censorius Christianus*, see Green 2009, 157.

15 On Shakespeare and the *Disticha*, see further Falk 1967 and on *Hamlet*, Barker and Chadwick 1993, 329, n. 12.

16 The translation comes from Lathrop 2005, 632.

17 On Cervantes and the *Disticha*, see Glaser 1954 and especially Taylor 1999.

18 The translation and discussion of the text come from MacCormack 2007, 63; the original can be found in Murra, Adorno and Urioste 1987, 59.

Almanack, and his translation would be the first of any Classical text produced in North America. Through Chaucer, Shakespeare, Cervantes, and now Franklin, the *Distichs* were firmly entrenched in the consciousness of Europe and the Americas, where they remained through the eighteenth and into the nineteenth centuries.

No one quotes the *Distichs* anymore, and scarcely anyone—beyond a few scholars—even reads them. Despite their ubiquity for so many centuries across Europe and in the New World too, a good many Classicists today have either never heard of them or never read them. The *Distichs* are no longer read in elementary Latin classes and have therefore fallen out of most people's consciousness;[19] moreover, a moralizing text that lacks an author or date and is written in simple Latin does not appeal to many philologists, while its unsystematic thought independent of any philosophical school renders it uninteresting to philosophers. Finally, some of those modern scholars who have looked at the collection have poured scorn on it, and only a few have deemed it worthy of their scholarship.

While the *Distichs* have loomed large and been admired in Western post-Classical education and literature, a fact acknowledged by scholars in those fields, the Loeb Classical Library—presumably reflecting a general attitude among Classicists—relegates them to the "Minor Latin Poets" volumes (1934). The entry for "Cato Dionysius" in Smith's *Dictionary of Greek and Roman Biography and Mythology* (1849) summarizes the differing attitudes towards the collection:

> The language has been pronounced worthy of the purest era of Latin composition, and declared to be a specimen of the worst epoch of barbarism. The adages themselves have been extolled by some as the dignified exposition of high philosophy; by others they have been contemptuously characterised as, with few exceptions, a farrago of vapid trash.

Nevertheless, this is a good time to be working on the *Distichs* for several reasons. First, reception has become increasingly important to Classics for intellectual and pragmatic reasons; second, scholarship on wisdom literature is burgeoning. Third, the *Distichs* offer rich insights into Roman social history. For, as the *Rhetorica ad Herennium* 4.17.24 tells us, "A saying is a pronouncement taken from life and it demonstrates briefly what is done or ought to be done in life" (*sententia est oratio sumpta de vita, quae aut quid sit aut quid esse oporteat in*

---

[19] I know of only one Classics course taught in North America that includes the *Distichs* in the syllabus: Edan Dekel's "Ancient Wisdom Literature," taught at Williams College. Domach 2013, an M.A. thesis, is among the most recent student work on the *Distichs*.

vita, breviter ostendit), and therefore the *Distichs*, like other wisdom texts, "reflects the values of its era. It is, in fact, a distillation (from the modern point of view, an adulteration) of many of the ideas and sentiments found in Augustan and Silver Latin literature."[20]

Beginning with the foundational work of Archer Taylor and Barrett Jere Whiting in the 1930s on proverbs in their socio-linguistic context, scholars of wisdom texts moved from simply cataloguing wisdom expressions and tracing their users to instead analyzing them as the products of particular societies and substantiations of belief.[21] Martin West's work on Hesiod as a writer of wisdom and John Barns' work on Greek gnomologia preserved on papyrus in Egypt have drawn Classicists' attention to scholarship on wisdom. More recently Nikolaos Lazaridis' linguistic analysis of Greek and Egyptian proverbs, which demonstrates how their interrelationship reflects Greco-Egyptian cultural exchange, bears witness to the importance and productiveness of that scholarship. In addition, good editions of several wisdom texts have appeared over the twentieth century, including Jäkel's edition of the *Sententiae Menandri* and, most importantly for this study, Boas' fine edition of the *Disticha Catonis*.[22]

Essential to any scholarship on ancient wisdom texts is Teresa Morgan's study of *Morality in the Early Roman Empire*, which draws on proverbs, fables and *gnomai* of the first two centuries CE to reconstruct a popular Roman morality and to produce "a map of the ethical landscape." Morgan succeeds in demonstrating the use of minor literary texts of this sort to social historians who are attempting to recreate the lives of ordinary Romans. I hope that the present study will complement and add to hers.[23]

As I explain in Chapter 1, the text as we currently encounter it has at its heart 144 hexameter couplets. These are the *Distichs*—the two-liners—and they are the focus of this study. Chapter 1 serves as an introduction for Classicists

---

[20] Hazelton 1957, 162, referring to wisdom texts.
[21] Scholars of Anglo-Saxon wisdom texts have been pioneers: see especially the work of Tom Shippey.
[22] An exception is the *Sententiae Publilii Syri*, excerpted from the Roman Republican playwright's mimes, which were last edited in the nineteenth century and have received treatment in only one monograph, Giancotti 1967, despite Archer Taylor's observation of their neglect back in 1934 (Taylor 1934, 9). The most recent brief treatments are Panayotakis 2010, 27, n. 52, and 50–56, and Bradley 2016 and 2019. A new translation for the Loeb Classical Library is anticipated (Bradley 2016, 663).
[23] Morgan 2007. Morgan's dating of the *Distichs* to the third century CE led her to omit consideration of it. Reichert 1956 presents snapshots of various aspects of Roman life derived from wisdom sayings; however, his work is impressionistic and unsystematic.

and scholars of later literatures to the *Distichs*—their form, content, and authorship—and argues for a new dating in the first century CE. It proposes, contrary to the historical and current consensus, that the *Distichs* were associated by their author not necessarily just with Cato Censorius, but perhaps in addition with Cato Uticensis, in order to increase their appeal among the reading public of the first century CE.

Chapter 2 considers the long tradition of wisdom literature, in particular that of paraenetic literature. It isolates the key characteristics of paraenetic texts: they are composed of a series of brief texts written in a literary style, phrased as instructions and/or reflections, and arranged thematically or alphabetically, that concern a wide range of topics and are authored by or attributed to a figure of wisdom. The *Distichs* demonstrate most of these characteristics, and their familiarity to ancient readers in search of wisdom as a paraenetic collection would have added to their appeal. But the *Distichs* lack arrangement and are written in hexameter couplets, a form that no other text of the genre uses exclusively.

Chapter 3 demonstrates that the author of the *Distichs*, far from being a barbarous writer, was a skilled poet who used the binarism of the hexameter couplet form and the maxims' content to maximize the impact of their messages. Finally, it proposes that the author intended for his work to be read by both adults and children.

Chapter 4 explores the collection's treatment of friendship. Friendship is a common theme in the collection, where it is presented not so much as a source of comfort and pleasure but rather as a bulwark against more powerful foes, as well as personal enemies of similar status. The importance of friends is clear in a society that the collection characterizes as paranoid, defensive, and suspicious. Advice on money—how and when to spend or save it—is the focus of Chapter 5. The *Distichs* reveal alternative attitudes to money to those found in elite writers, such as Cicero and Seneca, and make clear Romans' everyday anxieties about want. The concentration of maxims about money makes possible a sustained treatment of Romans' attitudes towards money, wealth, and personal financial management.

These two chapters explore the interrelationship of the maxims and Roman social history, in particular convergences with, divergences from, and additions to what we already know of Romans' thinking on two key topics: friendship and money. The first of these topics is well explored in the scholarship; it will be instructive to see what the *Distichs* might add to it. The second has been relatively less explored, and my discussion will demonstrate how the *Distichs* might contribute to new work that is beginning to consider it. I have limited myself to examination of two topics for reasons of space, but I am hopeful that these chapters might inspire others to use the *Distichs* for their work on many other topics besides. In chapters 4 and 5, I set the maxims in their Roman context and put them in conversation with contemporary or near-contemporary texts in order to gain a better understanding of attitudes towards the topics. These chapters will also offer the first modern extensive exegeses of the maxims.

The translations and transformations of the *Distichs* in the medieval period and beyond form the basis of Chapters 6 and 7. Editions, commentaries, and translations of the *Distichs* secured the collection's survival, and these chapters demonstrate how scholars and publishers collaborated to meet the demands of educators, pupils, and a wider consumer public across Europe and the New World to read and understand a text used for centuries as the first reader in Latin. It also demonstrates that the *Distichs* could be packaged and repackaged to meet the various needs of different audiences across time and space. The title of Chapter 6, which treats editions and commentaries, is to the point: the German "Fortleben" expresses more strongly than does English "survival" (or the oft used import "Nachleben") the fact that the *Distichs* enjoyed a wide and constant readership from the medieval period through to the eighteenth century. Chapter 7 turns to the enormous range and variety of translations and adaptations of the *Distichs*. Both chapters should be of interest to Classicists and those interested in the reception of Classical texts.

The *Distichs* are a *Roman* text, composed by a Roman for Romans perhaps in the first century CE. Read as a Roman text, the *Distichs* have much to tell us about contemporary Roman society, in particular how Romans, as a group, agreed it should properly function and the ways or circumstances in which it failed to do so. While wisdom collections are often attributed to or associated with a wise individual, the wisdom supposedly originating with that individual is more likely the product of society as a whole. Instead, therefore, of regarding each maxim in the *Distichs* as an instruction or reflection that "Cato" might have given or said, or even as the product of the Author's peculiar social outlook, rather we should consider each a "sententious generalisation," as Cavill puts it: a statement that encapsulates in memorable form the received wisdom on a topic of broad social import.[24]

---

[24] Cavill 1999, 9. The *Distichs* rely on generalizations for their broad appeal, and those generalizations are useful for us as reflections of Roman thought about Roman society. As MacMullen 1974, viii, notes, "At times it is possible to catch people of the past doing their own generalizing for us. They may do this in fiction, when authors try to present a situation that would easily be believed by their readers, and weave in details felt to be applicable throughout their

While scholars in the field of Classics have continued to pay little attention to wisdom texts—with the notable exceptions of Teresa Morgan, Nikolaos Lazaridis, André Lardinois, and Robert Knapp[25]—over the last two decades, scholars of Near Eastern and Old English literature have produced work that not only analyzes such texts in and for their social context, but also applies stimulating methods that lead to productive readings. Particularly important for my approach in Chapters 4 and 5 are studies of Old English texts that were inspired by mid-twentieth century work in folklore studies and anthropology. The studies of Paul Cavill, Tom Shippey, and Susan Deskis have been especially helpful.[26]

---

own world. Or they may do this in predictions, as astrologers, dream-diviners, and seers: to stay in business, such practitioners had to deal in probabilities. Or again, we can apply a sort of 'association test' to written sources of all kinds, through the study of pairs of words or pairs of ideas: 'rich and honored,' 'rustic and cloddish,' 'paupers and criminals.'"

25 Especially Morgan 2007, Lazaridis 2007, and Lardinois 1997 and 2001. Knapp 2011 draws on a wealth of evidence, including wisdom texts, as well as Jewish and Christian texts, from the first and second centuries CE to create a portrait of non-elite Romans that he summarizes thus (p. 11):

> Marriage is a good thing; monogamy is the norm. Loyalty in marriage is important. Wives are to be faithful, available and alluring; husbands chaste. Men reject the philosophic view that sex is a distraction done for procreation and without enjoyment. Chastity is valued, but does not extend to the point that male homosexual relationships and occasional male infidelity are unacceptable. Visiting prostitutes is a neutral activity, as is discussed elsewhere. Divorce is possible and acceptable. Lying, cheating, and stealing are in principle bad. Honesty in dealings within kinship groups and with socioeconomic equals or superiors is expected; however, business with others exists in an ambiguous state which allows 'sharp dealing' and deceit for personal gain. Fair and just treatment of all is good, although 'fair' is based on a distributive concept of justice. Acquisitiveness is a positive virtue; excessive acquisitiveness, i.e. avarice, and taking possessions that are not rightfully yours, is bad. For the more philosophically inclined, self-sufficiency is a moral commonplace.
>
> Self-confidence is a positive virtue, while arrogance and boasting, i.e. self-confidence outstripping appropriate expression according to socio-economic status, is a bad thing; humility is a commonplace (the opposite of excessive pride). A strong sense of self-worth is good. A person has the obligation to protect his standing (honor); almost any action is justified by this. But at the same time there is a sentiment for self-restraint, which is a common topos in popular philosophy. Drunkenness, for example, is frowned upon. Murder is bad. Minding one's own business is yet another common topos; gossip and being a busybody are bad. Taking care of those in need within your family, e.g. widows, is good. Looking to the welfare of those more distant from you is not good. Beyond immediate family, friends are highly valued. Indeed, friendship is another constant topos of popular philosophy and culture.

26 See especially Cavill 1998 and 1999, Shippey 1976 and 1994, and Deskis 1996. Lardinois 1997, 213, observes that postwar scholarship on *gnomai* now regularly considers them in their

Paraenetic texts encapsulate what a society collectively knows—they are part of "the social stock of knowledge," as Cavill puts it[27]—and as collections of statements of what that society knows it should do or tends to do, these texts help to define a society for itself. They also codify, institutionalize, and legitimate the relationships that a society agrees structure how its members interact (which in turn might make its members interact in that way). They are the result of a society's attempts to understand needs, desires, and experiences that are universal to humans, but that must be fitted to the cultural context of that society. The expression of the texts might appear universal, and an author might try to suggest that they are tried and tested and have authority apparently beyond the society of their target audience; yet they remain texts to be understood primarily within that society.

Aristotle tells us that the Greeks used statements of wisdom, such as those in the *Distichs*, as bons mots in social situations in order to insert a final judgment into a conversation in a witty and poetic way. He reveals to us that their effectiveness derives in part from the fact that so used, they offered an appeal to shared thinking.[28] Looking forward in time, physician Jean le Bon of Lorraine, a sixteenth-century French collector of proverbs, would declare proverbs—a subset of statements of wisdom—to be the "voix de ville" that "in any conversation might serve as the final arbiter and judge."[29]

For Romans, the *Distichs* would have been self-defining and self-affirming instructions and reflections. According to Cavill, "a maxim works by specifying the situation and involving the audience in a corporate statement of response." That response is formulated as a general principle, and so a statement of wisdom gains axiomatic force.[30] *Vox populi, vox Dei*. In specifying and responding, the *Distichs* define the world of first-century Rome—i.e., what is good vs. bad, wise vs. foolish—and order it accordingly. Through ordering the world and applying society's knowledge to its own ills, the *Distichs* state and solve its social problems. The *Distichs* are Rome's remedy for itself.

To understand that society, a Roman reading—as opposed to a Greek, medieval European or modern American reading—is essential. It is true that the generalizing principles of the *Distichs*, which are all relevant to Roman society,

---

social and linguistic contexts: good examples include Hamblenne 1973 and Bradley 2019 on Publilius Syrus, and Christes 1979 on using Syrus and also Phaedrus to understand the lived experiences of enslaved individuals.

27 Cavill 1999, 183, who is referring to Old English maxims.
28 Arist. *Rhet.* 1395a10–12.
29 I owe the reference and translation to Zemon Davis 1975, 240.
30 Cavill 1999, 52. The quotation is from Cavill 1999, 111.

have been useful also to European and New World societies and might, if more widely read, remain relevant today.³¹ But as a Roman collection, they reflect habitual and typified behavior among Romans. To be sure, much of the same behavior was found in other ancient cultures, was also habitual and typical, and is also treated in non-Roman wisdom literature, as I demonstrate in chapter 2. Yet this collection remains Roman, and my emphasis on its Roman-ness is important: as the anthropologists Arewa and Dundes have noted, earlier scholars' work on wisdom texts and utterances has sometimes offered anachronistic and culturally inappropriate interpretations, since their understanding has derived only from their own context.³² It is heartening to reflect, however, that recent scholars in Classics have been sensitive to context, as the work of Teresa Morgan in particular demonstrates.³³

One might counter that a Roman reading of the *Distichs* is unnecessary or even inappropriate, since so many of its messages have ancient precedents.³⁴ The precedents are certainly there, and it would be odd if they were not: the *Distichs* would otherwise lack the tradition that is so important for wisdom statements' definition and authority. Moreover, no society is so culturally or morally unique that its wisdom would be wholly without precedent. Yet, as I demonstrate in chapters 2 and 3, the form of the *Distichs*, which is strikingly idiosyncratic and of which the Author is very aware, reminds us that every couplet he composed is original.³⁵ While a good number of the couplets may be (conscious or unconscious) re-workings of earlier sentiments, the *Distichs* were composed by one person at one particular time: a Roman most likely in the first century CE, as I argue in chapter 1. He chose the sentiments and, as a Roman, they are the product of his Roman environment and should be read in that context. Indeed, Classicists have also become aware that, while the Romans were

---

31 Holiday 2016 and Pigliucci 2018 are among recent volumes that interpret (and sometimes misinterpret) ancient wisdom and offer it as a guide for modern living. The *Distichs* might be similarly used.
32 Arewa and Dundes 1964, quoted in Cavill 1999, 106.
33 Morgan 2007.
34 For example, Otto 1890 includes *DC* 2.8 among a series of expressions of the same idea, s.v. *tempus* 5 (p. 343). For a full list of references to the *Distichs*, see under *Cato, distich*, p. 407. Otto's magisterial collection of Sprichwörter offers ancient analogs to some of the *Distichs*, many of them Greek; those that predate the *Distichs* might have been sources, as might the *fontes* that Boas includes in his edition. But it is impossible to determine the influences on the Author.
35 In *DC* 4.49, he takes credit for both the brevity and bareness of his verses, as well as their couplet form.

great inheritors, especially of the Greek tradition, their inheritances need to be analyzed within their new context. Harriet Flower notes, "As elsewhere in Roman culture, patterns and forms borrowed and adapted from the Greeks need to be interpreted as fully 'Roman' within their new social and political context."[36]

The *Distichs* help us to understand the Romans. As Biville summarizes,

> Les proverbes et les sentences jouent aussi un rôle social capital, ils servent de repère d'identité culturelle, ils traduisent l'appartenance à une communauté (qui n'est pas seulement romaine mais gréco-romaine), l'adhésion à ses valeurs, l'ancrage dans ses traditions. Ils sont le symbole et la quintessence du monde qu'ils représentent.[37]

> The proverbs and sayings also play a role in social capital, they act as a benchmark of cultural identity, they express membership of a community (which is not only Roman, but Greco-Roman), adherence to its values, anchorage in its traditions. They are the symbol and the quintessence of the world they represent.

Paul Cavill has observed, in reference to Old English maxims, that "Ultimately it is the social context which makes sense of the poems, and the poems which make sense of the social context."[38] The interrelationship of the *Distichs* and their context may lure a reader towards the danger of circular reasoning: the *Distichs* tell us about Rome, which can tell us about the *Distichs*. But as "traditional forms of expression which reflect a socially sanctioned world view" (Cavill again), the maxims offer us a Roman world view—and my purpose in chapters 4 and 5 is to study the *Distichs* in order to understand Rome and not the other way round.[39]

With their imperatives and statements of wisdom, the *Distichs* promote social conventions or norms to the status of ideals, and the collection's ascription to "Cato" reinforces that idealization (even if one or both of the historical Catos would not necessarily have said or recommended these ideals). The notion that the *Distichs* can be read to understand Rome is further supported if one considers the power of social conditioning: a Roman's seemingly impersonal claim that "it is right to do X" could be reformulated "I am reporting that the society in whose culture I have been raised and socialized believes collectively that we should do X," and so the instructions and injunctions of the *Distichs* that "you

---

[36] Flower 1996, 118.
[37] Biville 1999, 13, who offers an overview of the importance of *sententiae* in Latin literature and Roman thought on pp. 11–14.
[38] Cavill 1999, 183.
[39] Cavill 1998, 631.

should do X" could similarly be reformulated as "the society in whose culture you have been raised and socialized believes collectively that you should do X."

As a text of the first century CE, the *Distichs* offer us an excellent opportunity to deepen our understanding of the beliefs and attitudes of Roman society during an important period. Yet there are limitations on their usefulness to us. First, their audience is limited: they offer advice to both children and adults, and so we might say that they were aimed at or spoke mostly to literate persons of all ages. Yet they offer advice only about enslaved individuals and wives, not to them.[40] We should imagine an audience of perhaps no more than free males, but of all ages.[41]

Second, while the *Distichs* describe the Roman world and offer solutions to its problems, they do not define every aspect of it nor offer a solution to every problem and cannot present a complete and unified picture of Roman society. Moreover, we cannot claim that there is an overarching moral or socio-political philosophy in the *Distichs* since the problems they identify and solutions they propose are not necessarily mutually compatible, and there are no programmatic statements of philosophy for the maxims. What we have instead is a series of commonplaces no less true, yet no more consistent than, for example, the sayings "too many cooks spoil the broth," and "many hands make light work."

Third, the *Distichs* are not always self-explanatory, and we should be aware of the fact that even those maxims that might seem obvious might be read differently by different readers—now and in the past.[42] We need then to be self-aware readers, cognizant of the assumptions and prejudices that come from our age, gender, and geographical, cultural, and socio-economic context. We should also recognize that our experience of the *Disticha Catonis*—as an anonymous text comprising a letter, *sententiae* and maxims, introduced as though

---

40 Maxims about enslaved individuals: *DC* 1.8, 1.37, 3.10, 4.44; about wives: *DC* 1.8, 3.20, 3.23, 3.12, 4.47.
41 The composition of the *Distichs* in Latin presumably places their Author and readership in the Western part of the Empire, though a lack of internal or external evidence precludes us from being more precise.
42 Zemon Davis 1975, 243–244, notes that users of early modern French proverbs or maxims seem to have had no problem with the possibility that they might change their meaning with a change in speaker (or that they might be inconsistent or overlap with others). More broadly, Langlands 2018, 62–64, draws attention to the "multivalency" of exempla, fables, and other vehicles of moralizing, noting that it "describes not only their capacity to be reinterpreted and redeployed in different contexts and to acquire new meanings over time (what we might term 'serial multivalency') but also their capacity to generate multiple interpretations within a single reader at a single reading (what we might term 'simultaneous multivalency')" (pp. 62–63).

from a father to his son, and attributed to "Cato"—is not the only one: it is possible Roman readers may have known the author's identity; they may not have read the letter and *sententiae* along with the couplets; they may not therefore have thought of the maxims' speaker or source in the role of a father and themselves as readers in the role of his son; and finally they may have been differently affected by the Catonian connection. They may also have come across the couplets removed from their textual setting, perhaps quoted in another text. In addition, a couplet might be interpreted differently by similar readers, even by two free male literate Romans. Of course, we cannot survey free male literate Romans to discover their different readings of or reactions to the same couplet. Finally, we should beware of over-reading the *Distichs*: an academic's take on a maxim might strike a Roman as amusingly over-analytical, which is how some scholars now regard the work of sixteenth and seventeenth-century French academics (or savants) on contemporary popular proverbs.[43] A light touch is needed.

A short text should produce a short book. As Charlotte Roueché has pointed out, there simply is not an audience for a book that offers an enormous commentary on a brief wisdom text.[44] Archer Taylor had noted that "The *Disticha catonis* [sic] inculcates many a moral principle in aphoristic form and even gave rise to a parody. Some proverbs trace back to the *Distichs of Cato*, but no one has yet appraised the value of that collection as a source of proverbs."[45] And this book is limited to that task: it introduces the *Distichs* and, for the first time, considers them in their Classical context.

This book does not trace the "origins" of the maxims, or rather cite instances of a maxim's particular idea back through Roman and Greek literature. That is an immense task perhaps better carried out as part of a collaborative project that uses digital text encoding, such as the Sharing Ancient Wisdoms project (SAWS), which is being carried out by a team from King's College London and the Universities of Uppsala and Vienna.[46] Besides, a printed book is surely now the wrong medium for such Quellenforschung. My more modest task is to analyze the maxims in their socio-historical context—a task that requires reading between their lines. After all, as the preface to the *Distichs* warns: "*legere enim et non intelligere neglegere est*" ("for to read and not to read between the lines is

---

43 See Zemon Davis 1975.
44 Roueché and Tupman 2011.
45 Taylor 1934, 10.
46 http://www.ancientwisdoms.ac.uk/library/, accessed 5/18/2022. Some of this task was undertaken by Otto 1890, who lists *fontes* for Roman sayings, an impressive work for its time.

not to read at all"). The collection will never again attain its earlier fame, but I hope that this book will at least make it better known among scholars of the ancient world and its reception.

Part I: **The *Distichs* and Paraenesis**

1 The *Distichs*

Modern texts of the *Distichs of Cato* are models of simplification and clarity: to the readers who choose to overlook the apparatus criticus (as many do), the text appears uncomplicated. They can be forgiven for thinking that the collection they see now is the same as that written nearly 2000 years ago, but they have been lulled into a false sense of textual security.

Modern editors present the *Distichs* as a collection of discrete parts: a passage of continuous prose, usually called the *Epistula*; a series of one-line phrases, often referred to as the *Breves Sententiae*; and four books of maxims in verse couplets clearly separated, with prefaces at the start of books 2, 3 and 4, and with each couplet within them in turn separated and numbered. The ordered state of most printed and online modern editions has created a false impression of the collection. But much of what is presented in those editions is the product of received assumption and speculation. This chapter presents and discusses the constituent parts of the collection and their connection with each other, the collection's development, and its title, author, and audience.

The texts of Chase (1922) and the Duffs (1934) remain the most accessible and consulted, yet both are out of date and have been superseded by that of Boas (1952).[47] His magisterial edition is available in most good university and college collections, but is no longer in print and besides, its language—it is written entirely in Latin—and technical discussion are off-putting to all but the determined and patient specialist. This chapter is therefore also devoted to simplifying, making more accessible, and updating Boas' work in order to explain what a reader may have seen two millennia ago.

---

47 Boas' work largely superseded that of Stechert 1912 and Schanz 1927, 34–41. Most of his large output is listed in the bibliography of this book; for an overview, see Bieler 1957, who offers summaries (and occasionally critiques) of the various articles. It is testament to Boas' work that there has been virtually no change to his text since the 1950s. My discussion of meter, below, adds to his attempts to secure an original text, free of later accretions.

The Text

Epistula

Readers of the *Distichs* encounter first this short paragraph of continuous prose:

> Cum animadverterem quam plurimos graviter in via morum errare, succurrendum opinioni eorum et consulendum famae existimavi, maxime ut gloriose viverent et honorem contingerent. Nunc te, fili carissime, docebo quo pacto morem animi tui componas. Igitur praecepta mea ita legito ut intellegas. Legere enim et non intellegere neglegere est.

> Since I have noticed how many people wander seriously astray on the path of good morals, I thought that help was needed for their reputations and concern for their good names, in particular so that they might live with glory and attain honor. Now I will teach you, my dearest son, how you may construct the character of your soul. Therefore, read my teachings so that you grasp their full meaning. After all, reading without reading between the lines is not reading at all.

This text may have been a letter—it is addressed to a son—and some manuscripts and modern editions title it the *Epistula*, though there is nothing in the text itself to confirm the label.[48] Letters are often found at the start of Greco-Roman works of *paraenesis*, and epistolary prefaces addressed to sons are especially popular.[49] The *Epistula*, then, is a fitting introduction to a moralizing self-help text.[50]

Marcus Boas has written of the *Epistula*'s "authenticity" (Echtheit), noting, for example, its complementarity to the final distich (*DC* 4.49, on which see

---

[48] Gibson and Morrison 2007 recognize that a text may not be a letter, even though it is customarily known as such. So, while the text presented above may be called an *epistula*, it may simply be a dedication.

[49] See Stowers 1989, 91–106. Isocrates's *Ad Nicoclem* is a well-known and early example of an epistolary preface to a paraenetic work. Letters themselves were also vehicles for advice or teaching, of which Aristotle's *Protrepticus* is our earliest extant example. On the importance of letter-writing in ancient philosophy, see Stowers 1989, 36–40; on letters in the Epicurean tradition and Seneca's use of letters, see Inwood 2007. On Horace's epistolary didactic poems, see Morrison 2007, 107–113. Generally, see Langslow 2007.

[50] On letters from fathers to sons, see Langslow 2007, 226 at n. 76. Ebbeler 2007, 304–305, notes the general popularity of letters from fathers to sons in the classical period and later. LeMoine 1991, 343 provides a useful listing of those that are best known. It is striking that the *Disticha* are in his list, since only the *Epistula* (and no other section) mentions fathers and sons, while some of the other works mention that relationship in the body of a text that is securely the work of its named author.

below).⁵¹ He regards the *Epistula* and the four books of maxims as belonging to a first stage of the text of the collection, with the three verse prefaces and *Breves Sententiae* gradually added by other persons. Yet there is no compelling evidence that the *Epistula* was written by the same person who composed the maxims, and in the absence of such evidence, and given the accretion of the prefaces and the *Breves Sententiae*, I regard it as more likely a later addition to the maxims. While there is no evidence to rule out that it was the work of the Author, there is also no evidence to prove that it was. Moreover, while the *Epistula* recommends its teachings (*praecepta*), it makes no reference to the unique form of the maxims that follow, and while the *Epistula* addresses a son, the rest of the collection is directed simply to an unidentified individual reader (although several of the maxims present their author as being older than his audience).⁵²

Some medieval manuscripts present the *Epistula* and *Breves Sententiae* under the title *Parvus Cato* and separate them from the maxims, which are called the *Magnus Cato*. This is not to suggest, however, that medieval copyists necessarily knew more about the text than we do today.⁵³ When or why the *Epistula* was composed is unknown, as is its author.⁵⁴ Otherwise, the *Epistula* is included with the maxims in our earliest manuscripts, which date to the late eighth century; by that date it was regarded by at least some as part of the collection.⁵⁵

Breves Sententiae

A series of fifty-seven prose instructions follows: the *Breves Sententiae*, or brief sayings.⁵⁶ As their name suggests, these are short, usually only two or three

---

51 Boas 1934, especially pp. 22–24.
52 The maxims are *DC* 1.16, 3.9 and 4.18; the observation is made by Cipolla 1880, 521, who goes on to show (pp. 521–522) how some of sentiments of the maxims and *Breves Sententiae* (on which, see below) accord with what we know of Cato Censorius's attitudes.
53 In the text accompanying Benedict Burgh's translation and commentary, for example, the collection was split in two.
54 On pseudepigraphic letters, see Gibson and Morrison 2007, 9; on prefatory letters, see Langslow 2007, 222, who provides an example of such a collection at p. 224, n. 67. Marcellus' *De medicamentis* is prefaced by a series of others' prefatory letters, some of which are genuine.
55 The dating is further supported by one epitome, the *Cato Novus*, whose first two lines contain references to father and sons. That work is attested in manuscripts from the ninth century. For a text of the *Cato Novus*, see Zarncke 1863, 31–48.
56 The manuscripts are A, B, C, and P. Manuscript A contains fifty-seven *Sententiae*; the remaining manuscripts omit 38a (in Boas's numbering). The *Sententiae* are found in all the manuscripts, except H, E, F, and K.

words; most comprise simply an object or adverb followed by a command or prohibition.[57]

There are two schools of thought on the relationship of the *Breves Sententiae* to the maxims that follow. The first, promoted by Erich Bischoff at the end of the nineteenth century, argues that the former summarize the latter.[58] Fully fifty-three of the *Sententiae* seem to do just that, and the remaining four perhaps summarized maxims, now lost, from what was originally a larger collection. Otto Skutsch, writing fifteen years later, was so convinced by the parallels that he proposed common authorship, but he has found no supporters.[59]

According to the second school of thought, matching *Sententiae* to maxims is easier in some cases than in others, and ninety-one maxims lack corresponding summaries in the *Sententiae*; the broad similarity in basic content does not prove common authorship or even that the *Sententiae* derive from the maxims. As Bischoff acknowledges, the *Sententiae* more closely follow the brief prose form of the *Dicta Septem Sapientum*, or *Sayings of the Seven Wise Men*, another paraenetic collection.[60] Their similarity in content to the maxims of the *Disticks* is coincidental, but not surprising: the mix of apparent influences suggests that wisdom collections could receive multiple influences and/or simply even draw on shared human notions of wise behavior.

Like the *Epistula*, the *Breves Sententiae* were probably a later addition to the *Disticks*, and their inclusion could have occurred easily: they may have been included before the maxims in an early manuscript; subsequent recopying created a connection between them, and the *Sententiae* became regarded as part of the *Disticks*. The question of their authorship is, I think, impossible to answer, and finding a date for them is also hard.[61]

---

57 Only a few entries extend to four or more words, for example, *patere legem quam ipse tuleris* (*Sent.* 49) and *illud adgredere quod iustum est* (*Sent.* 55). Examples include *deo supplica* (*Sent.* 1), *parentes ama* (2), *cognatos cole* (3), *saluta libenter* (9), *nihil temere credideris* (24), *neminem riseris* (31), and *minorem ne contempseris* (47).
58 Bischoff 1890, 20 and 53.
59 Skutsch 1905.
60 On the *Dicta Septem Sapientum*, see Fehling 1985 and Martin 1993. On the *Septem Sapientes*, see generally Althoff and Zeller 2006.
61 Bischoff 1890, 61–62, goes so far as to propose that because a significant number of the ninety-one maxims lacking *Breves Sententiae* concern friendship, which is badly needed and tested only in regular society, a monk must be their author. Bischoff 1890, 62, proposes a *terminus post quem* for composition of around 600 CE on the basis that some of the brief wisdom sayings of the Irish monk Columbanus (who died in 615 CE) resemble the maxims, but not the *Breves Sententiae*. Yet there is no compelling reason for why Columbanus should have necessarily wanted to incorporate the prose *Sententiae* into his verse.

The development in late antiquity of unitary books into miscellaneous books, i.e., those containing works by various authors copied at a single time, which became more common in the mediaeval period, may explain why the *Epistula* and *Breves Sententiae* were attached to the maxims. The maxims may have circulated alone shortly after they were composed; sometime later the maxims may have been included in miscellaneous books along with the *Epistula*, the *Breves Sententiae*, and other moralizing texts, such as those later included in the *Liber Catonianus* (on which see Chapter 7). The grouping into a miscellaneous book may have happened in the eighth century, when Armando Petrucci sees the most significant emergence of miscellaneous codices. This is also when our earliest manuscript of the *Distichs*—which contains the *Epistula* and the *Breves Sententiae*—was copied. Petrucci suggests that the development reflects an attitude among Christians that valued texts as part of a "stream" rather than as individual works of particular authors. There is, however, nothing to rule out an earlier date. As a result of the accretions, the singularity and authorship of the maxims and related texts would have become less important than the fact that they were all moralizing.[62]

Maxims

The maxims follow, 144 of them, divided into four books of 40, 31, 24, and 49 each, with their conclusions usually marked in our manuscripts. These conclusions are nearly always found at the same points, a fact that may raise the possibility that the book divisions we see in our modern editions appeared early.[63] Further support comes from imagining the collection as it was first read: on a papyrus roll. The reader of a papyrus roll might be able to view simultaneously two, three or four columns of between twenty-five and forty-five lines of verse.[64] Book 4, the longest of the *Distichs'* books at forty-nine maxims, if written in two or three columns, could therefore be visible in its entirety to the reader. Even the shortest, Book 3, at twenty-four maxims, if written in two columns, would not have been inappropriately short for viewing by itself. It is possible that the book

---

62 Petrucci 1995, 3–16.
63 *DC* 2.31a is occasionally presented as the first maxim in Book 3. This maxim reads as though it might be prefatory, and indeed is omitted along with some of the other prefaces in some manuscripts. See further Boas 1952, 144.
64 Van Sickle 1980, 5–7.

divisions are original and that book length was determined in part by the papyrus roll format.[65]

The order of the maxims within those books may not have changed significantly. Support for this notion comes from an ancient quotation from the *Distichs*. Vindicianus, *comes archiatrorum* to Valentinian II, quoted from *DC* 2.22.2 in the prefatory letter of his *De expertis remediis* dedicated to the emperor. The maxim should read as follows:

> *Consilium arcanum tacito committe sodali;*
> *Corporis auxilium medico committe fideli.*
>
> Entrust private deliberations to a discreet friend;
> Entrust your medical problems to a reliable doctor.

However, Vindicianus misremembered or misread the line, replacing *auxilium* with *exigua*, which he took from *DC* 2.9:

> *Corporis exigui vires contemnere noli;*
> *Consilio pollet, cui vim natura negavit.*
>
> Do not scorn the power of somebody small;
> He is rich in counsel, whom nature has denied strength.

Vindicianus writes: *Quod cum pati coepisset infirmus, flens et gemens illud Catonis saepe dicebat: 'Corporis exigua medico committe fideli'* ("But when the patient had begun to suffer, weeping and groaning he would often quote that saw of Cato: 'Entrust the smallnesses of your body to a trusted doctor'"). The confusion suggests that Vindicianus had seen the maxims placed close together, as indeed they are now.

There is ostensibly no preface to the first book of maxims, or at least none that our manuscripts clearly mark out as such. Boas has followed their lead: in his edition, he moves from the *Epistula*, through the *Breves Sententiae* and past an *incipit*, into the first book of maxims. Yet it is possible that the first maxim, *DC* 1.1, could be read as a preface, albeit one that is extremely brief.

> *Si deus est animus, nobis ut carmina dicunt,*
> *Hic tibi praecipue sit pura mente colendus.*

---

[65] Van Sickle 1980, 9–12, finds that Homeric episodic divisions allow for presentation of text in separate rolls of 500–600 lines each. The maxims, totalling nearly 300 lines, would need only a short roll, four feet in length.

> Reason is the god within us—that's what the poets say,
> So nurture it, put it first, and keep your mind pure.

The couplet introduces a nexus of ideas that will be key to the collection. First, the maxims that follow will appeal to and perhaps find a home in the reader's *animus*, i.e., good sense, sense of reason, or rationality. Use of the term *animus*, frequently employed in philosophical works, might suggest that the *Distichs* belong with them in philosophy, though the Author has borrowed the thought from Euripides.[66] Second, the Author claims that our good sense is the divine element within us and, as a result, it must be nurtured and privileged, with the mind kept pure. The necessity expressed in *colendus sit* (a passive periphrastic formed from a gerundive construction) requires that the reader dedicate himself to the collection. To follow it *pura mente*, with an untainted mind, the reader must banish all of his previous notions about how to live life: the Author's way of being requires total devotion.

This maxim might function as a preface to the first book and perhaps to the complete collection of maxims. I argue below for the singularity of the collection, i.e., authorship by one individual, on lexical, stylistic, and metrical grounds, and my argument is based on analyses of all 144 couplets. The meter of *DC* 1.1 seems consistent with the rest of the collection;[67] its vocabulary and syntax also seem to be straightforward. There is nothing in this couplet that suggests authorship by another person, and I will therefore assume that the Author of the rest of the collection wrote this couplet. Indeed, the placement of *DC* 1.1 at the head of the collection suggests that the Author wants to signal the collection's singularity. While his couplets may not constitute a comprehensive and internally consistent system of thought, they are all the work of one person and are meant to offer a guide to living. As such, his work stands in contrast to the collections of excerpts from Publilius Syrus, Cicero, and Seneca (among others) that were compiled later by editors.

Prefaces introduce Books 2, 3, and 4, and the preface to Book 2 is the fullest of the three:

> *Telluris si forte velis cognoscere cultus*
> *Vergilium legito; quodsi mage nosse laboras*

---

66 See Boas 1952, 34.

67 The first four feet in each line comprise two dactyls followed by two spondees. The simple repetition of patterns from the first line to the second is consistent with a trend found in the rest of the collection. The use of caesurae (three in the first line, one in the second) to emphasize the syntax is also consistent with the rest of the collection.

Herbarum vires, Macer tibi carmina dicit.
Si Romana cupis et Punica noscere bella,
Lucanum quaeres, qui Martis proelia dixit.
Si quid amare libet vel discere amare legendo,
Nasonem petito; sin autem cura tibi haec est,
Ut sapiens vivas, audi quae discere possis,
Per quae semotum vitiis deducitur aevum:
Ergo ades, et quae sit sapientia disce legendo.

If you happen to want to understand cultivation of the land
Read Vergil; but if you are striving to know better
The powers of plants, Macer sings his song to you.
If you want to learn about Rome's Punic wars,
Look for Lucan, who sings of the battles of Mars.
If you want a love affair or to learn about love by reading,
Seek out Naso; but if, however, this is your concern,
To live as a wise man, hear what you could learn,
So that you can lead a life free from wrongdoing:
And so pay attention, and learn from reading what wisdom is.

The importance of authority is the hallmark of this preface. It directs the reader looking for advice on specific topics to named authors (and alludes to specific texts). For each area of inquiry—farming, healing plants, wars, love—a poet is named: Vergil, Macer, Lucan and Ovid, respectively. But there is one exception: no poet is named as a source of wisdom; instead, there is simply a recommendation to read on.

There are several explanations for the omission: first, "Cato" is the implied source of wisdom, and as author of the maxims, does not need to be named. Perhaps he is even imagined as author of the preface; as such, he would not name himself. A second alternative would be that the maxims' author wrote the preface. This would signal an interesting self-referential play. However, nowhere else in the collection do we have further examples of such play. Moreover, the departure in metrical style from that of the maxims suggests that the preface was written later and by someone else: their metrical patterns are among those used least in the maxims.[68] Third, it might be possible that the

---

[68] Metrical analysis of the prefaces is difficult given their brevity; therefore, any analyses can yield only impressions, not conclusions. Analysis of the maxims is easier: the four most popular metrical patterns among the sixteen possible are *dsss*, *ddss*, *dsds*, and *ssss*, and they appear in fully 51% of the first four feet in the maxims. If the prefaces are the work of the maxims' Author, we would expect to find these patterns well-represented, especially if prefaces are expected to characterize the author's style. Significant divergences from some or all of these may suggest authorship by one or more other individuals. The preface to Book 2 provides a

preface has nothing to do with the maxims and that, like the *Epistula* and *Breves Sententiae*, it was simply added later as part of a miscellaneous codex. The apparently deliberate omission of Cato, however, makes this unlikely. Most likely is this final possibility: that the preface is acknowledging doubts about Cato's authorship and playing with them, and omission of his name leads the reader to wonder whether Cato is indeed the author. The preface was written later, and specifically for the collection, by someone who knew that the ascription of the collection to Cato was doubtful and wanted to play on that fact.[69] Indeed, most scholars believe that this and the prefaces to books 3 and 4 are later additions.[70]

While this preface reads as an introduction to the entire collection, no manuscript moves it to the beginning of Book 1.[71] The preface to Book 2 is followed in many manuscripts immediately, without any space, by the maxims of Book 2, though its syntactical and thematic integrity prevent the reader from trying to read it as part of the series of maxims that follows. The same cannot be said, however, about the preface to Book 3.

Hoc quicumque voles carmen cognoscere lector
Cum praecepta ferat, quae sunt gratissima vitae,
Instrue praeceptis animum, nec discere cesses;
Nam sine doctrina vita est quasi mortis imago.
Commoda multa feres, sin autem spreveris illud,
Non me scriptorem, sed te neglexeris ipse.

Reader, whoever you are, if you wish to understand this poem,
Since it contains teachings which are most helpful for life,
Form your mind with these teachings, and don't stop learning;
For to live untaught may seem like dying.
You would reap many benefits; but if, however, you should reject it,
You would be neglecting not me, as writer, but yourself.

---

good initial test: only four of its ten lines (1, 5, 8, and 9) contain patterns that appear in the eight most popular patterns of the maxims and only two that are in top four. Moreover, the ending of line 6 imitates that of line 10, which suggests that line 6 and therefore line 7 too were probably added later still.

69 It is possible, though unlikely, that the text of Cato alluded to here might be one of his lost or fragmentary works, such as the *Ad Filium*.

70 For example, according to Hunt 1994, 1, by the ninth century "the original distichs had been supplied with prefaces to the four books which constituted the collection." Later composition is further confirmed by a couple of errors: the first syllable of Macer should scan short, and Lucan wrote about civil wars, not Punic. As I discuss elsewhere (Connolly 2010), these are easily explained. Jacobs 2020, 24, sees in *Punica* a reference to Silius Italicus.

71 Boas 1952, 95, makes the claim.

The Preface to Book 3 comprises three hexameter couplets that seem most logically ordered as presented above, though some manuscripts reverse the order of the second and third, while others omit the third and fourth lines altogether. Boas includes them at the end of the second book (as *DC* 2.31a), while other editors place them at the start of Book 3's maxims (as *DC* 3.1).[72]

DC 1.1. had urged that the reader's *animus* is to be molded by learning, a notion found also in Preface 3, line 3 (*instrue praeceptis animum*). Learning should never cease (*nec discere cesses*), for to learn is truly to live; to live without teaching condemns one to a sort of death. The Preface's reasoning is not entirely logical: a good life depends upon learning, as does the mind, yet the relationship between the mind and life is not spelled out. But the overall message—that learning molds the mind and creates a true life—is intelligible and appropriate to the context. Indeed, Preface 3 promises teachings that are most helpful for life (*gratissima vitae*), a grand claim, but one that, like the rest of the Preface, is somewhat banal.

The reference to *carmen* in the first line of Preface 3 announces the collection as poetic, a fact that may have been alluded to in Preface 2, which in referencing Vergil, Macer, Lucan, and Ovid, all poets, perhaps places the Author in their company. Use of the singular noun, as opposed to the plural (*hoc...carmen* vs. *haec...carmina*) suggests that the author of Preface 3, at least, viewed the collection as comprising one poem, as opposed to multiple discrete couplets. The precise nature of that *carmen* is unclear: it may comprise all 144 of the couplets, arranged over four books or perhaps just the couplets in book 3. Alternatively, the Preface may have been a later addition that was moved from another text. Yet the content of the Preface complements the content of the collection so well that it seems purpose written.

Preface 3 is highly self-referential, as was Preface 2. Indeed, the reference to the preface's author—in the first person—in the final line is striking, since otherwise only *DC* 4.49, the final couplet of the collection, is self-referential.[73] In that line, the preface's author asserts that if the reader rejects it (*illud*), referring presumably to the poem (*hoc carmen*), he will not be neglected, but the reader will. The authorship of the Preface is uncertain: the manuscripts seem to disagree on its length and content, and its meter is not consistent with the maxims.[74]

---

[72] See also the discussion in Boas 1952, 142–144 and 148.

[73] It is just possible that the combination of the authorial self-reference and use of the verb *neglegere* is meant to look forward to the final couplet, on which see further below.

[74] While its metrical patterns are all among those favored by the maxims' Author, the repeated use of the weak caesura and the restriction of the bucolic diaeresis to only one line—the

For these reasons, Preface 3 is, I believe, probably a later addition, but one written expressly to accompany the maxims.

The contents and placement of the preface to Book 4 are also uncertain: it is found after Book 2 in a few manuscripts and separated among earlier books in others, and in yet other manuscripts it has lost two lines—the third and either the second or fourth; conjectures for the correct formulation of the fourth line vary.[75] In its fullest form it reads:

> *Securam quicumque cupis perducere vitam*
> *Nec vitiis haerere animo, quae moribus obsint,*
> *Haec praecepta tibi semper retinenda memento;*
> *Invenies aliquid † quo te vitare magistrum †.*
>
> Whoever you are who wishes to lead a life free from care
> And not in your mind cling to the vices that harm good character,
> Remember always to keep these teachings close to you;
> You will find something that will keep you from the schoolmaster.

This preface too was probably a later addition. The maintenance of the fiction of address to a younger reader is found nowhere else in the prefaces or maxims, only in the *Epistula*, and its metrical patterns are dissimilar to those of the maxims.[76]

Our manuscripts present to us a collection with a lot of prefatory material: a letter, the *Breves Sententiae*, and three prefaces. To understand this material as prefatory assumes that the maxims are the core of the collection, which may be a modern and therefore anachronistic attitude. But, with the exception of the *Breves Sententiae*, the letter and prefaces refer to teachings, and these must surely be the maxims. The brevity of the prefaces precludes knowing their authorship with any certainty, and while it seems likely that they were written for the collection, they were most likely composed later by one or more persons unknown. The *Epistula* might be viewed similarly, while the *Breves Sententiae* were probably a collection thematically similar to the *Distichs* that was later added to them.

The final maxim of the collection, *DC* 4.49, acts as an epilogue and was probably original to the collection (its meter is strongly reminiscent of that of

---

former avoided in the *Distichs*, the latter regularly employed—mark something of a departure from the maxims.
75 The details are given by Boas 1952, 190.
76 While the maxims contain as many diaereses as caesurae, this preface contains only two.

the other maxims), and it is found in a consistent form and position in all the manuscripts.

> *Miraris verbis nudis me scribere versus;*
> *Hoc brevitas fecit, sensus coniugere binos.*
>
> Do you wonder how I write verses in bare words?
> It's the brevity that does it, joining together two ideas.

The Author combines two ideas in the two lines of the maxim: first, that he is writing verses in bare words because he does not have much space and, second, that he is combining two thoughts in each couplet. The anacolouthon in the second line reinforces his goal of brevity: it comes even at the expense of syntax, as the syntax of the second clause does not follow logically from the first. *Hoc* ("this") in the second line exemplifies his goal of brevity, as it seems to do double duty, referring back to the infinitive *scribere* in the first line (namely, writing verses) and anticipating *coniugere* (joining ideas) in the second. Moreover, his use of the distributive *binos* (i.e., "two each") as opposed to the cardinal *duo* (meaning simply "two"), which would admittedly disrupt the meter, supports the idea that each line, both in this couplet and in the collection as a whole, contains a thought. The syntax of this couplet reinforces the characterization: it, like most of the maxims, contains a statement or instruction in one line and a subordinate explanation or justification in the other (see further Chapter 3).

While the Author's words may be bare—he uses little high-flown poetic vocabulary—he is certainly aware that he is writing in verse, as opposed to prose: so, for example, the homoeoteleuton in the first line (*miraris verbis nudis*) is reinforced by metrical position (each successive ending in *-is* comes at the beginning of a metrical foot). We see also that the homoeoteleuton in *versus* and *sensus* strengthens the relationship between them—one thought per verse—leaving *binos* the odd one out among the plural accusatives and therefore drawing attention to it. The fact that *binos* is the final word in the collection adds additional emphasis and characterizes the collection as a whole by its distichic form, a point to which I return in Chapter 3. The simplicity and brevity of *hoc*, referring to two aspects of the author's style, contrasts (perhaps humorously) with the multi-syllabic *brevitas*, a word whose form belies its meaning.[77]

---

77 On the importance of brevity to ancient wisdom, see especially the early statement of Demetrius, *De elocutione* 9.

The appearance of the first person, which is found otherwise only in the *Epistula* and Preface 3, has led some to wonder about its authorship or text.[78] Yet the couplet does not seem corrupt and there are more arguments for it being genuine than against. It engages so broadly with all the other maxims and is so cleverly self-aware in its vocabulary and composition—more so than the prefaces—that it is most likely genuine.

Title

No name exactly or wholly describes or encapsulates the nature of the *Distichs*: *apophthegmata* usually describes anecdotes that include sayings, but not the sayings themselves, and *chreiai* are basically synonymous with these. The term *gnome* is similarly broad: it is a statement on an ethical matter.[79] An aphorism encapsulates an ethical principle, but lacks the notion of instruction that defines many of the *Distichs*.[80] *Dicta* are simply sayings, though they can also refer to speeches; the broad scope of the term explains why the *Distichs* are sometimes known as the *Dicta Catonis*.

"*Disticha*" emerged as the most popular descriptive title for the maxims, a title that speaks to both their form and the absence of any other suitable Greek or Latin name. I use the term *Distichs* (the Anglicized form of *Disticha*) in this book to refer to the 144 couplets—the original contents of the collection—though for variety's sake, I also employ "maxim."[81] The latter term denotes a saying that both encapsulates and teaches a fundamental ethical principle in a non-prosaic style.

---

[78] Scriverius called it an epilogue (perhaps from a gloss, as Boas wonders), while Arntzenius believes it a later addition or at least corrupted.

[79] The classic definition is that of Aristotle, *Rhet.* 1394a21–25: ἔστι δὴ γνώμη ἀπόφανσις, οὐ μέντοι οὔτε περὶ τῶν καθ' ἕκαστον, οἷον ποῖός τις Ἰφικράτης, ἀλλὰ καθόλου, οὔτε περὶ πάντων, οἷον ὅτι τὸ εὐθὺ τῷ καμπύλῳ ἐναντίον, ἀλλὰ περὶ ὅσων αἱ πράξεις εἰσί, καὶ <ἃ> αἱρετὰ ἢ φευκτά ἐστι πρὸς τὸ πράττειν ("A maxim is an assertion—not, however, one about particulars, such as what kind of person Iphicrates is, but of a general sort, and not about everything (for example, not that the straight is the opposite of the crooked) but about things that involve actions and are to be chosen or avoided in regard to action"; trans. Kennedy 2007, 164–165).

[80] This list is taken from the excellent explanation of sometimes confusing and overlapping technical terms in Searby 2007, vol. 1, pp. 1–8.

[81] *Distichon* occurs in a few places in Latin literature: for example, in Donatus' and Servius' biographies of Vergil, the spurious epitaphs for the Gnat (*Culex*) and the poet himself are introduced with *hoc distichon*. Martial 8.29 refers to brief aphoristic *disticha* in what could be a reference to the *Distichs*; on this epigram, see further below.

Transmission

The *Distichs*, along with the *Epistula, Breves Sententiae*, and prefaces, have been transmitted to us through a large number of manuscripts. Indeed, in 2017, the University of Notre Dame's Digital Schoolbook Project had counted over 1,200 manuscripts, including full Latin texts and excerpts, translations, and commentaries in Latin and other languages.[82] The full Latin texts and excerpts can be divided into three *traditiones*, or families, all descended from the now-lost original text. The first, the *traditio vulgata*, is represented by 43 manuscripts dating from the ninth to the fifteenth centuries, while the second, the *traditio Barberina*, is represented by five manuscripts that date from the tenth to the fourteenth centuries, as well as some remnants preserved in a 1475 manuscript. The third *traditio*, Φ, is more complex. It has been established from a number of disparate sources: a series of abbreviated collections of the maxims (*syllogai*) dating to the ninth and eleventh centuries; three small collections of the maxims and *breves sententiae* of the eleventh to thirteenth centuries erroneously attributed to Cicero; a number of the maxims preserved in Alcuin; and finally, the maxims preserved in a Veronese manuscript (A) that dates to the eighth century and is our earliest manuscript.

In the *traditiones vulgata* (Ψ) and *Barberina*, the maxims are distributed unevenly and at random across four books, and there seems to be no organizing principle for their arrangement within the books.[83] The texts in these *traditiones* are remarkable for their consistency in the wording, number, and arrangement of the maxims. The manuscripts of *traditio* Φ are markedly different: they contain additional maxims or individual lines, and their arrangement only partially follows that of the other *traditiones*. A is the fullest witness to Φ; the others are *syllogai*, excerpts from the collection erroneously attributed to Cicero, and a number of maxims quoted by Alcuin.[84]

The text of A (MS CLXIII of Verona's Biblioteca Capitolare) has been important to scholars of the collection because, dating to the second half of the eighth century, it is the earliest surviving text of the work and a rich source of

---

[82] The bulk of these date to the medieval period, but a few fall as late as the nineteenth century.
[83] Only *DC* 4.49 seems to have been deliberately placed, its self-reflection perhaps explaining its position at the end of the collection. On the manuscript tradition of the *Distichs*, see especially Boas 1952, VII–XLIX. On the variant readings, see Boas 1915, 307–310. Boas 1952, XLII–XLVI and *passim*, also treats the individual maxims.
[84] On Alcuin and the *Disticha*, see Boas 1937, 19–20.

variant readings.⁸⁵ Yet scholars have paid less attention to its arrangement of the individual *disticha*, which may have been thematic. The editor of A may have been attempting to impose on the *Disticha* a more user-friendly organization. The maxims seem to fall into roughly thematic clusters of two, sometimes three. For example, in the first book of maxims in A, we encounter four maxims that treat the benefits of learning from others, then three that concern respect (as well as some additional lines not found in others manuscripts), three on the theme of pleasure, four on helping others, seven on the inconstancy and fragility of life, three on deception with words (as well as some additional lines), and finally two on justice (and a final additional line).⁸⁶ The editor's shifting of maxims—sometimes even individual lines—out of sequence and across books and his omission and addition of maxims or lines strongly suggest that he was aiming to group maxims by theme. Identification of those themes is sometimes difficult, but the shift from maxims dealing with the fragility and inconstancy of life to those concerned with deception with words, for example, is perceptible. It is striking that the compiler of A still divides the maxims among four books. The four-book structure seems irrelevant (or at least not obviously necessary) in any of the *traditiones*, but was perhaps preserved in A for the sake of familiarity.

Two puzzles remain. The first is the occasional thematic runs that must have been found in the Author's original text (which Boas terms Δ'), since they appear in *Vulg.* and *Barb.* It is not impossible that its compiler (who may have

---

85 A is dated to the ninth century most recently in Reynolds 1983, xxv. But the scholarly consensus is for a date in the eighth century: see Venturini 1929, 54; Lowe 1947, no. 516; Bischoff 1981, 30, n. 126. More generally on the manuscript, see also Carusi and Lindsay 1934, 8 and 19–20, with plate 38; Boas 1928, 61–63. On the contents of A, see especially Boas 1915, 297–310 (which is largely reproduced in Boas 1952, VIII–XXIX) and also Schenkl 1873, and Cipolla 1880, who discuss the *Disticha* generally and present a text from A. The small octavo codex contains thirty-five sequentially numbered folia, but is damaged at the beginning and the end, leaving the fourth book of the *Disticha* only partially intact; it is also missing two folia. Like our modern editions, the text of the *Disticha* in A comprises the *Epistula*, *Breves Sententiae*, and maxims, but its presentation of them differs in several respects: the *Breves Sententiae* and maxims are ordered differently; some of the maxims have been moved from one book to another; and a number of otherwise unattested distichic maxims and single lines have been added. In addition, a number of maxims found in the other *traditiones* are missing from their expected position, though the lacuna prevents us from knowing whether they were omitted completely or moved to a part of the text now missing.

86 A possible preface: *DC* 1.2; learning from others: *DC* 1.8, 1.9, 4.23, 1.10; respect: *DC* 1.13, 1.14, 1.12; pleasure: *DC* 4.24, 4.25, 2.8; helping others: *DC* 1.28. 1.15, 1.16, 1.17; inconstancy and fragility of life: *DC* 1.18, 1.19, 1.20, 1.21, 1.22, 1.23, 1.24; deception with words: *DC* 1.25, 1.26, 1.27; justice: *DC* 1.30, 1.31.

been the Author) put together some thematically-linked maxims, adding further maxims without any discernible principle for organization. Certainly, organization is found among ancient collections, more often than the lack of it, as we will see in the next chapter. The absence of any extant manuscripts closely related to A or fellow exemplars is also striking, given the greater incidence of thematic (or alphabetical) organization among wisdom texts.[87] Indeed, a few later translations of the *Disticha* were organized thematically, including some of our earliest German and French versions.[88] But perhaps we might attribute A's singularity simply to the comfort of familiarity: in an educational system that valued memorization, educators who had learned by heart the text arranged randomly might have resisted any new arrangement, even one appealing to logic.

According to Boas' stemma, reproduced below, the Author's original text of the *Distichs* is Δ', from which Δ and Bb' are recensions.[89] From the plethora of texts in the recensions Vulg. and Barb., it is likely that in Δ and Bb' and, by extension, Δ', the maxims are arranged in roughly the same order. The nature of recension Φ is harder to determine, though from the evidence of Σ and M, it seems likely that it too followed the organizing principle of Δ' but added maxims and also contained variant readings. A is an outlier: it presents the maxims in a different order, one that apparently skews more thematic than that of Δ', though the incomplete state of the manuscript prevents certainty. The order in A is apparently an innovation, one that reflects editorial intent rather than authorial. If it is not an innovation, then we would have to imagine that the editors of the other recensions, presumably Vulg. and Barb., intended to create a less ordered arrangement out of one that was more ordered.[90]

---

87 The other manuscripts in *traditio* Φ contain only brief excerpts from the *Disticha*; there is no other extant manuscript within that *traditio* that, like A, contains (or once contained) the complete text. Lowe 1947 describes A's script as "inexpert, individual pre-Caroline" and its parchment as "mediocre," and Venturini 1929, 51, notes that in the script "l'eleganza viene alquanto nascosta e turbata"; perhaps the manuscript was produced for individual or small-scale use and was itself never copied, like its fellow exemplars.
88 The various versions of the German thirteenth-century Rumpfübersetzung contained renderings of about one hundred maxims arranged thematically. See, for example, Heidelberg, Universitätsbibliothek, Cod. pal. germ. 341, fol. 71va-75rb, and Genf-Cologny, Bibliotheca Bodmeriana, Cod. Bodmer 72, fol. 34vb-38rb. A century later, Jean Lefèvre's French translation also reorders the maxims by theme. On all these texts, see Chapter 7.
89 See Boas 1952, XLI. I follow here Boas' 1952 edition and his stemma.
90 The stemma would presumably need to change to reflect the deviation of Vulg. and Barb. from A (and perhaps or presumably Φ).

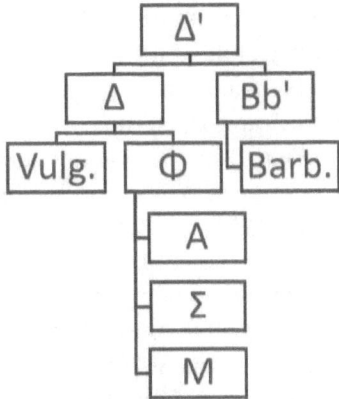

Fig. 1: Boas' stemma of the *Disticha Catonis*.

Assuming that A is the outlier, the apparent lack of arrangement in other manuscripts is probably older and perhaps original; the book divisions and order of the maxims within them may also be original.[91] The collection of 144 maxims transmitted in the *traditio vulgata* is probably as close as we will come to the text as it was first circulated, and it is remarkable for the integrity through its manuscripts of the sequence of maxims across the four books.

Authorship

Many Classicists assume the *Distichs of Cato* to be a work of Cato the Elder. This is in part because today we pay increasing attention to the full range of texts written by a particular author and are more open to moving beyond his canonical works to embrace those rarely read, including those we tend not to hear of during our education (and sometimes even beyond). It is also because Cato is an appropriate author: wise and opinionated, a father figure in the Republic, he was an author of moralizing texts, and it would not be a surprise if he had written the *Distichs*. But he did not.

---

91 The text of these manuscripts may not, however, be entirely original: Boas thinks that manuscript A contains older readings, such as *deos* instead of *deum* in *DC* 1.23.2. A full discussion of the nature of A and the difficulties facing readers of the manuscript can be found in Boas 1952, VIII–XVII.

With his best-known works, the *Origines* and *De agricultura*, the Elder Cato furnished his Roman aristocratic reader with an early history of his people and taught him how to be a successful farmer, the backbone of Roman society. In addition, Cato wrote or collected sayings, which may have constituted his *Ad filium*, a one-book collection of pithy sayings and advice. The Elder Pliny, Plutarch, and other writers quoted these sayings, but as Rossi points out, while they are apt for Cato, they are not necessarily his, and Plutarch himself notes that Cato collected Greek sayings translated into Latin.[92] None of the sayings attributed to Cato resembles any of the *Distichs* in either form or content.[93] Cato's *Carmen de moribus*, of which three fragments survive, all in prose, does not seem to be connected to the *Distichs* either: while the fragments seem to be moralizing, they also display an interest in earlier generations that is absent from the *Distichs*.[94]

Authorship by Cato the Younger also seems unlikely: while Plutarch quotes individual *sententiae* attributed to him (and these are unlike the *Distichs* in form), no collection of sayings is associated with him by an ancient source. Finally, Valerius Cato, the grammaticus and neoteric poet, is an unlikely choice for a moralizing collection. If he did write the *Distichs*, he was uniquely adept at restyling his meter: the hexameter of the *Dirae/Lydia*, which are sometimes attributed to him, is markedly different from that of the maxims.[95]

Our sole ancient reference to the *Distichs*'s association with "Cato" is in Vindicianus' letter, discussed above. He describes the maxim he (mis)quotes as *illud Catonis*, literally "that one of Cato."[96] Yet while Vindicianus believed "Cato" to be the author, by as early as the ninth century doubts were surfacing, when the commentator Remigius of Auxerre claimed that the attribution was

---

[92] Astin 1978, 183. Rossi 1924, 182. Plut. *Cat. Mai.* 2.4.
[93] The topics included religious law, medicine, and agriculture, none of which is addressed in the *Distichs*. On these topics in the *Ad filium*, see Astin 1978, 339.
[94] The fragments, preserved in Gellius *NA* 11.2, are discussed by Astin 1978, 186, Schönberger 1980, 388–390, and Sciarrino 2011, 156–162.
[95] On Valerius Cato, see Suet. *De gramm.* 11, with discussions in Bonner 1977, 62, and Robinson 1923. In his emphasis on brevity, Martial presumably had in mind the *De urbanitate* of Domitius Marsus, who was known, in turn, to have cited "Cato" on the definition of the *urbanus homo*. Hendrickson 1917, 90, thinks that the "Cato" in question was Valerius Cato, while Pliny the Younger (10.20[19]) asserts he was Cato the Elder. As the ancient source, Pliny is perhaps more credible; moreover, Valerius, as a Neoteric, simply does not seem to be a good fit to be an author of the *Distichs*. There is a discussion in Byrne 2004, 260.
[96] *Illud* could have referred to any number of terms, including *distichon* ("two-liner"), *dictum* ("saying"), or perhaps even *carmen* ("verse").

erroneous.⁹⁷ Indeed, there are no references to "Cato" in the maxims, and the *Epistula* (while not original) does not mention Cato, even if its author, inspired by the maxims' Catonian title, may have had him in mind. "Cato" is named only in manuscript titles, inscriptions, and subscriptions. The titles, some of which pertain to the entire collection, others only to the *Epistula* and *Breves Sententiae*, include the following (with minor variations omitted): *Incipit Dicta Marci Catonis ad filium sum, Incipit Marci Catonis ad filium libri, Incipit PP Catonis viri sapientis, Incipit prologus librorum Catonis Cordub*⁹⁸, *Incipiunt libri Catonis Philosophi, Marci Catonis ad filium salutem*, and *Praefatio in libro Catonis* (followed by *expliciunt precepta Catonis*).⁹⁹ None of these may have been part of the Author's original text: titles of ancient works are rarely original, and one becomes the standard only over time.

There is no early and reliable evidence of authorship by a historical Cato. The Catonian connection attested several centuries later in Vindicianus is instead one of association that probably originates with the Author, though need not.¹⁰⁰ That association may have been established through a descriptive title or even a false attribution, both potentially rendered in Latin with a simple genitive, e.g., *Disticha* (vel sim.) *Catonis*, meaning literally the *Catonian Two-Liners* or the *Two-Liners of Cato*. In that case, the reference to *illud Catonis* in Vindicianus could reflect an early title or a deliberately false attribution, with *illud* standing in for *distichon*. Additional support for *Disticha Catonis* as an early title is found in an epigram of Martial (on which see further below).

In the first century CE, the *Distichs* could have been associated with a historical Cato, who may have been the Elder, but may also have been the Younger. The former was "the ideal paternal educator," appearing in Plutarch and Cicero's works in this role,¹⁰¹ but Cato Uticensis was a paragon of virtue and wisdom in the first century CE and therefore a timely and appropriate muse for the *Dis-*

---

97 Hunt 1994, 1.
98 This title is found in ms Y, which belongs to a group of Gallo-Hispanic manuscripts of the collection (hence "*Cordub*").
99 These titles have been collected from Boas 1952, VIII–XLIX *passim*.
100 Cicero in his *De officiis* and *De oratore* refers to Cato's own collection of sayings. See Astin 1978, 186. If, as seems likely, Cato liked to collect sayings, we might posit a tradition of Catonian collections, in which he may have included some of his own sayings. The existence of such a collection could have set a precedent for the *Distichs*.
101 The quotation comes from Bernstein 2008, 207, who discusses depictions of Cato as an educator (pp. 209–215). Plutarch describes Cato's educational program for his son in his *Cato Maior* 20.3–6; as the central interlocutor in Cic. *De senectute*, Cato claims that young men delight in learning from their elders (8.26).

tichs.¹⁰² By the time Vindicianus (mis-)quoted the *Distichs*, he (and others) may have had in mind a Cato-type, an amalgamation of the historical figures and their reputations for ethical standards and wisdom.¹⁰³

While the *Distichs* have most commonly been associated with "Cato," other connections have been made: in one manuscript, a series of maxims from the *Distichs* are attributed to Cicero, and the *Distichs* have also been attributed to Seneca, most likely because of the existence of a pseudo-Senecan collection of *apophthegmata*.¹⁰⁴ They might also have been connected with Ovid, since several of his didactic texts are often found in manuscripts along with the *Distichs*.¹⁰⁵ Finally, in the sixteenth century, the collection was ascribed by Vinet to a certain "Dionysius." The attribution perhaps derives from confusion with a real-life Dionysius, Cassius Dionysius Uticensis, who was the author, according to Varro, of a translation of Mago of Carthage's earlier Punic work on agriculture—hence his agnomen. But there is no reason to believe that this Dionysius—or indeed any other—was the author.¹⁰⁶

---

102 See further Connolly 2012. Drogula 2019 claims that Cato Uticensis was better known as a traditionalist than a philosopher, a characterization that would still have contributed to his connection to the *Disticha*.

103 Although Remigius disavowed authorship by a historical Cato, the Catonian connection persisted into the medieval period and beyond. Indeed, the *Disticha* were to inspire later wisdom texts that associated themselves in title and tone with the figure of Cato (on which see Chapter 7); they also contributed to the evolution of an ahistorical Cato as a paragon of wisdom.

104 Cicero: Boas 1952, xxix–xxxv. The attribution to Seneca is made in a medieval schoolbook, Firenze, Biblioteca Riccardiana, MS 640, of which multiple copies must have been made and on which see Gehl 1989, 428. On the pseudo-Senecan collection, see Roussel 1994, 3. The connection of the *Disticha* to Seneca is not altogether unsurprising: the Author may well have been drawing on some thoughts expressed in the roughly-contemporary philosopher, as Bloomer 2015, 348–353 argues; the two writers may also have been expressing traditional and contemporary shared modes of thought (as the various exempla from Seneca in Boas 1952 suggest—e.g., on *DC* 3.4).

105 For example, the Paris manuscripts 7575, 8246, 8246A, and 8460 contain texts of the *Ars Amatoria* and *Remedia Amoris*, as well as the *Disticha*.

106 On the misattribution of the collection to "Dionysius Cato," see especially Boas 1930. On Cassius Dionysius Uticensis, see Varro, *de Agric*. 1.1.1. Additional explanations are: the name Dionysius may have been an old misreading of Dioreus, the author of a collection of moral texts that included *DC* 1.1; it may have derived from a confusion of Dionysius Uticensis with Cato Uticensis; it may have come from a misunderstanding of the front page of a Renaissance text of the *Disticha*: the page included an illustration of a Dionysiac temple labelled "Dionysius"; finally, it may have been taken from a book containing Ausonius' poem *Dionyson Indi vocant*, which preceded the *Disticha* and was titled in the contents as Dionysius, so that the following was seen:

The real Author—and the consistency of style across all 144 maxims points to a single author—most likely composed the maxims towards the end of the first century CE as a collection in four books, much as we see it now. Throughout this book I have referred to him as the Author—capitalized—for the sake of clarity and in a bid to recognize the authorial agency of this individual, even though he is anonymous to us and perhaps was to his ancient readers too. Yet, despite the Author's association of his maxims with or attribution of them to one or both of the Catos and his own anonymity, we can deduce a little from the nearly 300 lines of poetry he has left to us. He knew his meter well, using Vergil's hexameter as his model.[107] He was an effective stylist, writing with a simple vocabulary and an uncomplicated meter that supports a repetitive and unadorned syntax and that facilitates comprehension and memorization.[108]

The mere fact that the Author was literate and was apparently successful in circulating his work suggests that he most likely enjoyed high socio-economic status. His references to interactions with enslaved individuals may have been solely for the benefit of his slave-holding readers, though there is a good chance that he was a slaveholder himself. A date of composition in the first century CE suggests that the maxims that deal with gods, fate, and the afterlife were written by a pagan. But such claims should not be pushed too hard. A couple of the maxims offer advice on dealing with difficult wives, which might suggest that the Author was male, a claim that few would contest; one maxim refers to children, a second to parents. Perhaps, we might say, the Author was in middle age: he was a parent, and his own parents were still alive. But while this may be true, it does not need to be. Extrapolating the Author's biography is fraught with difficulty when his text derived much of its success from its appeal and appropriateness to a wide range of readers across time, space, cultures, and contexts.

Date

The *Distichs* have been dated usually to the third century CE, not on any evidentiary basis, but from a perception of their quality and an implied comparison with canonical Latin texts, which tend to date earlier. Moreover, the *Distichs* do

Dionysius ... 16
Disticha Moralia, vel Cato ... 265

---

107 See further Connolly 2011.
108 For example, not one of the Author's 288 lines requires protraction, correption, iambic shortening, *vel sim.*, in order to scan. On meter and style, see Connolly 2011 and 2013a.

not belong to a genre represented in the canon (such as epic, tragedy, oratory or even philosophy) and they lack the sophistication common to canonical texts. Viewed as sub-par, their association with a period of decline has been almost inevitable. The historiographically murky third century was once a convenient home for apparently sub-par poetry of uncertain provenance, and while the prejudice that produced such thinking has largely disappeared among scholars, the dating of the *Distichs* has remained.[109] But their apparent lack of sophistication is, I argue, a stylistic ploy to make them as accessible as possible to a wide audience, and their lexical, syntactical, and metrical simplicity is meant to maximize their efficiency as vehicles for communicating wisdom and advice.

The *Distichs* most likely date to the first century CE. Clues for this dating—evidence is too strong a term—are external, including quotations of the maxims and a reference to the collection in Martial, and internal, for example, from their meter. Vindicianus' letter, discussed above, supplies a terminus ante quem of 390 CE, the year of Valentinian's death, and his confusion of *DC* 2.22 and 2.9 strongly suggests that he knew not just these two maxims, but rather the *collection* of the maxims perhaps in its current form.[110] Another quotation, in a funerary inscription for the wife of a certain Q. Oppius Secundus, moves that terminus earlier. *CIL* 6.11252 is a prose text and is therefore quoting from the hexameter *Distichs* (and not vice versa); it therefore postdates the collection. Scholars argue over a date for the inscription of the first, third or fourth century; most recently, Massaro suggests a date towards the end of the first century CE.[111]

The inscription contains a number of quotations, including an almost complete line from *DC* 2.3:

> *domui aeternae consecratae*
> *Agileiae Primae q(uae) e(t) Auguriae,*
> *uxori supra aetatem castissimae et*
> *pudicissimae et frugalissimae, quae innocenter*
> *maritum et domum eius amavit, omnia de se*
> *merenti fecit Q. Oppius Secundus maritus et sibi.*
> *tempore quo sum genita, natura mihi bis denos tribuit*
> *annos, quibus completis septima deinde die resoluta*
> *legibus otio sum perpetuo tradita: haec mihi vita fuit.*

---

109 For example, Conte 1994, a well-respected and widely consulted reference work, claims that the *Distichs* were "assembled between the end of the second century and beginning of the fourth" (612).
110 Connolly 2013b.
111 Massaro 2007, 279. Colafrancesco 1986 also places this Roman inscription between 50 and 100 CE.

> *Oppi, ne metuas Lethen, nam stultum est, tempore et om-*
> *ni dunc mortem metuas, amittere gaudia vitae.*
> *mors etenim hominum natura, non poena est;*
> *cui contigit nasci, instat et mori. igitur,*
> *domine Oppi marite, ne doleas mei quod praecessi:*
> *sustineo in aeterno toro adventum tuum.*
> *valete superi et cuncti cunctaeque valete.*
>
> (CIL 6.11252 = CE 756 adn. = CE 1567)

To the eternal and consecrated house of Agileia Prima, also known as Auguria, a wife most chaste, modest and thrifty beyond her years, who blithely loved her husband and his house, Q. Oppius Secundus her husband put up all this about his deserving wife and for himself. When I was born, nature allotted me twice ten years; and once these were finished, on the seventh day, freed from these terms, I was delivered over to everlasting rest: such was my life. Oppius, do not fear death, for it is foolish, if you fear death at every moment, to lose the joys of life. For death is in the nature of mortals, it is not a punishment; whoever is granted life is condemned with death too. And so, my master and husband, Oppius, do not grieve that I have gone: I am ready for your arrival on our eternal couch. Farewell to those I leave behind, farewell my kinsmen and women.

Only the first three words differ from our text of *DC* 2.3:

> *Linque metum leti; nam stultum est tempore in omni,*
> *Dum mortem metuis, amittere gaudia vitae.*
>
> Let go your fear of death: it is foolish,
> Fearing death at every moment, to lose life's joys.

Not only does this inscription supply a terminus *ante quem*, it also provides our earliest evidence for a maxim in couplet form.[112]

Texts that quote from the *Distichs* are useful as evidence for dating. But just as importantly the nature and variety of them give us insights into the position held by the *Distichs* in Romans' popular imagination and shared cultural experience. Especially interesting is the misquotation of the *Distichs*, which suggests that those who quoted from the *Distichs* were more concerned with capitalizing on the cultural value of this respected text than with observing its correct form

---

[112] *Carmina Epigraphica* 857, l. 6, quotes *DC* 2.2.2, though the inscription cannot be dated (Colafrancesco 1986). Boas 1932a, 178–186, suggests that l. 51 of the Allia Potestas funerary inscription (*CIL* VI.37965 = *CE* 1988), Laedere qui *hoc* poterit *ausus quoque laedere divos*, is quoting *DC* 4.39.2: Laedere qui *potuit,* poterit *prodesse aliquando*. Horsfall 1985, 272, however, disagrees and believes that it derives simply from "a common type of formula."

and, crucially, that the *Distichs* were widely known soon after their composition.

In the inscription of Quintus Oppius Secundus, only the first three words in lines 10–11 differ from our text of *DC* 2.3. The inscription, which is probably Oppius' own composition, though it is also possible he had someone write it for him, is written as if to him by his wife. Oppius has kept the basic sentiment of the original *Distich*—do not fear death—but he has personalized the text, for example by including the vocative *Oppi* at the start of line 10. Then, in place of *linque metum*, literally "leave fear," Oppius has used a negative jussive subjunctive instead: *ne metuas* "do not fear."[113] It is impossible to know for sure why Oppius changed the text, but it is significant that he felt free to do so.

Oppius—and perhaps other Romans too—may have felt a sense of shared ownership of the *Distichs*. Early re-workings of lines from Vergil's *Aeneid* provide useful analogies for this notion. For example, a parodic spin on *Aeneid* 1.1 preserved in a graffito from Pompeii proclaims *fullones ululamque cano non arma virumq(ue)* ("I sing of fullers and the owl, not arms and the man").[114] The importance for us is that, first, the writer of the graffito had to assume his readers' familiarity with the original line for the parody to be effective. Second, the *Aeneid* had strong currency among Romans: it became an instant classic and straightaway an educational text. It was Vergil's, but it was also everyone's. Similarly, the *Distichs* seem early on to have been sufficiently popular that they belonged to everyone.[115]

---

113 Oppius has switched from the Latin *letum* to the Greek-derived *Lēthēn*, a Greek accusative form. The switch is striking: perhaps Oppius was showing off his learning, by favoring Greek over Latin. Perhaps he was claiming to see an etymological connection between them, though there is not one. He may have felt that *Lēthē*, the river that runs through the Underworld and brings forgetfulness to those who drink from it, had a gentler connotation than *letum*, simply "death". Yet he uses Latin *mors* just below, in line 12. A final possibility is that, in circulation at the time, there was an alternative text of *Distichs* 2.3 that substituted *Lēthēs* (the genitive form) for *leti*. This alternative reading would scan, but it is not recorded in any manuscripts. Such personification has precedents in the *Distichs*: in *DC* 4.10 and 4.30, the Author uses Venus and Bacchus as personifications of love and drunkenness.

114 On this and other re-workings in graffiti, see Milnor 2014, 238–272.

115 The inscription draws on a couple more texts: lines 12 and 13 are both adaptations from the Stoic philosopher Seneca, preserved in the *De Remediis Fortuitorum* 2.1 (*Morieris, ista hominis natura est non poena*) and *Epistles* 99.8 (*cui nasci contigit mori restat*). It is clear that Oppius liked philosophy and wisdom. But what is interesting is that he put Seneca and the *Distichs* together: a well-respected philosopher and a collection of commonplaces. The *Distichs* were held by some, at least, in high regard.

Another funerary inscription, *Carmina Epigraphica* 857, quotes from *Distichs* 2.2.

> *Hic s]ita sunt pia natorum dua cor[pora cara*
> *E]t matris myserae semper dilectae ma[rito,*
> *Nomina sub titulo quorum perscripta [leguntur,*
> *Quos pater infelix coniux myser ips[e locavit.*
> *Te quicumque legis pietatis nomine ad[hortor,*
> *Cum sis mortalis, quae sint mortal[ia cures,*
> *Et patrias admitte preces et parce s[epulcro.*

> Placed here are the two dutiful and dear bodies of my children
> And of my pitiful wife always beloved of her husband,
> Whose names are read written out in full under this inscription,
> Whom their unlucky father, pitiful husband has himself put here.
> You, whoever you are reading this, I urge you in the name of duty,
> You're mortal—concern yourself with mortal things,
> And grant a father's prayers and preserve this tomb.

DC 2.2

> *Mitte archana dei caelumque inquirere quid sit;*
> *Cum sis mortalis, quae sunt mortalia cura.*

> Quit seeking divine secrets and what heaven is;
> You're mortal—concern yourself with mortal things.

In the undated inscription, a man mourns his wife and two children. The inscription comprises hexameter couplets, with a final single line. In lines 5 and 6, the husband urges his reader, the passerby, to take care for the here and now, since he or she is mortal. The first line of *Distichs* 2.2 told the reader to stop thinking too much about the divine; the line is now replaced, in line 5 of the inscription, with an instruction to the reader to contemplate what follows, i.e., the quoted second line of the *Distichs* couplet. The replacement makes sense given the new context, and it serves to emphasize the quoted line. It also demonstrates, again, how the *Distichs* were seen as open to appropriation. Indeed, they were suitable for appropriation too: they are lexically and syntactically simple; there is also lack of enjambment—in other words, clauses do not spill over from one line to the next—and in a good number of the couplets, the lines can stand by themselves, independently, as is the case here.[116]

Vindicianus' misquotation is also significant for understanding the *Distichs'* early popularity. The fact that Vindicianus chooses to quote from the *Distichs* confirms what we might have guessed from their style and content: that they offered nuggets of wisdom that could serve as the moral of the story or as bons mots. Readers must have found their clear and easy-to-follow formulations of frankly pedestrian wisdom especially apposite. The *Distichs* do not offer much original thought—and that is perhaps why they are so successful. They present the obvious in a readily accessible, memorable, and recognizable package that can be used in multiple situations, from funerary inscriptions to letters, and as a rhetorical or lyrical florilegium.

But if they are so easily memorable, Vindicianus would surely not have misquoted them. Perhaps an explanation for his error lies in the idea that the *Distichs* as a collection are more important and significant than their text. The authors of the inscriptions personalize the text of the *Distichs*; Vindicianus privileges the *Distichs* over their text. These are different aspects of the same phenomenon, namely that ancient Romans had a *sense* of the *Distichs*, a feel for them, a notion of them. They could alter or misremember the text of couplets to make them their own without losing their readers' ability to recognize them as being from the *Distichs*. The *Distichs* were so well known that Romans could even misquote and garble them—in a letter to an emperor no less—and the reader could still expect to recognize them because the reader probably knew them by heart and needed only a few words to recall the rest. Indeed, the *Distichs* were so well known and thus open to appropriation that those who quoted them felt free to alter their meaning, even radically.

---

116 The inscription is fragmentary, and line 6 is incomplete. The editors have supplemented it from the *Distichs*, which is understandable, but it is just possible that the inscription contained a different verb, which would be a variant reading or another example of appropriation and adaptation. Inscriptions in Latin seem to have been common vehicles for maxims, as had been inscriptions in Greek, on which see Tsagalis 2008, 9–15. The husband and Oppius were not alone in including wisdom in an epitaph. Another example is *CIL* 11.600 (ca. 30 BCE), the epitaph of C. Castricius, whose agnomen Agricola was possibly meant to associate him with Roman Republican wise landowners, such as the Elder Cato. Agricola dispenses wisdom that Buecheler, the editor for *CIL*, likens to the *Sententiae Septem Sapientum*, though Agricola claims that his wisdom is his own and not acquired at the hands of teachers—and indeed Buecheler's heavy supplements to the fragmentary text may have been made with the *Sententiae* in mind. On the inscription, see also Chevallier 1997, 55.

Commodianus, the third-century Christian poet, quoted the *Distichs* correctly and inserted them—together with their correct classical hexameter—into his not-so-classical verse. He was well read and fond of quoting or at least alluding to a host of classical Latin authors, including Lucretius, Cicero, Vergil, Manilius, Ovid, Seneca, Lucan, Martial, and Juvenal, as well as more contemporary Christian writers, including Justin, Tertullian, Minucius Felix and Cyprian.[117] The quotation of *DC* 3.17 is among the most substantial found in Commodianus' poems and provides evidence that the *Distichs* found favor early on with Christian writers, a fact crucial for their preservation.

Commodianus has reworked the imperative *damnā* ("condemn") into the present participle form *damnans* ("condemning") to fit his syntax. In so doing, he has rendered the line a simple circumstantial subordinate. Now, the *Distichs* derive their memorable force from their expression as imperatives and gnomic

---

117 Most scholars now date Commodianus' *floruit* to the mid-third century; see especially Poinsotte 1996, 272–273. According to Poinsotte 2009, xi–xii and xxxviii–xli, there are examples of thoughts or expressions in the *Instructions* influenced by Lucretius, Cicero, Vergil, Manilius, Ovid, Seneca, Lucan, Martial, and Juvenal, all of whom were writers of the first centuries BCE and CE, excepting the last. The Christian writers influential on the work—Justin, Tertullian, Minucius Felix, and Cyprian—are more contemporary with Commodian. There are further examples of shared wording between Commodianus and the *Disticha*, though they are less significant, and some are probably not quotations at all, but simply verbal coincidences. Among the most substantive are:

> *Apol.* 67: *Estote prudentes, quod imminet ante videte*
> *DC* 2.27: *Quod sequitur specta, quodque imminet ante videto;*
> *Illum imitare deum, partem qui spectat utramque.*
> *Instruct.* 1.32.1–2: *Si locus aut tempus favet aut persona provenit.*
> *Iudex esto tuus. Quod nunc extolleris inde?*
> *DC* 1.14: *Cum te aliquis laudat, iudex tuus esse memento;*
> *Plus aliis de te, quam tu tibi, credere noli.*
> *Apol.* 15: *Quis melior medicus nisi passus vulnera victor?*
> *DC* 4.13: *Auxilium a notis petito, si forte labores;*
> *Nec quisquam melior medicus quam fidus amicus.*
> *Instruct.* 1.35.15–16: *... gustat unde licet, ille*
> *qui Deos adorat vetitos, mala gaudia vitae.*
> *DC* 4.17 : *Si famam servare cupis, dum vivis, honestam*
> *Fac fugias animo, quae sunt mala gaudia vitae.*

The references are from Boas 1952, LXXII–LXXIII. Opelt 1988, 147, believes that funerary inscriptions are the source of Commodian and the *Disticha*'s shared vocabulary, phrasing, and notions. On Commodianus' use of the *Disticha*, see also Bloomer 2017, who considers him within his North African context.

statements. But in borrowing this line, Commodianus has taken away its force. This is a completely new use of the *Distichs*—and a strange one too. Even more strange is that Commodianus has altered the sense of the original. So in *DC* 3.17, we read

> *Quod merito pateris, patienter ferre memento,*
> *Cumque reus tibi sis, ipsum te iudice damna.*

> Whatever you deserve to suffer, tolerate it;
> Be your own defense, but be judge and jury too.

The sense is this: you have done something wrong and, as a result, have suffered an unpleasant consequence, perhaps even a punishment, and you should tolerate what you have justly deserved. Whatever actions you undertake, when you go to defend yourself, put yourself also in the position of prosecution and judge—that is to say, try to consider whether criticism, even punishment, of you is justified. Following this advice, you will modify your future behavior.

Commodianus says something quite different:

> *Omnia suspensus vivis in ardore lucrorum;*
> *Cumque reus tibi sis ipsum te iudice damnans*
> *Oculorum acies nunquam satiatur avara*
> *Nunc ergo si credeas et cogites vana cupido est*   5
> *Congerere nimium sub fragili vita moranti.*

> In thrall to everything, you live enamored by profit; and whenever you defend yourself, acting as your own prosecution and judge too, the greedy sights of your eyes are never satisfied.

Now the line castigates the reader for acting as his own defense, prosecution, and judge: appropriating all three roles, he is unable to place limits upon himself. In Commodianus' reworking of the line, the reader will consistently fail to moderate his future behavior. Commodianus has reworked the distich he quotes, but has undermined both the expression and the message of the original. Perhaps he knew them so well that he could even use their text against their message. This may have been accidental: he knew the text, but neglected to think about its meaning. Alternatively, it could be ironic quotation, i.e., when Commodianus quotes the *Distichs*, he does so in order to challenge their meaning.

Soon after their composition, several centuries later, and even far beyond that, the *Distichs* were so well known that a single line from them could be effective in multiple ways. It could connote wisdom, as well as a shared educational and cultural tradition; it could also suggest an idea, as well as transmit a specific message: when Commodianus quoted *DC* 3.17, there was a general sentiment he wanted to express, and he remembered the text of that couplet as connoting a mix of general ideas about judgment, self-knowledge, and evaluation of one's actions.

We might say something similar about the other quotations: they too are drawing on the *Distichs* as a wisdom collection and a source of authority. For first Oppius, then for the unknown husband bereft of his wife and children, and finally for Vindicianus, the *Distichs* either exactly expressed or generally reflected a sentiment they wished to communicate. The quotations and misquotations of the collection, while few in number, demonstrate that it was respected, effective, and so well known that this anonymous text soon became everyone's: a literary possession of the Romans first would become a literary possession of Europe and beyond for many centuries thereafter.

Oppius' inscription helps to give the *Distichs* a terminus ante quem sometime in the first century CE. An allusion to the *Distichs* in Martial 8.29, which circulated in December 94, supplies confirmation and adds precision. As was first discussed by Herrmann, there is a strong possibility that Martial 8.29 was written in response to *DC* 4.49:[118]

> *Disticha qui scribit, puto, vult brevitate placere.*
>   *Quid prodest brevitas, dic mihi, si liber est?*

> Whoever writes two-liners, so I think, wants to please by being brief.
>   But what good is brevity, tell me, if it comes in a tome?

In his first line, Martial suggests that two-liners are pleasing to the reader on account of their brevity. The public seems to have liked its poetry snappy and to the point, and it is unsurprising then that the aim for brevity was a trope among epigrammatists, especially Martial, who addresses that aim appropriately in his own two-liner.[119] In the second line, the poet adds a caveat: two-liners are popular, but massing them into a book is inappropriate.

Martial's choice of the Greek word *disticha* is unusual, and its prominent position places additional emphasis upon it. With this word and the abstract noun *brevitas*, a key term in *DC* 4.49, we have an allusion to the final *Distich*. That allusion is complex, but it may tell us something about the circulation of the collection in 94 CE.

---

118 Herrmann 1950, 117.
119 On this epigram, see most recently Schöffel 2002, 276–280.

Martial is, I think, poking fun at poets' circulation of their epigrams. Wanting to please his readers, he has produced brief epigrams like 8.29. Yet he has taken those poems and massed them together in a book, the very practice he derides in 8.29. We can understand his reasons for doing so: an individual epigram might be made public first at a reading, but afterwards circulating it would be difficult. Custom suggested that it would circulate best in a book, a *liber*. But producing a book would undermine the poet's public rejection—in his own epigrams, no less—of such a practice. Martial has, with a wink, summed up the plight of the ambitious epigrammatist.

But he is also poking fun at the circulation of the *Distichs*. As I argued above, the *Distichs* were authored by one person. It is impossible to know his methods of composition and circulation, but at some point his individual couplets were gathered into one collection of four books.[120] Martial's epigram may be alluding to the individual four books or perhaps to the collection as a whole, but the point is clear: distichs may be brief, but a whole book of them is not, and that book—perhaps one or more of the four or the *Distichs* as whole—was already circulating by 94 CE.

Martial makes particular fun of *DC* 4.49's use of *brevitas*. The word's form contradicts its meaning: comprising three syllables, it is hardly brief. In his own two-liner, Martial includes the word not once, but twice, perhaps to emphasize the duality of the epigram, certainly to point up that *brevitas*, as the signature of a distich and indeed of the *Distichs*, has been undermined by the fact that there are so many in a book.[121] Oppius' inscription and Martial's epigram together may provide *termini ante quem* in the late first century CE for the composition and circulation of the *Distichs*. A *terminus post quem* could come from the collection's meter.

A comparison of the metrical patterns used in the *Distichs* with those employed in a range of other hexameter texts dating as late as the sixth century reveals that the predilections of the collection's Author in this regard are most similar to Germanicus' *Aratea*, Manilius' *Astronomica*, Vergil's *Georgics* and, in particular, his *Aeneid*. The fact that most of these works cluster around the start

---

120 The couplets may have initially circulated individually in some way; or they may have first circulated in books; alternatively, the couplets may always have circulated in four books contained within one collection.

121 Of course, we cannot be sure that Martial had read the *Distichs*, and it is possible that he is referring instead to collections by other epigrammatists, as well as his own. Garthwaite 1998, 169–170, instead reads Martial 8.29 with 9.50 as part of a poetic conversation with the poet's contemporaries.

of the first century CE might point to a contemporary date for the *Distichs* also.¹²² The earliest of these works, the *Georgics*, perhaps first circulated in 29 BCE, and we might then posit a terminus post quem of that year. However, the greater metrical similarity of the *Distichs* to the *Aeneid* makes 19 BCE more likely. Similarities to the *Aratea* and *Astronomica* suggest that the Author may have been writing in the first century CE, by which time the *Aeneid* had been established widely as a metrical model.¹²³

The *Distichs'* meter is important for establishing a possible period for their composition, and analysis of it helps to reveal some of the ways in which the Author used the form of his *Distichs* to complement their messages, as I discuss further below in Chapter 3. It can even be used to determine whether additional couplets found in some manuscripts are original.

The meter of the *Distichs* is remarkably simple and consistent, more so than in any other work of Latin poetry.¹²⁴ The key characteristics of that meter are as follows: the eight most common combinations of dactyls (*d*) and spondees (*s*) in the first four feet of each dactylic hexameter line (of which there are 288) are *dsss*, *ddss*, *dsds*, *ssss*, *sdss*, *dssd*, *ddds*, and *ssds*.¹²⁵ The resulting abundance of spondees in the lines of the *Distichs* relative to those of other Latin poetic texts creates a slow, plodding meter that encourages the reader to consider each word in turn. This slow deliberateness is in turn supported and strengthened by the Author's apparent desire to include multiple points of articulation in each line that serve to mark off key words. He makes generous use of caesurae, in particular, strong caesurae in the third foot of his lines, and in about one third of those, he follows with a monosyllabic word, a combination rare in other authors. The result is lines that are split halfway, usually where there is a syntactical break. The Author also makes frequent use of diaereses to isolate key words, and over one half of his lines contain bucolic diaereses, which also help to create an emphatic point of articulation. To further underscore the articulations

---

122 On the meter and date of the *Disticha*, see Connolly 2011.
123 On the meter of the *Aeneid* and its imitators, see generally Duckworth 1969.
124 For a full discussion of the meter of the *Distichs*, see Connolly 2011, in which the meter of the *Distichs* is found to be simpler even than that of the *Ilias Latina*, which Dickey 1999, has described as containing "some of the easiest classical-sounding Latin poetry in existence."
125 Every line of the *Distichs* is in hexameter and has a dactyl in the fifth foot, without exception. The percentages of lines represented by the eight most common metrical patterns in the first four feet are as follows: *dsss* (19.1%), *ddss* (12.85%), *dsds* (9.72%), *ssss* (9.03%), *sdss* (8.68%), *dssd* (7.29%), *ddds* (6.25%) and *ssds* (5.21%).

created by caesurae and diaereses, the Author avoids elision, and only seven of his couplets contain enjambment.[126]

The final couplet of the collection provides a broadly representative example of the Author's meter. Foot divisions are marked with /, caesurae with //, and diaereses with |.

Mira/ris // ver/bis // nu/dis // me/ | scribere/ | versus?
Hoc // brevi/tas // fe/cit, // sen/sus // con/iungere/ | binos.

Each word in these two heavily spondaic lines is separated from the words preceding and following by either a caesura or diaeresis, and the result is a couplet that takes time to say, forcing the reader to reflect on each word he encounters.

Eight maxims and two lines that are found in manuscripts belonging to *traditio* Φ and the *traditio Barberina* do not appear in the *traditio vulgata*.[127] Of these, only one, *DC* 3.1a in Boas' numbering, shares the favored metrical patterns of the maxims (*ssss* in the first line and *ddds* in the second); like the *Distichs*, it also contains caesurae and diaereses in both lines and lacks elision, thus separating off each word.

Fortu/nae // do/nis // sem/per // par/ | esse // me/mento:
Non // opi/bus // bona/ | fama // da/tur, // sed/ | moribus/ | ipsis.

The first three caesurae in the second line, however, are weak, which is a marked departure from the predilection in the *Distichs* for strong caesurae. The three elisions of *DC* 1.27a render it a likely addition:

Contr(a) homi/n(em) astu/tum // no/li // ver/sutus // ha/beri :
Non // cap/tare // ma/los // stul/t(um) est, // sed/ | velle // no/cere.

Moreover, the phrasing of the second line might remind the reader of *DC* 3.23.2 (*Namque malum est, non velle pati nec posse tacere*). If this maxim is a later addition, it was the work of someone who knew the *Distichs* well. Three maxims, *DC* 1.12a, 1.14a, and 1.14b, which appear only in manuscript A, all contain a

---

126 A caesura marks a break between words that occurs within a metrical foot and creates a pause in the line. A diaeresis marks a break between words that coincides with the end of a metrical foot and also creates a pause. Elision is the merger of two words by the substitution of the end of the final syllable of the first with the vocalic opening of the second. Enjambment is the continuation of a syntactical unit across two or more lines. For a succinct introduction to scansion of Classical Latin hexameter verse, see especially Garrison 2004, 175–177.

127 The additional maxims are *DC* 1.12a, 1.14a, 1.14b, 1.27a, 3.1a, 3.21a, 3.21b and 4.25a. There are also additional lines: *DC* 1.31a and 2.21.3.

first line whose metrical pattern is among the most favored in the *Distichs*, but a second whose pattern is not.[128] Moreover, they are so closely related in theme to the widely attested maxims that precede them that they are most likely later additions to A's archetype. The same is true of *DC* 1.27a.

Finally, three additional couplets—*DC* 1.31a, 2.21.3 and 4.25a—are unlikely to have been composed by the maxims' author because they are clearly lines adapted from the *sententiae* of Publilius Syrus.[129] Similarly, *DC* 1.40a.1 is identical to Hor. *Epist.* 1.2.57, and since no other maxim in the collection is so derivative, it should be regarded as a later addition.

With the exclusion of these additional couplets and lines, we are left with a corpus of 144 couplets that are consistent in their meter and, as I demonstrate in Chapter 3, in their lexical and syntactical simplicity too. These couplets are most likely original to the collection, i.e., they were all composed by the Author. They are the original *Disticha Catonis*.

Looking back over all these clues, the following picture emerges. The *Distichs* is a text whose meter is modeled on Vergil's *Aeneid*. An almost complete couplet is quoted in an inscription perhaps of the first century, and a poem of 94 CE may refer to the collection. Vindicianus, an educated man, quoted from the collection in the late fourth century, ascribing the quotation to "Cato". This picture suggests a date of the first century CE, rather than of the third.

A new date for the *Distichs* has significant implications: it places them in the broad context of a plethora of texts of the first centuries BCE and CE that may have provided inspiration for their style and phrasing. It also provides the scholar the opportunity to consider the *Distichs* and the broad themes they tackle in light of a density of texts that does not exist in the third century. Chapters 4 and 5 demonstrate how considering the *Distichs* within their new context allows us to set their messages alongside and often in contrast to those of contemporary texts and to reveal some of the attitudes of their audience.

---

128 *DC* 1.14a is patterned *ddss* (which ranks second most popular in the *Distichs*) and *dsdd* (ranked below eighth in the *Distichs*); *DC* 1.14b is patterned *dssd* (ranked sixth) and *sdds* (ranked below eighth); *DC* 1.40a contains *ddss* (ranked second) and *sdsd* (ranked below eighth); *DC* 3.21a contains *dsss* (ranked first) and *dsdd* (ranked below eighth).
129 *DC* 1.31a is inspired by Publilius Syrus 399, *DC* 2.21.3 by Publilius Syrus 75, and *DC* 4.25a by Publilius Syrus 443. For Syrus, I follow the numbering system in Duff and Duff 1934.

Audience

We know already of several of the *Distichs*' readers. The first is Q. Oppius Secundus, who quoted a (modified) couplet on the funerary inscription to his wife. Nothing is known about this individual, except that he had also read Seneca and Silius Italicus, whom he also quotes.[130] Three Oppii Secundi are known to us: a freedman priest of Augustus, a centurion who was perhaps also a member of the praetorian guard, and another praetorian.[131] These men—who are not necessarily related—are not of the highest social status, but they are educated. Our earliest known reader, then, was interested in philosophy, was educated, and, with priests and military officials possibly in the family, was perhaps a man who held a low-level magistracy in or near Rome, where the inscription was found.

The next known reader is Commodianus. A Christian convert later in life, he was well-read in earlier Classical pagan literature and roughly contemporary Christian texts. His geographical origins are obscure, though suggestions have ranged from Syria to North Africa, and with his quotation we may have evidence for the collection's wide geographical spread.[132] Our final known reader is Vindicianus, an educated man of high socio-economic status. And we can add another probable reader too: Valentinian II. Even if Vindicianus did not know for sure that Valentinian had read the *Distichs*, he certainly felt confident in assuming he had.

Over the course of perhaps 300 years, the *Distichs* were read by a man probably from Rome of middling status with a private interest in philosophy, a pagan-turned-Christian poet, a doctor who wrote medical treatises and was physician to an emperor, and finally the emperor himself. This is an audience of mixed economic and social status, religion, and geographical background, not all of whom necessarily had a strong interest in moral, philosophical, or ethical texts. The *Distichs*, then, seem to have enjoyed a wide audience that was deeply

---

130 For a discussion of the inscription's quotations, see Langford Wilson 1911, 168–169. On the philosophy of the piece, see Pleket 1983, 251.
131 The freedman is L. Oppius Secundus, who is attested in 25 CE at Caere in *CIL* 11.3613 and *ILS* 5052; see Papi 1994, 165. The centurion, another L. Oppius Secundus, is attested in the legio VII Gemina between the reigns of Galba and Trajan; see Le Roux 1972, 105, and Palao Vicente 2006, 194. The praetorian is G. Oppius Secundus, who is attested on an inscription from Annecy, France, on which see Serralongue, Faure, and Bertrandy 2004.
132 Poinsotte 1996, 278–279, suggests that Commodian was born in Syria and subsequently settled in Africa. Some early manuscripts have a Spanish provenance (Bischoff 1981, 170–171), but this fact cannot point to a Spanish origin for the collection or its particular popularity there.

familiar with them. That familiarity is most easily explained if they were a school text.

There is compelling circumstantial evidence that makes it highly likely that the *Distichs* were used in Roman schools.¹³³ The content of the *Distichs* is uncontroversial, offering sound advice that avoids any overt philosophical or political polemic; the sentiments are basic, sub-philosophical common sense, and thus are suitable reading for an audience of children. Even those maxims that give modern readers pause have good Classical precedent. For example, *DC* 3.3 (*Productus testis, salvo tamen ante pudore, / Quantumcumque potes, celato crimen amici* "When brought to court as witness, though your shame has never yet been compromised, / As far as you can, hide the wrongdoing of a friend"), which might strike us as advocating that witnesses withhold information to protect their friends, instead speaks to the ancient anxiety, voiced by Cicero, and Gellius, about the relative claims of justice and friendship.¹³⁴

The *Distichs*, with their brief verse couplets and simple phrasing of instructions as reflections or imperatives, could be learned easily in school. We know from Seneca the Younger that *gnomai* were learned by heart in Roman schools: *ideo pueris et sententias ediscendas damus et has quas Graeci chrias vocant, quia complecti illas puerilis animus potest, qui plus adhuc non capit* ("and for that reason we give the boys sayings to learn by heart and what the Greeks call *chreiai*, because a boy's mind can get to grips with them, though it cannot handle much more").¹³⁵

Indeed, from at least the second century CE, Roman schoolchildren followed the model of the Greeks in reading and learning by heart *chreiai* or *gnomai*, edifying statements of wisdom.¹³⁶ For example, in Lucian's *Anacharsis*,

---

133 On the *Distichs* in ancient education, see Bonner 1977, 173; Marrou 1956, 365; and especially Bloomer 2011, 139–169. It is tempting to assume that widespread use of the *Disticha* throughout the medieval period and beyond might be a remnant of their use by the Romans, but as Glauche 1972, 617, notes, "Vielmehr ist mit einem völligen Neuansatz in vorkarolingischer Zeit zu rechnen."

134 Cic. *Off.* 3.43–44, and *Amic.* 61; Gell. *NA* 1.3. *DC* 3.3 is discussed further in Chapter 4. Another way to approach ethically ambiguous maxims is to consider that they may have been useful for *aetiologica*, exercises whose precise nature is unclear, but which may have required pupils to explain *sententiae*, in particular those that were paradoxical, seemingly non-sensical or somehow controversial. On definitions for *aetiologica*, see Bonner 1977, 258, and Bons 1992, 205–206.

135 Seneca, *Ep.* 33.7.

136 On the use of *gnomai* in Greek and Roman education, see especially Morgan 1998, chap. 4, and Wolff 2015, 150, who notes that Augustus recommended adults read them too and share them with the rest of their household (Suet. *Aug.* 89.4).

Solon tells the title character that the Greeks recite to boys "sayings of wise men" (σοφῶν ἀνδρῶν γνώμας), which they have put into meter to aid their memory, in order to encourage them to imitation.[137] There were plenty of Greek *gnomologia* (see Chapter 2), such as the Bouriant papyrus, which contains a series of monostichs whose first letters spell out the alphabet from alpha to omega, so creating a brief set of readily memorable pieces of wisdom for an educational context.[138] The *Distichs* provided a similar store of *gnomai* for the Latin classroom. Alternatively, the *Distichs* could have aided children's handwriting: we learn from Seneca that moralizing verses were used as copying exercises.[139]

The *Distichs* likely enjoyed a readership beyond the schoolroom, and adults may have been the original intended audience. Indeed, as Raffaella Cribiore points out, paraenetic collections were read by children and adults alike.[140] The short collection is just the sort of text one might expect to find in the house of a family eager or concerned to act properly and look after itself, and it would have appealed to a broad audience: several maxims are directed at husbands and a couple at slaveholders; one maxim has advice for the father who lacks sufficient money for a specialized education for his children; and while no entries are directed at senators, equestrians, decurions or other members of the political and social élite, we know that they were among the readership. The fact that there are no entries aimed explicitly at women or enslaved individuals should not surprise us.[141]

Leo Perdue, in a study of Biblical wisdom, notes that paraenetic texts might be used to direct young members of society at a liminal point in their development, but equally could help to remind adults how to behave or reorient them if they had lost their way.[142] The *Distichs*, then, might have told a Roman man and

---

[137] Lucian, *Anacharsis* 21; the reference is from Bonner 1977, 172.
[138] A text of the papyrus is in Jäkel 1964, 5–6; Bonner 1977, 173, has a discussion.
[139] Seneca, *Ep.* 94.9. See Bonner 1977, 173–176. Williams 1977, 271, suggests that the late Ptolemaic or early Roman *Deir al-Bahri Ostracon*, comprising a few lines of advice directed to a male audience about women, may have been a schoolboy copy of a paraenetic text; this too may have been an exercise in handwriting. Paraenetic texts were used earlier, in Hellenistic Egypt, as reading exercises, on which see Barns 1951.
[140] Cribiore 2001, 178–179.
[141] To husbands: *DC* 1.8, 3.20, 3.23, 3.12, 4.47; to slaveholders: *DC* 1.8, 1.37, 3.10, 4.44. It is possible that the second line of *DC* 3.23 was directed to wives (I am grateful to Ronald Mellor for the observation), but husbands are the more likely addressees.
[142] Perdue 1981, 248–253.

his family too how they should behave in order to find success, security, and happiness in Roman society.

Ostensibly a guide to better living, the *Distichs* could in addition serve a practical purpose. According to Quintilian, *sententiae* were employed in legal trials and political speeches.[143] They could also be useful for the Roman man looking for an easy way to show off his erudition and social skills.[144] For example, in Athenaeus' *Deipnosophistae*, a speaker recounts at dinner the witticisms of courtesans, a scene that Laura McClure claims is meant to parody Cynic philosophers, who may perhaps have sprinkled their dinnertime talk with aphorisms; in Petronius' *Cena Trimalchionis*, we find the dinner host self-consciously composing two hexameter lines and one pentameter (a puffed-up mashing of a hexameter couplet and an elegiac couplet), whose feeble profundity underwhelms.[145] With their rhythm and brevity—which the Author himself points out in his final maxim—individual lines or an entire couplet from the *Distichs* could easily have been dropped into conversation by Romans eager to impress.

---

143 See especially Quint. *Inst.* 8.5.
144 Adrados 2009, 59, claims that in the *Dicta Septem Sapientum* and other wisdom texts we can find "the influence of symposiastic elements (related of old to maxims, similes, anecdotes, etc.)."
145 Ath. 577d–85f; on this passage, see McClure 2003. Petr. *Sat.* 55.

2 Ancient Wisdom

> Science is organized knowledge. Wisdom is organized life.
> Immanuel Kant

The previous chapter argued for understanding the style of the *Distichs* as informed by the desire of the Author to create a collection for readers that would be easy to read, understand, and remember. In this chapter, I argue that the form of the *Distichs* and its content were also informed by the text's long generic tradition; but the collection's more immediate Roman context should not be neglected. The *Distichs* express a universal wisdom and they can profitably be read with and against other wisdom collections. But it is useful also to read them with and against contemporary texts, since the Author, while drawing on the store of available ancient wisdom, will have drawn from it selectively to suit his needs, his audience, and his time. This latter fact will have contributed to their appeal for Romans.

This chapter falls into three parts: the first is an analysis of the *Distichs* within the paraenetic tradition (the first such analysis), in which I set out key similarities and differences between the *Distichs* and various paraenetic texts in order to understand and appreciate what is traditional and what is distinctively innovative about them. The second contains a brief consideration of the *Distichs* as a store of universal wisdom, and I argue that the universality of many of the *Distichs'* messages must help to explain their appeal, but I also note that approaching the *Distichs* simply as a store of universal wisdom presents a barrier to understanding the possible reasons why this collection was appreciated by its original Roman audience. In response, in the third section, I present an assertion for the need for considering the *Distichs* in a Roman context and as a text that held appeal for Romans.

Ancient paraenesis

No one extant ancient text emerges as a model for the *Distichs*, a collection of two-line maxims in hexameter couplets written on a wide array of topics by an anonymous Author to no specified audience. To be sure, an immense wisdom tradition stretches back before the *Distichs*: Near Eastern and Greek, and Biblical too, as well as Republican Roman. Wisdom in the ancient world has been expressed in a variety of forms: proverbs, beatitudes, questions, riddles, instructions, didactic narratives, disputations, panegyrics, anecdotes, philosophical discourses, fables, theodicies, and omens are all included.¹⁴⁶ In addition there are paraenetic texts: miscellaneous and assorted collections of precepts and admonitions that concern the regulation of human behavior.¹⁴⁷ The *Distichs* are a paraenetic text. But it is striking that of the texts in the paraenetic tradition, few share more than a couple of the collection's characteristics.

With a possible date of the first century CE, the *Distichs* may have been composed at a moment in which there was strong interest in wisdom and especially in paraenesis. The *Sententiae* of Publilius Syrus were circulating from the late Republic. These are probably the best-known work of Latin paraenesis thanks to their inclusion in the modern *Wheelock's Latin* series as simple and pithy selections of "real" Latin that supply examples of grammatical points, as well as insights into Roman views. Drawn from the mimes of the Republican playwright, the *Sententiae* as a collection were perhaps inspired by earlier Greco-Egyptian *gnomologia*. The approximately 800 lines are arranged alphabetically and cover a wide array of topics: relationships, fate and fortune, abstract concepts such as justice and fairness, and the realities of servitude and freedom. Hamblenne seems to suggest that the compiler of the *Sententiae* took excerpts from Publilius and repackaged them as one-line maxims in response to a phenomenon upon which Seneca the Elder (*Contr.* 7.3.8) comments: namely that young rhetors of the late Republic were fond of employing *sententiae* and *bons mots* in their speeches, a practice whose popularity Hamblenne attributes to the political circumstances, presumably because it allowed for safety in allusion and subtlety, yet drew force from the authority of the past.¹⁴⁸

Around the close of the Republic and through the beginning of the first century CE, Tiro, Trebonius, and Furius Bibaculus were apparently collecting the witticisms of Cicero; Julius Caesar compiled *apophthegmata*, which included

---

146 Some of the items in this list come from Perdue 2008, 7. The best brief overview of ancient wisdom literature is in West 1978, 3–25; see also Roos 1984, 14–25. For a more detailed treatment, see especially Perdue 2007 and Clifford 2007. Russo 1997 offers a survey of the various distinctions that have been drawn between maxims, proverbs, and apophthegms in Greek literature. Wilson 2022 offers a selection of key ancient wisdom texts, along with brief discussion.
147 The term is used by Gammie 1990. Another term that could equally be used is "conduct books," though this is more usually applied to texts of the medieval period and later.
148 Hamblenne 1973, 632. On the *Sententiae*, see now the extensive and sensitive treatment by Bradley 2019.

material from Cicero; a collection of the orator Domitius Afer's sayings was in circulation; and C. Melissus, a freedman of Maecenas, compiled anecdotes.[149]

The *Sententiae Varronis* might seem to date to this period too, though little is understood of this fragmentary collection of just over 150 brief sayings.[150] From this collection, despite all the uncertainty, and the others attributed to Roman historical figures, we can reconstruct a cultural landscape in which Romans enjoyed their wisdom in the form of *sententiae* apparently from famous authorities. The *Distichs* belong to and were inspired by that landscape.[151]

Gnomologia found in Roman Egypt continue the earlier Hellenistic tradition through the first few centuries CE.[152] Also in Egypt, the *Wisdom of Solomon* (or *Book of Wisdom*), found alongside Proverbs in the Septuagint (as discussed above) and written between 37 and 41 CE (or perhaps in the first century BCE), was very much a product of the Greek East: despite its Jewish framework, it was concerned with theodicy and wisdom more broadly, but was also influenced by Greek philosophy. Scholars disagree on the categorization of the text as wisdom literature, but I suggest we can include it among the contemporary texts that may have influenced the Author of the *Distichs* or, more likely, contributed to a broader interest in wisdom across the Roman world in which the Author also participated.[153] The choice of Cato, a wisdom figure of old, to be the Author's referent authority makes sense given the appearance perhaps around the same time of the eponymous *Wisdom of Solomon* and given Cato's apparent status as the first paraenetic author in Latin. By the time the *Distichs* were in circulation, the wisdom tradition was well established in the Roman world, including in Italy.

---

149 There is a brief history of the text of the *Sententiae Varronis* in Knapp 1913; its many Senecan parallels are discussed in Germann 1910, 1–6, and a text is given on pp. 30–42. Tiro's collection: Quint. 6.3.5; Macrob. *Sat.* 2.1.12; Trebonius' collection: Cic. *Ad Fam.* 15.21.1–3. Domitius Afer: Quint. 6.3.42. C. Melissus: Suet. *Gram.* 21. The references come from Teuffel 1872. The ancient references, in particular those of Quintilian, place a *terminus ante quem* of the later first century CE for some of these collections.

150 A text of the *Sententiae* is available in Riese 1865, 265–272. According to Knapp 1913, 373, who provides a helpful overview of the *Sententiae Varronis*, no ancient authority quotes from the collection as we have it now. Moreover, it is unclear that any of it is really Varro's, and it also shares sentiments with Cicero, Horace, and especially Seneca. On the Senecan borrowings and the text more generally, see Germann 1910.

151 Single-author (or single-authority) collections of prose maxims and anthologies attributed to multiple authors were also in circulation. Adrados 2009, 74, provides a list.

152 Examples include P.Oxy. 42.3004, which dates probably to the first century CE.

153 Clifford 1999 considers the Wisdom of Solomon to be wisdom literature; Burkes 2002 sees connections between the text and apocalyptic literature, as well as wisdom literature.

Roman paraenesis comprised, on the whole, long series of brief statements in prose (with the notable exception of Syrus) that were attributed to wisdom figures or, more widely, to cultural authorities or excerpted from their writings, and sometimes apparently addressed to a junior. The texts contain wise reflections or instructions on a wide range of topics; they may be arranged alphabetically, thematically, or as is occasionally found, without any discernible organizing principle, but they do not form a continuous narrative. The sentiments and topics of the *Distichs* place them squarely within the Roman tradition of paraenesis.

Form

Yet the *Distichs* stand out from the Roman and broader ancient Mediterranean paraenetic traditions because of their form: as a series of discrete hexameter couplets, they are unique.[154] Much paraenetic literature is also in verse or, at least, written in an elevated literary style: as John Foster has argued, the distinct categories of verse and prose may not even have existed in all literatures.[155] For example, Mesopotamian texts (e.g., the *Instructions of Shuruppak*) are grouped into balanced clusters of words.[156] Egyptian instructional texts, with only few exceptions, are in a literary style, which is characterized by significant patterns in accentuation and pauses and signaled by the organization of a text into couplets and stanzas: for example, the lines of *P.Louvre* 2414 group themselves into units of two or more lines, and it is commonly accepted that the *Counsels of Wisdom*, *Counsels of a Pessimist*, and the *Hymn to Ninurta* are in a literary

---

154 There are broad surveys of the paraenetic traditions of the Near East in Kitchen 1977 and Lambert 1960, of Egypt in Lichtheim 1973 and 1983, in the Bible in Kitchen 1998, and in the Greek world in Lardinois 2001 and Adrados 2009, 47–76.

155 Lichtheim 1973, vol. 1, 11–12, identifies three styles: prose, orational (to which she assigns Instructional texts), and verse. I follow Foster 1977, 31, n. 10, in grouping the latter two into a non-prose style.

156 On the *Instructions of Shuruppak*, versions of which survive from ca. 2500 BCE in Sumerian and Akkadian, see Lambert 1960, Alster 1974, and Römer and Burkard 1990, 48–67. According to Lambert 1960, vi, meter in Akkadian is indicated by "a certain schematic balance of words" that groups words into cluster divided by caesurae. He signifies that a text is in verse by reproducing the transliterated version in columns, and in his collection, Akkadian popular sayings are in prose, while proverbs are in verse. Identifying texts written in prose or verse or an elevated literary style can be difficult for readers, especially if they lack knowledge of the languages in which some of these texts were written; moreover, editors may ignore line breaks in the original and present their edited version as continuous text.

style.[157] Distinguishing between styles becomes easier for us when we reach Greek texts, in which a simple distinction may be drawn between prose and verse.

Demotic and Greek *gnomologia* of the Hellenistic period, such as the inscription Hasluck no. 3 and the *Commandments of Sansnos*, include prose texts written in an elevated style that seems to characterize gnomic texts.[158] Other paraenetic texts, however, are in verse: for example, the *Theognidea* are elegiac, presumably on the model of epigrams, with which paraenetic literature may overlap.[159] Moving into the Roman period, we find more texts in verse, both in Latin and Greek, such as papyrus texts P.Oxy. 42.3004–6 and P.Oxy. 50.3541, and the verse collections of the *Sententiae Menandri* and the *Sententiae* of Publilius Syrus. The latter collections are mostly in iambic trimeter, presumably because of their dramatic origins.[160] Hexameter was the meter of choice for the paraenetic fragments of sixth-century BCE lyric poet Phocylides and the Hellenistic *Sententiae* of Pseudo-Phocylides.[161] Of all wisdom texts, aside from the *Distichs*, only Pseudo-Phocylides' *sententiae* are wholly in hexameter.

---

157 Texts and translations of Egyptian paraenetic texts are found mostly in Lichtheim 1973 and 1983, Kitchen 1979, and Simpson 2003. On the *Counsels of Wisdom*, see Lambert 1960, 100ff., and Pfeiffer 1955, 426–427. A translation of the *Hymn to Ninurta*, along with notes, is available in Lambert 1960.
158 Hasluck 1907. On the Commandments of Sansnos, see Oikonomides 1980.
159 The *Theognidea*, a collection of advice and other poems totaling about 1400 lines, may contain poems written by Theognis; others certainly post-date him. The collection's fragmentary state precludes us from understanding the prominence of maxims within it.
160 Hellenistic poets seem to have favored elegiacs and iambics probably under the influence of drama. On meter in gnomic poetry, see Gerhard 1909, 253–255, and Lardinois 2001, 97–105, especially 103. Epigrams, like paraenesis, are short and pithy, but they lack the exclusive focus on wisdom and advice that defines paraenetic texts. But they share with paraenesis the goal of brevity: according to Cyrillos, *AP* 9.369, "The two-line epigram is very beautiful; but if you go beyond three, you're talking epic, not epigram." The *sententiae* of Phoinix of Colophon (on whom see Gerhard 1909) are in iambic trimeter. The list in Adrados 2009, 71–73, of iambic trimeter maxims of the Roman imperial period seems often to draw from New Comedy. Some of the *Sententiae Menandri* are drawn from the plays of Menander, though the rest are pseudepigraphic, and the collection was probably formed through gradual accretions of material. On the *Sententiae*, see Görler 1963, Jäkel 1964, Pompella 1997, Mariño Sánchez-Elvira and García Romero 1999, Liapis 2002 and 2007, and the essays in Funghi 2003, vol. I, part I.
161 On the fragments of Phocylides, see West 1978, 167. On the *Sententiae* of Pseudo-Phocylides, most likely the work of a Jewish writer, see Wilson 1994 and also van der Horst 1978. A fragment of the collection is found in the preface to the third book of the Sibylline Oracles, on which see Buitenwerf 2003, 53 and 84, n. 59.

Hexameter is, of course, the meter of epic, satire, and—importantly for our purposes—didactic, and it is tempting to associate Greco-Roman paraenesis with the didactic tradition.[162] After all, Hesiod's *Works and Days*, an epic poem containing many aphorisms, could also be classed as didactic or even gnomic.[163] Yet hexameter is also associated with utterances of truth: according to the prophetess Boio, the Hyperborean Olen was the first speaker of Delphic oracles *and* the inventor of hexameter, while in another tradition, hexameter is found first in the oracle of Gaia. It is the usual meter for oracles, though elegiacs and iambics are also occasionally found.[164] Finally, hexameter is archaizing, since it was the meter of Homer and Hesiod: paraenetic texts written in hexameter are thereby endowed with the authority of age.

The couplets of the *Distichs* are unique among paraenetic texts.[165] To be sure, the couplet is a key feature of early paraenesis: Lambert describes it as "exceedingly common" in Babylonian wisdom texts and according to Kitchen it

---

162 Gnomic utterances sometimes fill the second half of hexameter lines in Homer; on this phenomenon, see West 1978, 211.

163 Aphorisms in the *Works and Days* include ll. 28–29, 30–32, 405–409. Wilson 1994, 18, identifies a genre of "gnomic poetry," which contains gnomic statements formulated as poems or hymns; written in hexameter, elegiac couplets, or sometimes in iambic meters, the best-known examples include Hesiod's *Works and Days*, the *Comparatio Menandri et Philistionis* (which is transmitted with the *Sententiae Menandri*), the *Theognidea* (which Wilson 1994, 18, believes is "actually an anthology of gnomic poetry"), and the *Sententiae* of Pseudo-Phocylides. On Greek gnomic poetry, see especially Russo 1997. Dracontius (fifth/sixth century CE) uses hexameter for his school exercises (the *Deliberativa* and *Controversia*, two poems that are included among his *Romulea*), a choice that may be informed by Classical precedents for exercises, but more likely by the poems' epic and mythological characters. For a text of Dracontius, see Wolff 2002.

164 The myth of Olen is told in ap. Pausanius 10.5.7–8; the myth of Gaia is found in Plut. *Mor.* 402D. On meter in oracles, see Parke 1945. The possible connection to oracles was noticed already by Schrevelius in his introduction to Ampzing's 1632 translation:

Vitam denique quae ferunt beatam,
Haec sunt quae brevibus Cato libellis
Versu compare posteris reliquit,
Quorum singula Delphici fuere
Oracli vice gentibus togatis.

Finally, those things that bring a blessed life are what Cato left to posterity in verse in his brief little books; some of these were, for the Romans, like a Delphic Oracle.

165 Other poets who write in hexameter couplets are Leonidas of Tarentum and Serenus Sammonicus, though their works do not contain any sustained paraenetic utterances.

is the "dominant favourite in most periods" in Egyptian paraenetic texts.[166] Yet for all the popularity of the couplet, it was almost never the exclusive structural form, and while many texts contain many couplets, complete units of thought tend to comprise groups of two or three couplets, rather than one. In the Hellenistic period, the distich begins to give way to the monostich: in Demotic texts, for example, increasingly we find monostichs grouped in pairs that are not related logically or syntactically, but simply by topic or through parallel structure.[167] The *Distichs* are apparently the first Roman purpose-written unitary paraenetic text, and they adopted the apparently pre-Hellenistic distichic form, allowing each couplet to offer advice, reflection, or even both: most of the maxims contain an instruction in one line, followed by a gnomic reflection, explanation or justification in the next. We might consider paraenetic monostichs as one half of a distich, in which the explanation or justification has gone unexpressed.[168] The Author of the *Distichs*, in an attempt to offer as much clarity as possible, may have adopted the distich in order to explain and justify his messages.

The organization of material in paraenetic texts follows a few patterns. Egyptian and Biblical texts can comprise a single series of maxims (as is the case with most) or two or three discrete sections (or books), or four or more sections (the least common arrangement). Sometimes these sections have their own distinct theme along with sub-titles or numbered chapter headings (such as are found in the late Ptolemaic P.Insinger), though the topics themselves are arranged haphazardly, without any sense of organization.[169] Alternatively maxims may be arranged by initial letter or sign (for example, the *sententiae* of Publilius Syrus and Menander, and the first-century CE P.Oxy 42.3004), though they

---

[166] Lambert 1960, vi, who points out that units of one and three lines are also found in Babylonian texts. On the distich in Egyptian texts, see Kitchen 1977, 89. Recognition of the dominance of the distich is due to Foster 1977, a work that builds on his analysis of another text, the *Hymn to the Inundation* in Foster 1975. He notes (1977, 12) that a couplet can comprise "two independent clauses in coordination," though one clause in subordination to the other is the more common formulation. Among the texts that contain distichs are Ptahhotep, Shuruppak, Amenemope (chap. 9), Ahiqar (113), *Pap. Louvre* 2414, Ankhsheshonqy, and Proverbs. (The list is from Kitchen 1977.)

[167] On Hellenistic-era distichs, see Kitchen 1998, 355. For a detailed examination of the form of Egyptian and Greek paraenesis (with a focus on proverbs), see Lazaridis 2007. On Demotic monostichs, see Lichtheim 1983, 10–12.

[168] Lazaridis 2007, 177–182, raises the possibility of every proverb being bipartite; I add the suggestion that bipartism suggests a distichic structure.

[169] Kitchen 1977, 86–87. Fox 2011, 5, notes that the most recent scholarship views *Proverbs* as being arranged in "thematic or associative clusters."

are rarely alphabetized beyond that; sometimes maxims beginning with the same letter may be organized thematically.¹⁷⁰ Otherwise, paraenetic texts lack any discernible organizing principle, which is unsettling to modern readers: we are accustomed to narrative sequences or sustained treatments of topics rather than seemingly haphazard statements about randomly repeating topics. Though of course, these texts may have been arranged in a way that is no longer obvious to us.

The Author may have followed the tradition of some paraenetic texts in choosing apparently not to organize his material beyond separating it across books. But he may have been inspired also by miscellanies, such as Pamphila of Epidauros' *Historica Hypomnemata*, a mid-first century CE prose collection of interesting information she claimed to have picked up from her husband and those around him.¹⁷¹ Photius (Phot. Bibl. cod. 175) describes the content of her work as "mixed together" (συμμιγῆ) at random and without topical arrangement and reports that Pamphila considered "mixture and variety more charming than unity" (χαριέστερον τὸ ἀναμεμιγμένον καὶ τὴν ποικιλίαν τοῦ μονοειδοῦς).

Reconsidering the *Distichs* similarly as a miscellany, rather than a collection lacking organization, encourages us to consider the effects of mixture and variety on the reader. According to William Fitzgerald and Teresa Morgan, paraenetic and other moralizing texts were probably read in sequence from the beginning.¹⁷² The reader of the *Distichs*, working through the text in order, rather than seeking out maxims by topic (or some other criterion), might have found that the miscellaneous quality of the collection—mixing topics within and across books—stimulated him and relieved him of potential boredom. Such stimulation may have been especially useful in a classroom setting, but could also have been appreciated by adult readers.

Fitzgerald suggests that miscellaneity might also increase a work's appeal to a variety of readers;¹⁷³ similarly, Photius notes that Pamphila's work was useful for broadening the learning (εἰς πολυμάθειαν) of her readers. Readers of the *Distichs*, moving through the collection sequentially, encounter advice on myriad aspects of life, some that might be immediately helpful, others potentially useful in the future; some maxims might be relevant to some readers, other

---

170 Taylor 2005, 14–17, notes that at least one of Sumerian proverb collections is arranged by initial sign.
171 The fragments of Pamphila's work are collected in Müller, *FHG* 3.520–522 (now conveniently available at http://www.dfhg-project.org/DFHG/index.php, accessed 5/18/2022). For a discussion, see especially Müller-Reineke 2006, 649–651.
172 Fitzgerald 2016, chapter 5, especially p. 149, and Morgan 2007, 257–273, especially p. 267.
173 Fitzgerald 2016, 161–162.

maxims to others. Through miscellaneity, the Author has created for his collection a world of advice (albeit a partial one) whose variety mirrors the world of problems and anxieties his various readers might at some time encounter.

We might push the effects of miscellaneity further: it also provides the reader with opportunities to encounter maxims on similar themes in different contexts, leading to a gradual broad layering of advice. As Scott DiGiulio notes in his study of Aulus Gellius' *Noctes Atticae*, itself a miscellany of information without obvious organizing principle, "information is introduced in different contexts and patterns, which the reader is left to recognize; these patterns encourage the reader to contemplate the reapplicability of that information he is learning."[174] Searching for such patterns in the *Distichs* might be fruitful, though we should remember that the Author did not necessarily intend for the reader to experience the collection in that way.

Universality

It is clear that the *Distichs* share similarities of form with various works of paraenesis, though determining how those similarities came to be is difficult: in the absence of a statement from the Author, we cannot know how familiar he was with the paraenetic tradition—Roman, Greek or earlier and from farther afield—and which texts he may have read. It is reasonable to assume that an educated individual intending to write paraenesis knew at least something of the tradition, though his choice of hexameter and his use of couplets exclusively may have been driven not so much by tradition, but rather by the desire to produce a reader-friendly educational text.

Questions of the relative importance of influence and purpose are also relevant to the *Distichs*' content. There is a marked similarity in thought and occasionally expression between paraenetic texts, so much so that some scholars assume not just the transmission of ideas through a tradition, but also modes of expression and even direct borrowings. For example, Miriam Lichtheim argues for an international milieu of Aramaic, Egyptian, and Greek writers of wisdom texts, whose sharing, she believes, is noticeable in, for example, common phrasing and imagery.[175] Tradition, influence, and perhaps even borrowing too, are characteristics of paraenesis, a genre in which most texts are anonymous; as

---

[174] DiGiulio 2020, 261. For an excellent overview of Classical miscellanism, see Heath 2020, 23–32.
[175] Lichtheim 1983, 107.

a result, one might expect paraenetic texts to be prone to alteration. Yet compilers, it seems, wanted to transmit texts faithfully.[176] For example, the *Sententiae of Menander* is a composite collection of maxims composed at different times, though perhaps simply in two blocks. While no other ancient paraenetic collection seems to have been rewritten or otherwise significantly altered, new collections might be formed out of earlier ones, and one maxim might be found in more than one collection.[177]

Determining the extent of the influence of earlier paraenesis on the messages of the *Distichs* is difficult. To be sure, tradition plays a significant role in the development of ancient paraenesis, as indeed it does in every genre. Francisco Adrados has argued for influence from Near Eastern wisdom texts onto Greek, then Indian, and finally Byzantine successors, which was helped by translations.[178] For example, the *Sententiae Menandri* and *Sententiae Sextii* were translated into Coptic; the former was also aped by a later Syriac writer (the "Syriac Menander"), while the latter was also translated into Latin, Armenian, and Coptic.[179] The work of Greek writers was influential on Roman writers and compilers of wisdom. Indeed, Teresa Morgan sees in many of the *Distichs* translations of *sententiae* culled from Menander's plays.[180] There are, to be sure, many echoes and parallels with the *Sententiae Menandri*—as there usually are between paraenetic texts—though direct translations are harder to discern.[181]

Paraenetic authors' fondness for borrowing from earlier texts and even translating them is closely connected to a tradition in paraenesis of conservative content and expression. For example, Mesopotamian proverbs were also socially conservative in content, never proposing any innovations in behavior or viewpoint.[182] Some Hellenistic paraenesis drew from an existing store of tradi-

---

176 Searby 2007, 89, who is referring to West 1973, 16–17.
177 Taylor 2005, 25.
178 Adrados 2009.
179 Some of the Sumerian proverbs reappear much later in Syriac, according to Alster 1997, xviii–xix.
180 Morgan 1998, 145.
181 *Sententiae* from the plays of Menander that are paralleled or echoed in the *Distichs* are (following the numbering of Edmonds 1957): M 165 and *DC* 1.40; M 188 and *DC* 4.13.1; M 205 and *DC* 1.12; M 206 and *DC* 1.31; M 309 and *DC* 1.28; M 391 and *DC* 2.1; and M 407 and *DC* 2.28 and 4.5. A text of the *Sententiae* is also available in Pernigotti 2008. Calboli 1999, 28–30, points out that there are similarities between *sententiae* expressed in various dramatic works (including Euripides, Terence, and Syrus), but they are different enough in expression that translation can be ruled out.
182 For example, the *Sumerian Proverbs* were written and continued to be transmitted in a language no longer spoken, and the *Instructions of Shuruppak* were ascribed to an individual so

tional sayings: Demetrios of Phaleron compiled a collection of gnomic statements and instructions, some of which were drawn from the *Dicta Septem Sapientum*.[183] The long circulation of the *Sententiae Menandri* and the inclusion of many Greek paraenetic texts in Stobaeus' florilegium of the fifth century CE tells us that the content of collections remained useful for a long time and probably therefore either looked back in time or stuck to contemporary mores.

Yet the similarities of thought we can discern between the *Distichs* and earlier paraenetic texts may not all be the result of deliberate borrowing: they may also appear independently across societies.[184] Taking two common topics as an example, Lichtheim notes that "right speech and right silence were universal sapiential topics in which even close parallels need not indicate borrowing."[185] Lazaridis also allows for the possibility that different peoples across time and space can hold similar views and express them in similar ways:

> ... the high degree of similarity observed among the themes of the Egyptian and Greek proverbs, or even with regard to their binary type of structure, seems to point towards a common ground not only in literary expression, but also in human logic and concerns. In other words, such types of similarity depict proverb production as a common phenomenon of human societies. On the other hand, similarity in the type and use of metaphors, and of the association between an image and a characteristic of humanity ... may be explained as the result of a common manner of experiencing the Mediterranean scenery and of relating it to human action and its ethics. Finally, similarities in the manner of presenting, and maybe also of using, this common sort of literary material, such as the similar, loose form of the Egyptian and Greek collections examined, may be the result of a general inter-cultural influence and exchange that could have happened in this or an earlier historical point of contact between these two literary traditions.[186]

---

long dead that he may never have existed. Indeed, the fact that Sumerian proverbs were written in a language that (according to scholarly consensus) was dead suggests that they were never used by the man in the street or even in an educational setting.

183 On conservatism in Mesopotamian proverbs, see Alster 1997, xxiv; on Hellenistic conservatism, see Perdue 1981, 242–243.

184 For examples of themes appearing across cultures and traditions, see especially the collection of Düringsfeld and Reinsberg-Düringsfeld 1872.

185 Lichtheim 1983, 47. When we look beyond the Mediterranean world, we find still more similarities between texts: between the Indian Bārhaspatya-sūtras (on which see Bhattacharya 2002) and contemporary Hellenistic *gnomologia*; between the Qur'anic Sura of Luqman's brief instructions to a son from a quasi-historical sage and the wisdom of Solomon (on which see Kassis 1999, 47–54, and Williams 2000), and between the Turkic Dīwān Luġāt at-Turk of Maḥmūd al-Kāšġarī and Egyptian wisdom (see Dankoff 1981, 89). Yet the similarities may derive from wisdom that is not peculiar to any one local tradition.

186 Lazaridis 2007, 242.

The notion of a universal wisdom may help to explain why, as Richard Hazelton has observed, there are "few precepts in the *Disticha* that do not have equivalents in *Proverbs*."[187] If the *Distichs* were composed in the first century CE, it is unlikely that the Author was Christian and unlikely that he had read the Hebrew Bible.[188] A direct tradition between the two works should therefore be ruled out, and we should be careful not to assume that similarities of thought and expression in two works are necessarily the result of one borrowing from the other.[189]

A related reason for the apparent plethora of similarities among paraenetic texts comes from the fact that paraenetic literature tends to cover a wide range of topics. There are of course exceptions: some offer precepts only appropriate for a ruler (the "mirror of princes") or for someone in a particular situation, such as a pupil in a scribal school.[190] But from Sumerian to Roman collections, paraenesis tends to be concerned with the human lifeworld in general. Lichtheim's listing of the topics found in classical Egyptian Instructions is generally applicable also to the Hellenistic and Roman-era texts that succeeded them and summarizes well their range:

> They had enjoined to respect parents and elders; to love one's family; and to instruct the young. To be helpful and generous to neighbors, friends, and the poor. To be respectful and discreet in dealing with superiors. To shun greed, gluttony, and lechery. To refrain from deceit and cheating. To avoid anger, quarrelling and violence. Nor to fear the morrow and not be dismayed by misfortune. To respect the gods and trust in divine justice ... Self-control, moderation, and modesty were at all times the central virtues from which others flowed, notably respectfulness, peacefulness, loyalty, and discretion. The active, outgoing virtues also appeared in clusters and were viewed together: industry and generosity, be-

---

187 Hazelton 1957, 163, n. 30.
188 The apparent connection between the *Distichs* and a Biblical text helped make them palatable to later periods and ensured their survival, yet later commentators (and educators) still felt compelled to Christianize the collection through their comments and glosses, presumably because of the connection of the *Distichs* to the pagan "Cato." On the commentaries and glosses, see the final chapter of this book. The collection spoke strongly to Christians, but that fact does not make it a Christian collection or a pagan collection with Christian accretions (*pace* Morgan 2007, 87).
189 Otto 1890 offers ancient analogs to some of the maxims, many of them Greek; those that predate the *Distichs* might have been sources. For a full list of references to the *Distichs*, see under *Cato, distich*, p. 407. Boas 1952 offers *fontes* for many of the *Distichs*, but we should be careful not to assume that they were sources for the Author.
190 "Mirror for princes" texts, common especially in the Egyptian tradition, include the *Instruction to King Merikare*, the *Loyalist Teaching*, the *Instructions of Amenemhat*, and the *Instructions of Amennakhte*. Texts for scribal pupils include the Egyptian *Instruction of Khety* and *Instructions of Amennakhte*.

nevolence and justice, honesty and courage. The principal vices stood out just as clearly: Greed, avarice, and gluttony were inseparable; lying and cheating went hand in hand; and so did anger, quarrelsomeness, and violence. Altogether, the most lauded virtue was self-control, and the most sharply castigated vice was greed.[191]

Despite all these similarities between the *Distichs* and other paraenetic texts (whatever their origin), there are differences too. For example, cosmic order, an important part of the wisdom literature of the Old Testament and Christianity, is scarcely mentioned in the *Distichs*, leaving little sense of the sources of justice and of right and wrong. Furthermore, while much Near Eastern wisdom literature emphasizes tradition and memory, there is very little about either in the *Distichs*.[192]

Paraenetic literature often looks back and rarely proposes action that is progressive. The similarities of the *Distichs* to earlier paraenetic texts helped to root them in the paraenetic tradition, endowed them with authority, and lent them a reassuring conservatism. Yet at the same time, as I will argue in Chapters 4 and 5, the *Distichs* are never out of step with the present. They are therefore—as Leo Perdue has argued for Mesopotamian and Biblical wisdom and Pierre Hamblenne for the *sententiae* of Publilius Syrus—a good mirror for the beliefs of the time and society in which they originated.[193]

As suggested above, the Author presumably knew of earlier paraenetic texts. His choice of hexameter couplets, lack of apparent organization, avoidance of figurative language, and embrace of a wide range of topics all suggest that he knew of them and was influenced by them. He perhaps drew some of his content from those texts, what I would call the universal store of wisdom, as well as paraenetic material from other sources, such as proverbs and texts from other genres. If he did, his selections will have been determined at least to some extent by the fact that he was a Roman writing for a Roman audience. In addition, he may have added original material, some of which may coincidentally and unintentionally have resembled material from earlier texts. That original material was Roman. Comprising original Roman material and selections from earlier material that were determined at least in part by the Author's context, the *Distichs* are a Roman text.

---

191 Lichtheim 1983, 113–114.
192 Perdue 2008.
193 Perdue 1990, 26, observes that paraenetic texts can be non-traditional, even subversive, but those are a small minority.

3 Style

> *Miraris verbis nudis me scribere versus?*
> *Hoc brevitas fecit, sensus coniungere binos.* (DC 4.49)
>
> Do you wonder how I write verses in bare words?
> It's the brevity that does it, joining together two ideas.
>
> *Quod nimium est, fugito, parvo gaudere memento;*
> *Tuta mage puppis est, modico quae flumine fertur.* (DC 2.6)
>
> Avoid excess and rejoice in restraint:
> A boat is safer carried on a gentle current.

Set alongside earlier and contemporary paraenetic texts, the *Distichs* stand out for their consistency: every one of them is a hexameter couplet constructed from one of a small number of combinations of clauses: either a statement of wisdom that is accompanied by an explanation, justification or limitation; or an instruction that is explained, justified, limited or simply accompanied by a statement of wisdom.[194] These combinations are also found in the illustrations that accompany Aristotle's discussion of enthymemes, and indeed the *Distichs* could themselves be used as illustrations of the enthymeme. They are, to use a popular descriptor, textbook. As I will argue in this chapter, it is their syntactical simplicity and regularity, along with other characteristics of their style, that helped to make the *Distichs* widely read and familiar among Romans and thereafter.

In his *Rhetoric*, Aristotle defines the maxim (γνώμη) as "concerning people's actions and what they should choose to do or avoid doing" (περὶ ὅσων αἱ πράξεις εἰσί, καὶ <ἃ> αἱρετὰ ἢ φευκτά ἐστι πρὸς τὸ πράττειν). He notes that the maxim can form one part of an enthymeme (ἐνθύμημα); the other part is the syllogism (συλλογισμός), which provides an explanation and justification for the enthymeme as a whole (προστεθείσης δὲ τῆς αἰτίας καὶ τοῦ διὰ τί ἐνθύμημά ἐστιν τὸ ἅπαν: "when the explanation and justification are added, the whole thing is an enthymeme") and therefore the maxim in particular. According to Aristotle's definitions, every one of the *Distichs* is an enthymeme, both those

---

[194] In grammatical terms, the first combination comprises a syntactically independent statement and a syntactically dependent clause that may be conditional, final (i.e., expressing purpose), causal (including a clause that is introduced with a causal conjunction, such as *nam* ("for"), temporal, concessive or relative. The second combination comprises a clause containing an imperative verb that is followed by a syntactically dependent clause that may be conditional, final, causal, temporal, concessive or relative, or by an independent clause.

that contain wisdom statements and those that formulate their wisdom in an instruction.[195] Moreover, the maxims Aristotle uses as illustrations are brief—the longest is twelve words, but most are six or seven—and he encourages his reader to keep their accompanying syllogisms brief too, even when the maxim's message is not obvious (περὶ δὲ τῶν μὴ παραδόξων ἀδήλων δὲ προστιθέντα τὸ διότι στρογγυλώτατα: "when they are not paradoxical, but unclear, the reason should be added as concisely as possible").[196]

The philosopher discusses enthymemes as a rhetorical tool for persuading the listener, rather than as a moral-educational tool. This context is important for understanding why he claims that "using maxims is appropriate for the time of life of older people" (ἁρμόττει δὲ γνωμολογεῖν ἡλικίᾳ μὲν πρεσβυτέρων, Ar. *Rhet.* 2.21.9): he is not claiming that children should not learn them, but rather that mature individuals, such as those imagined as the authors of ancient wisdom collections, should employ and teach them. The Author had perhaps read his Aristotle.

Aristotle was not the only possible guide for the Author. The *Rhetorica ad Herennium*, dated to the 80s BCE, was perhaps as familiar to the Author as was Aristotle. The opening of the relevant discussion in the *Rhetorica* begins with a definition of the statement of wisdom (*sententia*, corresponding to Aristotle's γνώμη) that is remarkably similar to that of Aristotle: "a maxim is a saying drawn from life, which shows concisely either what happens or ought to happen in life" (*sententia est oratio sumpta de vita, quae aut quid sit aut quid esse oporteat in vita, breviter ostendit*). Yet the author of the *Rhetorica* acknowledges that sometimes there may be a statement of wisdom "that is strengthened by the addition of an explanation" (*quod confirmatur subiectione rationis*), a formulation that is found repeatedly in the *Distichs*. Finally, he notes that wisdom may sometimes be presented with two closely related ideas presented as a pair (*dupliciter*), accompanied by a reason or not; this latter formulation is also found in the *Distichs*.[197]

The significance of these discussions in Aristotle and the *Rhetorica ad Herennium* is that they suggest the Author's formulation of the *Distichs* was not by chance, but carefully planned. Indeed, it was so carefully planned that the con-

---

195 Ar. *Rhet.* 2.21.6 provides an example of a maxim couched as an instruction: ἀθάνατον ὀργὴν μὴ φύλασσε θνητὸς ὤν ("since you are mortal, do not covet immortal riches").
196 One of the illustrations is Ar. *Rhet.* 2.21.2: χρὴ δ' οὔ ποθ' ὅστις ἀρτίφρων πέφυκ' ἀνήρ παῖδας περισσῶς ἐκδιδάσκεσθαι σοφούς ("no right-minded man should ever have his children taught to be uncommonly wise"), quoted from Eur. *Med.* 294–295. The quotation above is from Ar. *Rhet.* 2.21.7.
197 *Rhet. ad Her.* 4.17.24.

sistent meter, structure, and combinations of clauses might appear monotonous, the product of a lack of imagination or confidence. Instead, however, we should attribute the collection's consistency to a desire to adhere to established modes of presenting wisdom that were acknowledged as effective by no less authorities than Aristotle and the author of the *Rhetorica*.[198] Those modes were to continue: in his analysis of Old English wisdom, Paul Cavill identified formulations that we find also in the *Distichs* and indeed throughout the paraenetic tradition: enthymemes (do X, since Y is the result, according to his definition), conditions (if you do X, then Y results), obligations (you should do X in order for Y to happen), particular maxims (it is the mark of X to do Y), and general maxims (it is the mark of an X person to do Y).[199] Indeed Teresa Morgan suggests that wisdom texts have a normative grammar, an idea that is useful for the *Distichs*, whose repeated syntactical constructions and patterns suggest that their Author strove to create a core of modes of expression for his wisdom.[200]

Thus far in this study, I have assumed an audience of readers for the *Distichs*. Of course, in the ancient world texts were also heard—far more so than today.[201] Orality is a formative element of the paraenetic tradition, informing some of its key aspects, such as a lack of named author for many works (including the *Distichs*) and the openness of their texts to accretions. Applying criteria from Walter Ong's seminal *Orality and Literary* for identification of a text as oral or oral-like reveals that the *Distichs* work well as an "oral text"—i.e., one that may be written, but is well suited to be spoken, heard, and repeated.[202] For example, Ong characterizes oral texts as aggregative rather than analytic: soldiers are characterized by being labeled brave, rather than through analyses of the condition of soldiery and the nature of braveness. An oral text has a form that adds, rather than subordinates, syntactical units, as we will see demonstrated

---

198 Another important discussion is in Aphthonius, *Progymnasmata* 4. For a philosophical treatment of the logic of the enthymeme, see Burnyeat 1996, who notes that an enthymeme is a statement, but one that in a rhetorical work is part of an argument. It is not a strictly logical proof for a *gnome*, but is meant to persuade a general audience listening to a speech and is therefore convincing according to common sense, likelihood, and reasonableness. Aristotle himself became associated with collections of sayings, some his, though not all: see Searby 1998.
199 Cavill 1999, 48.
200 Morgan 2007, 182–183.
201 On modes of receiving texts in the Roman world, see generally Johnson 2010.
202 The criteria are drawn from the summary in Cavill 1999, 169–170, of Ong 1982, 37. It remains true that the *Distichs* are known today as a written text and that our only knowledge of their use in the ancient world comes from written quotations.

by the *Distichs* in the discussion that follows. Ong has found oral texts to be full of redundancy or repetition, and several couplets in the *Distichs* contain similar messages and repeated phrasing. Oral texts are conservative, and the *Distichs* do not advocate revolutionary or unusual behavior. Oral texts are concerned with the human lifeworld, i.e., what is familiar, and Aristotle had noticed this was true also of maxims:

> ἔστι δὴ γνώμη ἀπόφανσις, οὐ μέντοι οὔτε περὶ τῶν καθ' ἕκαστον ... καθόλου ... περὶ ὅσων αἱ πράξεις εἰσί, καὶ <ἃ> αἱρετὰ ἢ φευκτά ἐστι πρὸς τὸ πράττειν.
>
> A maxim is an assertion—not, however, one about particulars ... but of a general sort ... about things that involve actions and are to be chosen or avoided in regard to action.[203]

Finally, according to Ong, oral texts are homeostatic, i.e., concerned only with the present, rather than the past or distant future, and they are situational rather than abstract, a description that suits the *Distichs* well.

In the final couplet of the *Distichs*, DC 4.49, quoted at the start of this chapter, the Author refers to several aspects of his style: "Do you wonder how I write verses in bare words? It's the brevity that does it, joining together two ideas." His words are bare and his maxims brief, and they contain two ideas. I will explain in this chapter how the Author's choices of form, syntax, meter, and lexical choice—essentially of style—made his *Distichs* effective as both a written and an oral text.[204]

---

203 Arist. *Rhet*. 21.2. The translation is from Kennedy 2007, 164–165.
204 To analyze an author's style requires more than just a close familiarity with a text. A person recognizes the texture of a piece of writing from noticing in an unsystematic way repetitions in proximity, thematic unities or series, and features that strike them as unusual for the author, genre, period, or culture. The result is an overall impression of a work that may differ from one person to another depending on taste, experience, and cultural context. Producing lists and tallies, however, that focus systematically and employ statistical methods is more objective, though this method too has its flaws: the focus points and analyses are chosen, not predetermined, and interpretation of the results cannot be wholly objective. But it is a start. Much of this chapter is indebted to the analysis in Cavill 1999, chap. 5, of the language of Old English maxims, and to Haag 2002, which offers an analysis of the language of the *Distichs* and two German translations.

Syntax

The most common couplet construction in the collection comprises an instruction in the first line, followed by a statement of wisdom in the second.[205] Perhaps the Author found that maxims containing an instruction and a statement have the greatest impact when they appear in that order: the reader's mind is struck first by the instruction, usually rendered with an imperative, which provides an urgent and impactful expression; pausing to wonder at the reason or justification for the instruction, he comes to the gnomic second line, whose reflective force is strengthened by its second position, allowing him to dwell on it, and also by its universality.

Statements of wisdom help to announce and establish paraenetic texts as sources of authority, while instructions render them practical instruction manuals and didactic aids. The Author uses them together in his *Distichs*, and the combination is also a highly effective vehicle for his advice. The Author does not need to use instructions to impress his messages upon his readers, though instructions are effective in the classroom, perhaps more so than statements of wisdom. Instructions offer immediacy and impact; statements of wisdom lend the collection a more philosophical flavor. Together they create a collection that not only instructs, but also educates a wider audience by providing food for thought. They also help the Author to construct his syntax around similar phrasing across couplets. His phrasing of instructions provides a good first example.

Instructions

The Author employs a variety of ways to express instructions, the most common of which is the future imperative.[206] He favors the future imperative over the

---

[205] Of 144 total maxims, in 70 one line is filled by an instruction, the other by a gnomic reflection; in 8 the instruction and reflection are divided unevenly across the couplet. In a few more, the structure is found, but it does not coincide with the line division. The order of the lines in maxims so constructed is potentially reversible thanks to the coincidence of their syntactical and line divisions. Yet the manuscripts are nevertheless almost universally consistent in their order.

[206] On imperatives, see especially Gildersleeve 1895, §§266ff., the study by Risselada 1993, and the discussions in Löfstedt 1966 and Vairel-Carron 1975. I use the terms "future" and "present" imperative because they are familiar to most readers, though they are admittedly imprecise. The future imperative is known as the second imperative in Gildersleeve's terminology

present, disregarding any difference in meaning between them.[207] Granted, the most common future imperative forms are *esto* and *memento* ("be" and "remember" respectively), for which a present imperative form is not used, and they constitute the majority of future imperatives in the *Distichs*.[208]

Even aside from these, which have either no attested or regularly employed present imperative forms, the Author of the *Distichs* seems to favor future imperative forms more than do other Latin authors, when their works are assessed as a corpus. Granted, their rates of incidence in the *Distichs* are too low for serious statistical analysis; but it is possible at least to gain an impression of some of the Author's preferences.[209] He disproportionally favors future imperatives (56% of his imperatives are future; the figure is 15% for the rest of the corpus), and even when he prefers the present imperative form of a verb, he does so less strongly than the corpus. Imperative forms of *facere* ("to do") prove exceptional: he shows a stronger preference for the present tense than does the corpus (82% in the *Distichs* versus 57% in the corpus). This may be because *facere*, unlike other verbs, can combine with another verb in the subjunctive mood to create an imperatival periphrasis, which the Author likes to employ. In the *Distichs*, the present imperative *fac* appears only twice by itself, but 7 times in conjunction with a subjunctive; *facito* never appears by itself, but twice in conjunction with a subjunctive. I will return to a possible explanation shortly.

One reason for the Author's preference for future imperatives could be associative: future imperatives are often found in legal texts, most notably the

---

and Imperative II in Risselada's, while the present imperative is called a first imperative by Gildersleeve and Imperative I by Risselada.

207 Future imperatives, though often translated simply as denoting action that will happen, is likely to happen, or tends to happen, can often express "contingent fulfillment." By contrast, the Latin present imperative is an absolute imperative and expresses an expectation of "immediate fulfillment." The distinction is barely perceptible in the *Distichs*.

208 Among the imperative forms in the *Distichs*, *esto* and *memento* predominate, with 8 and 19 instances respectively out of a total of 48. A small number of future imperatives seem to have contingent circumstances, including *DC* 1.15, 18, 20, 24; 3.3; 4.13, 23, 26, and 36. And then conversely many maxims containing present imperatives also contain overtly or implicitly contingent clauses, including, for example, *DC* 1.9, 1.19, and 1.28. Indeed, we even find present and future imperatives in same maxim with no clear distinction in meaning, such as *DC* 2.27, 3.18, and 4.7.

209 The figures for the corpus of Latin literature are based on my analysis of data derived from the Packard Humanities database, accessed through the Perseus project (http://www.perseus.tufts.edu/hopper/collection?collection=Perseus:collection:Greco-Roman, accessed 5/18/2022). The database, which is not comprehensive, omits the *Distichs*. Table 1, included at the end of this chapter, contains the full data.

Twelve Tables, where their contingency is particularly apt, and so the Author may have been keen to capitalize on the connection and lend the *Distichs* an air of authority. Indeed, Tom Shippey notes that maxims aim at "a definitive, even quasi-legal tone."[210] The force of the future imperative would have been further strengthened by readers' familiarity with the writing of Cato the Elder, who is among its most frequent users, and by its association with older speakers and an archaizing style.[211]

A second explanation is metrical. The Author likes to set future imperatives at the end of his hexameter line, often using infinitives or adjectives in the preceding position in order to fill out the dactylic fifth and trochaic or spondaic sixth feet. For example, *memento* can fit the last three metrical positions of the line—indeed, *memento* is in the final position 17 times out of 19, and *esto* 5 times out of 8—and before that he usually places an infinitive, whose long penultimate vowel (which appears in most present active infinitives) and short final *e* begin the fifth dactylic foot of the line.[212]

> *Officium alterius multis narrare memento* (DC 1.15.1)
> *Accipito placide, plene laudare memento* (DC 1.20.2)
> *Si potes, ignotis etiam prodesse memento* (DC 2.1.1)

The other common future imperative, *esto*, nicely fills the final two positions, and the Author is then free to fill the preceding foot with a trisyllabic word, as he does in 4 out of 5 cases. For example,

> *Cum fueris felix, semper tibi proximus esto* (DC 1.18.1)
> *Fortius ut valeas, interdum parcior esto* (DC 2.28.1)
> *Gratior officiis, quo sis mage carior, esto* (DC 4.42.1)

By placing future imperatives at the end of the line, the Author creates a pattern around them that, through repetition, becomes familiar in the reader's mind. The pattern also emphasizes the imperatival force of the line and so helps char-

---

210 Shippey 1976, 19, who treats Old English maxims. On the use of maxims in legal trials, see, for example, Arewa and Dundes 1964, 70, on Nigerians' use of proverbs in place of precedent.
211 Clackson 2011, 513. In his *De agricultura*, a work of just over 15,700 words, Cato uses the future imperative a little over 1,100 times.
212 Of the remaining imperatives, 8 out of 21 are found at the end of a line. *Memento* ("remember") commonly appears at the end of a line in other authors too, and according to Newlands 2011, 171, "the archaic imperative *memento* always occurs at line end in hexameter poetry," citing *TLL* viii 653.64–65 for the claim. By comparison, only 5 out of 67 present imperatives in the *Distichs* that could have taken the final position in the line in fact do so. In the *Distichs*, *memento* in final position is preceded by an infinitive 15 out of 17 times.

acterize the collection as instructive. As we will see, the Author repeats other metrical patterns to aid his readers' memory and for emphasis. The Author also employs additional types of imperatival formulation, including gerundives and a form of *debere*.[213] The resulting range of expressions creates syntactical variety that is balanced by the employment of patterns.

Prohibitions (negative instructions) are also variously expressed.[214] Just over half comprise *noli* (itself an imperative, literally "do not want!") followed by an infinitive. The Author often places *noli* in the middle of the line, where it serves to demarcate the core message of the line from additional material.[215] To fill the rest of the line, he usually places the infinitive next and finishes with a disyllabic or trisyllabic word: for example,

> *Adversum notum noli contendere verbis* (DC 2.11.1)

In the next example, placing *noli* in the middle, and at the end of a sense unit, emphasizes the verb and helps to structure the rest of the line as containing two equally important messages:

> *Incusare deum noli, sed te ipse coerce* (DC 1.23.2)

The Author also uses the iussive subjunctive for prohibitions, though it was apparently out of fashion: Cicero had largely eschewed it in the late Republic.

---

[213] Gerundives are used in *DC* 1.1.2; 2.5.2, 20.2; 4.15.2, 23.2 and 45.1; an impersonal verb appears in *DC* 4.29.1; *debet* is used in *DC* 1.6.2; *DC* 2.8 uses *nolo* followed by a subjunctive in a complementary final clause. As Gildersleeve notes (§546, R.2), when a verb of wishing (or its negative) is followed by a simple present subjunctive in the complementary final clause, the force is imperative. On subsidiary directions (or illocutions), which express instructions without using an imperative, see Haag 2002, 6, who refers to Risselada 1993, 55, though most of the latter work is devoted to such instructions.

[214] Gildersleeve counts six ways of forming a prohibition in Latin: *ne* followed by a present imperative, *ne* followed by a future imperative (which he notes is not contingent), *noli(te)* followed by an infinitive, *ne* followed by a present or perfect iussive, and finally *non* followed by a future indicative. The first and second appear only once each in the *Distichs* (*DC* 3.10 and *DC* 1.2, respectively), and the last not at all. Gildersleeve identifies the first as mostly poetic or colloquial, which might explain its rarity in the *Distichs*, which are neither colloquial nor especially poetic. According to Gildersleeve, the second formulation is not contingent; in the *Distichs* it is used with *esto*, which further reduces any notion of contingency.

[215] *Noli(te)* mid-line followed by infinitive: *DC* 2.11.1, 12.1; 4.18.1, 35.1; not followed by infinitive: *DC* 1.23.2; 3.20.1; 4.10.2. *Noli(te)* in initial position preceded by infinitive: *DC* 1.13.1, 14.2, 19.2; 2.4.1, 9.1, 25.1, 26.1; 4.34.1; not preceded by an infinitive: *DC* 2.21.1. In initial position: *DC* 2.20.1; 3.4.1; 4.3.2.

Its popularity in the *Distichs* might suggest an attempt by the Author to write in an old-fashioned style and so endow his collection with authority.[216]

Statements of wisdom

Cultivating authority seems also to be an aim in the Author's formulation of statements of wisdom. Rendering them universal—i.e., without time or application specific to only one or a few people—plays a key role in that process. The Author renders every verb in the *Distichs* in the present tense and so avoids any sense of a past that is potentially irrelevant to the reader because it is fixed and therefore anachronistic or outdated, or any sense of a future that, by its very nature, cannot be known for certain. The Author also chooses the indicative mood to state simply what is—not what might be—and thus render each statement of wisdom a statement of truth. The choice of the third singular for the person of the verb in his statements of wisdom—with only a few exceptions—results from the Author's tendency to use unidentifiable persons as subjects, such as "men," "the man who," and "no one"; identification of any particular person would limit the scope of the reflection. Otherwise, he eschews any mention of persons, employing abstract nouns instead.[217]

---

216 Prohibitions containing iussive subjunctives in the present tense: *DC* 1.17.1, 22.1, 25.2, 29.2, 35.1; 2.31.1; 3.1.1, 2.1, 12.2, 19.2, 24.2; 4.22.1, 27.1, 38.2, 47.2. Perfect tense: *DC* 1.25.1, 30.1; 2.29.1; 3.7.1, 3.10.2. Subjunctive forms are also found following *fac/facito* (see above). Cicero uses this formulation in only 2% of his prohibitions, a finding that Risselada 1993, 140–141, uses to claim that *ne* followed by a iussive subjunctive loses its early popularity by the time of Classical Latin; in the *Distichs* it accounts for 40% of prohibitions. Lines containing present iussive subjunctives seem not to be formulated according to any patterns; the five lines containing perfect subjunctives, however, are metrically similar: in every case, the verb fills the fifth foot and some of the fourth too. For example, *DC* 1.25.1: *Quod praestare potes, ne bis promiseris ulli* ("When you have something to give, you cannot give it twice over").

217 Aristotle notes that gnomic statements deal with generalities (*Rhet.* 1394a1); the *Rhetorica ad Herennium* notes that they are "taken from life" (*sumpta de vita*; *Rhet. Her.* 4.17.24), which also suggests generality. In just the first ten couplets of *Distichs* Book 1, we find the abstract nouns *quies* ("quiet", *DC* 1.2), *utilitas* ("usefulness", *DC* 1.6), and *sermo* ("speech") and *sapientia* ("wisdom") (both *DC* 1.10). Both Aristotle and the author of the *Rhetorica ad Herennium* use examples of statements of wisdom that employ third singular present indicative verbs and third person pronouns. Otherwise in Book 1, *DC* 1.5.2's awkward anacolouthon produces as subjects unspecified *homines* (understood from the previous line) and *nemo*; the subjects of *DC* 1.3, 1.7 and 1.8, *ille...qui*, *sapiens*, and *mulier*, are also unspecified. The subject of the remaining maxim, *DC* 1.4, is contained within its impersonal verb *conveniet*. Only two statements of wisdom in the *Distichs*, *DC* 4.37.2 and 4.40.2, employ the second person singular, which by specify-

Unspecified actors are often given attributes that are defined by their behavior. For example,

Virtutem primam esse puta compescere linguam:
Proximus ille deo est, qui scit ratione tacere. (DC 1.3)

Holding your tongue—that is a chief virtue;
He is closest to a god who knows when to keep quiet.

The authority of the statement in the second line derives from its timelessness and also from its insularity: all we know and need to know of *"ille"* is that he is closest to a god and that he knows when silence is needed.[218]

In many of these formulations, the first part of the line, which establishes a characterization ("he who..."), closes at the third-foot caesura, while the second part, which illustrates the characterization, follows. The Author employs this simple pattern of defining an adjective with an action nineteen times to instruct his readers about what is good, bad, stupid, etc.[219] The result is statements of wisdom that, being aggregative rather than analytic, according to Ong's formulation, are more readily understandable to the reader than are reflections upon the abstract notions of good, bad, and stupidity.[220]

---

ing a single reader, risks lessening its universal application and therefore force. First person plurals in *DC* 2.10.2 and 2.24.2 lend universality by expressing a wisdom that is not impersonal and timeless, but collective and immediate.

218 The Author may have been following earlier models: several of Aristotle's exemplary statements of wisdom are constructed as "he is ... who does ..." including

οὐκ ἔστιν ὅστις πάντ' ἀνὴρ εὐδαιμονεῖ
("he does not exist who is blessed in all things"; *Rhet.* 1394b, quoting Eur. *Sthen.*, *TrGF* 661)

οὐκ ἔστιν ἀνδρῶν ὅστις ἔστ' ἐλεύθερος
("he does not exist among men who is free"; *Rhet.* 1394b, quoting Eur. *Hec.* 864)

Similarly in the *Rhetorica ad Herennium* we find

non solet is potissimum virtutes revereri qui semper secunda fortuna sit usus
("he tends to revere virtues least who has always enjoyed favorable fortune"; *Rhet. Her.* 4.17)

219 *DC* 1.3.2, 4.2, 5.2, 7.2, 17.2, 22.2, 30.2; 2.9.2, 14.2, 15.2, 16.2; 3.21.2; 4.1.2, 4.2, 5.2, 13.2, 22.2, 39.2, 46.2.
220 On the usefulness of avoiding abstraction in inculcating morals, see especially the discussion in Langlands 2018, 64–65, on Valerius Maximus' exempla. It is true that we sometimes find instead of a person an abstract noun, such as *utilitas*, *sapientia*, *fides*, or *ira* ("usefulness,"

Ong identified oral texts as more additive than subordinative. We see addition rather than subordination in two important aspects in the *Distichs*: first, at the couplet level, while there is plenty of syntactical subordination, it is simple, and the containment of subordinate clauses in their own lines gives the reader the sense that they have been added to the couplet's main message; second, at the level of the collection, simple addition—in which one couplet follows another without any sense of progression and without theme or logic—seems to be the organizing principle.

Lexical Choice

Aristotle claims that statements of wisdom held especial appeal for regular folk: "rustic types are especially fond of maxims and make them appear, just like that" (οἱ γὰρ ἀγροῖκοι μάλιστα γνωμοτύποι εἰσὶ καὶ ῥᾳδίως ἀποφαίνονται).[221] It seems likely that the Author of the *Distichs* had perceived the same phenomenon: he complements repeated formulations and syntactical structures with a simple vocabulary.

Determining the commonness of vocabulary is hard, and even a comparative approach is hampered by a lack of texts analogous to the *Distichs*. But it does appear that the *Distichs* contain, with only a few exceptions, words found regularly in other Latin texts.[222]

"wisdom," "trust," "anger," respectively). See *DC* 1.6.2, 10.2, 13.2, 32.2, 36.2, 39.2; 2.1.1, 4.2, 6.2, 8.2, 11.2, 18.2, 23.2, 25.2, 26.2, 28.2; 3.4.2, 13.2, 22.2; 4.20.2, 27.2, 29.2, 31.2. For example,

> *Contra verbosos noli contendere verbis:*
> *Sermo datur cunctis, animi sapientia paucis.* (*DC* 1.10)

> Don't try to out-talk a talker:
> We all have tongues in our mouths, but few wisdom in our brains.

Neither Aristotle nor Ps. Cicero includes examples of this sort, but the Author of the *Distichs* seems sometimes to have found them useful, perhaps because they provided variety in a collection of maxims.

[221] Arist. *Rhet.* 1395a. For that reason, they are especially useful for appealing to an audience that "on account of its coarseness" (διὰ τὴν φορτικότητα; Arist. *Rhet.* 1395b1) wants to hear its opinions validated.

[222] Two words in the *Distichs* are strikingly uncommon: *dapsilis* ("bounteous") in *DC* 1.40 and *officiperdus* ("sponge") in *DC* 4.42. The latter appears only here and in a gloss on Isidore by Scaliger, who presumably knew it from the *Distichs*; manuscripts are divided on whether it should be one word or two, but otherwise all reproduce it.

Verbs

Verbs provide a good first example of the Author's lexical strategy. The verbs appearing most frequently are (in order) *esse, nolle, meminisse, posse, facere, velle, fugere, discere, ferre, loqui* and *vivere* ("to be," "not to want," "to remember," "to be able," "to do," "to want," "to escape," "to learn," "to bear," "to speak," and "to live," respectively).[223] In Publilius Syrus' *Sententiae*, forms of *esse* are as common as they are in the *Distichs* and they account for roughly same percentage of words overall in the *Distichs* and Syrus (5.5–6%).[224] But the other most common verbs (roughly second through fifth place) in Syrus account for between 0.6–0.5% of all words, while in the *Distichs* they account for 1.5–0.8%. Or to put it another way, in the *Distichs*, we find an overall smaller pool of verbs and greater repetition among them.

Repetition of *esse*, *posse*, and *facere* in the *Distichs* is unsurprising, as is that of *nolle*, which is used to express prohibitions. The high incidence of *meminisse*, mostly in the future imperative form *memento* ("remember"), speaks strongly to the admonitory tone of the collection and to the Author's goal to have the reader learn its contents—i.e., to receive, reflect upon, and remember them. The frequency of *discere* ("to learn") also speaks to the didactic importance of the collection, as does the appearance of *velle* in this list, which in the *Distichs* seems most often to mean "to aim at, to have as one's object."[225]

---

[223] The incidences of the verbs are as follows: *esse* appears 106 times, *nolle* 28, *meminisse* 19, *posse* 18, *facere* 16, *velle* 13, *fugere* 9, *discere* 8, *ferre* 6, *loqui* 6, and *vivere* 6.

[224] The most common verbs in the *Sententiae* include *esse, facere, peccare, posse, habere, cogere, fieri, imperare, nescire, timere, velle, quaerere, vincere,* and *accipere* ("to be," "to do," "to do wrong," "to be able," "to have," "to compel," "to become," "to order," "not to know," "to fear," "to wish," "to ask," "to overcome," and "to receive," respectively). The *Sententiae* are a useful comparative text: they pre-date the *Distichs*, but are in Latin and in verse. My analysis of the *Sententiae* is rougher than that for the *Distichs*: for the purposes of quick identification, I have identified and analyzed words from their first five letters, not the entire word (while grouping together dissimilar present and perfect stem forms of the same verb). The same sort of analysis on *Distichs* produces roughly comparable results to my earlier and more precise analysis, but the results are admittedly not identical.

[225] *OLD*, s.v. *volo*, 16. The verb is being used in a similar way in *DC* 3.16:

> *Iudicis auxilium sub iniquitate rogato;*
> *Ipsae etiam leges cupiunt, ut iure rogentur.*

> In adversity seek the help of a judge;
> Even the laws themselves wish to be called upon rightfully.

Together with *velle,* the repetition of *ferre* ("to bear, put up with") and *fugere* ("to escape, flee") commends the reader to aim at certain things, escape others, and put up with yet others. The Author of the *Distichs* does not have as a goal that his reader should follow his heart's desire; rather, the goal is to live wisely.[226]

A final small point on imperatives: they are all singular, that is, addressed to a single "you," not to a group.[227] Wisdom texts, on the whole, assume an individual as their audience, and the result is that their advice feels more personal and targeted.

Nouns

An analysis of the rates of incidence of the ten most common nouns in the *Distichs* reveals them to be *tempus* ("time"), *vita* ("life"), *amicus* ("friend"), *res* ("thing, matter, affair"), *animus* ("mind"), *mors* ("death"), *homo* ("man"), *deus* ("god"), *vis* ("strength, power") and *verbum* ("word").[228]

From this list it might seem that the *Disticha* are focused on the broad themes of human existence—gods, men, death, and time. We should be cautious about characterizing texts on the basis of an analysis that relies simply on calculations of frequency: isolated words, while repeated often, may not reflect a text's themes, motifs, and concerns, and so tell us what a text is "about."[229]

---

226 The only appearance of the verb *optare* ("to desire") comes in *DC* 2.31, where the reader is warned that unattainable desires come to the mind while awake, but the attainable reality is revealed only in dreams.

227 Latin does not use the second person plural form to express formality.

228 In the *Distichs,* *tempus* appears 16 times, *vita* also 16, *amicus* 15, *res* 14, *animus* 13, *mors* 11, *homo* 10, *deus* 9, *vis* also 9, and *verbum* 8. References to gods (sometimes in the singular) are also frequent, appearing nine times, with additional named references to Bacchus, Venus, and Janus.

229 The most common nouns in the *Aeneid* and their incidences are as follows: *aurum* 904, *altum* 866, *Aeneas* 848, *arma* 554, *caelum* 546, *ora* 526, *bellum* 511, *auris* 465, *deus* 450, *pater* 393, *dictum* 370, *manus* 268. These figures were taken from the Perseus Digital Library (http://www.perseus.tufts.edu, accessed 5/18/2022). *Vir* does, of course, appear in the *Aeneid,* but perhaps only 171 times (the number is difficult to confirm without a full study of the poem, as the Perseus vocabulary tool seems to have confused forms of the nouns *vir* and *virus*). So, while most of the commonest nouns in Vergil's *Aeneid* reflect the main concerns of the poem—its hero Aeneas, weapons, the sea, the sky or heavens, shores, war, etc.—a few do not, such as ear and hand (or band), while man (*vir*) is noticeably absent from the list in a poem intensely focused on the psychological and ethical development of a mortal.

But the above lexical analysis, albeit briefly done, does confirm some of the chief themes of the *Distichs*: notably friendship and mortality.

Among the nouns, there are also those that refer to people who might populate the reader's world: spouses, enslaved individuals, doctors, and parents, as well as slaveholders (including the reader imagined as one) and teachers. This list is no surprise, comprising as it does household members, as well as authorities in learning or wisdom. Significantly, figures from the worlds of government or commerce are absent: the world of the *Distichs* is concerned with a person's most immediately personal interactions.[230]

Adjectives and adverbs

Adjectives also reveal the themes of the *Distichs*.[231] Among the collection's common adjectives, *carus, malus, bonus, adversus, exiguus, longus, notus* and *tacitus* ("dear," "evil," "good," "hostile," "small," "long," "familiar," and "silent," respectively), there are associations with, among other topics, modesty, familiarity, and speech. Those that characterize—i.e., excluding relative and interrogative adjectives, which are functional, but including demonstratives—help to suggest to the reader who or what should be emulated ("the good man") or avoided ("the evil man"), and who can be trusted ("someone who is known") or not ("a hostile person"), etc. Some adjectives in the couplets fall naturally into opposing pairs: *malus* vs. *bonus* ("evil" vs. "good") *carus* vs. *adversus* ("dear" vs. "hostile"). These pairs suit and further strengthen the collection's binarism, which I discuss further below.

---

[230] Spouses: *coniunx* and *uxor* appear three times each; enslaved individuals: *servus*, four times, and *famulus*; doctors: *doctor* and *medicus*; parents: *parens*, three times, *pater* and *mater*; master: *dominus*; teacher: *magister*. There are also references to an *auceps* and a *poeta*; while the reader might recognize these terms, it is unlikely they encountered them regularly. The collection also contains many references to unspecified, and therefore generalized, men and also some women. Indefinite pronouns and substantives include: *amicus* ("friend") and *homo, femina*, and *mulier* (terms for men and women). *Homo* appears multiple times, usually referring to a man, though it might refer more widely to a person; *vir*, which is gender specific, appears only once.

[231] The adjectives, many of which can also be used as pronouns, and the numbers of their incidence are as follows: *ipse* 19, *multus* 12, *carus* 8, *ille* 8, *malus* 8, *bonus* 7, *quicumque* 7, *alter* 6, *nullus* 6, *adversus* 5, *aliquis* 5, *plus* 5, *unus* 5, *exiguus* 4, *hic* 4, *is* 4, *longus* 4, *notus* 4, *quaesitus* 4, *tacitus* 4. Adjectives that are almost always used as substantives, for example *amicus* and *bona* (in the neuter plural, meaning "goods, property"), are excluded.

Adverbs in the *Distichs* are so few that one is seldom repeated. Only a handful appear three or more times, including *praecipue* ("especially") (3 times), *rursus* ("again") (4), *saepe* ("often") (3), and *semper* ("always") (10). It is unsurprising that *semper* should be the most common adverb: adverbs of generalization and frequency produce "probability statements" that are taken as rules of thumb—not laws or scientific principles, but general principles that have greater force because they are based on common experience and common sense and also because one's own experience cannot contradict the principle.[232] We might say, then, that the Author of the *Distichs* is keen to establish a timeless wisdom for his maxims: he establishes what *always* happens.

Lexical density

Lexical density, that is, the ratio of unique words in a text to the total word count, can provide a measure of readability: the more unique words a text contains, the more lexically sophisticated it is, and the lower its lexical density. The length of a text has some impact on density: the proportion of new words in a text becomes smaller as the text increases in length and as, therefore, the proportion of new commonly occurring or relevant specialized words shrinks. Even accounting for the impact of the collection's briefness, the density of the *Distichs* is unusually high, and they are therefore unusually readable.[233] The following graph, which plots the lexical densities of fourteen poetic texts or collections (from left to right along the *y*-axis, Horace, *Carmen saeculare*; the *Distichs*; Ovid, *Ibis*; Claudian, *Rape of Persephone*; Vergil, *Eclogues*; Persius, *Satires*; Statius, *Achilleid*; Phaedrus, *Fables*; Catullus; Juvenal, *Satires*; Martial; Vergil, *Aeneid*) of differing length, illustrates the point. The *x*-axis represents lexical density; the *y*-axis represents total word count; the dotted line shows the mean of all the texts. The point representing the *Distichs*, which has been circled, is furthest from the line, demonstrating that the *Distichs*, of all the texts, have an unusually high lexical density.[234]

---

232 The expression comes from Cavill 1999, 46.
233 The only other text in this sample that is out of position is Vergil's *Eclogues*, which is unsurprising given the simplicity of the shepherds' songs.
234 The figures that generated the graph can be found in Table 2, at the end of this chapter, with lexical density calculated to two decimal places. Figures are from the Perseus Digital Library (http://www.perseus.tufts.edu, accessed 5/18/2022), and the texts correspond to the dots, moving along the *y*-axis.

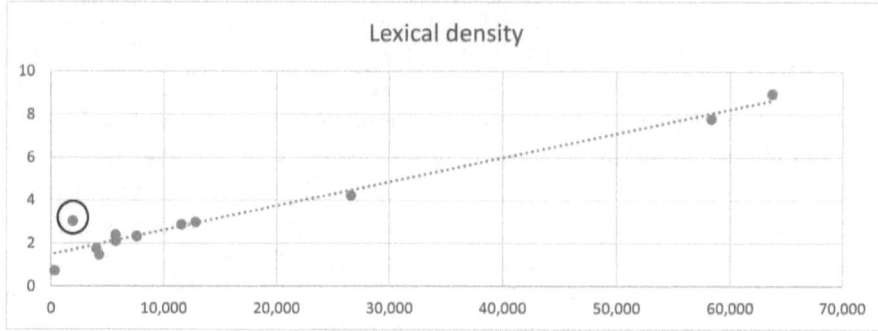

Fig. 2: Lexical density of select poetic texts and collections.

One result of high lexical density is similarity of expression and repeated phrasing, a feature of the *Distichs* that Ong associates with oral texts. Another result is similarity in message, which Ong has also observed in oral texts.

Stylistics

Proverbial language

The collection contains only a few proverbial lines (which is good news for the soundness of the lexical analysis).[235] One couplet refers to a fowling scene.[236] With this line, the Author is not assuming a reader used to seeing or participating in hunting for birds. Rather, he assumes that his reader has been exposed to similar imagery elsewhere; and besides, fowling is an activity easy to imagine

---

235 It is certainly the case that we find occasional proverbial expressions or notions: e.g., being a judge to oneself (*DC* 1.14). I am more concerned, however, with complete lines of verse that draw on imagery outside the immediate context of a person learning morals. On definitions of proverbs and their impossibility, see Taylor 1962, 3. On the difference between a proverb and a maxim—the former is expressed metaphorically and may be paraphrased by the latter—see Barley 1972, 739.
236 *DC* 1.27:

> *Noli homines blando nimium sermone probare;*
> *Fistula dulce canit, volucrem dum decipit auceps.*

> Don't think well of someone whose talk is all flattery:
> The fowler's pipe sings a sweet song, when he's beguiling a bird.

even without specialized knowledge or exposure.[237] Three other couplets contain proverbial lines drawn from seafaring.[238] A final couplet borrows proverbial

---

237 Martial uses the same image in 14.216:

> Auceps.
> *Non tantum calamis, sed cantu fallitur ales,*
> *Callida dum tacita crescit harundo manu.*

> Fowler. A bird is deceived not only by reeds, but by song, while the cunning snare grows thanks to his silent hand.

On the uses and significance of hunting imagery in didactic poetry, see most recently Whitlatch 2013 and Green 2018.

238 The first couplet is *DC* 4.31:

> *Demissos animo et tacitos vitare memento;*
> *Quod flumen placidum est, forsan latet altius unda.*

> Remember to steer clear of the depressed and taciturn:
> Though a river is calm, its current may lie more deeply hidden.

According to Otto 1890, 139, no. 680, Curtius attributed the metaphor to the Bactrians (Curtius 7.4.13: *quod apud Bactrianos vulgo usurpabant, canem timidum vehementius latrare quam mordere, altissima quaeque flumina minimo sono labi,* "they used this commonly among the Bactrians, that a timid dog barks more fiercely than bites, and that the deepest rivers flow with the least sound") who presumably had a reputation for employing sayings. The second couplet is *DC* 2.6

> *Quod nimium est, fugito, parvo gaudere memento;*
> *Tuta mage puppis est, modico quae flumine fertur.*

> Avoid excess and rejoice in restraint:
> A boat is safer carried on a gentle current.

The maxim contains a sentiment *nil nimis* ("nothing in excess") that is found in Terence, Cicero, and Seneca, according to Otto 1890, 243, no. 1229. Surprisingly, the imagery used in the *Distichs* to illustrate the sentiment is found nowhere else. The third couplet is *DC* 4.33:

> *Quod potes id tempta; nam litus carpere remis*
> *Tutius est multo quam velum tendere in altum.*

> Stay within your capabilities: it is much safer to row
> Near the shore than to set sail for the deep.

language from a striking personification, found as early as the fourth century BCE, of Opportunity or Chance, which is represented as having hair in front but being bald behind.[239]

In the *Distichs*, a proverb takes up one line (or so) of a couplet and is a statement of wisdom. It has a primary meaning, related to fowling or sailing, for example, but also a secondary meaning that is revealed thanks to an introductory instruction or statement. For example, in those couplets that draw on nautical imagery, the proverbial lines warn that the reader must beware strong undercurrents in seemingly calm waters, stay safe in a boat by cleaving to a middle course, and avoid danger by rowing close to shore rather than setting sail into the deep. These are their primary meanings. But in each case, the first line or clause guides us to secondary, wider meanings: avoid the depressed and laconic, reject excess in favor of still delightful moderation, and attempt only what is achievable. Proverbs always carry primary and secondary meanings. But the Author's addition of a line that offers a straightforward direction reveals his desire to guide readers and avoid having them miss his messages.

The first of this group of proverbial maxims, *DC* 2.6, which I also included at the head of this chapter, serves as an example of how a metaphorical maxim can be read on three levels: first, as a literal warning to sail a modest course, second as a general urging not to trade contented moderation for risky excess, and finally perhaps as a reflection of the Author's own approach to his writing: his "unadorned words" (*verba nuda*) delivers his messages successfully; a more ambitious stylist might have failed in the task.

A glance back at earlier wisdom literature reveals, however, a wealth of proverbial language. The Author's almost complete avoidance of it—in 139 of his

---

This maxim contains imagery that (surprisingly) is also unique. The Author of the *Distichs* seems, then, unconcerned with creating a collection that draws from paraphrases of or expands existing proverbs or sayings.

239 *DC* 2.26:

Rem, tibi quam scieris aptam, dimittere noli;
Fronte capillata, post haec occasio calva.

Don't let slip away what you know is right for you:
Opportunity has hair at the front, but is bald in the back.

On earlier and subsequent uses of the image, see the opening of this book's Introduction, as well as Otto, 1890, 249, no. 1262, which lists *DC* 2.26.

144 couplets—perhaps suggests that he wanted his collection to be accessible. His readers should not have to work hard.[240]

Negatives

The overall tone of the *Distichs* is negative. Tallying the incidence of negating words among the 144 couplets in the collection, we find that roughly 60% contain at least one negating word, usually an adjective or adverb, such as *nemo, nihil, ne, non, nullus, numquam, nusquam, nisi,* etc. ("no one," "nothing," "lest," "not," "nothing," "never," "nowhere," respectively).[241] The predominance of negatives among the *Distichs* is unsurprising: this is a collection of simple instructions and reflections.

Possible reasons for the Author's tone may be, first, that Romans were accustomed to hearing both encouragement and admonishment at school. Alternatively, negative instructions or statements from an authority figure may be more immediately effective and memorable than positive statements of encouragement. For example, among children in a classroom setting, reprimands produce more on-task (i.e., "better") behavior than do either praise alone or no reprimands and no praise; adding praise to reprimands produces little immediate effect, but it does maintain on-task behavior as reprimands are gradually removed.[242] While reprimands are not identical to prohibitions, nor praise to positive instructions, they do share the goal (and perhaps effect) of steering a child or indeed adult away from or towards a behavior or activity. Finally, the predominance of couplets containing negatives seems to contrast with the generally encouraging and upbeat tone of modern self-help tomes. We are unused to the guardedness and caution that pervades the collection, though it presumably found a positive reception among ancient audiences.

---

240 Shippey 1994, 295–296, describes the mental work that readers must do with every maxim: having perceived its basic message, they must reformulate it to apply it to general circumstances and once again to particular circumstances.
241 86 couplets contain at least one negative word; 58 do not. These figures provide only a rough impression of the tone of the *Distichs*, as they include maxims that have a negative tone, though their message might be positive, and they leave out couplets whose message is negative though they lack negating words. An analysis that includes negatively toned words would better reflect the overall tone of the collection, though its objectivity might be questionable.
242 Acker and O'Leary 1987; Pfiffner and O'Leary 1987.

Binarism

The notion that humanness—the condition of being a homo sapiens—is the basis for modes of thought was explored by Lévi-Strauss in his work on binary structures in the languages and cultures of various "primitive" peoples.[243] While Lévi-Strauss has been attacked both for his reliance on too few example cultures (especially native American) and for the possibility that binarism is a trait of males, but not necessarily females, the notion of binarism has found significant favor among not only anthropologists, but scholars in other fields too.[244]

Lévi-Strauss's binarism is helpful for exploring several aspects of the *Distichs*: firstly, their bipartite structure, comprising two clauses, one usually subordinate to the other; secondly, their distichic (i.e., two-line) form; and thirdly, the oppositions either expressed or implied in the *Distichs* between, for example, good and bad men, wise and foolish men, life and death, and certainty and chance.[245] The simplicity of these contrasts is helped by the lack of references in the *Distichs* to the state or politics; their focus—like oral texts—is intensely on the self and one's immediate community in the here and now. The Author's adherence to all three aspects throughout the collection renders it consistent and predictable and so makes its messages more accessible and memorable to its readers. Binary oppositions in subject matter are not unique to the *Distichs*: according to Leo Perdue, a binary opposition lies behind every work of paraene-

---

[243] Lévi-Strauss 1963, chap. 5, deals with the fundamental importance of binary thinking that is reflected in cultural practice, myth, and ways of considering the world. For a summary of arguments in favor of and against Lévi-Strauss, see Trigger 2003, especially 3–11.

[244] An example of the fundamental importance of binarism in language acquisition and especially reasoning is found in the fascinating study of Gazzaniga and Miller 1989 on the recognition of antonymy in a commissurotomy patient's brain.

[245] For example, *DC* 1.11 comprises in each line an instruction and a purpose clause:

Dilige sic alios, ut sis tibi carus amicus;
Sic bonus esto bonis, ne te mala damna sequantur.

Value friends to be valuable to them—and to you;
Being good to good people will shield you from heavy losses.

In addition to the contrast between good and bad in the second line, the couplet's parallel syntax allows for a comparison of *bonus esto* to *dilige alios* and comparison of *sis tibi carus amicus* with *mala damna sequantur*. The simple construction of the couplet helps to formulate a complex (and perhaps repetitive) message: being kind but not overly so to others is what brings personal benefits; you should treat good men in the same way to avoid bad consequences, which is also a personal benefit.

sis, and the result, as he explains, is that "paraenesis presents a group ethic designed to maintain a clear differentiation between in-group and out-group."[246]

The features identified above help the *Distichs* to function well as a text to be read or spoken, and to be understood and memorized, not just by Romans, but readers in later centuries too, as Chapters 6 and 7 describe. Their adoption is also explained by the appeal of their subject matter, to which I turn in Chapters 4 and 5.

Tab. 1: Data for lexical density chart.

Text	Total word count	Lexical density
Horace, *Carmen saeculare*	313	0.716
Disticha Catonis	1,930	3.03937
Ovid, *Ibis*	4,032	1.782
Claudian, *Rape of Persephone*	4,269	1.461
Vergil, *Eclogues*	5,757	2.383
Persius, *Satires*	5,769	2.096
Statius, *Achilleid*	7,598	2.339
Phaedrus, *Fables*	11,562	2.885
Catullus	12,857	2.972
Juvenal, *Satires*	26,564	4.219
Martial	58,314	7.792
Vergil, *Aeneid*	63,719	8.957

---

246 Perdue 1981, 255. On binarism in the *Distichs*, see further Connolly 2013a.

Tab. 2: Verbs with imperative forms in the *Distichs* and the corpus of Latin literature.

Verbs with imperative forms in the *Distichs*	Distichs				Latin literature			
	Present		Future		Present		Future	
	Number	Percentage	Number	Percentage	Number	Percentage	Number	Percentage
Accipere	0	0%	1	100%	367	99%	5	1%
Cavere	1	50%	1	50%	232	83%	48	17%
Celare	0	0%	1	100%	40	40%	60	60%
Docere	0	0%	1	100%	58	98%	1	2%
Facere	9	82%	2	18%	457	57%	342	43%
Fugere	4	57%	3	43%	93	91%	9	9%
Laudare	0	0%	1	100%	11	31%	24	69%
Petere	0	0%	2	100%	76	67%	38	33%
Perspicere	1	50%	1	50%	10	100%	0	0%
Putare	1	25%	3	75%	719	97%	25	3%
Rogare	0	0%	1	100%	57	77%	17	23%
Silere	0	0%	1	100%	6	100%	0	0%
Timere	0	0%	1	100%	33	77%	10	23%
Videre	0	0%	1	100%	469	95%	26	5%
All verbs	16	44%	20	56%	3375	85%	612	15%

Part II: **Content and Context**

4 Friendship

> *Consilium arcanum tacito committe sodali;*
> *Corporis auxilium medico committe fideli.* (DC 2.22)
>
> Entrust private deliberations to a discreet friend;
> Entrust your medical problems to a reliable doctor.

In the pragmatic and jaded world of the *Distichs*, friendship could offer solidarity, financial help, and emotional support. *DC* 2.22, the couplet quoted above, makes the point that just as they entrust their plans and intentions to reliable friends, so patients should happily entrust their bodies to doctors.[247]

The *Distichs* that concern friendship offer an opportunity to consider how the collection might increase our understanding of the topic and, in particular, what anxieties surrounded it. I discuss here those entries that deal with friendship, as opposed to any other relationship, and that deal with it explicitly.[248] I consider the maxims within the context of informal friendships, and the precise natures of the friendships described or assumed in the maxims will be explored in this chapter. I omit patronage from my discussion. A significant number of the maxims concerning friendship are concerned with reciprocity, as I will discuss, and they may have been of use to patrons and clients in navigating the social obligations between them. But patronage, in its various manifestations, could also entail political, economic, and legal obligations, which may have impacted the social interactions of patrons and clients, and these are not dis-

---

[247] This is the couplet garbled by Vindicianus, court physician to Valentinian II, in his dedication to the emperor. He quotes it to make the point that doctors should give their patients only those treatments they wish to receive, but he might also be alluding to an actual or wished-for friendship with Valentinian. The encouragement to trust a doctor runs counter to the well-known mistrust of medical practitioners, voiced most famously by the Elder Pliny (*HN* 29.16–23).
[248] I have selected couplets that contain key words including *amicus*, *sodalis*, *socius*, and *contubernalis*. The Author uses the first three as near synonyms. On the terminology of friendship, see Williams 2012, especially 40–44, though *socius* receives scant attention, presumably because it rarely appears in his chosen sources. *Familiaris*, another (near) synonym, does not appear in the *Distichs* because it will not scan. One couplet, *DC* 4.36, appears in Boas 1952 as *Est iactura gravis quae sunt amittere damnis, / Sed tibi cum valeas semper superesse putato.* Chase and the Duffs print and/or translate these lines. Pepin and Marchand, however, read a different second line (Boas' 4.36a): *sunt quaedam, quae ferre decet patienter, amici.* I follow Boas 1952 and therefore omit *DC* 4.36 from my discussion of friendship.

cussed explicitly in the *Distichs*.[249] Discussion of the maxims, therefore, in the context of patronage risks being incomplete and potentially misleading.

The discussion that follows considers the *Distichs* in the context of contemporary attitudes towards friendship as understood in wisdom texts, moralizing texts, inscriptions, and dedicated discussions of the topic. A date in the first century CE would put the collection in the general temporal context of a number of key Roman treatments of friendship, most notably Cicero's *De amicitia*, which presumably remained well known into the following century. Contemporaries or near-contemporaries also include Publilius Syrus, Valerius Maximus, Phaedrus, Babrius, Seneca, Martial, and Plutarch, whose reflections on friendship offer useful comparisons with or to the *Distichs*.[250] I have omitted from my discussion references to friendship in other texts that are not set within large-scale treatments of friendship or reflections in wisdom collections. There are, to be sure, plenty of insightful references to friendship outside of such contexts, though their lack of sustained discussion of friendship renders them on the whole less useful.[251]

The couplets that concern friendship fall into three rough groupings by focus: on reciprocity, on the benefits that friendship brings, and on problematic friends.

Reciprocity

A first set of couplets concerning friendship introduces us to a key feature of Roman friendship as presented in the *Distichs*: reciprocity.

DC 1.11

> *Dilige sic alios, ut sis tibi carus amicus;*[252]
> *Sic bonus esto bonis, ne te mala damna sequantur.*

---

249 These obligations, manifested through "the *reciprocal* exchange of goods and services" are claimed by Saller 1982, 1, as a defining feature of patronage.
250 I have omitted the epigrams attributed to Seneca, as there is general agreement that they post-date Martial (Holzberg 2004; Breitenbach 2009, 6).
251 On friendship in the Roman satirists, for example, see Mayer 1989.
252 This is a difficult couplet to translate: *tibi* seems to be an ethical dative (or something akin to it), but its precise relationship to *carus* is unclear. A similar construction with a similar theme is found in Hor. *Epist.* 1.18.101: *te tibi amicum* ("being a friend to oneself," trans. Mayer 1989, 13).

> Value friends to be valuable to them—and to you;
> Being good to good people will shield you from heavy losses.

This couplet is crucial for understanding the Author's treatment of friendship and could even be considered programmatic. His use of economic language is striking. *Dilige* means "put a high value on," either literally or figuratively, and when used figuratively, the verb then comes to mean "love," with an affection that comes from choice rather than from any familial bond.[253] The reader is told to put a high value on or love others so that one becomes a friend who is *carus*, "of high value." If taken literally, then a friend who is *carus* might literally offer the possibility of financial security or perhaps under certain circumstances, financial gain.[254] The assumption behind *dilige* and *carus* in economic terms is that friendship is a reciprocal relationship, in which friends offer each other benefits, in the form of material goods or services or advice or loyalty, with the understanding and assumption that the exchange is reasonably balanced.[255]

The inclusion of *tibi* underscores the importance of reciprocity: undervaluing the size of the benefit a friend deserves will lose that friend's loyalty and redound to the reader's disadvantage. The second line also contains economic language: *damna* may mean "losses," and the reader is advised that if he is to avoid losses, he should be "good to good men" and so do good to those who do good things. This advice presumably holds true because good people follow the conventions of reciprocity in friendship, while bad people fail to reciprocate, thereby inflicting losses on their friends.[256]

---

253 Hellegouarc'h 1972, 145, cites Isidore of Seville on the difference in meaning between *amare* and *diligere*: "'*amare*' is naturally planted in us, but '*diligere*' is by choice" (*amare nobis est naturaliter insitum, diligere vero electione*, Isid. *Diff.* 1.17). According to Hellegouarc'h, the verbs are often used interchangeably. Williams 2012, 224–225, however, follows Cicero in contrasting *amare* and *diligere* as to "love" and to be "fond." The distinction is not crucial here; more important is the Author's emphasis on affection.

254 Several of the couplets may contribute to the debate: *DC* 1.11, 1.35, and 4.42 (among others) have ambiguous language that may be construed in an economic sense or not.

255 For a list of the possible favors that friends might do, see Verboven 2002, 65–66. Hellegouarc'h 1972, 148–149, notes that *diligere* was a term in vogue in the early Empire, especially in philosophical texts. As a term for affection by choice, its analogue is *caritas* (and by extension *carus*), a relationship paralleled by *amare* and *amor*.

256 Cicero, *Amic.* 18, makes the basic point that only good men can really be friends. *DC* 4.8 (*Quod donare potes gratis, ne vende roganti, / nam recte fecisse bonis, in parte lucrorum est*. "Give for free what you can to whomever asks; / If you do right by good men, that is to your gain") lacks any reference to friends, but echoes the message of the initial couplets: that gaining friends should be regarded as a financial plus. The connection to friendship is made

The emphasis in *DC* 1.11 is on the centrality of reciprocity to friendship, as well as on the benefits and dangers of friendship. The couplet can be read in purely economic terms, though it does not have to be. Yet the very ambiguity, most obvious in the word *carus* ("dear") which denotes firstly a high value and secondarily an emotional worth, suggests that Roman friendship was primarily and essentially reciprocal, and only secondarily and not necessarily emotional.[257] The ambiguity also serves as a reminder to modern readers of the difficulties of the language of friendship: Latin terms connected to friendship need to be understood within their broad social, cultural, and political context, but that context is not monolithic, and terms might be multivalent within it.[258]

Seneca advises Lucilius to judge a potential friend (*delibera ... de ipso*)—and presumably not his worth—before entering into friendship, as does Plutarch, in his essay on telling flatterers from friends, who warns that a friend must be examined early, not in a time of need. Cicero simply recommends being careful and looking for someone who is true.[259]

DC 1.35

> *Ne dubita cum magna petas impendere parva:*
> *his etenim rebus coniungit gratia caros.*

> When looking for large returns, don't hesitate to make modest investments:
> It's with spending, you see, that favors bring dear friends together.

The text is awkward, and Boas 1952 acknowledges that the lines seem not to belong together (and indeed Chase, the Duffs, and Marchand substitute and translate an alternative second line), but perhaps some sense might be drawn from the couplet as presented.[260] The second line establishes friendship as the theme, while the first sets up economic language as the vehicle. The first line could refer simply to financial investment, but the investment may also be in a friendship—whose payoff, as we have seen, might be financial. The second line

---

stronger by the inclusion of *bonis* ("good men"): for the Author, the benefits of friendship accrued from making friends with good men.

257 The English term "dear" carries a similar double meaning, though its economic sense is admittedly somewhat dated.
258 On the nuances of friendship terms and the importance of contextualized readings, including across genres and media, see especially Williams 2012.
259 Sen. *Ep.* 3.2; Plut. *Mor.* 49D–E; Cic. *Amic.* 95). On discerning flatterers from friends, see also generally Konstan 1996.
260 Chase 1922, Duff and Duff 1934, and Marchand.

suggests that making these investments (taking *parva* or indeed the entire first line as the antecedent of *his...rebus*) will help to bring a valued (*carus*) friend closer, i.e., it will stimulate valued friends to greater reciprocity, which may yield significant returns. The Author, however, sees utility as the primary motivating factor in friendship, and nowhere does he mention love.

Publilius Syrus echoes this couplet's emphasis on reciprocity. Asserting that there is no better purchase than a firm friend, he uses strikingly economic language: loyal friends have to be bought, but they are the best use of one's money.[261] Claiming that it is easy to find people who can do you favors by cultivating those who have a record of doing them, he places significant emphasis on reciprocity and the expectations that come with it, while implying that not everyone always manages or is willing to respond in kind.[262] He also points out that those accommodated in times of safety will offer aid in times of adversity.[263] Syrus also acknowledges the appeal of friendship's emotional support: "There's comradeship in tears when a pitying heart recognizes the piteous."[264] The fragments of Syrus are culled from mimes, and his *sententiae* were therefore voiced by dramatic characters; without their contexts, we cannot know whether they were uttered seriously, in jest, or with irony. But the collection of them as *sententiae* suggests that they were all later, at least, taken seriously.

A fable of Babrius also highlights the importance of reciprocity for building trust in a friendship:

> λέοντι προσπτὰς αἰετῶν τις ἐζήτει
> κοινωνὸς εἶναι. χὠ λέων "τί κωλύει;"
> πρὸς αὐτὸν εἶπεν, "ἀλλ' ἐπ' ἐνεχύρῳ δώσεις
> τὠκυπτέρῳ σου μὴ μεθιέναι πίστιν·
> πῶς γὰρ φίλῳ σοι μὴ μένοντι πιστεύσω;"

> An eagle flew up to a lion and asked him to be his partner. "I don't see why not," replied the lion. "But first you must give me your long wing-feathers as a pledge that you will keep your promise. How will I be able to trust you as a friend if you do not stay here with me?"[265]

The eagle will receive the lion's protection, which presumably will entail some potential unspecified sacrifice on the part of the lion. But the lion will make

---

261 Syrus 53.
262 Syrus 225.
263 Syrus 245.
264 Syrus 143: *Contubernia sunt lacrimarum ubi misericors miserum adspicit.*
265 Babrius 99 = Perry 335 = Gibbs 50. Trans. Gibbs 2002.

such a sacrifice only if the eagle demonstrates a reciprocal willingness to sacrifice something, in this case, his wing-feathers. For the lion, without such a sacrifice as a pledge, there can be no friendship.

Cicero regards friendship differently. In his *De amicitia*, our most extensive ancient treatment of friendship, he includes among his definitions of friendship that it is "the greatest possible community of interests, wishes and opinions" (*voluntatum studiorum sententiarum summa consensio*) (*Amic.* 15).[266] He sees affection as the origin of friendship and looks askance at the idea that utility should be its motivation, arguing instead that reciprocity, with all its advantages, should be a result of friendship.[267] Elsewhere in the work, Cicero has Laelius see love as the primary cause of friendship, but grants that the advantages derived from friendship are a natural consequence.[268] For all his high-flown assertions about the primacy of affection, in his *De inventione* Cicero does, however, acknowledge that friendship may have different impetuses, when he offers to discuss elsewhere the claim that friendship may be sought for either emotional intimacy or practical advantage.[269]

Seneca takes a stronger position on affection versus reciprocity. In his *Epistulae Morales*, promoting the Stoic view that friendship should offer simply the pleasure of company, he strongly opposes the Epicurean promotion of the practical benefits of friendship that derive from the exchange of favors, and claims instead to seek friends whom he can follow into exile and for whom he will even

---

[266] Cicero offers two further definitions of friendship: "For friendship is in fact nothing other than a community of views on all matters human and divine, together with goodwill and affection" (*est enim amicitia nihil aliud nisi omnium divinarum humanarumque rerum cum benevolentia et caritate consensio*) (*Amic.* 20) and "one's desire for good for someone, for the sake of doing good to the person one loves and with reciprocal desire" (*voluntas erga aliquem rerum bonarum illius ipsius causa quem diligit cum eius pari voluntate*) (*De inv.* 2.166). All translations from Cicero's *De amicitia* are from Powell 1990.

[267] Cic. *Amic.* 29.

[268] Cic. *Amic.* 26. The same point—that friendship begins with affection and reciprocity is natural consequence—is found also in *Amic.* 32. Cicero asserts the primacy of emotion, not practical advantage, in friendship also at *Fin.* 1.66, *Leg.* 1.49, and *Nat. D.* 1.122.

[269] Cic. *De inv.* 2.166. While noting that he had already dealt with obligations in friendship in *De amicitia*, Cicero does not wholly neglect the topic in *De officiis*. Though his thoughts about friendship in *De officiis* are suited to his focus on public office, he promotes first the traditional notion that friendship is ideally founded on affection and in its counsel, support, and enjoyment offers greater comfort to men than any riches, while also acknowledging the role of reciprocity. On the ideal of friendship based on mutual affection, see Cic. *Off.* 1.55, 1.56, 1.58; 2.30. On reciprocity, see Cic. *Off.* 1.56.

die.²⁷⁰ Some years later, Plutarch recognizes the importance of emotional intimacy as well as reciprocity: "But true friendship seeks after three things above all else: virtue as a good thing, intimacy as a pleasant thing, and usefulness as a necessary thing, for a man ought to use judgement before accepting a friend, and to enjoy being with him and to use him when in need of him."²⁷¹

An explanation for why reciprocity is important to the Author and others might be inferred from Plutarch, who notes that while true friendship is built on mutual affection and shared interests, with reciprocity following easily from that, the flatterer (or false friend), lacking the ability to engage later in reciprocity, must resort to empty flattery in order to ingratiate himself and initiate something like friendship.²⁷² A friend who can reciprocate is perhaps a friend who is more likely to be intimate and offer protection.²⁷³ In their discussions on the centrality of emotional intimacy in friendship, both Cicero and Plutarch stress fellow feeling and shared interests. The Author does not.

DC 4.42

Gratior officiis, quo sis mage carior, esto,
Ne nomen subeas, quod dicunt, officiperdi.

Return favors and so make yourself a better friend;
That way, people won't call you a sponge (as they say).

This couplet, while not naming friends directly, uses the language of reciprocal friendship—*officium, carus,* and *gratia.*²⁷⁴ The Author uses *officium*, a term for a

---

270 Sen. *Ep.* 9.10. I omit from discussion Seneca's *Quomodo amicitia continenda sit* as it is preserved only in fragments.
271 Plut. *Mor.* 94B: ἐπεὶ δ' ἡ ἀληθινὴ φιλία τρία ζητεῖ μάλιστα, τὴν ἀρετὴν ὡς καλόν, καὶ τὴν συνήθειαν ὡς ἡδύ, καὶ τὴν χρείαν ὡς ἀναγκαῖον δεῖ γὰρ ἀποδέξασθαι κρίναντα καὶ χαίρειν συνόντα καὶ χρῆσθαι δεόμενον. The translation is from Babbitt.
272 Plut. *Mor.* 51B–C.
273 It might, of course, be objected that Plutarch is writing about Greek culture, not Roman. For the purposes of this discussion, we should therefore be cautious about placing too much emphasis on his treatment of the topic.
274 *Officiperdus* is a hapax legomenon. Its suffix *-perdus* is perhaps to be translated as *–losing*. (So, for example, Lewis and Short, s.v. *frugiperdus*, fruit-losing, a translation of the Homeric ὠλεσίκαρπος; also *officiperdi, qui sui laboris non habent remunerationem*, Gloss. Isid.) *Officiperdus* may describe someone who squanders others' favors or someone who fails to capitalize on his own favors to others. I have kept my translation ambiguous in order to communicate that the reader is simply inept at exchanging favors. On these terms and others pertaining to Roman social and political relations, see especially Hellegouarc'h 1972.

favor that has been prompted by social obligation and will generate a reciprocal favor. *Gratia*, which appeared in *DC* 1.35 and is found here in adjectival form, denotes the goodwill that is the driving force of reciprocity.

The Author does not use anywhere the term *beneficium*, a favor free from any obligations and expecting no return. The omission is simple to explain: *beneficium* will not scan in a hexameter line. But a result of its absence is that the reciprocal exchange that takes place within friendship is emphasized over the free granting of favors.[275] In his *De beneficiis*, Seneca provides examples of the exchange of *beneficia* between *amici* ("friends"), but also between slaveholders and enslaved individuals, and fathers and sons, and some of what he writes about is germane to our discussion.[276] For example, as Griffin puts it, "Seneca likes to emphasize that a *beneficium* differs from an *officium* precisely in that it is given without prior obligation (*Ben.* 3.18.1), that it goes beyond the duties prescribed by any social role (3.21.34), and that it creates bonds of friendship (2.18.5; 2.21.2...)."[277] Seneca notes that *beneficia* should not always be reciprocated and also that being in a state of obligation fosters friendship; paying back a friend might suggest a discomfort with the obligation, a discomfort that may jeopardize the relationship.[278] Cicero, according to Griffin, "regards conferring a beneficium as 'in our power', i.e. a free act not dictated by obligation (*Off.* 1.48), whereas *officium* is an action dictated by obligations relating to social roles and relationships or obligations of gratitude for previous benefits."[279]

---

275 *Beneficium* and *officium* are both used in political, commercial, or other professional contexts, and it is these that Seneca discusses in his *De beneficiis* (*On Favors*). Indeed, as Konstan notes, Seneca rarely discusses friendship in that work (Konstan 1997, 127). Cicero's interest in exploring personal obligations in the context of public office was made clear in an earlier letter to Atticus (*Att.* XVI.14.3), in which Cicero had proposed to his friend that the Greek καθῆκον could be rendered with the Latin *officium*; Atticus had wondered whether *officium*, which presumably was used mostly in the private sphere, could adequately apply to public life, as καθῆκον routinely did. Cicero replies *praeclare convenit* ("it fits perfectly", trans. Shackleton Bailey) since we speak of *consulum officium, senatus officium, imperatoris officium* ("consuls' duty, the Senate's duty, a general's duty"). I owe the reference to Griffin and Atkins 1991, xx.
276 Konstan 1997, 127–128, notes that there is only one mention of friendship in the work; Wolkenhauer 2014, 26–38, agrees that *De beneficiis* has little to do with friendship, yet he points out that the ways in which the ancients used terms might not match up with our modern conceptions and might not be consistent with each other. I use *De beneficiis* not as a text about friendship, but as a text that helps us reflect on friendship.
277 Griffin 2013, 22–23.
278 Sen. *De ben.* 4.40.
279 Griffin 2013, 23.

While neither consistently maintains the distinction they both claim, Seneca and Cicero agree that *beneficium* denotes a good or service freely given and received that is independent of any reciprocal bonds or other expectations, while *officium* is a favor given or received out of expectation and obligation. While the Author of the *Distichs* never uses the term *beneficium*, he does use *officium* in *DC* 4.42, a key couplet for understanding friendship in the collection. Indeed, the Author's emphasis on reciprocity and expectations suggests that he may have considered *officia* as more essential than *beneficia* to his conception of friendship.[280] One reason for that preference may be socio-economic: Griffin points out that "*beneficium* was an important word for the members of the Roman governing class. It was widely used in public life, where it could be synonymous with high office and privileges."[281] But the Author of the *Distichs*, by contrast, never explicitly engages with that milieu. His lessons on friendship were instead suited to Romans at a number of different socio-economic levels.

DC 3.9

> *Cum tibi divitiae superent in fine senectae,*
> *Munificus facito vivas, non parcus, amicus.*

---

280 Dixon 1993, 462, following Michel 1962, 511–512, has different definitions of *beneficium* and *officium*: "To be wealthy and powerful meant that certain demands could be made on one (*beneficia*) and that one could require certain services in return (*officia*)." Hellegouarc'h 1972 defines *officium* as "un action louable en faveur de quelqu'un," (p. 152) while *beneficium*, following Sen. *De ben.* 3.9.1, is "un acte purement spontané" (p. 162). Wolkenhauer 2014, 37, makes the helpful point that the paucity of words in the Latin language means that terms may bear a wide range of meanings and may necessarily have to generalize relationships. For a treatment of gift exchange with reference to anthropological approaches, see Dixon 1993, who (p. 457) quotes from Gregory 1982, 51: "The gift transactor's motivation is precisely the opposite to the capitalist's: whereas the latter maximizes net incomings, the former maximizes net outgoings. The aim of the capitalist is to accumulate profit while the aim of the 'big-man' gift transactor is to acquire a large following of people (gift-debtors) who are obligated to him."

281 Griffin 2013, 108. According to Griffin, Seneca aimed to underplay the term's socio-political connotations and establish it more widely as an ethical construct. The most concise formulation of Seneca's shifting of the locus of *beneficia* is at *De ben.* 6.34.5: *in pectore amicus, non in atrio quaeritur* ("it's in hearts that one looks for friends, not in reception rooms"). (See also Sen. *Ep.* 19.11.) I owe the references to Griffin 2013, 311. In book 3 of *De beneficiis*, Seneca considers *beneficia* between fathers and sons and even between slaveholders and enslaved individuals. *Beneficia* were also of interest to Syrus, though understanding the relevant *sententiae* in his collection is difficult: their contexts are lost to us, leaving their speakers—men, women, elites, non-elites, enslaved individuals—and their motivations unknown.

> If you have abundant wealth in your final years,
> Be a friend generous, not stingy, with your favors.

The key term in this couplet is *munificus,* used to describe a person who fulfils his obligations or performs the duties of his office, and thus by extension it means generous, bountiful and, of course, munificent. In the context of friendship, those obligations might be the exchange of gifts, and here the Author commends generosity, not meanness. Exact monetary exchange is not expected (and is perhaps not possible), and indeed a wealthy man is encouraged to give a lot, perhaps more than he receives. *Munificus* may, of course, be translated simply with our cognate "munificent" and the notion of exchange elided, but the Author's choice of a multivalent word is surely deliberate.

DC 2.1

> *Si potes, ignotis etiam prodesse memento:*
> *Utilius regno est, meritis adquirere amicos.*
>
> If you can, remember to help strangers:
> Attracting friends by kindness is more beneficial than power.

What is the point in being nice to strangers? Because they might become friends. The sentiment is simple, perhaps too simple, and the careful choice of vocabulary—*prodesse* ("be of service") and *meritis* ("favors")—suggests that the message is more complicated. Doing a service to a stranger will render him a friend—and the service is now regarded as a favor, which should be reciprocated. To help a stranger is ultimately to help oneself.

Utilius makes clear the focus on self-interest: having power might inspire someone's loyalty or obedience, but perhaps little more; doing favors, by contrast, sets up a reciprocal relationship with that person and an expectation of reasonable evenness of exchange. Inclusion of the word *regnum* in the *Distichs* might take on additional significance with a new date of composition in the first century CE: the reciprocity of friendship is desirable, as is the ideal of balance; one person's domination over another is not.[282]

---

282 *Regnum* might be referring to the Principate, by contrast to the Republic, and perhaps the Author is responding to anxiety about new power structures. Augustus and at least some emperors enjoyed wide popularity, despite vocal and highly literate aristocratic opposition, yet the political and social turmoil of the late Republic and early Empire surely remained a source of anxiety to many. Insincere friends have long been regarded as a problem for rulers: see, for example, Cic. *Off.* 3.84, who quotes Accius: *Multi iniqui atque infideles regno, pauci benivoli*

The emphasis on favors might lead the reader to wonder whether financial stability (or even wealth) should be the most important thing to look for in a prospective friend.

DC 4.15

> *Cum tibi vel socium vel fidum quaeris amicum,*
> *non tibi fortuna est hominis sed vita petenda.*

> When looking for an ally or a loyal friend,
> Don't look at the man's fortunes, but at his life.

The collocation *vel socium vel...amicum* is striking.[283] *Socii* were partners, often in business or politics, and their relationship was bound in law by obligations and also protected by law. *Amici* might also be *socii* and vice versa, but the relationships were distinct.[284] The significance for this couplet is that the same advice applies to both groups: do not be concerned with a man's wealth, but rather his experience.

Wealthy supporters and loyal friends might be advantageous to the reader, and indeed financial health would seem to be an important factor in a relationship built on reciprocity. Yet the Author tells the reader to be concerned instead with a potential friend's life, i.e., his experiences and habits (or lifestyle, in modern parlance). This is a suggestion that appeals to us: friends should be chosen for who they are, not what they are.

The Author sets the bar for friendship high: reciprocity and trust are essential. The fact that the Author never discusses friendship explicitly within the context of formal patronage or within the exchange of services such as advocacy makes his emphasis on reciprocity all the more impressive: friendship in the *Distichs* that is non-formal and non-familiar is still strongly centered on reci-

---

("Kings have many enemies and traitors, few friends"). Cicero discusses the pitfalls for tyrants of using their power rather than genuine friendship to engender loyalty in their subjects in *Amic.* 52–53. According to Powell 1990, 105, the theme is commonplace.

283 The phrase *socii et amici* is found in the language of Republican international relations, and while its meaning is contested, it either describes "those *amici* who were bound to assist Rome with military help" (as Matthaei 1907, 184, puts it) or is a synonym for *amici*, while simple *socii*, appearing as a discrete term, were a distinct group. Mommsen 1887, 593–594, follows the former definition, while Matthaei follows the latter.

284 For a good overview of *societas*, see Verboven 2002, 275–286. *Hospitium*, another relationship that partially resembles and overlaps with *amicitia*, is absent from the *Distichs*, as is the related *hospes*. On *hospitium*, see Nicols 2001.

procity. The Author also avoids any mention of friendship within the family (i.e., blood and marriage relations), except for noting its potential conflict with the loyalty of spouses.

The Author does not separate out entirely reciprocity and emotional intimacy in friendship. Nor do Cicero, Seneca, and the others, and it is the sometimes-competing demands and expectations of intimacy and reciprocity that lead these authors to reflect upon their relative importance. While Cicero might urge emotional intimacy as the motivating factor for and basis of friendship and Publilius Syrus might pay greater heed to the role of reciprocity, they both acknowledge both elements.[285]

Friendship's benefits

The next set of couplets tells the reader what a friend is or does and outlines what a friend might reasonably be expected to offer.

DC 2.22

> *Consilium arcanum tacito committe sodali*
> *Corporis auxilium medico committe fideli.*
>
> Entrust private deliberations to a discreet friend;
> Entrust your medical problems to a reliable doctor.

---

[285] Friendship of utility or advantage was familiar to Cicero: his letter of January 62 BCE to Q. Caecilius Metellus Celer, *Fam.* 5.2, is a study of the breakdown of such a friendship. At the core of the letter is Cicero's account of his enmity with Celer's brother. That enmity has spilled over into the friendship between Cicero and Celer and has raised suspicion, reproach, and now even hostility on the part of Celer (so Cicero claims) and perhaps on Cicero's part too. Celer claims that he has been reconciled with Cicero (§1), though as Cicero claims later in the letter (§5), he never thought that the friendship had been broken. Yet even if not broken, the friendship has clearly been strained: Cicero interprets Celer's letter to him as suggesting that they have different definitions of reciprocity in friendship (§3), but more likely the problem lies in the parties' differing interpretations of the exchanges and slights that Cicero catalogues. Cicero closes the letter by asking that Celer recognize Cicero was entitled to help (§10) and by claiming that he willingly remains as friendly as is possible and will sooner give way to Celer's brother than jeopardize the friendship. Cicero's friendship with Celer was most likely not based on intimacy and affection; it was more likely a political friendship, based instead on alliance and practical need—and possibly some community of feeling too. This was a friendship closer to that envisaged by the *Distichs*' Author than to the idealized friendship of *De amicitia*.

This couplet was discussed earlier in Chapter 1: Vindicianus, physician to the fourth-century emperor Valentinian II, had drawn on it in a dedicatory letter to the emperor, but confused it with another, *DC* 2.9.[286] Vindicianus' interest was in the second line; ours is with the first. The Author's comparison of the close-mouthed buddy to a trusted doctor might tell us about the preferred qualities of a close friend: first, he should be able to keep secrets; second, he should be able to offer advice or solutions to problems or anxieties based on experience or good sense. With the qualifying *tacito* ("discreet") the Author acknowledges that not all friends can keep secrets, and broadcasting one's concerns or problems can be, as *DC* 2.9 tells us, a bad idea. Having friends can be beneficial, but only when the reader discerns how the relationship with each should be managed.

The Author's (near-)contemporaries also voice the benefits of the friend as confidant. For Cicero, friendship offers an opportunity to have a sounding board and to share openly ideas and experiences.[287] Publilius Syrus recognizes the benefits of trusting a friend and recommends that we commit ourselves to friendship so deeply that a friend could never become an enemy.[288] Similarly, he asserts that trust breeds trust.[289] Finally, according to Syrus, "Whoever fears his friend does not know the force of the word."[290] Seneca makes openness a requirement of friendship, telling Lucilius that he must share all his concerns and thoughts.[291] Plutarch also recognizes the need for openness: a true friend will offer criticism and disagreement, not simply nod assent to one's plans. He too uses a medical analogy: in offering criticism, sometimes painful, the friend is like a doctor.[292]

---

[286] *DC* 2.9: *Corporis exigui vires contemnere noli; / Consilio pollet, cui vim natura negavit* ("Do not scorn the power of somebody small; / He is rich in counsel, whom nature has denied strength").

[287] Cic. *Amic.* 22: *Quid dulcius quam habere quicum omnia audeas sic loqui ut tecum?* ("What is more pleasant than to have someone with whom you can safely talk about anything whatever, just as with yourself?").

[288] Syrus, 300: *Ita crede amico, ne sit inimico locus* ("So put your trust in a friend that there is no room for an enemy").

[289] Syrus, 576: *Qui timet amicum, amicus ut timeat, docet* ("Whoever fears his friend teaches his friend to fear").

[290] Syrus, 592: *Qui timet amicum, vim non novit nominis*.

[291] Sen. *Ep.* 3.2–3.

[292] On openness, see Plut. *Mor.* 53B; on the friend as doctor, *Mor.* 55A.

DC 4.13

> Auxilium a notis petito si forte labores;
> Nec quisquam melior medicus quam fidus amicus.

> When in trouble, seek help from those you know;
> There is no better doctor than a loyal friend.

Like *DC* 2.22, this couplet equates the powers of doctors and friends. In the earlier couplet, the reader was encouraged to consult his friends in deliberations; in *DC* 4.13 he should ask friends for help if he is struggling. Friends provide practical advice and help, and they might provide emotional support too. Indeed, while the couplet advises the reader on how he should use his friends, it also conversely teaches him how to be a friend.

Cicero also expresses the idea that friends help those in need and claims that the counsel of friends can overcome the wickedness of enemies.[293] But Publilius Syrus warns that "Ruin reveals whether you have a friend in deed or in name." For Syrus, a good friend will stick with you even when your finances suffer,[294] and indeed, dire straits—real or feigned—offer the opportunity to find out whether a friend is true.[295]

DC 2.22 and 4.13 set high expectations of what friends should do, and they might make it hard to find a true friend.[296] Yet the following couplet suggests that a friend's qualities should be immediately obvious.

DC 4.28

> Parce laudato, nam quem tu saepe laudaris,
> Una dies, qualis fuerit, ostendit, amicus.

> Go easy on praising someone: the person you praise often
> Needs only one day to reveal what sort of friend he is.

According to this couplet, a good friend reveals his goodness to the reader quickly—in only one day. That fast-occurring demonstration of goodness comes

---

[293] Cic. *Fam.* 1.6.
[294] Syrus, 41: *Amicum an nomen habeas, aperit calamitas.* The ruin may be financial: *calamitas* often connotes financial misfortune, though it does not have to.
[295] Syrus, 134.
[296] According to Plutarch's *De amicorum multitudine* (*On Having Many Friends*), a person can have only very few, perhaps only one, really close friend (*Mor.* 94 A). See also Phaedrus 3.9.5–7 = Perry 500 = Gibbs 94.

about because of the friend's good character, not as a result of the reader's lengthy flattery of him. *Qualis amicus* ("what sort of friend") implies that some friends are better than others, but happily for the reader, their relative goodness becomes apparent quickly.

A good friend, as we have learned, is akin to a doctor: able to offer sound advice and helpful support. We also learned that a friend's life(style), not his wealth, should be the reader's prime concern. Good friends are easily identified, and they are expected to give a lot to a friendship—sometimes a surprising amount.

DC 3.3

> *Productus testis, salvo tamen ante pudore,*
> *Quantumcumque potes, celato crimen amici.*
>
> When brought to court as witness, though your shame has never yet been compromised,
> As far as you can, hide the wrongdoing of a friend.

The comment by Remigius on *celato crimen amici* summarizes the couplet nicely: *ne coram aliis videaris mentiri, videlicet ut alii nesciant crimen amici quantumcumque potes celare studeas; sin autem alii sciverunt, cave ne videaris mentiri* ("Lest you seem openly to others to be lying, granted that others do not know your friend's wrongdoing, you can try to cover it up as much as you can; but if others do know about it, make sure you are not seen to be lying"). Yet Remigius does not pick up on the significance of *productus testis*: this couplet does not simply deal with keeping quiet friends' wrongdoings, in the spirit of *DC* 2.7. Rather, *productus testis* places the couplet in the context of the lawcourts and, in so doing, renders this one of the most challenging couplets in the collection.

The reader is encouraged to help his friend as much as he can—even though his decency (*pudor*) has not before been jeopardized. Helping his friend might endanger his decency, and this is a source of anxiety for someone of unblemished reputation.[297] But the Author seems to encourage his reader, placing the only limit on his response as *quantumcumque potes* ("as far as you can"). In this

---

[297] In this couplet, *pudor* seems to denote a sense of decency that would be injured if the reader lowered himself to wrongdoing on behalf of his friend. This type of *pudor* is discussed in Kaster 2005, 47, in the section, "*Pudor* and Discreditable 'Lowering' of the Self."

couplet, friendship is valued highly, and its demands of loyalty compete with those of the state and the rule of law.[298]

Cicero treats at length the issue of friendship's demands, especially when those demands may require wrongdoing. For example, a person might ask a friend to commit a wrongdoing, and refusal would lead that person to call the loyalty of the friend into question. In *De amicitia*, Laelius recalls Scipio as saying that "Great divisions would arise, often with justification, when people were asked by their friends to do something that was not right, to help them in illicit pleasures or to assist them in doing wrong to another. Those who refused to do such a thing, however honourably they may be acting, nevertheless are accused of deserting the duties of friendship by those with whose wishes they were unwilling to conform."[299]

A little later, Laelius claims that there is no excuse for wrongdoing; friends should neither ask for nor carry out shameful acts.[300] Yet Cicero recognizes the problem of divided loyalty: to truth and justice on the one hand, and to friendship on the other, and he allows for some wrongdoing provided that it is not extreme.[301] Elsewhere, in *De officiis*, Cicero advises that should a person be asked to act as judge of his defendant friend, he should leave this much for friendship's sake: he will privilege the veracity of his friend's case and arrange a favorable time for the trial as far as the laws allow. He claims that doing everything a friend asks would create conspiracy, not friendship.[302]

Plutarch takes a harder line on the matter: he records that Pericles, in response to a friend who asked him to lie under oath, asserted that "he was a friend as far as the altar," and twice elsewhere Plutarch claims that he would have been tougher than the general.[303] Valerius Maximus, by contrast, in his account of Gaius Blossius' unwavering loyalty for his dead friend Tiberius Grac-

---

[298] *DC* 3.3 has a companion in *DC* 1.31, which sets the limits on what the reader should expect to be asked for. It suggests that the reader should expect only to be asked for things that are rightful and/or honorable and, if they are not, he can refuse. Likewise, the reader knows that the requests he makes of friends—or whomever—are limited by these conditions. Cic. *Amic.* 82, makes the same point.

[299] Cic. Amic. 35: *Magna etiam discidia et plerumque iusta nasci, cum aliquid ab amicis quod rectum non esset postularetur, ut aut libidinis ministri aut adiutores essent ad iniuriam; quod qui recusarent, quamvis honeste id facerent, ius tamen amicitiae deserere arguerentur ab iis quibus obsequi nollent.* The translation is from Powell 1990.

[300] Cic. *Amic.* 37 and 40.

[301] Cic. *Amic.* 61.

[302] Cic. *Off.* 3.43–46. See also the discussion and references at n. 235 above.

[303] Plut. *Mor.* 186 C 3. The translation is from Babbitt. Plutarch criticizes Pericles over this apophthegm at Plut. *Mor.* 531 C and 808 A.

chus, praises Blossius for supporting his friend, despite what Valerius views as his treacherous behavior. He reflects that Blossius privileged his friendship over even his life, preferring not to save himself by an honorable silence or careful speech.[304]

Valerius adds another story and in particular a phrase that might help us to rethink *DC* 3.3. Brutus, pursued by Antony's henchmen, hid himself inside a dark building; Terentius, taking advantage of the gloom, posed as Brutus and offered himself to be killed. His plan failed: he was recognized, and Brutus instead was killed. Here is the key factor: the attempted deceit, described by Valerius as a "loyal lie" (*fidele mendacium*), was solely on Terentius' initiative and not sought by Brutus.[305] Analogously, a similar deceit should be volunteered by the *Distichs*' reader, not sought by his friend.

For the Author, volunteering deceit—up to a certain point—is acceptable; deceit that is excessive or that has been undertaken in response to a request is not. But if this couplet still makes the modern reader uneasy, the next reminds the reader that he should always put himself first in friendship.

DC 1.40

> *Dapsilis interdum notis et carus amicis*
> *Dum fueris dando, semper tibi proximus esto.*
>
> From time to time, feast and gift friends and acquaintances;
> But always put yourself first.

This is a curious couplet: its opening word *dapsilis* is unusual—and an especially unusual choice for the *Distichs*, which contain little lexical variety (see the earlier discussion in Chapter 3). Boas' edition shows us that some manuscripts were unsure of its spelling and glosses were required to explain its meaning. While unusual, it is especially apt for this maxim about friendship. Here, the Author instructs the reader to be highly valued (*carus*) to his friends with his gifts (*dando*, literally "by giving"), but also to be *dapsilis* to his acquaintances. As the manuscript glosses explain, to be *dapsilis* is to be a generous dinner host, one who spends freely on entertaining. Therefore, the maxim suggests that investing money on occasional dinners for acquaintances and giving gifts to friends are activities to be encouraged. But the goal of those activities (and per-

---

304 Val. Max. 4.7.1. Valerius' hard line on loyalty to friends is made clear in his reference at 4.7.7 to the law of friendship (*iure amicitiae*).
305 Val. Max. 4.7.6.

haps, it is implied, others too) is always to put oneself first.[306] Even apparent generosity must always pay dividends for the giver; outright altruism is not encouraged.

The image of the bountiful host is found in Publilius Syrus too: "The tenth hour finds more friends than the first."[307] The message complements that of the *Distichs*: the tenth hour, roughly the time for dinner, attracts friends who are presumably false; the first hour attracts fewer friends, though perhaps they are more genuine. Similarly, Syrus warns that "Your table brings more friends than does your head."[308]

In *De amicitia*, Cicero presents his readers with three opinions on friendship:

> First, that we should have the same attitude towards a friend as we have towards ourselves; second, that our goodwill towards our friends should correspond equally and fairly to theirs towards us; third, that a man should be valued by his friends at precisely the value he puts upon himself.[309]

Powell, who notes that these opinions found favor variously with Aristotle and the Epicureans, sees reciprocity as their common factor.[310] But Cicero prefers that friends not think in such terms.

Yet in a striking shift from *De amicitia*, Cicero in *De officiis* treats more pragmatically the risks of excessive generosity between friends: it might deplete the personal property that would otherwise be transferred to relatives and it might encourage friends to plunder or misuse property (whether their own or others' is left unclear).[311] The Author also notes these risks in *DC* 1.40, and Syrus, in the same vein, advises, "Be of service to your friends without harm to yourself."[312] With reciprocity at the heart of friendship, as it is for the Author, the reader must cultivate friends, but also protect himself.

---

306 Unlike Duff and Duff, Chase, and Marchand, I take *notis* and *amicis* as distinct substantives.
307 Syrus, 173: *Decima hora amicos plures quam prima invenit*.
308 Syrus, 549: *Plures amicos mensa quam mens concipit*. The dinner table as a venue for tests of friendship is found also in Babrius' fable of the lion, fox, and monkey (Babrius 106 = Perry 337 = Gibbs 19). The warning is found again in Seneca, *Ep.* 19.11 and Martial 9.14. Plutarch recognizes the role of hospitality in gaining friends at Plut. *Mor.* 175E4. Conversely, the appeal of dining with established friends is described in Cicero, *Fam.* 9.24.3 and Seneca, *Ep.* 19.10.
309 Cic. *Amic.* 56: *ut eodem modo erga amicum adfecti simus, quo erga nosmet ipsos, alteram, ut nostra in amicos benevolentia illorum erga nos benevolentiae pariter aequaliterque respondeat, tertiam, ut, quanti quisque se ipse facit, tanti fiat ab amicis*.
310 Powell 1990, 106.
311 Cic. *Off.* 1.44.
312 Syrus, 54: *amicis ita prodesto, ne noceas tibi*.

How to be a friend

The next set of couplets concerns the ways in which a friend should manage his own behavior in order to maintain and derive the greatest benefit from friendships.

DC 2.7

> *Quod pudeat, socios prudens celare memento,*
> *Ne plures culpent id, quod tibi displicet uni.*

> Conceal embarrassments discreetly from supporters,
> Lest many scorn what should be your shame alone.

The Author's choice of *socios* in this couplet is striking. *Amicos* ("friends") would have fit the meter and the overall sense of the couplet, yet he chooses instead a word that brings additional nuance. The term *socius*, on which see also the discussion on *DC* 4.15 above, was regularly a partner, but could in addition or instead be (more closely) a friend or (more distantly) an acquaintance, but certainly a supporter, someone who should be on the side of the reader. In this maxim, *socii* are not intimates in our modern sense, people with whom the reader might share his triumphs, upsets, and embarrassments; rather they are people who will offer support—yet perhaps only as long as the reader is careful (*prudens*) to manage his appearance before others.

DC 1.34

> *Vincere cum possis, interdum cede sodali,*
> *obsequio quoniam dulces retinentur amici.*

> Though you can outdo him, now and again yield to a buddy,[313]
> As friends are kept sweet by obliging them.

Friends are kept happy not just through the even exchange of favors, but also by parity in, for example, wealth, looks, strength, athletic ability, or rhetorical skill. Parity is unlikely to be maintained in all respects, all the time: no pair of friends can always balance their successes and shortcomings. But they can use

---

[313] This is the term used in Marchant, which does not seem to be bettered. Pepin has "comrade," Duff and Duff "mate," and Chase "friend." I follow Williams 2012, 40, in taking *sodalis* as connoting one of a group of companions; he translates the term as "pal" (p. 145).

obsequium ("obliging," i.e., meekness, generosity, and praise) to balance their own occasional superiority. The resulting friendship is not a relationship that is simple, intimate, and born of affection; nor is it a relationship based on substantive reciprocity. Rather, it is a bond between two people that is founded on a careful balancing of their strengths in order to foster mutual security.

DC 2.10

> *Cui scieris non esse parem te, tempore cede:*
> *victorem a victo superari saepe videmus.*

> Sometimes give victory to the person clearly your inferior;
> We often see a victor vanquished by his victim.

This couplet may contain an additional explanation for the advice in *DC* 1.34: since fate is so changeable, individuals' strengths may change; forgoing victory from time to time will help ensure that opponents who may be stronger in future are more likely themselves to forgo victories.

Problematic friends

The reader who follows the Author's advice thus far will become adept at managing his friendships. He might encounter problematic friends, but the Author has advice for him on these too.

DC 1.20.

> *Exiguum munus cum dat tibi pauper amicus,*
> *Accipito placide, plene laudare memento.*

> When a poor friend gifts you something small,
> Remember: receive it gently and praise it fully.

Munus denotes a gift, one that is given as a duty or in expectation of a return. It may also signify a gift that is given without expectations, though this meaning seems to be less common.[314]

The Author acknowledges that friendship, even with its expectations of reciprocity, may exist between individuals of differing economic status, and when

---

[314] *OLD*, s.v. *munus* 5.

it does, its rules change. The reader is reminded of this fact: he must accept a meager gift in a gentle way and demonstrate effusive gratitude; he must acknowledge the inability of his friend to abide by the rules of reciprocity, but also then recognize his attempt. The couplet complicates basic reciprocal friendship by placing a value on the gift, as well as on affection, whose value in friendship some Romans apparently did not acknowledge. The value of that affection for the reader, should he be the wealthier of the friends, derives from its contribution to his reputation in the community as a gracious friend.

This maxim responds to anxieties about the appropriate response to an otherwise reliable friend who has given a too-small gift and/or the appropriate response to the possibility of friendship with an economic unequal. In *De amicitia*, Cicero points out that a friend's ambitions and desire for money might breed discontent within friendship.[315] But he simply encourages that friends try to overlook their uneven status.[316] The Author, by contrast, takes a more practical and realistic approach.

DC 1.23

Si tibi pro meritis nemo respondet amicus
Incusare deos noli, sed te ipse coerce.

If no friends repay your favors,
Do not blame the gods: keep yourself in check.

The previous couplet proposed that in an economically unequal friendship, the wealthier friend should be gracious toward the poorer. This couplet encourages restraint. The context is again economically equal friendship, in which one friend has not reciprocated at all or perhaps not reciprocated fully to another's gift. *Nemo* ("no one") intensifies the scenario: the reader does good things for multiple friends, yet none responds appropriately. The reader might restrain himself by keeping quiet and not voicing his displeasure. Hiding his displeasure does not necessarily solve the reader's problem in the long term, but it might preserve his reputation in the community. Alternatively, he might rein in his future gifts, a practical solution to this breakdown in reciprocity, since his gifts might create unreasonable expectations of his less fortunate friends. Whichever of these is the more likely, the couplet warns that reciprocity among friends cannot always be expected. Blaming the gods is foolish, according to the Au-

---

315 Cic. *Amic.* 34.
316 Cic. *Amic.* 69.

thor, who takes the problem away from the divine level and places it squarely in the realm of humans. In the *Distichs*, humans must solve their own problems. Cicero also notes that failure to reciprocate is a common problem, but chides those who complain about it:[317] a friend helps when asked; he should not expect anything in return.[318]

DC 1.9

> *Cum moneas aliquem, nec se velit ille moneri,*
> *Si tibi sit carus, noli desistere coeptis.*
>
> Your advice falls on deaf ears?
> If he is your friend, don't stop trying.

If a friend does not want to receive advice, no matter: the reader should try to persevere; that is his responsibility in friendship. Cicero also encourages friends to be liberal with advice and even to be forceful in giving it.[319] Similarly, Publilius Syrus advises that a person is right to consider a friend's wrongdoing as his; not to do so—and presumably not to warn against the wrongdoing—is to assume the fault himself, though he cautions that pointing out a friend's weakness will lose his loyalty.[320]

DC 4.41

> *Damnaris numquam post longum tempus amicum:*
> *Mutavit mores, sed pignera prima memento.*
>
> Never condemn a long-time friend:
> He has changed his behavior, but remember his first assurances.

The reader worries that his friends might change. The Author counters that while a friend's *mores* might change, a friendship does not. This is striking: while a person's behavior might change so that it eventually becomes obnoxious, the exchange of money, services, and support at the heart of reciprocal friendship should be expected by both sides to continue. Perhaps a person who was good enough to enter into a friendship long ago has the capacity to return

---

317 Cic. *Amic.* 71.
318 Cic. *Amic.* 44.
319 Cic. *Amic.* 44. He later repeats the idea at *Amic.* 88–89.
320 Syrus 522 and 634.

to his former goodness. More likely, the Author is suggesting that while a friend's character may have apparently changed, he should still have some of the commendable qualities that he demonstrated at the beginning of the friendship.

Cicero also acknowledges that friendships may come and go as people change.[321] He observes that people cast off old friendships and take on new ones as their fortunes change and their *mores* too.[322] But he advocates taking longer to determine whether a person will be a good friend: "Therefore it is a wise man's duty to hold back the first rush of goodwill, as he would hold in the reins of a chariot, in order that one may test the characters of one's friends, as one tries out a team of horses, before pursuing friendship."[323] Publilius Syrus takes a hard line on errant friends, claiming that if a person tolerates his friend's faults, he makes them his own; though elsewhere he tempers his tone, suggesting that a man should be aware of his friend's faults, but tolerate them.[324]

The context for the Author's concern with leniency to a long-time friend may be discerned from a comment of Plutarch: long-time friends have been tested, yet the current (νῦν, i.e., late-first/early-second century CE) fashion is to make friends in drinking houses, gymnasia, and markets—not a foundation on which to build lasting friendships and long-term trust.[325] I will return to this point shortly.

DC 1.26

Qui simulat verbis nec corde est fidus amicus,
Tu qui fac simile: sic ars deluditur arte.

If someone talks like a friend, but isn't one at heart,
You do the same: then your deceit will deceive his.

The Author has identified another anxiety: someone calls himself a friend to the reader, but has failed to be loyal. The reader had expected loyalty and had perhaps already done favors to his apparent friend, but when the loyalty was not reciprocated and the favors not returned, the reader was at a loss.

---

321 Cic. *Amic.* 33. See also *Amic.* 76–77.
322 Cic. *Amic.* 54.
323 Cic. *Amic.* 63: *est igitur prudentis sustinere ut cursum, sic impetum benevolentiae, quo utamur quasi equis temptatis, sic amicitia ex aliqua parte periclitatis moribus amicorum*. The translation is Powell 1990.
324 Syrus 10 and 56.
325 Plut. *Mor.* 94A. Some of Plutarch's concerns were anticipated in Sen. *Ep.* 19.

In *DC* 1.23, the reader was advised simply to restrain himself in the face of friends' meanness; in this couplet, the reader is advised to beat his so-called friend at his own game: "then your deceit will deceive his." The Author emphasizes that the "friend" had proclaimed himself as such, but had dissembled: for that he deserved also to be deceived. The Author seems to find fault not with unequal exchange of favors, but with deceit.

Cicero agrees that deceit and pretense have no place in friendship, but goes on to note that friendship has to originate from affection, not a calculation of need.[326] Indeed, according to Syrus, no one returns to a reliable friendship with an enemy.[327] The Author takes a more pragmatic approach: rather than simply break off the friendship, the reader should deceive a deceitful friend; he should use friendship for his own benefit, as his so-called friend did for his.

DC 4.47

> *Cum coniux tibi sit, ne res et fama laboret,*
> *Vitandum ducas inimicum nomen amici.*
>
> If you have a wife and don't want your property and reputation to suffer,
> Don't consider as friend the man who claims to be one—avoid him.

Friendship might offer a multiplicity of benefits, but could also risk harming a household. Women's propensity to squander their husband's property is a common trope in literature condemning women and marriage (for which Juvenal's sixth satire is the *locus classicus*). If we understand the couplet as implying that the reader's spouse and friend (who might be a man or a woman)[328] might enter into some sort of relationship, and if that relationship were sexual, the cuckolded reader's reputation would suffer; if it were platonic, we might imagine the wife giving gifts to the friend, in which case the reader's property would also suffer.[329] The Author's play on words—the term "friend" is itself unfriendly—suggests that with women around, there is no such thing as friendship. The Author recommends, then, that friends and spouses be kept separate and per-

---

326 Cic. *Amic.* 26–27.
327 Syrus, 106. On the centrality of trust and honesty in friendship, see also Babrius' fable of the wolf, the fox, and the trap (Perry 345).
328 Williams 2012, chapter 4 *passim*, presents epigraphic evidence for men's friendships with women, as well as men.
329 There have been several interpretations of this ambiguous couplet, for which see Boas 1952, 257.

haps that his reader should not even mention his friends to his wife—or should at least remind himself of the dangers of friends in the context of the home.

Fables, *gnomai*, and proverbs

As is apparent from the discussion above, the couplets that concern friendship are variously echoed by (near-)contemporaries or contradicted by them. The Author's attitude towards friendship seems most closely aligned with Publilius Syrus, less so with Seneca, and it contrasts markedly with much of Cicero.

Teresa Morgan, in her 2007 *Popular Morality in the Early Roman Empire*, gathered and analyzed a wealth of proverbs, *gnomai*, fables, and *exempla* from the first few centuries CE. The chronological spread of her material over several centuries sets it in contrast to Cicero's *De amicitia*, Seneca's moral epistles, and the *Distichs* too. For this reason, I simply summarize Morgan's conclusions on the theme of friendship in order to offer a broad sense of the ways in which the *Distichs* are similar to or differ from her material.

Like the *Distichs*, the proverbs also encourage that "everyone needs friends," "good men tend to band together," good men "also sympathize with those in the same plight," "'friends hold all things in common'," friends should be hospitable, "friendship is not only natural and agreeable, it is also politically expedient," and "friends sympathize with one another and feel pity and grief at each other's suffering."[330] The proverbs also encourage sharing with friends (something not encouraged in the *Distichs*) and harming one's enemies (another omission from the *Distichs*), but they omit any mention of dealing with deceitful friends or finding friends. Most strikingly, as Morgan notes, "It may surprise Greek and Roman historians that proverbs do not have more to say about 'strict reciprocity', which is not a strong theme."[331]

In fables, friends "may be of similar or dissimilar status, but [their] relationships are distinguished from other social relationships by being positively reciprocal. When it works, friendship is a thoroughly good thing; fables, however, have more to say about its difficulties."[332] Having mentioned earlier in this chapter a number of fables that echo, refine, or refute the *Distichs*' messages, I add

---

330 Morgan 2007, 39–40, who draws mainly from Zenobius' second-century CE collection of material probably dating back to the third century BCE. A text of Zenobius' collection is available in Leutsch and Schneidewin 1839. Among these Zenobian proverbs Morgan cites on the theme of friendship are 1.14, 1.18, 1.62, 1.7, 1.9, 2.42, 2.46, 3.51, 4.12, 4.79, and 5.98.
331 Morgan 2007, 55.
332 Morgan 2007, 68.

here simply Morgan's reflections that deceit and trickery are the fables' main concerns with friendship and they have little to say that is positive.[333] In that, they stand in contrast with the *Distichs*' acknowledgement of friendship's benefits.

Gnomai, for Morgan, are "moralizing quotations," synonymous with *sententiae*.[334] Key themes relevant to the *Distichs* include the search for good friends (Morgan summarizes: "One must test one's friends thoroughly before committing to them"), loyalty ("once committed, one must be absolutely loyal"), trust ("'Whenever a man speaks fair while doing evil, and does not escape his neighbour's notice, he will get double evil back,' say three fragments") and reciprocity (according to Morgan, the *gnomai* emphasize "the connection between human and material resources in Graeco-Roman minds and the possibility that friends to whom one is generous may respond in kind").[335] Like proverbs and fables, but unlike the *Distichs*, *gnomai* have much to say about enemies.[336] Of *exempla*, which she draws mostly from Valerius Maximus and Plutarch (see above), Morgan summarizes that they are concerned with friendship in times of adversity (among other themes less relevant here).[337]

On friendship in these various texts Morgan reflects, "We are told not only that friendship is a good thing, but that we should be cautious and slow in making friends, test them thoroughly before trusting them and make sure to keep them sweet by helping them in need."[338] There is nothing here that too strongly contradicts the *Distichs*, though the latter's focus on reciprocity, its lack of interest in enemies and enmity, and its more encouraging tone mark it out as a significant new addition to early imperial moralizing texts.

---

[333] Morgan 2007, 68–70.
[334] Morgan 2007, 84.
[335] Morgan 2007, 98–102. Among examples she cites are Goodspeed 1905, *P.Flor.* XXII (= *P. Brookl.*) 28 and 30, all of which date to the third or fourth centuries CE (along with *P.Bour.* I); and *Ad Nic.* 27 (Keil 1884). Morgan supplies many examples of reciprocity in the *gnomai*, though only a few refer to friendship explicitly. Her interest in reciprocity extends beyond friendship, which explains her inclusion of broader examples than my discussion permits. One that is relevant here, *P.Bour.* I 17, dates to the fourth century CE.
[336] *DC* 4.47 is one of only two couplets to contain references to enmity. The other, *DC* 2.15, whose context is the law court, does not concern enmity in opposition to friendship.
[337] Morgan 2007, 141–142.
[338] Morgan 2007, 167.

Differences in notions of friendship across times, places, and cultures complicate our understanding of an ancient form of a social institution. Ancient Roman *amicitia* seems to be a multivalent term: for example, one ancient author notes that it can encompass everything from an acquaintance characterized as "brief vote-catching" to a genuine friendship built on affection.[339] As we have seen above, the *Distichs* emphasize reciprocity, as do Publilius Syrus and the fables of Babrius and others, while Cicero's *De amicitia* emphasizes affection.[340] Possible explanations for the difference in approach between the *Distichs* and *De amicitia* are that the *Distichs*, which post-date *De amicitia*, reflect changes to friendship; that the *Distichs* and *De amicitia* belong to different genres; and that the intended audience of the *Distichs* may have been broader than that of *De amicitia*.

According to John Crook, "The distinction between the gratuitous services of status-equals and the paid services of status inferiors had partly ceased to be real even in Cicero's day and grew steadily more unreal."[341] This development may have affected the nature of some Roman friendships, as the reciprocity of friendship increasingly resembled the exchange of services that took the place of monetary exchange and may have become interchangeable with it. Similarly, for Jacques Michel, Roman society became gradually less cohesive in the early Empire than it was in the Republic and the circles within which Romans formed relationships became larger. This is the context for Plutarch's observation that friendships in his time were being formed from chance meetings under trivial circumstances. Romans' reliance upon socially accepted notions of reciprocity

---

339 [Cicero], *Comment. pet.* 29: *multis et variis amicitiis* ("many friendships of different sorts"). Political and genuine friendship are contrasted in chapter 26; "brief vote-catching" is Shackleton-Bailey's rendering of *brevem et suffragatorium*. The purported author is Cicero's brother, though his authorship and the text's date have been widely doubted. See also Brunt 1965, 20: "The range of amicitia is vast. From the constant intimacy and goodwill of virtuous or at least of like-minded men to the courtesy that etiquette normally enjoined on gentlemen, it covers every degree of genuinely or overtly amicable relation." See in addition Hellegouarc'h 1972, 143ff.
340 The different emphases of our ancient texts are mirrored by a similar split among modern scholars: Konstan 1997 emphasizes the role of affection in ancient friendship, while Verboven 2002, in his study of friendship in the economic and legal spheres, places greater emphasis on material obligation. On friendship, see especially also Peachin 2001, Fitzgerald 1997, and Williams 2012. There is a helpful survey of bibliography in Evenepoel 2006.
341 Crook 1967, 238–240.

was beginning to break down, and payment of lawyers' honoraria, for example, once a matter of course, now needed protection and enforcement.[342]

Michael Peachin sees another development through the late Republic and early Empire, in which friendship comes to stand in place of bureaucratized systems of support, reward, and promotion. Such a development could have spurred the strong emphasis on reciprocity in the highly pragmatic *Distichs*.[343] Granted, it is impossible to determine whether the *Distichs* do indeed reflect the changes Crook, Michel, and Peachin identify, but their advice on friendship would have helped readers to navigate them.

Cicero and Seneca, writing philosophy, emphasize the primacy of affection; proverbs and fables stress reciprocity, as do the *Distichs* and the collection of Syrus' *sententiae*, the text closest to the *Distichs* in form. The emphasis in other earlier paraenetic literature on practical advice and pragmatism might suggest that the Author's focus on reciprocity was motivated to some degree by genre and tradition. It may also have been more grounded in mundane everyday experiences than was Cicero's philosophy. As Jonathan Powell notes, ancient philosophical accounts "are too generalized to do real justice to experience."[344] Indeed, documentary texts seem to bear this out. For example, inscriptions from Rome, mostly of the first two centuries CE, as I discuss shortly, and Egyptian papyri from a much longer span of time, both attest to the recognition of bonds of friendship, usually practical bonds, as well as the social importance of the relationship, which seems to have ranked closely with family ties.[345]

Cicero's correspondence and, in particular, his *De amicitia* and *De officiis* stress the importance of friendship in the public and personal lives of high-status individuals, who will have made up a significant portion of his readership. Some of those same readers may well have encountered the *Distichs* too. Yet the *Distichs* were probably also read by literate lower-status individuals, and they will have been especially interested in their practical focus: as Jerry Toner has so vividly demonstrated, life for the Roman lower classes was precarious as a result of financial insecurity and physical vulnerability from lack of easy access to law and legal protection.[346] They will have derived especial benefit from reciprocal friendship.

---

[342] Michel 1962, 554 (on paid employment replacing gratuitous services), 577 (the erosion of friendship after the beginning of the Empire), and 584 (the breakdown of reciprocity).
[343] Peachin 2005, 257. Wolkenhauer 2014 places this development in the early Empire.
[344] Powell 1995, 44.
[345] On papyri, see Evans 1997, and on inscriptions from Rome, Caldelli 2001 and now especially Williams 2012, chapter 4.
[346] Toner 2009, 26–31.

The attitude towards friendship reflected in the *Distichs* demonstrates closer affinities with the proverbs and fables than with Cicero's *De amicitia*.[347] It is tempting, then, to imagine that the audience for the collection is wider than it may have been for Cicero's more philosophizing work, but we can make no definitive claims. Many of the problems surrounding friendship that are tackled by the *Distichs* had been anticipated by Cicero in his *De amicitia*, and the overlap between them suggests they were both dealing with common anxieties and concerns. But the Author was perhaps taking an approach to friendship that would have resonated with a less elite audience: the *Distichs* emphasize utility or advantage, an approach to friendship that Aristotle and Cicero in his *De amicitia* characterize as typical of the common man.[348] Paul Veyne's study of "middling plebeians" under the Empire includes discussion of the *Distichs* that, at three pages, is one of the longest recent treatments of the collection. In it he claims that the *Distichs* were read by "la plèbe moyenne."[349] I agree that some of the *Distichs* may reflect a middling plebeian mentality, certainly more so than does Cicero's *De amicitia*; but the readership of the *Distichs* was not necessarily confined to that group. Indeed, we know that the court physician Vindicianus certainly and the emperor Valentinian II perhaps were familiar with them. Moreover, the pragmatic messages in the collection and the Author's presentation of them may be a reflection not simply of the readership, but also of the genre, which had broad appeal.

The contribution of the *Distichs* to our understanding of ancient friendship is to add another voice to the mass of relevant texts dating to the late Republic and early Empire. While Cicero and Seneca's discussions of friendship loom large in the minds of modern scholars, less attention is paid to roughly contemporary texts with popular appeal, such as Syrus' *sententiae* and the fables. The emphasis in the *Distichs*' treatment of friendship is on reciprocity, as is the case with other more popular texts and will help to strengthen arguments that Roman friendship took very seriously reciprocity, yet also acknowledged the benefits of emotional intimacy that characterize friendship today.

---

347 Michel 1962, 512, for example, claims that Cicero's *De amicitia* addresses the elite and reflects their concerns.
348 Classifying *De amicitia* as philosophy might be a stretch: Powell 1995, 40, n. 20, describes the second half of the work as "a compendium of popular wisdom." Deskis 1996, 107 notes that many medieval proverbs express wariness of reciprocal obligations in friendship: "Apparently the mere connection of the ideas of friendship and wealth sufficed to evoke the negative connotation of purchased, and hence unstable, loyalty."
349 Veyne 2000, 1193–1194.

My discussion in this chapter reconfirms that, as Morgan had seen was the case with fables, proverbs, and *gnomai*, encouragement towards reciprocity and self-interest is common in texts from the wider wisdom genre and additionally among those from other genres that also enjoyed wide appeal. My discussion also raises the question, however, of whether the attitudes towards friendship expressed in the wide range of texts I have referenced are reflective more of an actual divergence of ancient views on friendship or rather of generic conventions and expectations. If there is anything that might move us closer to one of these alternatives than the other, it might be documentary evidence, which points to the former, though we might counter that generic conventions are at play in those textual sources too.

Craig Williams devotes a chapter of his study of Roman friendship to an extensive discussion of commemorations of individuals as friends (*amici* and *amicae*) in Latin funerary inscriptions of the first and second centuries CE.[350] Friendship's importance is made clear by the fact that individuals commemorated not only their family members, making space for them and their descendants in a tomb, but also their friends (albeit in significantly smaller numbers). The emphasis on reciprocity in friendship in the *Distichs* and elsewhere might encourage us to consider funerary commemoration a final act of reciprocity to *amicis bene merentibus* ("well deserving friends"), in the ubiquitous formulation. The *Distichs*' intense interest in friends—more so than in spouses—confirms the importance of friendship as a social institution and offers potential explanations for it: friendship that was centered around reciprocity might offer social and economic security, a benefit that would not have been lost on Romans outside the socio-economic elite. We saw that *DC* 4.47 treats the possibility of a reader's spouse subverting his friendship with a man to her husband's detriment; the Author's warning about mixing spouses and friends might find its context in the many inscriptions that Williams shows commemorating family members alongside friends.

Arguing that discussions of Roman friendship have been too heavily reliant on philosophical texts, Williams notes, "We must always be sensitive to distinctions between prescriptive and descriptive language, between ideal and practice, with its frequent self-authorizing claims on truth."[351] His study of the inscriptions, to be sure, moves us closer to an understanding of friendship through descriptive language. Yet it is striking that the Roman friendship presented through the prescriptive language of the *Distichs* seems to hew closer to

---

350 Williams 2012, 259–354.
351 Williams 2012, 21.

that experienced by the population of the inscriptions (as well as that reflected in Morgan's sources) than that of Cicero and Seneca. The *Distichs* may have been offering advice on friendship that was closer to the lived reality of many of its readers than were the idealizations of philosophers.

5 Money

The *Distichs* are unusual for their sustained advice on management of personal finances and attitudes towards money and personal financial management, i.e., the best ways to spend, save, and manage money; management of money and its effects on reputation; and the significance of money to an individual, his psyche, and his relationships. This is largely because the (near-)contemporary texts of Cicero, Seneca, et al. tend towards abstract and philosophical discussions of money. The *Distichs'* advice, by contrast, is pragmatic. Examining what the *Distichs* have to say on the topic is useful because a date for the collection in the first century CE puts them in a socio-economic context of enormous interest to historians, including economic historians, and while the *Distichs*, unlike the sources preferred by economic historians, cannot offer us data for that period, they do offer a useful and interesting complement to those sources.[352]

The twenty couplets in the *Distichs* that concern money seem to group naturally around few topics, though there are some overlaps between them. Most provide practical advice on personal finance, but a few offer recommendations for changing or adopting a particular attitude towards money. Given the apparent paucity of advice from elsewhere, it is easy to understand the appeal of the *Distichs*: they tell the reader what to do and also what to think.

I proposed at the end of the previous chapter that the audience of the *Distichs* is wider than that of, say, Cicero or Seneca, encompassing both the socio-economic elite—the senators and equestrians—and the lower ranks, including literate individuals from Veyne's "plèbe moyenne" or examples of what Augustine would much later term the *tenuis municeps* ("straitened town-councilor").[353] These readers were presumably living above subsistence level, but the *Distichs* will give us additional clues that will round out our understanding of their fi-

---

[352] Followers of New Institutional Economics (NIE) are especially supportive of approaches that consider economics in the context of and as resulting from human behavior. I use the word "attitudes," an admittedly nebulous term, to describe the various impacts—social, cultural, cognitive, political—on individuals' economic decision-making. The study of such attitudes might naturally fall into the economic sub-field of behavioral economics, but I am hesitant to use the term because it has been applied almost exclusively to the modern world and relies on modern theories and assumptions, as well as rigorous statistical methods, that are difficult to apply to an ancient context. The possibilities for applying approaches from behavioral economics to ancient economies are, however, promising and highly appealing. The movement towards NIE and the need for it among scholars of the ancient economy are discussed by von Reden 2002 and 2010 and Aarts 2005.

[353] Veyne 2000, 1193–1194. Augustine, *Conf.* II, iii, 5.

nances and financial dealings, as well as their attitudes towards their finances in the economic context of the first century CE. I will set the maxims alongside scant references in other texts in order to explore how the advice given in the *Distichs* responded in particular to the needs and anxieties of a subset of this larger audience and reflected their attitudes.

Contemporary and near-contemporary texts useful to my discussion include Valerius Maximus' *Facta et dicta memorabilia* and, though they post-date the *Distichs* a little, Martial's epigrams.[354] Cicero, to be sure, references money in various works, though he offers no sustained discussion of the topic comparable to those on friendship. The references are densest in his *Letters*, and they derive from his own immediate personal context.[355] That context is interesting and important, and yet the information that arises from it is so specific that it cannot sit easily alongside the more extensive and general discussions and reflections in Valerius Maximus, Martial, Seneca, and others. Also largely absent from this chapter are fables, which contain almost no explicit references to money.[356]

As befits a wisdom collection that has plenty of simple advice for action, the *Distichs* offer the reader instructions for managing his money and spending it wisely, advising him when to save or at least be frugal, when to spend, and when to divest. Saving receives the greatest emphasis.

---

354 Valerius Maximus is a useful virtual interlocutor with the Author in this chapter on money. He completed his work on famous deeds and sayings in 31 CE and is therefore perhaps a rough contemporary of the Author. He offers apparently non-controversial positions and hews to traditional Republican Roman values. The nature of Valerius Maximus' text—a list of *exempla* and *dicta*—could arguably place it in the wisdom tradition, perhaps even in the paraenetic tradition, alongside the *Distichs*. According to Walker 2004, xxi, Valerius was writing for new imperial administrators of modest backgrounds: "The work of Valerius Maximus was tailored to meet the social anxieties and insecurities of the people who belonged to this new administrative class. Valerius enabled them to project a good image of themselves in society." These administrators may have been reading the *Distichs* too. Valerius selects exemplary deeds and sayings from particular individuals across the span of ancient Mediterranean history as embodiments of good and bad. Those individuals are often semi-mythologized and therefore function similarly to the Author's generalizing and gnomic "the man who...," as exemplars of broad applicability. On Valerius Maximus and exemplarity, see especially Langlands 2018 and Murray and Wardle 2021.
355 Dixon 1986, a survey of correspondence concerning Tullia and Terentia, makes clear the frequent connection of Cicero's comments on money to his own family matters.
356 Many of the fables could, to be sure, be inferred as referring to money, but, as fables, they are open to multiple interpretations.

Saving and spending

DC 2.17

> *Utere quaesitis modice: cum sumptus abundat,*
> *labitur exiguo, quod partum est tempore longo.*
>
> Spend your savings carefully: when costs are overflowing,
> What you saved over a long time floats away in a moment.

The couplet warns the reader to be careful with what he has acquired: without a budget, spending always outpaces saving. Yet managing a budget requires some basic mathematical skills and financial literacy. For example, even basic accounting may have been difficult: bankers did not send customers statements or even keep them; it was the customer's responsibility to know how he stood.[357] We have plentiful references to accountants, accounts managers, bookkeepers, and comptrollers, all of whom were trained in managing and overseeing budgets. These individuals tend to be enslaved individuals and freedmen working for their elite (former) slaveholders.[358] But there is less evidence of non-specialists planning their own finances and using budgets. According to Marrou, the average Roman who had received a basic education knew nothing of arithmetic beyond the names of numbers and fractions and simple functions (i.e., addition and subtraction).[359] Horace suggests that this knowledge might have equipped him to look after his interests, though the claim is probably overstated.[360] To

---

[357] According to Andreau 1999, 45, who uses Plautus as evidence.

[358] Latin has an array of terms for individuals associated with managing accounts. On the *ratiocinator*, see Cic. *Att.* 1.12.2; Columella, *Rust.* 3.3.7; Ulp. *Dig.* 14.4.5.16. The *procurator* was the manager of a rural estate (Varro, *Rust.* 3.6.3) or an *insula* whose apartments were presumably being rented out (Petr. 96.4); see further Jones 2006, 60–61, on evidence for *procuratores* in the archive of the Sulpicii at Puteoli. On the *tabularius*, see Casson 1965, 35. The *dispensator*, referenced in Petr. 29.4 and Gaius *Inst.* 1.22, managed the finances of a household or an organization. According to Martial 10.62.4, the *calculator* taught arithmetic, though he might also be an accountant. See also Marrou 1956, 555, n. 13. According to Sidoli 2015, 387–390, basic arithmetic would have been taught at the elementary level, but the skills needed for accountancy would have been acquired in more specialist schools. On enslaved individuals and freedmen trained in accounting, see Forbes 1955, 342–343.

[359] Marrou 1956, 271.

[360] Hor. *Ars P.* 325–332. The context of Horace's claim might undermine it: he is lamenting the fact that boys from elite families learn fractions with the result that, now arithmetically minded, they can look after their interests (*rem poteris servare tuam*), but also hanker after wealth, rather than appreciate poetry.

learn anything more complex, a Roman needed lessons with a specialist teacher of arithmetic, a *calculator*.[361] According to Martial, those lessons were popular, though we cannot know how many free persons used their services.[362]

In *DC* 2.17, the Author has a simple message: watch your savings and keep a check on your spending. Cicero, by contrast, writing for an elite audience in *De officiis*, expresses a complex of ideas that reveal the conflicts in elite attitudes towards money: he pours scorn on taking too much of an interest in financial matters, noting waspishly that some people discuss making and investing money more keenly than any philosopher expounding on a topic; yet he allows that it is a good idea to take some notice of these topics. Money is useful, not interesting, and he notes parenthetically that he wished those same people would talk also about how to spend money, a comment that might suggest Cicero and some of his peers pour scorn on those who manipulate their finances, but make no practical use of them. Alternatively, he and others may have been critical of profligacy and wanted people to be more judicious with their money.[363]

DC 3.21

> *Utere quaesitis, sed ne videaris abuti;*
> *qui sua consumunt, cum deest, aliena sequentur.*
>
> Spend your savings, but don't broadcast if you used them up:
> When you reduce them to nothing, you'll need chase after what is not yours.

The previous couplet advises the reader to spend carefully, otherwise his money will run out. *DC* 3.21 deals with the consequences: he will have to go after what is not his. Savings are to be spent—like Cicero, the Author believes that money is to be put to use, not kept for its own sake. But the reader should not appear to waste them, for people will worry that he is after their savings, and he will need to look deserving when asking for their help.

Abuti and *consumunt* add color to this couplet. The inclusion of *abuti*, glossed by a commentator as *contra usum uti* ("to use contrary to what is expedient"), suggests that the reader should recognize there are generally acknowl-

---

361 Marrou 1956, 271.
362 Martial 10.62.4. Of course, there must have been free persons gaining extensive education in mathematics, including mathematicians. But their numbers are unknown.
363 Cic. *Off.* 2.87. Cicero's jibe at money-minded individuals works because he mockingly compares finance enthusiasts' love of the mundane to philosophers' passion for lofty subjects. At *Att.* 14.12.3, he contrasts business-types and philosophers again in a discussion of Gaius Vestorius, a wealthy entrepreneur in Puteoli. For more on this individual, see Jones 2006, 40.

edged sensible ways to spend, just as Cicero had suggested.³⁶⁴ *Consumunt* also implies not just spending, but, with the verbal prefix *con-* connoting force, spending in the wrong way: too quickly, too much, or on the wrong things. The same commentator glosses *aliena sequentur* with *coguntur mendicare* ("are compelled to go begging"): in his world, a needy person goes begging without any expectation of reciprocation (as *mendicare* connotes begging for alms). Yet the reader of the *Distichs* was unlikely to go begging for handouts from strangers; he was more likely to ask friends, and the reciprocal friendships he enjoyed with them expected a return. As a result, a person needed to appear worthy and reliable in order to ask for money.

Personal debt was a key financial issue in the late Republic and early Empire. An influx of wealth from imperial expansion had resulted in changes to rural landholding patterns and the wider economy, including an increase in the incidence of personal debt.³⁶⁵ The personal financial situations of many individuals were affected, as the political importance of cancellation of debts at that time attests.³⁶⁶ To be sure, debt has always been a significant topic in personal finance, and economic developments of the period need not necessarily have driven the Author's composition of this couplet. But if his couplets were meant to respond to contemporary anxieties, then *DC* 3.21 may be significant for adding to our understanding of the broader economic context and of the impacts of contemporary periodic economic instabilities on individuals' financial wellbeing.

Those anxieties are voiced also among the Author's (near-)contemporaries. For example, the wealthy Seneca warns that the more money a man owes you, the more hostile he becomes towards you.³⁶⁷ Indebtedness breeds anger and resentment, and the Author is wise to warn against it. In Seneca we also find

---

364 The comment is to be found in ms. W. See Boas 1952, 180.
365 According to Bang 2009, 202–203: "The phase of most explosive commercial development is not the peaceful Principate but the war-ridden late Republic." Kay 2014, 5, confirms that this is now the scholarly consensus. Yet according to Howgego 1992, 5, the annexation of Egypt led to increases in property values at Rome, giving some nobles additional money to lend and others an incentive to borrow, especially as interest rates fell. On the ease of borrowing around that time, see Mrozek 1985, 311.
366 On luxury from conquest and on contemporary debt, see especially Sall. *Cat.* 9–13. See also Frederiksen 1966, Crawford 1971, and Stewart 1995. Harris 2006 and, to a lesser extent, Kay 2014 regard the economy of the late Republic and early Empire as centered on credit. On the various non-monetary financial instruments available in the first century CE, including transferal of debt, see von Reden 2012, 276–279. On the periodic economic crises of the first century CE, see Kay 2014 and Elliott 2015 and 2020.
367 Sen. *Ep.* 19.11.

echoed the Author's warning that his reader's spending habits will draw scrutiny if he asks for money. Using the example of the apparently wealthy man heavily mortgaged, Seneca warns his own wealthy reader that he will need to assess a potential debtor's assets and liabilities.[368]

Writing perhaps not long after the *Distichs*, Martial has much to say on the topic of money. In one poem, he tells us of the pest who repeatedly asks for money despite rebuffs, while in another, he complains that, having bought an estate, he cannot get a loan, despite his newly acquired assets; in yet another, he calls out a man who had offered to lend him money, but has now reneged.[369] Reading Martial, indebtedness and periodic want appear a standard part of Roman life, including for a man with sufficient resources to purchase an estate: he even celebrates the return of the dole, which gives him more than the handouts and meals he receives as the client of a wealthier man.[370] A man such as Martial might hope that his acquisitions and investments would raise his socioeconomic status, yet he complains of declining opportunities for social mobility.[371]

DC 2.6

> *Quod nimium est fugito, parvo gaudere memento:*
> *tuta mage est puppis, modico quae flumine fertur.*

> Avoid excess and rejoice in restraint:
> A boat is safer carried on a gentle current.

This couplet is highly unusual for the *Distichs*: it is one of only five to use proverbial or metaphorical language.[372] It warns against excess, which could be taken in financial terms, but may also be taken more broadly.

---

368 Sen. *Ep.* 87.5–6. The wider context of Seneca's warning is that creditors must assess a person's worth in precise economic terms, since a person with the trappings of wealth may appear credit-worthy, but already carries heavy debts. Such calculations, however, have no place in friendship for Seneca, who rails against assessing a man as a friend on the basis of his credit worthiness. The Author of the *Distichs*, among others, would presumably feel differently.
369 Mart. 4.15; 6.5; 7.92.
370 Mart. 4.26.
371 Martial 5.81. The context of Book 5, in particular poems 25, 27, and 38, is the renewed enforcement of the Lex Roscia theatralis. According to Malnati 1987, these poems confirm that Martial sees status as dependent upon money.
372 The others are *DC* 1.27, 2.26, 4.31, and 4.33. *DC* 4.3 (*Cum sis incautus nec rem ratione gubernes, / Noli fortunam, quae non est, dicere caecam*), which also contains proverbial language, includes the image of a helmsman, though the transferred sense of a governor may be meant

With its nautical imagery, the couplet can be understood as concerning money (though it does not have to). Shipping was an enormous source of profit in the ancient world.[373] But it was also a source of risk, as investments in financing marine cargo were easily undone by shipwrecks. The economic importance of shipping in antiquity is hard to overstate: goods moved more swiftly by water than by land, and the expansion of the Roman Empire in the first centuries BCE and CE, in particular to Egypt and North Africa, greatly increased the volume of Mediterranean trade. At the same time, detailed knowledge of maritime routes was crucial, as evidenced by the existence of ancient maritime guides, such as that of Timosthenes of Rhodes.[374]

Behind the imagery of *DC* 2.6 is a basic idea: sailing in gentle waters, i.e., those with a calmer current, will result in a slower speed and therefore a slower journey, which might reduce the profits to be made over a season. Yet such a journey will also carry less risk of shipwreck. Conversely, a trip in more powerful waters might be speedier and therefore potentially more profitable, but also riskier.[375] The sailing imagery enables the Author to advise his readers not to spend so much that they risk ruin. Financial highs and lows are to be avoided; instead, readers should exercise restraint so that their income and outgoings remain constant and steady.

Similarly, in *Epistle* 19, Seneca urges Lucilius to retreat from public and professional life and from the demands of earning ever more money and ever more prestigious titles. He likens retirement to the safety and calm of a harbor after a voyage on the seas and reminds Lucilius of the risks he has taken for the sake of

---

here. Outside the *Distichs*, the ship may stand for the state, the human body, or the means to completing a risky undertaking. For references and analysis, see especially Fantham 1972. The commonness of these images suggests that the Author did not have to assume nautical knowledge among his readers. The departure and arrival of large boats would have been a spectacle that was well known: Seneca (*Ep.* 77.1–3) claims that the entire population of Puteoli came to the harbor to see the arrival of the first grain boats of the season. This is an exaggeration, but a significant one nonetheless. I owe the reference to Jones 2006, 26–27.

373 According to the Plebiscitum Claudianum (219–218 BCE and later reaffirmed in the Lex de repetundis of 59 BCE), no senator or son of a senator could own a *maritima navis*, which was a ship presumably capable of sailing the Mediterranean, Adriatic, or Aegean. But members of the senatorial order were able to use agents to act on their behalf.

374 I am grateful to Duane Roller for the reference.

375 Horden and Purcell 2000, 137–143. Sirks 2002 claims that the importance of a standard sailing season is overstated and that maritime traders continued to operate outside it. Maritime loans functioned differently from regular loans: the security on the loan was the cargo itself; in the event of shipwreck, the creditor both lost his initial investment and the possibility for claiming the security. The possible return on investment was high, but so were the risks.

money.[376] There is no need to take such risks: their impetus is a desire for luxury, which can be easily avoided. For example, Maecenas (Seneca's bête noire) should have avoided luxury, which necessitated risk-taking, and stuck closer to the shore.[377]

The Author has suggested that saving is a good thing. But he also acknowledges that there are appropriate times to spend and provides guidance on when a person should do so.

DC 2.5

> *Fac sumptum propere, cum res desiderat ipsa:*
> *dandum etenim est aliquid, cum tempus postulat aut res.*
>
> Don't wait to spend when circumstances require;
> Expenses are necessary when timing or the issue demands.

It is timing (*tempus*) and circumstances (*res*) that ask (*desiderat, postulat*) for money to be spent, as this couplet states in both lines (which are somewhat repetitious). The purpose of the couplet is to explain that expenses should be justified not by individual desire, but by external circumstances. Some spending may therefore be necessary, but it is to be reserved for such moments.

DC 3.9

> *Cum tibi divitiae superent in fine senectae,*
> *munificus facito vivas, non parcus, amicus.*
>
> If you have abundant wealth in your final years,
> Be a friend generous, not stingy, with your favors.

DC 2.5 recommends that spending should be reserved for when the time or circumstances demand; *DC* 3.9 offers an example of the right time: in old age. Yet the advice here is not to use the money for living expenses upon retirement or

---

376 Sen. *Ep.* 19.2 and 19.8.
377 Sen. *Ep.* 19.9. Seneca also criticizes Maecenas' dissolute lifestyle in *Ep.* 114. On Seneca and luxury, see Fitzpatrick 2011, 32. Valerius Maximus provides examples of extravagance, luxury, and self-indulgence in 9.1, singling out Gaius Sergius Orata and his expansive heated baths and desire for fresh seafood, the actor Aesopus for his love of outrageous foods, and others for ostentatious clothing, jewelry, homes and gardens, and tapestries. At *H.N.* 33, Pliny rails against luxury as a perverted use of money; on this complex passage, see von Reden 2010, epilogue.

significant healthcare costs, largely modern phenomenona.[378] Rather the Author has different ideas: old age is the time to spend money on your friends.

Spending during one's lifetime makes sense: wealth is no use in death, and money is more usefully and profitably shared with friends while you are alive than once you are dead. Friends will, as we saw in the previous chapter (in which this couplet was also discussed), reciprocate not only financially, but perhaps also with their time and affection—a significant emotional benefit in old age. Indeed, spending on friends is probably more beneficial than spending on oneself, which may be the implication in this couplet. Behind this couplet there may also be an expectation that older people should be generous, and that while a younger person should save for difficult times, old age was a time for sharing.

Thus far we have considered the wisdom of knowing when to save or spend. But the Author also advocates divesting property when necessary:

DC 1.6

Quae nocitura tenes, quamvis sint cara, relinque:
utilitas opibus praeponi tempore debet.

Give up what is bad for you, even if it was dear:
Sometimes usefulness must trump cost.

In this couplet, practicality trumps financial considerations. The neuter plural *nocitura* (rendered singular in the English) suggests that we are to think first of objects that might harm rather than intangibles, such as behaviors or ways of thinking. These objects might be valuable, but even expensive things may be harmful, and despite the advice of earlier couplets to save, here the reader learns that owning items of value is not necessarily always a good thing. Examples might include excessively rich foods, an estate at Baiae, or perhaps a pantomime troupe. The first may be detrimental to the health; the second and third may expose their owners to bad behavior.[379]

---

378 For many individuals of lower socio-economic status, retirement would have occurred only as a necessity arising from infirmity. Cokayne 2003, 83–85, notes that the elderly were often viewed as misers, but that their concern for money may have been the result of real economic insecurity.

379 See, for example, Plin. *Ep.* 7.24, in which Pliny expresses concern about the potential effects of a young man's exposure to his grandmother's pantomime troupe. Sick 1999 helpfully questions whether scholars have been too hasty in associating a wealthy person's engagement with the theater with moral laxity.

The juxtaposition of *utilitas* (utility or usefulness) and *opes* (wealth, riches) in the second line of the couplet is curious because these terms are neither exact opposites nor mutually exclusive. Yet the Author sets them in contrast. If we take *utilitas* here to connote practicality or usefulness on a physical level (i.e., to the body) and *opes* to refer to the intangible notion of wealth and its advantages, then the Author is advising the reader to put his physical self before his financial health. While the message to divest certain valuable items may seem to run contrary to the Author's exhortations to save, there is a common message: the reader must monitor and manage his income and expenses so that they provide him the maximum benefit not only financially, but physically and perhaps morally too.

For Seneca, riches are not a good (in the Stoic sense of the word) and cannot make a person good. But they are necessary or desirable, as well as useful, and they can make life more comfortable.[380] Yet Seneca also supports Posidonius' position that riches drive people to bad deeds: "riches...inflame our minds, they breed pride, they attract envy, and they so disturb the intellect that a reputation for wealth gives us pleasure, even when it is bound to harm us."[381] In a similar vein, Phaedrus warns of the envy that wealth attracts: two mules, one proudly carrying money, the other barley, were set upon by robbers; the first was attacked and his money stolen, while the second was overlooked. The moral: "This fable proves that there is little risk in being poor, while being rich can get you into trouble."[382] Wealth is not wholly a positive; rather, its dangers are to be understood and acknowledged. The *Distichs* join Seneca and Phaedrus in revealing the anxiety among Romans over wealth: it was necessary or desirable, but it also had potentially deleterious effects on a person.

Financial management, according to the Author, seems thus far to have the twin ends of avoidance of want and maintenance of wellbeing. But if the reader finds himself in financial need, he will wonder what he is to do.

---

380 Sen. *De vita beata* 24.5.
381 Sen. Ep. 87.31: *divitias...inflant animos, superbiam pariunt, invidiam contrahunt, et usque eo mentem alienant ut fama pecuniae nos etiam nocitura delectet*. The translation is from Inwood 2010, 53.
382 *Hoc argumento tuta est hominum tenuitas, magnae periclo sunt opes obnoxiae*. Phaedrus 2.7 = Perry 491 = Gibbs 411. The translation is from Gibbs 2002.

Want

DC 1.21

> *Infantem nudum cum te natura crearit,*
> *paupertatis onus patienter ferre memento.*
>
> Birthed by Nature, as a baby you lacked clothes;
> So bear the burden of poverty with patience.

The Author warns that wealth is not something to be expected: we are born without it, as a baby is born without clothes. A lack of wealth, like a lack of clothes, is the natural state. Yet both are uncomfortable and, in the normal course of things, to be avoided. Poverty must be borne with patience, as acquiring money can take time.

The Roman socio-economic elites were very few in number; those in the middle—Veyne's "plèbe moyenne"—were more numerous; Romans living just above or below subsistence level were many.[383] Perhaps the Author is right: in the Roman world, poverty was the natural state. Yet since literate readers of the *Distichs* were probably in the first or second groups, it seems odd that they should need to be reminded to bear poverty patiently. One explanation could be that the Author is thinking of poverty in relative terms: as a lack of what others—i.e., the elites—have, rather than an absolute want of food, shelter, and material goods. This explanation is especially relevant to the times: with the annexation of Egypt and the pax Augusta came an influx of wealth into the Roman Empire that improved the lives of many. Those left out may have been impatient with their lot. Another explanation comes from a consideration of the couplets discussed so far in this chapter. The reader addressed by them is an individual who needs to save money—his wealth is not so great that he can spend without limit. If, as his fortune changes, his savings run dry and he does

---

[383] For a division of the Roman population by wealth, see Scheidel 2006, 41–42. According to Garnsey and Saller 1987, 51–53, the majority of Romans were at risk of "chronic want," and the relative stability of the first century did not significantly improve the financial lot of most inhabitants of the Empire. Von Reden 2012, 279, offers support for this notion, observing that "Most examples we have for Roman credit fall in the category of consumption loans," i.e., they cover personal debts and shortfalls in personal expenses; they are not investment loans.[383] According to Dio Chrysostom 7.103–7, the poor of the early Empire must pay for everything— rent, food, clothes, firewood—except water, leaving them wholly reliant on a steady income and stable markets. I owe the reference to Hollander 2007, 112. MacMullen 1974, 12–14, offers a striking account of abject poverty in rural Roman Egypt.

not receive help, he may be vulnerable to poverty. But he knows that his fortune may change again, and he becomes impatient for that to happen.

The notion of accepting poverty patiently rather than, say, fighting it might strike us today as odd. Yet perhaps the Author is not advocating a total lack of resistance to it, but rather is encouraging his readers to live with poverty in the right way. Indeed, *patienter* should make us think not of patience, but rather an ability to withstand poverty, to live with it until better times return.

Understanding attitudes towards poverty from contemporary sources, especially literary sources, is difficult. From his work on this problem (which includes reading texts that are not contemporary with the *Distichs*), William Fitzgerald concludes that, in the minds of the elites, the poor are generally mean, though certain among them might have some dignity, including semi-mythologized figures such as the honorable man of self-imposed humble circumstances called to military or public service and the real-life poor who refrain from protesting at their condition, but bear it with equanimity.[384]

Valerius Maximus, in his survey of the honorable and notable, reflects upon the first group. He begins by praising the material simplicity of their lives:

> omnia nimirum habet qui nihil concupiscit, eo quidem certius quam <qui> cuncta possidet, quia dominium rerum conlabi solet, bonae mentis usurpatio nullum tristioris fortunae recipit incursum. itaque quorsum attinet aut divitias in prima felicitatis parte aut paupertatem in ultimo miseriarum statu ponere, cum et illarum frons hilaris multis intus amaritudinibus sit referta et huius horridior aspectus solidis et certis bonis abundet? quod melius personis quam verbis repraesentabitur.[385]

> A man who longs for nothing obviously has everything, and even more securely than a man who owns every possession. The ownership of possessions tends to fade away, but the enjoyment of a sound mind is not subject to the attacks of misfortune. So what is the point in regarding wealth as the highest point of happiness or poverty as the lowest level of misery? The happy appearance of the rich is filled with lots of inner bitterness whereas the scruffy look of the poor is enriched with firm and lasting advantages.[386]

He follows with a string of examples of famous and praiseworthy Republican generals and magistrates who had few material assets and scant income, including Valerius Publicola and Menenius Agrippa. Valerius wonders why Romans do not cease to pour scorn on modest means. After all, we might add,

---

[384] Fitzgerald 1996, especially pp. 391–394.
[385] Val. Max. 4.4.pr.
[386] The translation is from Walker 2004.

some of them were worthy individuals, an idea that was presumably unfathomable to some wealthy Romans.

Seneca summarizes the elite position towards the real-life poor: "in poverty the only kind of virtue is not to give up and not to be overwhelmed."[387] As a result, the happy poor are frequently romanticized and idealized.[388] So, for example, the poor farmer of the *Moretum* lacks meat in large quantities, yet he is somewhat satisfied with what little he has.[389] According to some scholars, the poem is a romantic fiction; but others hold that in its apparent realism, it may have been meant as a riposte to the even more rose-tinted view of poverty presented, for example, in Ovid's account of Philemon and Baucis.[390]

Definitions of poverty may be absolute or relative.[391] For example, the Multidimensional Poverty Index of the Oxford Poverty & Human Development Initiative (OPHDI) uses the following absolute criteria for calculating poverty in developing countries:

> No household member aged 10 years or older has completed five years of schooling...any school-aged child is not attending school up to the age at which he/she would complete class 8...any child has died in the family in the five-year period preceding...any adult under 70 years of age or any child for whom there is nutritional information is undernourished in terms of weight for age...the household has no electricity...the household's sanitation facility is not improved..., or it is improved but shared with other households...the household does not have access to safe drinking water...or safe drinking water is more than a 30-minute walk from home roundtrip...the household has a dirt, sand or dung floor...the household cooks with dung, wood or charcoal...the household does not own more than one radio, TV, telephone, bike, motorbike or refrigerator, and does not own a car or truck.[392]

---

387 Sen. *De vita beata* 22.1: *in hac [paupertate] unum genus virtutis sit non inclinari nec deprimi.*
388 It is significant that descriptions of the happy poor are placed usually in mythological and timeless rural contexts: they are fictional constructs removed from the historical reality of the restive urban poor or the agricultural laborers who worked on elite estates.
389 *Moretum* 55–56.
390 Fitzgerald 1996 surveys scholars' approaches to the *Moretum*. Ovid's account of Philemon and Baucis is at *Met.* 8.611–724, in which the pair join the ranks of the fictional happy poor as they make light of their poverty and bear it with equanimity (especially ll. 633–34). The Roman locus classicus of the theme of happiness in a simple life is Hor. *Sat.* 2.6. The Augustan elegiac poets take up the theme (e.g. Tib. 1.5), as does Martial (2.90 and 10.96).
391 Larsen 2015, 7–8, observes three ways in which someone can be described as a *pauper*: they are destitute, they lack the means to maintain their current status (e.g., an equestrian who has fallen on hard times), or they are financially wealthy, but voluntarily frugal.
392 These definitions have been reproduced from Alkire and Robles 2017, 5, table 1.

Yet poverty is also relative: for Merriam Webster, for example, it is "the state of one who lacks a usual or socially acceptable amount of money or material possessions." According to this definition, social convention determines poverty, and social convention is local and necessarily relative. Notions of relative poverty emerge within a society: feeling poor might be different from being poor.[393] This surely would have been the case for elite Romans, whose understanding of the lived realities of the poor would have been limited. Changes to their standards of living might have left them feeling poor, but they were still far from the experiences of the absolutely poor.

In a complex epigram (8.19), Martial reports that a certain Cinna wants to appear poor, presumably because such elegant slumming is in vogue for the wealthy. Yet Martial observes that those who want to appear wealthy, but are not, must also feign poverty. Cinna is one of those wannabes, and so this man, who is poor but wants to appear wealthy, must fake being poor. But how poor is Cinna? He cannot be so poor if he is trying to mingle with and become one of the wealthy. His adoption of a faux poverty, which is most likely not the same as real poverty, also suggests that he has the means to alter his lifestyle and manipulate his circumstances.[394]

Relative poverty appears in another epigram (11.32) of Martial: Nestor, presumably a wealthy man, wants to have a place among regular folk, and he has relinquished the trappings of wealth: the toga, furniture, and enslaved individuals. But Martial tells him that "having nothing is not poverty, Nestor" (*non est paupertas, Nestor, habere nihil*). Rather, as *DC* 1.21 suggests, poverty is a state that results from a lack of immediately accessible cash, something that does not afflict Nestor and is not necessarily permanent. But poverty may also be a state of mind, and that definition could be helpful for understanding *DC* 1.24, discussed below.

---

393 Research has found that rates of poverty determined by asking people whether they feel poor and those determined by welfare metrics may be broadly similar: see, for example, Pradhan and Ravallion 2000 and Ravallion 2012. Yet such outcomes may be attributed in part to people's recent and increasing access to information, especially online, about the living conditions of others.

394 A modern analogue to ancient faux poverty can be found in American fashion of the 1990s. Beginning in the 1980s, residents of the Pacific Northwest had worn tough workwear that was appropriate for their jobs in the logging and aviation industries. Young people in the region began to adopt these clothes in their leisure time as a mark of regional pride and a reaction to the glitzy excess of contemporary high fashion. In the 1990s, as interest in the popular culture of the Pacific Northwest grew, wealthy individuals across the U.S. adopted the look, and high-priced faux workwear appeared on catwalks and in mainstream fashion.

DC 1.24

Ne tibi quid desit, quaesitis utere parce,
utque quod est serves, semper deesse putato.

To keep from being in need, don't spend all you have;
To keep what you have, think yourself always in need.

The Author tells the reader that spending what he has acquired will put him at risk of being in need, that is, with neither immediate cash nor reserves on which to draw. In the second line, he proposes a way to avoid the problem: the reader should think of himself as always in need and so strive to maintain his supply of saved money. With this couplet, the Author sets out a long-term plan for financial health: the reader should never consider himself comfortable. Such advice assumes that some of his readers could not expect to have such substantial and permanent financial resources that they need never save.

Seneca echoes the Author's advice and confirms his notion of poverty: in *Epistle* 20, he encourages Lucilius to ensure that his expenses are appropriate and proportionate, making sure that no one area—clothing, household maintenance, food, family support—should considerably exceed the others.[395] But the wealthy Stoic philosopher goes further, suggesting that Lucilius should be content with the "goods," here non-material ones, that he can find within himself and, more than that, he should strive to be content with little when around him are riches.[396] This is because, while Lucilius should not adopt poverty because it is inherently better, he should be prepared for it, so that he can bear it more easily.[397]

DC 1.28

Cum tibi sint nati nec opes, tunc artibus illos
instrue, quo possint inopem defendere vitam.

You have sons, but no means? Teach them a trade,
So they can avoid a life of want.

The message sounds simple and obvious: children from families that are not wealthy may face financial insecurity, but learning a trade will mitigate it. The

---

395 Sen. *Ep.* 20.7.
396 Sen. *Ep.* 20.8 and 10.
397 Sen. *Ep.* 20.12.

Author assumes a juxtaposition: between on the one hand wealth that has been acquired through trade and on the other wealth that has been inherited and perhaps grown through an elite occupation. With a father still alive, sons in their father's power (*in patria potestate*) could borrow money, although this was becoming more difficult during the course of the first century CE. By the time of the *Distichs*, Roman fathers who were legally independent (*sui iuris*) were in most cases not responsible for their children's debts beyond what they had given them as an allowance (*peculium*).[398] Sons of modest families needed to find their own sources of income both while their fathers were alive and after they had died. The fathers who followed the Author's advice were acting not because of any legal responsibility, but rather out of parental concern.[399] They stand in contrast to the fathers of Roman comedy, miserly individuals who denied their sons access to their wealth even after death. Both groups of men were anxious that their sons should not depend upon them, though for quite different reasons.[400]

The Author perhaps assumes that individuals who inherited their father's wealth (*opes*) would avoid financial insecurity, while those who could not rely on such a financial cushion but had a trade or skill (*ars*) would also enjoy a life free from want. The two groups are drawn too simply, but perhaps the Roman world of the first century CE was indeed one in which inherited wealth tended to be sufficient to offer financial security and in which skilled men could find stable employment. Yet the socio-economic elites were critical of those who performed labor for compensation: to them, a man tending to his plot of land was a noble farmer, but the worker in a foundry was contemptible and base.[401]

The term *ars*, when connoting an occupation or activity, is broad: it may refer generally to education or more narrowly to a defined body of knowledge and

---

398 With the Senatus consultum Macedonianum, passed during the reign of Vespasian, sons faced tough restrictions, as they were barred from using their inheritance to pay off debts incurred during their father's lifetime. I think it likely that the *Distichs* were composed before the Senatus consultum Macedonianum.

399 By contrast, the Rabbinical maxim, T. Kid. I, 11, warns that "A man is obliged to teach his son a trade, and whoever does not teach his son a trade teaches him to become a robber" (trans. Montefiore and Loewe 1974, 444.) I owe the reference to MacMullen 1974, 97.

400 Cantarella 2003, 293–294, lists sources from comedy and indeed elsewhere for financially needy sons and offers the example of the accused in Cicero's *Pro Sexto Roscio Amerino*, a man accused of committing parricide in a bid to pay off his debts.

401 A full treatment of attitudes towards banausic occupations is Cuomo 2007, 7–40. On the stigma associated with certain professions, such as tanning and undertaking, see especially Bond 2016.

skills and the resulting trade or occupation.⁴⁰² Others use the term *ars* more widely to denote a job or occupation. Livy, for example, uses it in connection with cooks for hire: beginning in 187 BCE, "cooks were being hired, and what had once been a service (*ministerium*) began to be considered an *ars*."⁴⁰³ *Ministeria* were duties performed especially by enslaved individuals; but now cooks, presumably freeborn or freed, were hiring themselves out, and their work was considered skilled.

A reference by Pliny the Elder pushes the elevation of cooking from *ministerium* to *ars* forward perhaps to the first century BCE.⁴⁰⁴ A little later certain services, such as advocacy, changed from *officia*—acts expecting reciprocity, but still discretionary—to fee-based services, whose terms and compensation were gradually enforced.⁴⁰⁵ These two developments—the transformations of some *ministeria* and *officia*—suggest that the first centuries BCE and CE may have seen significant changes in the nature of work and its compensation.⁴⁰⁶ Such changes may have been taking place alongside significant shifts in patterns of landholding following the civil wars of the first century BCE and the influx of wealth with the pax Augusta. It is possible that while some readers of the *Distichs* found themselves newly enriched, others were less lucky and needed now to navigate a new world of jobs, trades, and services.

In Petronius' *Cena Trimalchionis*, the freedman guests discuss trades that include undertaking, barbering, auctioneering, and lawyering. All are presented, presumably ironically, by the freedmen as honorable and desirable occupa-

---

402 See, for example, Cic. *Mur.* 30.
403 Liv. 39.6.9: *coquus...in pretio esse, et quod ministerium fuerat, ars haberi coepta*.
404 Weissenborn 1875, 8, refers to Plin. *H.N.* 18.108: *nec cocos vero habebant in servitiis, eosque ex macello conducebant* ("and in fact their cooks were not enslaved: they hired them at the marketplace").
405 Michel 1962, 554; Coffee 2017.
406 A comment in Martial might reflect these changes. At 3.7, he reports that hangers-on are lamenting the decline in hand-outs; one of them suggests that handouts should now become salaries. The joke is that the hanger-on no longer receives money as a spontaneous (though expected) recognition for his talents and therefore wants a dependable salary instead. But behind the joke might be the serious suggestion that the talents of hangers-on (including poets and other entertainers) should be recognized and compensated, since they play an important role in the social economies of wealthy households. Under Nero, hand-outs (*sportulae*) were no longer to be paid all in kind, but at least partly as cash, and some had objected to this monetization of a polite exchange. Yet when Domitian briefly reversed Nero's decision, apparently requiring compensation through meals, financially unstable hangers-on were once again vulnerable to wealthy individuals' failure to recognize adequately and discreetly their presence and contributions. On these developments, see especially Harrison 2001, 300–306.

tions that (should) ensure financial wellbeing.[407] One freedman announces that he will teach his son a trade—perhaps he will be a barber, auctioneer, or lawyer. He twice asserts that a trade offers financial security: only death can take it away.[408] The notion is echoed by Phaedrus, who tells the story of Simonides shipwrecked but, despite his losses, able to support himself from his talents as a poet; the moral is that an educated man or a skilled man trained in a trade has riches always within himself.[409] Indeed, the Author himself echoes the sentiment later in the collection:

DC 4.19

Disce aliquid, nam, cum subito fortuna recessit,
ars remanet vitamque hominis non deserit umquam.

Pick up a skill: Fortune may suddenly desert you,
But a trade never leaves in the lurch a man who makes his living.

It is tempting to assume that members of the socio-economic elite will have found fault with DC 1.28. In *De officiis*, Cicero gives examples of trades and occupations that he finds becoming and unbecoming to a free person. In the second group are "collecting harbour dues, or usury," as well as reselling, unskilled labor, handicraft, luxury supply, entertainment, and other activities that incur others' displeasure, such as the services provided by "fishmongers, butchers, cooks, poulterers, fishermen... perfumers, dancers, and the whole variety show," and small-scale trade.[410] Cicero does not criticize all occupations: he regards some as unworthy of any individual, while others are inappropriate only for his peers. While he may have refined the Author's advice, he would not have rejected it. Among the readers of the *Distichs*, members of the elite are likewise unlikely to have disagreed completely with this couplet, simply understanding that it was not relevant to them. But for the rest, it apparently offered helpful advice. Perhaps among them were Romans who were sufficiently close in status to the elites that they felt compelled to look askance at earning a living, yet were unable to live off inheritances and landed wealth.

---

407 Petr. 38 and 46. On the marginalized status of undertakers, see Lindsay 2000, Bodel 1994, 72–80, and 2000.
408 Petr. 46.
409 Phaedrus 4.23 = Perry 519 = Gibbs 412: *homo doctus semper habet divitias in se*. On Romans' attitudes towards work, see Joshel 1992, 62–69.
410 Cic. *Off.* 1.150. The translations are from Griffin and Atkins 1991. On the passage, see Griffin and Atkins 1991, 58, and Dyck 1996, 333–338.

DC 1.39

> *Conserva potius, quae sunt iam parta labore;*
> *cum labor in damno est, crescit mortalis egestas.*

> Preserve, if you can, what you gained with labor;
> When labor is in want, the poverty of men increases.

The message of this couplet seems simple: be sure to build up savings from your labors, since working to make up for losses is especially hard. The final two words of the couplet, *mortalis egestas*, are striking. The phrase is found elsewhere only in Vergil's *Georgics* 3.318–20: "And so make every effort to ward off ice and snowy winds in order to reduce their need for human help" (*ergo omni studio glaciem ventosque nivalis, / quo minor est illis curae mortalis egestas, / avertes...*).[411] The phrase may have been in the minds of some readers of the *Distichs*. But whereas in the *Georgics*, *mortalis* is in the genitive case, modifying *curae*, in the *Distichs* it is nominative, modifying *egestas*, and that results in an ambiguity of meaning: it can mean "the needs of man" or "a need for men." When a man must toil to make good the losses he has incurred, *either* the threat to his very life increases *or* his need for the help of others is greater.[412] Following the first translation, threats to the man's life may come as a result of increased working hours (which leads to deprivation of sleep and rest), a need to take on more physically demanding work, or a reduction in available food and shelter. The second translation leads us to understand that under such circumstances the man needs more help from others.[413] The second is the more awkward of the two, but it is also more reminiscent of *Georgics* 3.319, which may have been operative in readers' minds.

---

411 Greenough 1900 translates the subordinate clause, "the less they crave man's vigilance," and Fairclough 1916 formulates his translation similarly. Kline 2002 has "So because they need man's attention less, protect them / with all due care, from the ice and snowy winds." Servius' comment on the phrase reflects the ambiguity by glossing it with another ambiguous phrase: *quo minus est illis curae mortifera egestas, si diligens circa eas fueris, necessitas mortalitatis minor est* ("in order to reduce your herd's concern for *mortalis egestas*: if you have been attentive to them, there is less *either* need for mortals *or* inevitability of death").
412 Published translations of this couplet reflect more or less the ambiguity: Chase 1922 translates "dire want"; Duff and Duff 1934 "want"; Marchand "human need"; Pepin 1999 "poverty of men."
413 A third reading might be possible by translating the Latin as "the lack of mortals," and the couplet now warns that when Romans labor to pay off their debts, fewer people are willing to help them, since they tend to shun debtors.

Yet another reading comes from remembering Syrus, *Sententiae* 11: "Debt is for a freeborn man a bitter servitude" (*alienum aes homini ingenuo acerba est servitus*). The reader will have to labor to make up for his losses because he has had to take out debt and must now work harder to pay off the interest.[414] Even a brief period of want could have long-lasting effects: as Greg Woolf observes, "Impoverishment carried with it the threat of a form of social death. For the grandest Romans it would entail formal expulsion from the senate, or even the equestrian centuries and a consequent check on careers in the public or the emperor's service, as well as the inability to sustain reciprocal exchanges of the kind needed to maintain social intercourse with one's peers."[415] Forced out of the circles in which he had cultivated his creditworthiness, the suddenly impoverished Roman would have found it especially hard to regain his former economic status.[416]

DC 3.11

> *Rebus et in censu si non est quod fuit ante,*
> *fac vivas contentus eo, quod tempora praebent.*

> If your possessions and property are not what they once were,
> Be satisfied with what your circumstances offer you now.

This couplet emphasizes the fact—presumably grounded in reality—that fortunes could change. Social mobility—upward or downward—in antiquity was, we understand, more limited than in the modern era, but we have examples from ancient literature of characters who fell on hard times, as well as those who moved up in the world.[417] The second line makes the basic point that the

---

414 According to Andreau 1999, 141, referring to Johnson 1936, 452–454, "We know that in Roman Egypt, in poor and working-class communities, many loans were remunerated, not by interest, but by work or services."
415 Woolf 2006, 91–92.
416 Garnsey and Saller 1987, 123, note that "for reasons that are not clear senatorial families disappeared at an average rate of 75 percent per generation"; some of those reasons were surely financial, and the financial pressures on many senatorial and equestrian families must have been considerable. Frederiksen 1966, 128–138, points out that insolvency might cause elite Romans to lose their place in the Senate, any public office they might hold, and their personal property; other Romans might face debt bondage or even private imprisonment, despite their possible illegality.
417 Unfortunate characters include Vergil's goatherd Meliboeus in *Eclogues* 1 and Petronius' unlucky freedmen, among them the undertaker mentioned above (Petr. 38), Julius Proculus (50–51), and Plocamus (63); the upwardly mobile include Meliboeus' interlocutor Tityrus and

reader should be satisfied with what he has. Just as other authors, most notably Seneca, had lauded the happy poor for their satisfaction with little, so the Author encourages his reader to be content with what he has. He perhaps also recognizes that improving their financial lot is in part outside a person's control.

DC 4.35

> *Ereptis opibus noli maerere dolendo*
> *sed gaude potius, tibi si contingat habere.*
>
> Don't wail with grief when someone makes off with your property;
> Instead be glad, if you happen to have anything left.

The message of this couplet is similar: changes in wealth may come with changes in fortune, and wealth is not something we can always control. But when his wealth is reduced, the reader should use the opportunity to feel gratitude for what is present, instead of feeling anger over what has been lost.

The nature of the theft to be imagined by the reader might range from land confiscation, akin to that alluded to in Vergil's first *Eclogue*, to a mugging on the street.[418] Most likely, given the implied scale of the loss—it is possible that the reader will be left with nothing—and given the emphasis elsewhere in the *Distichs* on modest wealth, this couplet more likely points to cash wealth stored on the person or in a strongbox and therefore highly vulnerable. This scenario could have been a real possibility for many readers of the *Distichs*.[419]

Seneca, who was far removed from the risks of personal ruin as the result of theft, reminds his readers that the possession of wealth is not a blessing. In a letter on superficiality and not understanding the true worth of things, he discusses man's obsession with wealth and exclaims, "The possession of riches means even greater agony of spirit than the acquisition of riches. And how we sorrow over our losses—losses which fall heavily upon us, and yet seem still more heavy! And finally, though Fortune may leave our property intact, what-

---

Petronius' luckier freedmen, Pompeius Diogenes (38), Chrysanthus (43), and Hermeros (57–58). The scholarship on Roman social mobility is large, but see, for example, Hopkins 1965, Weaver 1967, and Purcell 1983, and more recently on *collegia* as a means of social mobility, see Perry 2006, 508–511.

418 On the land confiscations, see especially Osgood 2006, chap. 3.

419 At Petr. *Sat.* 43, the freedman Phileros wonders at the fact that someone had 100,000 sesterces in ready cash at his home. I owe the reference to Mrozek 1985, 313–314. On urban theft in the Roman Empire, see Fuhrmann 2011, chap. 3. For a helpful list of ancient references to burglary and muggings, see Holleran 2011, 257, n. 73.

ever we cannot gain in addition, is sheer loss!"[420] He closes the letter with a statement that a person should be content with the prosperity he has and a wish that those who long for wealth might discuss that longing with rich men.[421] For once, the *Distichs* skew philosophical, siding with Seneca in a rejection of righteous outrage at personal privation.

Wealth

DC 3.12

> *Uxorem fuge ne ducas sub nomine dotis,*
> *nec retinere velis, si coeperit esse molesta.*
>
> Don't marry a wife for the sake of her dowry,
> And don't keep her if she now causes you trouble.

The reader should not take a wife for the sake of money and should not remain married to her if she becomes troublesome. The theme is an old one: the well-dowered wife and her belittled husband are stock characters in Roman comedy.[422] The couplet's second line, commending that the reader divorce a troublesome wife (*uxor molesta*) draws on another old theme—that of the nuisance wife.[423] Indeed, the couplet's timelessness might warn us off reading it closely

---

420 Sen. *Ep.* 115.16: *Maiore tormento pecunia possidetur quam quaeritur. Quantum damnis ingemescunt, quae et magna incidunt et videntur maiora. Denique ut illis fortuna nihil detrahat, quidquid non adquiritur damnum est.* The translation is Gummere 1917.
421 Sen. *Ep.* 115.17.
422 According to Plautus (*Aul.* 534-35), "women with large dowries slay their husbands with misfortune and financial loss" (*dotatae mactant et malo et damno viros*).
423 *Molestus* (and its related forms) appear quite frequently in ancient literature, most often applied to women. For example, in Plautus' *Casina*, Cleostrata asserts that she does not want to inconvenience Alcesimus' wife by insisting that she come over to visit (545): "I don't want to be any trouble to her; I'll see her later" (*molesta ei esse nolo: post convenero*). But in inconveniencing her own husband, who had been looking forward to an afternoon of secret passion at Alcesimus' house, she is trouble (*molesta*) to him. According to Gellius' description (*NA* 1.17.1) of Xanthippe, wife of Socrates, "She is said to have been most peevish and quarrelsome and she gushed out day and night womanish anger and irritations" (*morosa admodum fuisse fertur et iurgiosa, irarumque et molestiarum muliebrium per diem perque noctem scatebat*). Catullus complains of lack of empathy in a girl who refuses to conspire in his claim to have bought litter-bearers while in Bithynia (10.33-34): "But you're badly lacking in wit and you're a pain, and with you around we can't let things go" (*sed tu insulsa male et molesta vivis, per quam non licet esse neglegentem*). In *Pro Caelio*, Cicero has Clodius ask his sister (36), "Why are you trou-

for insights into gender roles in marriage in the context of the first-century CE.[424] We might do better to think about the couplet in purely financial terms: birth, family connections, gender-specific virtues, looks, and disposition were significant in the selection of a spouse to differing degrees for different individuals, but financial security will have been important for most.[425] Yet, as the Author urges here, finances should not be put before personal happiness.

Several couplets in the *Distichs* are concerned with adopting a healthy attitude towards money. For example, *DC* 4.1

> *Despice divitias, si vis animo esse beatus,*
> *quas qui suspiciunt, mendicant semper avari.*
>
> If you want to be rich in the mind, look down on wealth:
> Those who look up to it are forever greedy beggars.

The sentiment is simple: do not covet wealth, as you will always want more, and that will make you unhappy. But the couplet has been carefully composed. For example, the contrast between *despice* ("look down") and *suspiciunt* ("look up") is underscored by the fact that they are both compounded forms of the verb *specere*. The Author also contrasts *divitias* ("wealth") and *animo...beatus* ("rich in mind"), juxtaposing material and immaterial bounty. A third contrast occurs in the last clause: *mendicant* ("beg") suggests people down on their luck and perhaps deserving of pity. But the clause has a sting in its tail in *avari* ("greedy"): the reader must not covet wealth, otherwise he risks becoming a "greedy beggar."

---

blesome to this man, who spurns you?" (*cur huic, qui te spernit, molesta es?*). The term was also applied to marriage, though rarely in public, hence the apparent shock at a speech by censor Q. Caecilius Metellus Macedonicus (Gell. *NA* 1.6.2–3), in which he claimed that "If we could do without wives, fellow citizens, we would all be free of that trouble" (*si sine uxore possemus, Quirites, omnes ea molestia careremus*).

424 It is tempting, for example, to try to read this couplet in the context of Augustus' efforts to increase marriage and the birthrate (on which see Milnor 2005, chap. 3). Perhaps some Romans were reluctant to divorce in order to find happiness in a new marriage, while others were chary of marrying, lest they also meet with unhappiness. But this is a stretch.

425 On selection of a spouse, see especially Treggiari 1991, chap. 3. Women's behavior in marriage (which was, almost without exception, *sine manu* in the first century CE) will have varied in part according to their legal status (i.e., whether or not they were *sui iuris*, on which see Gardner 1986 and Dixon 1992, which was in turn impacted by the decline of *tutela*, on which see the helpful introduction in Crook 1986, 62–67), their location in the Empire (see, for example, Cotton 1993 and Connolly 2004), among other factors.

Seneca provides a historical example of the Author's point: after campaigning against Darius and the peoples of India, Alexander the Great was left poor because he continued to need to expand his empire and therefore lacked satisfaction with what he had.[426] Seneca observes that "money never made a man rich; on the contrary, it always smites men with a greater craving for itself."[427]

The Author encourages the reader to be content without wealth, but this is not quite the same as the advice of Seneca and others. Seneca encourages his reader that, following the teachings of great men, he adopt poverty and hardship—for example, meager, cheap food, and rough clothes—for just a few days so that he can confront his fears of want before returning to a life of plenty.[428] For some elites, poverty is a philosophical tool, their unassailable wealth providing security while they contemplate; the Author, by contrast, encourages his readers to be content without wealth they do not have. For Seneca, wealth is not a good and cannot aid in becoming and being a good Stoic; it is only an accessory to a person.[429] The Author's goal is also happiness, but the point is stated in a less philosophically sophisticated way.

DC 4.4

Dilige denarium, sed parce dilige formam.
Quam nemo sanctus nec honestus captat habere.

Love money, but don't love the feel of it in your hands.
A man of scruples and honor doesn't yearn for cash.

---

[426] Sen. *Ep.* 119.7.
[427] Sen. *Ep.* 119.9: *neminem pecunia divitem fecit, immo contra nulli non maiorem sui cupidinem incussit*. The translation is from Gummere. Valerius Maximus makes a similar point (9.4.pr): "Avarice will be dragged out too. It searches for hidden profit and greedily devours an obvious prey. The pleasure of ownership does not make it happy; the desire for gain makes it miserable" (*protrahatur etiam auaritia, latentium indagatrix lucrorum, manifestae praedae auidissima uorago, neque habendi fructu felix et cupiditate quaerendi miserrima*). The translation is from Walker 2004. Von Reden 2010, 186–198, observes that some ancient writers connected the beginning of man's decline with his invention of currency. For example, according to Pliny *H.N.* 33.48, "with coins came the first beginnings of greed, along with the idle wealth that came with the invention of usury, and this did not happen gradually, but rather with a certain feverishness there blazed no longer simply greed, but rather a hunger for gold" (*sed a nummo prima origo avaritiae faenore excogitato quaestuosaque segnitia, nec paulatim: exarsit rabie quadam non iam avaritia, sed fames auri*).
[428] Sen. *Ep.* 18.5–7.
[429] Sen. *Ep.* 87.18.

This couplet contains another warning not to covet wealth, and the Author seems to connect it back to *DC* 4.1 with alliteration of the opening words of both couplets: *despice divitias* and *dilige denarium*.[430] But refining his stance in *DC* 4.1, the Author asserts here that his reader may desire money, though he should not love the sensation of having cash.[431] Perhaps he is warning his reader against appearing both covetous and ostentatious for keeping his wealth in cash rather than spending it. The Author's emphasis on the physicality of money might also be motivated by his and others' feelings about different kinds of wealth: negative towards cash wealth and positive towards landed wealth.

There is also a warning here against wanting to become rich. The unimportance of wealth is a common theme among Roman writers. For example, Valerius Maximus dedicates a chapter of his work on memorable deeds and sayings to "people who were born in humble circumstances but ended up famous," in which there is little mention of wealth; rather attainment of office is the reward for their respectability, wisdom, and leadership ability.[432] A little later he provides examples of virtuous Republican men who refused to be compromised by money.[433] One might argue that their reverence for glory and integrity over money should be placed in the context of their probable financial security, but Valerius Maximus notes that the plebs too have demonstrated self-restraint (*continentia*): for example, Pyrrhus was unable to buy the loyalty of the people of Rome; similarly Marius and Cinna were unable to buy off the plebs.[434]

---

[430] The only other example of alliteration at the start of a line comes at *DC* 4.17.2: *fac fugias...*

[431] I follow the commentators in understanding *formam* to refer to the appearance and feel of coins (Boas 1952, 197–199), rather than beauty (e.g., the beauty of women, whose affection might be expensive to purchase and maintain). The syntax of *parce dilige* is awkward, as the commentators note, and some editors proposed ending one clause with *parce* and beginning another with *dilige*.

[432] Val. Max. 3.4: *quo <e>venit ut et humili loco nati ad summam dignitatem consurgant*. Conversely, Valerius Maximus reports that men born to illustrious families who nevertheless fell into disgrace did so because of military cowardice, lack of personal hygiene, lust, and profligacy. Inclusion of the latter, the only failing with immediate financial repercussions, reveals that lack of wealth is not a fault (as the Author allows in *DC* 4.4), but a misuse of wealth is. For example, Valerius Maximus reports (3.5.2) that "people were angry at the idea that [Quintus Fabius Maximus] would waste all that money on his vices, since it should have been used to advance the splendor of the Fabius family" (*dolenter enim homines ferebant pecuniam, quae Fabiae gentis splendori servire debebat, flagitiis disici*). The translations are from Walker 2004.

[433] Val. Max. 4.3.

[434] Val. Max. 4.3.14.

DC 4.5

> *Cum fueris locuples, corpus curare memento:*
> *aeger dives habet nummos, se non habet ipsum.*

> You may be wealthy, but be sure that you're healthy too:
> A rich man who's sick has cash, but he doesn't have himself.

This couplet should be placed in the context of several social realities: first, sickness was an ever-present reality; second, the wealthy were not insulated from sickness. *Curare* ("care for") may allude to a third, the importance in ancient medicine of the prevention of illness through correct diet and exercise, which would help to maintain the balance of the humors and therefore one's health. The message of the first line is simple: wealth cannot prevent or remove illness. The second is less so. In "*se non habet ipsum*" ("does not have himself"), the Author suggests that to be healthy—to have no sickness—is the ideal state, and to be healthy is to have oneself, i.e., to enjoy the greatest benefit and pleasure of life. But being wealthy cannot bring health or overcome sickness. Seneca goes further: "If you compare all the other ills from which we suffer—deaths, sicknesses, fears, longings, the endurance of pains and labours—with the evils which our money brings, this portion will far outweigh the other."[435]

Reputation

As was clear from the previous chapter on friendship, a considerable number of the maxims in the *Distichs* are concerned with reputation, and a person's attitude towards money and his financial undertakings, activities, and actions seem to have played a significant role in others' judgements of him.

DC 1.29

> *Quod vile est carum, quod carum vile putato:*
> *sic tu nec cupidus nec avarus nosceris ulli.*

---

[435] Sen. *De tranq.* 8.1: *nam si omnia alia quibus angimur compares, mortes, aegrotationes, metus, desideria, dolorum laborumque patientiam, eum iis quae nobis mala pecunia nostra exhibet, haec pars multum praegravabit.* The translation is from Basore. The basic sentiment— that being content with poverty is better than suffering with wealth—is restated at *De tranq.* 8.4 and 8.9 and found also at *Ep.* 19.7.

> Reckon what is worthless to be dear, and what is dear to be worthless:
> And you will be known to all as neither greedy nor grasping.

Avarice and parsimony are both reprehensible. To avoid them, the Author tells his reader, he should not be wasteful with or dismissive of things that have little value, and he should not be too covetous of objects that have significant value. The couplet is (relatively) elegantly expressed, with chiastic repetition in the first line and alliteration in "n" and "c" in the second. But the sentiment is somewhat pedestrian, and the Author is not alone in his censure: (near-)contemporary condemnations of cupidity are widespread.[436] He does not tell us why greed and avarice are bad, but rather warns of their repercussions for the reader's reputation.

DC 2.19

> *Luxuriam fugito, simul et vitare memento*
> *crimen avaritiae; nam sunt contraria famae.*

> Steer clear of indulgence, but also avoid any charge
> Of stinginess: neither is incompatible with a good reputation.

In similar fashion, the Author emphasizes not the inherent wrong of indulgence and stinginess, but rather their harm to a person's reputation.

DC 3.8

> *Quod tibi sors dederit tabulis suprema parentis*
> *augendo serva, ne sis quem fama loquatur.*

> Whatever fate has given you in your parent's will,
> You must protect and grow to avoid a bad reputation.

---

[436] Among the most forceful expressions are Cic. *Tusc.* 3.5: "Than these two diseases (and I am leaving out others) illness and greed, can there be any more grievous to the body?" (*quibus duobus morbis, ut omittam alios, aegritudine et cupiditate, qui tandem possunt in corpore esse graviores?*). See, in a similar vein, Martial 3.12 and 3.13. Pliny the Younger will later make the same point (*Ep.* 2.6.7): "And so remember that nothing is to be avoided more than that strange union of luxury and meanness; by themselves and separate these are most shameful, even more so when joined together" (*igitur memento nihil magis esse vitandum quam istam luxuriae et sordium novam societatem; quae cum sint turpissima discreta ac separata, turpius iunguntur*).

The Author's concern with reputation appears again in *DC* 3.8. Behind this couplet is presumably the attitude that an inheritance is family money that should, as far as possible, be preserved through future generations; as a result, heirs should carefully manage and invest their inheritance.

Wealth acquired during one's lifetime and not through inheritance can be spent, and indeed some should be used, otherwise the reader will gain a poor reputation, as the Author explains in the following couplet:

DC 4.16

> *Utere quaesitis opibus, fuge nomen avari;*
> *quid tibi divitias, si semper pauper abundas.*
>
> Put to work the wealth you have acquired and avoid being called a miser;
> What's the point of riches, if you're always the poor rich guy?

The Author's concern is well-founded: Martial complains of a certain Caecilianus, who has come into money and become a miser; elsewhere he uses mismanagement of meager means as a way to characterize someone as being of poor judgement.[437] The Author emphasizes the public face of personal financial management because good management helps to preserve a person's *nomen*—literally his name, but by extension his creditworthiness—and also because it may characterize him in a positive way more broadly and thus contribute to his reputation.[438]

The *Distichs* bear out William Harris' claim that one's reputation was crucial to financial undertakings.[439] The Author's emphasis on reputation was surely

---

437 Mart. 4.51; in 2.51, Hyllus spends his last denarius not on food, but on sex. On this and other examples, see Woolf 2006, 95–97.
438 On *nomen* as "credit-worthiness," *OLD* s.v. *nomen* 22d. Greek uses similar terminology, including εὐγνώμων ("having a good financial reputation," among other meanings) and ἀγνώμων (sometimes "not credit-worthy"). See, for example, *P.Bad.* 2.35.10 (87 CE), in which ἀγνωμοσύνη is translated by Bagnall and Cribiore 2008, B2.4, as "unkindness," though "financial instability" might be more suitable to the context. I owe the references to David Ratzan. On the importance of a Roman's name, see Mart. 5.82 and the discussion later in this chapter. Kay 2014, 109, cautions that *nomina* should be translated not as "outstanding loans" (Harris 2006, 9), but as "an entry in an account book," though, as Kay acknowledges (2014, 115–116), *nomen* may be used for an entry in an account book that is for a loan.
439 Harris 2006, 6–7; see also MacMullen 1974, 65. At *Fam.* 5.6, Cicero claims that creditors consider him a *bonum nomen* ("good name") because he supported them during his consulship (I owe the reference to Hollander 2007, 52), but at *Att.* 12.3.2 he worries that auctioning one of his debts would discredit him (on which see Kay 2014, 239). Cicero had good reason to be wor-

meant to appeal to readers who were familiar with indebtedness and were anxious about it. Indeed, the financially related *Distichs* acknowledge the importance of personal debt both to one's reputation and in the wider Roman economy.

Thus far the emphasis in couplets that concern money has been on the reader's own financial behavior. But *DC* 2.8 is concerned with the behavior of others and its impact on the reader:

DC 2.8

> *Nolo putes*[440] *pravos homines peccata lucrari:*
> *temporibus peccata latent et tempore parent.*
>
> Don't think that wicked men gain from their misdeeds:
> These lie hidden for a while, but in time are revealed.[441]

In this couplet, the reader is imagined as assuming that men might benefit from corruption, but he learns that corruption does not pay. He might be either a potential victim or a possible miscreant, and in the second line the Author acknowledges that sometimes wrongdoing may lie hidden, but encourages or warns his reader that in time others notice and the wrongdoing must be corrected.

Behind this couplet may be an anxiety about the acquisition of wealth, in particular over whether there are right ways and wrong ways to gain money. Some of those wrong ways—through corruption and plunder, for example—and the moral degeneracy attendant upon them are explored fully by Sallust and

---

ried: in *Clu.* 12.38–39 he tells us that debtors' reputations were posted on the *columna Maenia* (see Andreau 1999, 12). Bang 2011, 260–261, surveys the epigraphic evidence that traders were keen to advertise themselves as most reliable (*fidelissimi*), since personal networks were essential for success in the ancient marketplace (Bang 2011, 289), and there is evidence for cults of the goddess Fides among traders (Rauh 1993, 111–112). Jones 2006, 74, demonstrates that a significant number of the loans in the Sulpicii archive used sureties as security that could be sued for any outstanding debts. The prominence of sureties further underscores the importance of personal standing in business, as well as the ability to maintain strong networks.

440 *Nolo putes* is preferable to *nolo putare* and *noli putes* on metrical grounds and is permissible too: *volo* (and presumably *nolo* too) can have a final short *o* according to Gildersleeve 1895, § 707.5.2. On the construction of prohibitions using *noli* followed by a verb in the subjunctive mood, see Gildersleeve 1895, § 271.1, n. 2.

441 *Parent* is ambiguous: it can mean both obey and also to appear or be seen. I have tried to keep something of the Latin's ambiguity in the English.

Cicero.[442] Less well explored is the concern that is presumably behind this couplet: that gaining wealth by dishonest means is unfair, though that unfairness is not always punished. The Author nods to it, but given the constraints of the couplet form, does not elaborate.

The *Distichs* add to our understanding of experiences in the credit-reliant economy of the first century CE, and they reinforce William Harris' claim of credit's ubiquity in the contemporary Roman economy, as well as Jerry Toner's emphasis on the prevalence of debt and the notion that between 10% and 44% of borrowers defaulted in any given year.[443] The advice in several couplets to accrue savings also sounds simple, though among people so regularly indebted, the possibility of saving may have unrealistic. The Author urges his readers to avoid risk, simple enough advice, but there is more to it: risk presupposes an investment that might lead to either windfall gains or indebtedness. Toner also emphasizes the precariousness of life for non-elites and the importance of a trade for increasing and ensuring one's income.[444] The *Distichs* provide supporting evidence. They also offer a counterpoint to ancient elites' criticism of those who must work in a trade because they are not self-sufficient. The Author's encouragement to learn a trade reflects both his characteristic pragmatism, but also his appeal to wider audience than that of, say, Cicero's *De officiis*. Yet because being poor was not always simply a condition, but could sometimes also be a pose (or lifestyle choice), the Author's apparent targeting of an economically insecure audience may have a literary purpose too: to the elite reader, advice ostensibly for his socio-economic inferiors might feel quaintly simple and homespun, reminiscent of less affluent times.

The advice of the *Distichs* on personal finances—to manage one's spending, to save when possible, to avoid risk, and to be content with what one has— and other topics too could find broad support not only among a wide readership at that time, but indeed for many centuries to follow, as the following chapters show.

---

[442] See especially Sall. *Cat.* 9–13; also Cic. *Verr.* I, especially 4, for a list of Verres' alleged misdeeds, among them ruination of others to his financial benefit.

[443] Toner 2009, 1. On the lived experiences of Roman non-elites, see also MacMullen 1974, Woolf 2006, Morgan 2007, and Knapp 2011.

[444] Similarly, Knapp 2011, 23–33 and 97, draws on the *Carmen Astrologicum* to demonstrate that men of the middling sort worried about debt, unemployment, and underemployment. Knapp 2011, chapter 3, surveys sources for the views of the poor about their condition and, with a nod to Teresa Morgan, uses fables to demonstrate views of the poor on such topics as risk, religion, and friendship.

Part III: **Reception**

6 *Legere et intelligere*: Editions and Commentaries for Schools and Homes

In the afternoon sun, boys sit in rows of uncomfortable wooden benches trying to concentrate on the words of their teacher. Standing at a lectern, he reads aloud the next lesson of the day: "Love your dear parents with a piety not feeble, and don't offend your mother when you want to be good to your father." Glancing down at the copious notes before him, he intones to the boys: "'Feeble.' What do we mean by that? Sluggish. 'Piety' is, of course, affection and fondness. 'Dear parents' are not just fathers; no, Cato here means father *and* mother. And when he says 'father', well, grandfather would suit just as well." He paraphrases the maxim and follows with an illustration of its message from the Bible. The boys then repeat the maxim, impressing it into their minds: tomorrow morning, they will be asked to recite this and many others. The year is 1200 in Iceland. But it could also be 1300 in France, 1400 in Spain, 1500 in Italy, 1600 in England, or even 1800 in America. The maxim is *DC* 3.24, and the notes are the commentary of Remigius. The lesson here is Latin, but similar lessons that used translations of the maxims were taught in most of the proto- and modern European languages, and even when the teacher was not using the *Distichs*, he (and later she) taught lessons influenced by it.

The *Distichs* did not enjoy the reception of, say, the *Aeneid*: they were not translated or transformed by the greatest literary talents in Europe, the new renderings becoming masterpieces in their own right; there is no glittering literary path like that leading from Vergil through Dante and Petrarch to Dryden (and beyond). Instead, this chapter and the one that follows tell of the career of a less starry, though highly marketable text that was the first "real Latin" text read by students from all over Europe for about 900 years. Erasmus was its best-known editor and publicist, yet he apologized for his labors.[445]

The sheer scale of the afterlife of the *Distichs* is well expressed by Infantes:

> Si añadimos las traducciones vernáculas, las citas en todo tipo de obras y autores, su utilización en contextos doctrinales, morales y literarios, las influencias textuales y, además, nos asomamos bibliográficamente al siglo siguiente, la lista es a todos luces inabarcable y los impulses iniciales de investigador se vuelven de inmediato en pesimistas perspectivas. Su nombre evoca un océano de libros y manuscritos que inunda la Europa medieval y re-

---

[445] Erasmus' work with the *Distichs* (and his embarrassment about it) will be discussed further through this chapter.

nacentista, no obstante, entre tan vastas aguas parecen existir dársenas donde in[i]ciar su estudio.[446]

If we include the vernacular translations, quotations in all types of text and authors, their use in educational, moral, and literary contexts, textual influences and, moreover, we take a look at the bibliography of the following century, the list is clearly endless, and the initial impulses of the researcher turn immediately to a feeling of pessimism. Its name calls up an ocean of books and manuscripts that flood medieval and renaissance Europe, though in the midst of such vast waters there seem to be docks from where a study can begin.

Mindful of Infantes and not wishing to overwhelm the reader, I present here merely an overview, albeit a substantial one, of the *Distichs* after the Classical period. My survey is structured around the claim that the long-lasting prominence of the *Distichs* as a text read in classrooms and beyond derives from the fact that they were well suited to successive educational systems and curricula. Their ubiquity appealed to print publishers, and I demonstrate that their adaptability to different types of publication made them especially lucrative.

Using the *Distichs*

Medieval Period

Our earliest evidence for the use of the *Distichs* as a teaching tool appears with Remigius' commentary in the ninth century, though the collection may have been used in schools for several hundred years before that.[447] It was certainly well known at the time by educated individuals: the opening words of the first maxim, *Si deus est animus*, was the commonest *probatio pennae*, the phrase written by a scribe in the margin of a text as he tested a new pen, and is found

---

[446] Infantes 1997, 840. One dock that is eagerly anticipated is Martin Bloomer's forthcoming guide to medieval and Renaissance commentaries and translations of the *Distichs*.

[447] Chase 1922, 4, asserts that it was used in Irish monastic schools in the seventh century, directing the reader to Goldberg 1883, 8, and Schanz 1927, 37, for the evidence. Neither of them, however, supplies it. A possible substantiation for Johnson Chase's claim comes from the fact that the *Proverbia Grecorum*, a collection of brief *sententiae* with a terminus ante quem of 775 CE, has an Irish (not Greek) origin (on which see Brunhölzl 1975, 192). Perhaps there was a tradition of teaching with sentential texts in early medieval Ireland. On the pre-medieval period, see also the brief survey of Hallik 2007, 1–2, and now especially Bloomer 2015 on the survival of the text in late antique Spain.

as early as the sixth or seventh century in a Visigothic manuscript of Augustine's *Enarrationes in Psalmos*.[448]

Our knowledge of education before the end of the Carolingian period is very patchy. We know that lay people in France and Italy may have received some basic instruction from a teacher, but they were educated mostly at home. Education was available in monastic schools, though lay parents might be frustrated by the emphasis on religious, rather than elementary education.[449] The *Distichs* were certainly being read, since they are found in some lists of authors, but it is difficult to know whether there was widespread knowledge of them in schools since we have no evidence of set lists of educational texts.[450] Moving forward in time, it seems that the *Distichs* were finding a place in schools, most likely because they were so well suited to contemporary pedagogical techniques. In the *Colloquia* of Ælfric Bata, the monk and educator of early eleventh-century Britain, a master tells his pupils to learn their set-pieces because "to read books and not to comprehend them, is to neglect them."[451] The line comes from the *Epistula* of the manuscripts of the *Distichs*, and perhaps Ælfric assumed pupils would know the text. The *Distichs* themselves were, as we saw in Chapter 3, well-suited to memorization.

In the post-Carolingian period, lay schools were established, first in Italy where a strong literary culture had persisted through the post-Classical period, and then in France at the end of the eleventh century.[452] While the earliest known manuscripts of the *Distichs*, which date to the ninth century (and perhaps even the eighth), may have been produced for educational purposes or simply as editions for libraries (usually monastic ones), the sudden increase in extant manuscripts from the tenth and eleventh centuries could be explained by the needs of teachers in these schools, who favored pagan texts, perhaps in

---

448 Bischoff 1938, 11, n. 20, refers to the Visigothic manuscript, Autun 107 = *CLA* VI (Lowe 1947), 729, where Lowe calls the Catonian phrase "the medieval scribe's favourite *probatio pennae*." Lutz 1957, 145, n. 57, referring to its frequency, mentions that it appears in the text of a work of Remigius. On *probationes pennae*, see Lindsay 1923, 29–30, and also the references in Lesne 1938, 334, n. 3. According to Robinson 1939, 60, the first verse of *Distichs* book 4 was the second most popular *probatio pennae* in Autun 107.
449 See Riché 1962, 177–178.
450 On the debate over the extent of knowledge of the period, see the summary and bibliography of Hazelton 1957, 160, n. 13, and also Schindel 1983, 431. On surviving reading lists of the Carolingian period, see Glauche 1972, 619–620 and *passim*.
451 On the *Colloquia*, see Lapidge 1982, 100–101; the translation is from p. 103. See also Gwara and Porter 1997.
452 On the growth of lay schools, see Riché 1962, 179–180.

reaction to the clergy's earlier stranglehold on education. That the *Distichs* were among these texts is clear from their inclusion during the eleventh to thirteenth centuries in the reading lists of the German scholar-monk Otloh of St. Emmeram (despite his opposition to teaching from pagan texts),[453] the French cleric Aimericus,[454] the educationalist John of Salisbury, who was active in Britain and France, and Freidank, a didactic poet,[455] and Eberhard (or Evrard), a grammarian, both Germans.[456] The *Distichs* also appeared in the lists of textbooks owned by what is now Gonville and Caius College, Cambridge, and Merton College Grammar School, Oxford.[457] Evidence that the *Distichs* were read in southern Europe, as well as the north, comes from an unlikely source: in fourteenth-century Portugal, king Pedro I prohibited unauthorized instruction of scholars, students, and children outside public places, specifying the *Distichs* among texts that should not be taught.[458]

The teaching of Latin was an essential part of post-Carolingian education: in the eleventh and twelfth centuries, *illitteratus* denoted not an inability to

---

[453] See Bizzarri 2002, 130.
[454] On Aimericus of Angoulême's *De arte lectoria* of 1086, see Manitius 1931, 180–182 and Hazelton 1957, 157, n. 3.
[455] See Brunner 1965, 28.
[456] In Evrard's *Laborinthus* (ll. 603–4) "Cato" is associated with the Latin adjective *catus* and, by extension, the *Distichs*:

> *Semita virtutum catus est Cato, regula morum,*
> *Quem metri brevitas verba polire vetat.*

> Wise Cato is a course in virtues, a pattern of behavior, and the brevity of the meter prevents him from polishing his words.

Faral 1924, whose text I quote here, notes, "On remarquera que, dans son énumération, Évrard caractérise chaque auteur par un adjective, un nom ou un verbe dont la racine fait allitération avec le nom propre." The association appears also in the *Accessus ad auctores* (on which see further below) and the introduction to Remigius' commentary: *a Graeco venit catus, id est ingeniosus*.
[457] MS Cambridge, Gonville and Caius College 385 (early thirteenth century). The reference is from Hunt 1991, 79. The manuscript was given to the college, then known as The Hall of the Annunciation of the Blessed Virgin Mary, in the late fifteenth century. For a full description of the contents, see James 1908, 441–446. Merton College Grammar School bought a "Cato" in 1308–1309 for 2d, on which see Leach 1911, 220.
[458] For a text and discussion of the law, see Martins 1968, 107.

read, but ignorance of Latin.[459] For students of Latin during this period, drills were drawn most often from ethical or moralizing texts, and the *Distichs* were an obvious choice—even though they were pagan.[460] Indeed, non-Christian authors were an important source of medieval ethical instruction,[461] and in this period the *Distichs* further benefited from a narrowing and solidification of Classical texts in the canon.[462] These were included in the twelfth-century anonymous *Accessus ad auctores* (which comprised brief introductions to authors) and in the educator Conrad of Hirsau's *Dialogus super auctores*.

The introduction to the *Distichs* in the *Accessus* reads as follows:

Duo Catones erant Romae, Censorinus Cato et Uticensis Cato. ideo Censorinus dicitur Cato quia bonus iudex erat, et bene et iuste de omnibus iudicabat. ideo autem Uticensis Cato dicitur quia devicit Uticam que est regio in Romano imperio. set Censorinus Cato cum videret iuvenes et puellas in magno errore versari, scripsit hunc libellum ad filium suum, insinuans ei rationem bene vivendi, et per eum docens cunctos homines ut iuste et caste vivant. alii dicunt quod huic libello nomen non ab auctore set a materia sit inditum: catus enim sapiens dicitur. dicitur autem scripsisse ad filium suum, ut eo utiliora collegisse videatur. materia eius sunt precepta bene et caste vivendi. intentio eius est representare nobis qua via tendamus ad veram salutem, et diligenter eam appetamus, et omni studio inquiramus, non ad tempus, set perseveranter. utilitas est hunc librum legentibus ut vitam suam instituere agnoscant. ethice subponitur quia ad utilitatem maxime nititur. premittit itaque prologum in quo nos attentos, dociles, benivolos fieri desiderat. quippe dum dicit 'graviter,' attentos nos reddit. dum vero dicit ubi errorem illum intellexerit, scilicet 'in via morum,' in ipsorum morum consideratione dociles nos reddit; dum autem vocat nos filios, dicens 'filii karissime,' benivolos nos reddit.[463]

There were two Catos at Rome, Cato the Censor and Cato of Utica. Cato the Censor is so named because he was a good judge and he made just decisions about everyone well and justly. On the other hand, Cato of Utica is so called because he conquered Utica, which is an area in the Roman Empire. But when Cato the Censor saw that boys and girls were behaving most poorly, he wrote this little book to his son introducing to him a system for living well, and through it teaching all men to live according to justice and virtue. Some say

---

459 See Riché 1962, 180–181, and Grundmann 1958. For excellent overviews of the *Distichs* in education from the twelfth to the sixteenth centuries, see Thomson and Perraud 1990, 1–48, and Cannon 2016, 159–257.
460 Mettmann 1960, 101, notes that both religious wisdom—from the Bible, especially the Old Testament and the various sources of Solomon's wisdom—and "pagan" wisdom, such as the *Distichs*, informed the development of western gnomic literature.
461 See the general essay of Delhaye 1949.
462 Glauche 1972, 636: "Um 1100 ist der Kanon der Schulautoren insofern abgerundet, als im Bereich der römischen Klassiker, der *aurei auctores* bei Aimeric, hernach keine nennenswerten Neuzugänge erscheinen, bei denen eher eine rückläufige Bewegung zu beobachten ist."
463 The text is from Wheeler 2015, 32–33.

that the name of this little book was given not from the author, but from the material: for a wise man is called 'catus'. Moreover, it is said that he wrote to his son in this manner so that he might be seen to have gathered together rather useful information for him. Its material is instructions for living well and virtuously. Its purpose is to present to us by what route we may come to true wellbeing, and how we may aim for it with attentiveness and we may apply ourselves completely to exploring it, not just in the moment, but sticking with it. The usefulness to those reading this book is that they might recognize how to set their lives on a foundation. It is categorized in ethics because the goal of its strenuous efforts is usefulness. In this way, it puts at the start a prologue in which it expresses the wish that we might become engaged, readily teachable, well disposed. Indeed, when it says 'seriously,' it renders us engaged; but when it tells us where it has understood that errant behavior to reside, that is to say, 'on the path of good behavior,' it renders us teachable as we contemplate that very behavior. Moreover, when it says 'dearest son,' it renders us well disposed.

The *Accessus* to the *Distichs* reveals how the fundamental questions addressed in the Introduction to this book were addressed early: aside from recognizing that the *Distichs* are a collection of common-sense advice, this text also understands that they were not authored by Cato the Elder (or Younger).[464] Yet it sees the *Distichs*, together with the *Epistula* and prologues, as a unified whole. It also points out that the *Distichs* are addressed to girls as well as boys, despite the fact that several maxims are directed to husbands and none to wives.[465]

According to Conrad of Hirsau, students should read Donatus (a grammar) and then move on to the *Distichs* as a first text, before tackling Aesop and Avianus. Only later would they reach the authors favored by Latin teachers today, such as Cicero and Vergil. Conrad also advises that readings of Church texts should be spiced up (his metaphor) with secular texts to drive pupils on.[466]

The *Distichs* also benefited from educational techniques that were in vogue. Texts were expounded by teachers (rather than read and analyzed by students) in a three-stage process that Hugh of St. Victor, in his twelfth-century *Didascalion*, describes:

---

[464] There is a fuller discussion of the *Accessus* in Wheeler 2015, 129–134. While the author of the *Accessus* recognized that Cato might not be the author of the *Distichs*, many others did not: for centuries, they believed the *Distichs* were the work of the wise "Cato", a characterization that led to and was reinforced by the conflation in the medieval period and later of Cato Censorius (or Elder) and Cato Uticensis (or Younger) into one Cato-type, a paragon of wisdom and virtue. On the development of the Cato-type, see Carron 2009.
[465] The maxims directed to husbands are *DC* 1.8, 3.20, 3.23, 3.12, 4.47.
[466] On these texts, see Perraud 1988, 84. On *accessus* in general, see Wheeler 2015, 1–24.

expositio tria continent: litteram, sensum, sententiam. littera est congrua ordinatio dictionum, quod etiam constructionem vocamus. sensus est facilis quaedam et aperta significatio, quam littera prima fronte praefert. sententia est profundior intelligentia, quae nisi expositione vel interpretatione non invenitur. in his ordo est, ut prima litteratura, deinde sensus, deinde sententia inquiratur. quo facto perfecta est expositio.

Exposition has three aspects: the words, the sense, the message. "Words" refers to the appropriate arrangement of words, which we also call "construction." "Sense" is a certain natural and obvious indication of meaning, which the words make literally clear. "Message" is a deeper meaning which comes only from exposition or interpretation. Once this is done, the exposition is complete.

The *Distichs*—brief, simple maxims—were perfectly suited to this process, and the schoolroom scene sketched at the start of this chapter illustrates its second stage.[467] By the end of the thirteenth century, the *Distichs* were being taught at schools across most of Europe and were firmly ensconced in the curriculum as one of the first Latin readers.[468]

Christian texts became more popular in curricula of the fourteenth century,[469] but the *Distichs*, along with Aesop and Avianus, held on.[470] They remained a primary reader in the rise of Humanism and the classical revival in Italy in the century that followed; at the same time, formal education was reaffirmed in Northern Europe by the Brethren of the Common Life, a Catholic group Dutch in origin, of which Erasmus was a member. One result of these two movements was a more regularized pattern of learning across Europe, in which the *Distichs* were a key text. For example, in England, of thirteen reading lists that date to the fifteenth century, the *Distichs* are missing from only five, and they are the only Roman-period text included.[471] Reading lists across Europe were probably similar, since we know that English lists tended to originate on the continent.

---

467 Justice 2015, 76–77, wryly notes that medieval commentaries made the *Distichs*, a collection that aimed at "a contented selfishness," mean whatever the commentator (and his readers) wanted them to mean.
468 For example, we know that the *Distichs* were being read in the thirteenth century, even in the smallest schools. See Beets 1885, 6.
469 On broad educational trends of the fourteenth and fifteenth centuries, see generally Bonaventure 1961.
470 For a brief and convenient overview of the *Distichs*' popularity at the time of Chaucer, see Brusendorff 1929.
471 The list comes from Bonaventure 1961, 7–8. The *Distichs* usually appear incomplete, however, as the Parvus or Magnus Cato. In the late medieval period in Germany, the *Cato moralis*, as it was most commonly known, was also split into two: the *Cato parvus* was for youngest children, while *Cato metricus* was reserved for more advanced pupils. See Schindel 1983, 443.

Most texts on those lists were in verse, presumably because they were easy for both teachers and students in a program that emphasized memorization.[472] Children had to memorize texts and their explanations as homework, with morning classes devoted to recital.[473] It is possible that this is how Dante first encountered the collection.[474]

The maxims were included in florilegia, including the twelfth-century *Flores auctorum* of the *Florilegium Morale Oxoniense* (Ms. Bodl. 633). The popularity of such collections has sometimes worked to undermine the integrity and survival of their source texts, and the *Distichs* might have run this risk: in the *Flores auctorum* we find single lines of the *Distichs* excerpted from their couplets and even two lines drawn from different couplets but presented together.[475] The collection's use in schools and the ready availability of copies seem, however, to have helped ensure the relative stability of the text. Translations of the *Distichs* were soon included in the new vernacular florilegia of the high medieval period, which helped to ensure their inclusion in the wisdom traditions—and therefore minds—of post-Classical and post-Latin Europe.[476]

---

[472] Bonaventure 1961, 15.
[473] On the *lectio* and "les methodes d'enseignement," see Paré et al. 1933, 109–137.
[474] On Dante, his presumed exposure to the *Distichs* through education, and contemporary use and attitudes towards the *Distichs*, see Gianferrari 2017.
[475] For example,

Cum dubia incertis versetur vita periculis, (DC 1.33.1)
In morte alterius spem tu tibi ponere noli. (DC 1.19.2)

Since life is uncertain and filled with unknowable dangers,
Do not rest your hopes on someone else's death.

is followed by

Cum dubia et fragilis sit nobis vita tributa, (DC 1.19.1)
Pro lucro tibi pone diem quicumque laboras. (DC 1.33.2)

The life we are given is fickle and frail,
Consider each day a bonus, whatever it may bring.

[476] On the *Distichs* in florilegia, see Talbot 1956, 15–20. Excerpts from Everard's translation of the *Distichs* were included, for example, in the late twelfth or early thirteenth-century *Enseignements de Robert de Ho* (on which see Young 1901). Everard's translation is discussed further in the final chapter.

Renaissance

The Renaissance saw an overhaul of the medieval curriculum, though the *Distichs* were still found in curricula after a basic grammar and were now usually accompanied by the *Auctores*.[477] Their use continued in schools in Italy, in Germany, where they were listed in school ordinances across the country,[478] in England, where Edward VI apparently knew the collection by heart at the age of nine,[479] and in Spain and Portugal, probably thanks to the editions of the educationalist Lebrijo.[480] From there the *Distichs* spread to Latin America. In 1577, Mexican Jesuits included the *Distichs* in their curriculum (behind only Aesop), which in turn led to the printing of editions in Mexico—a sensible step since copies of the *Distichs* were being shipped to the new world by the hundreds: in 1600 one ship, the Espíritu Santo, which was bound for the West Indies, had on board 248 copies.[481] The text may also have been brought south to Peru, where the Andean lord Guaman Poma de Ayala, the author of a 1615 Andean history that equated the Incas and Romans temporally and culturally, mentions that in his culture's past, "boys and children were instructed and taught with chastisement as Cato of Rome did, who provided good examples and taught his children, so they were well brought up."[482]

The Renaissance saw only slight changes in pedagogical technique: according to the popular sixteenth-century English grammar of Brinsley, the teacher

---

[477] On the *Distichs* in this period, especially in Italy, see Schindel 1983, 448, Grendler 1989, 178-198, and Gehl 1993, 107-127. Gehl 2008 is a study of the production and sale of educational texts in early modern Italy Europe that is posted online at http://www.humanismforsale.org/text/, accessed 5/18/2022; the *Distichs* feature prominently in several chapters.

[478] Brunken 1987, 555-556. On use of the *Distichs* in German schools after the Reformation, see Sowards 1985, xlv.

[479] Baldwin 1944, 206-207. Edward was able later to quote from the *Distichs* to his former tutor. On the *Distichs* in Britain in this period, see Baldwin 1944, 595-606. Alongside the *Distichs*, students also read Culmannus' *Sententiae Pueriles*, which aped the *Distichs*' format.

[480] Taylor 2004, xiv-xix. On school education in Spain in this period, see Bartolomé 1993, 195-214. Generally on the survival of the *Distichs* in Spain, see Civil 1996.

[481] The first text was called "Fabulas"—probably those of Aesop—and was followed by the *Distichs*, Cicero, Vergil, Ovid, Gregory Nazianzus, Jerome, Ambrose, and Verinus, as well as "Marcial purgado". See Taylor 1999, 81, referring to Osorio Romero 1980, 96-97. The reference to the Espíritu Santo comes from Civil 1996, 258.

[482] The quotation comes from Guaman Poma's *Nueva Crónica* (Murra et al. 1987, 59), translated by MacCormack 2007, 63. MacCormack mentions that while Guaman Poma includes the name of Cicero, Josephus, and others in his chronicle, he is unlikely to have read them. He may, however, have read the *Distichs*, given its wide distribution across Europe, including Spain.

read a text aloud, construed and parsed it, and then translated it; pupils were supposed to memorize it and perform the same tasks without the text.[483] At this time, second year pupils at elite schools such as Eton and Winchester spent weekdays and Sunday studying rules of grammar and construing Aesop, with Saturday dedicated to repetition of and examination on four maxims of the *Distichs*.[484] The *Distichs* were also being used in a similar curriculum in universities: at Jean Sturm's Strasbourg, France's College de Guyenne, and at the Spanish Universidad Menor de Burgo de Osma.[485]

During this time, the *Distichs* were championed as an aid to learning Latin by several important educators and thinkers, including Melanchthon[486] and Luther, who asserted that the *Distichs*, along with Aesop's *Fables*, were good teaching material for those who declined anything else and that they held better insights into wisdom than did the monks' faulty pronouncements on God.[487] It was thanks to Luther's influence that the *Distichs* were the first Latin text read in sixteenth-century Denmark and Norway.[488] Since the *Distichs* seem to have been palatable to even the most reluctant learners, they were included in the *Ratio studiorum*, a common European curriculum. They received a further boost from the efforts of Montaigne in France and Simón Abril in Spain, among others, to persuade the European elites that Latin was the essential professional language for would-be clerics, administrators, politicians, and courtiers. As knowledge of Latin became a status symbol for the educated elite—the Renais-

---

483 Baldwin 1944, 581–591.
484 Leach 1915, 302–304.
485 On the *Distichs* in Spain at this time, see Infantes 1997, 846, who refers to Bartolomé 1993, 211–212. On the *Distichs* in university courses in Spain (and probably elsewhere), see Bartolomé 1993, 211.
486 On Melanchthon, the Reformation humanist educator who was close to Luther, see Brunken 1987, 555. He expresses his enthusiasm for the collection in the *Corpus Reformatorum* 10, 101.
487 Luther, *Genesisvorlesung* 9.12-16: "And so it is sufficient if to those wishing to learn nothing else, you give them the poetry of Cato, or Aesop, whom I consider the better teacher of correct behavior" (*Itaque satis fuerit, si nihil aliud volentibus discere proponas Catonis carmen, aut Aesopum, quem meliorem morum magistrum esse iudico*); the reference is from Brunner 1965, 28. Luther goes on to recommend Cicero for older readers. Luther, WA 46:670: "Die Barfuesser Monche sind viel blinder gewesen denn die Heiden...Es ist eben das erkentnis Gottes, das auch die Heiden gehabt haben, ja, Cato ist viel besser gewesen, der gesaget hat: *Si deus est animus, nobis ut carmina dicunt etc.*" (The barefoot monks were, then, far blinder than the pagans...It is precisely their understanding of God that the pagans had too; indeed, Cato was much better, who said: If good sense is divine, as the poets tell us etc.) I owe the reference to Springer 2011, 9; the text is from Knaake 1883, 670.
488 On use of the *Distichs* in sixteenth-century Scandinavia, see Fink-Jensen 2021, 18.

sance *litterati*—the language was increasingly taught in schools and universities. And not just to the elites: in his autobiography, the humanist scholar Thomas Platter, who tells of his childhood spent in poverty, recalls that the *Distichs* were one of the favored texts in charity schools.[489] Adults who wanted to better themselves also discovered their advantages, and as we will see, editions were produced to help them too.[490]

Early Modern Period

The increase in numbers of self-educators and their reliance on printed texts parallels a change in pedagogical technique in the sixteenth and seventeenth centuries. The French educator Cordier recognized that when students learned *viva voce*, they failed to develop good orthography and script (which were increasingly important as bureaucracies grew), and so recommended that they have access to print editions of texts and complete written exercises.[491] A rare example of these comes from the 1600 schoolwork of Simon VII, Count of Lippe-Detmold, complete with corrections from his teacher. After writing out a couplet from the *Distichs*, Simon parsed each word in detail, referenced relevant syntactical points from his grammar, and finally paraphrased the couplet phrase by phrase before translating it into German and thus demonstrating he had learned the couplet's moral lesson. From the syntax exercise, we know that Simon was referencing Melanchthon's *Praeceptoris Germaniae*, a grammar that would remain popular into the nineteenth century, not just in Germany, but in Scandinavia too.[492]

---

[489] Brunken 1987, 555.
[490] Bartolomé 1993, 203–205, who also stresses the *Distichs*'s popularity with Jesuit educators. According to Mead 1939, 37, in the fifteenth century 360 editions of Donatus and 280 of the *Doctrinale* of Alexander de Villa Dei (a twelfth-century grammar) were produced, but only 135 of the *Distichs*. There are fewer editions of the *Distichs*, a text, than Donatus and the *Doctrinale*, which were grammars. But what is important is that more editions of the *Distichs* were produced in that century than of any other Latin text.
[491] Baldwin 1944, 599.
[492] Fink 1991, 70–76 presents and analyzes the exercise, which is preserved in Landesbibliothek MS 131. Baldwin 1944, 600–606, describes similar exercises in England at the time, which were known as "posing Cato," and presents the following example:

> Q. What thing ought to be chiefe unto us?
> The worship of God.
> Q. *Da sententiam.*

Other aids too may have helped teachers and students with such exercises. For example, Hoole's parallel text and English translation (resembling a Loeb edition) was needed, according to Hoole, because the shortage of such versions had made them "excessive dear." It was aimed at young boys, as well as university students with rusty Latin, rural schoolmasters lacking the necessary skills to teach, adults wanting to brush up their Latin, and adult self-teachers. Sixteen editions were produced from 1659 until 1749.[493]

Despite the increased importance of the written word, many children were still being taught also to speak Latin. For example, in Colonial American grammar schools, Latin courses began with a grammar and then moved to a text, which might be the *Distichs*.[494]

Modern Period

The modern period has seen the popularity of the *Distichs* wane. As the educational system broadened gradually in the nineteenth and twentieth centuries to include further branches of learning, so the learning of Latin declined, and far fewer children have learned from the *Distichs*. As new editions, commentaries, and translations of the *Distichs* have fallen in number—and those of the *Aeneid*, *Catilinarian Orations*, etc. have risen—so the collection has fallen even further from favor. Boas' edition is now out of print, and for many years the only text in print has languished in the *Minor Latin Poets* volumes of the Loeb Classical Library, an ignominious fate for formerly one of the most widely read Latin texts.

R. *Cultus Dei praecipuus.*
Q. *Da carmen.*
R. *Si Deus est animus nobis,* &c.
Or alternatively, pupil may be asked:
What Verses in *Cato* have you, to prove that the worship of God must be chiefly regarded?
A. *Si Deus est animus.*
What against sleepinesse and idlenesse? A. *Plus vigila semper,* &c.

493 Green 2009, 161, who mentions the text in connection with adult self-education.
494 Other choices included the *Confabulatiunculae Pueriles* or the colloquies of Cordier, both of which aimed at improving speaking in Latin. See Monroe 1911, 119.

Editions

The ubiquity of the *Distichs* in curricula across Europe for many centuries guaranteed a constant market for editions of the text. The impetus for new editions came from successive educational movements, but also from the realization that the *Distichs* could be packaged along with other improving texts for schools or in inexpensive anthologies for adults.

Manuscript editions of the *Distichs* used in schools had textual companions, including grammars, word lists, and texts from a range of Classical and post-Classical authors.[495] The poems of Eugenius Toletanus (seventh century) are found so often with the *Distichs* that one of them was once mistakenly believed to be the fifth book of the collection.[496] The number of manuscript editions of the *Distichs* increases dramatically in the thirteenth century when the text is fully entrenched in the educational system along with a core group of texts known collectively as the *Liber Catonianus*.[497] This package of set texts could be copied, recopied, and distributed among schools as a reader, and indeed we find it in France and England and later spreading to Germany.[498] It could be adapted to new curricula and tastes: in the ninth century it comprised just the *Distichs* and Avianus' fables, and it was probably enthusiasm among educators for a classroom-ready reader that led to the addition of Theodulus' *Eclogue*, Maximian's *Elegies*, Statius' *Achilleid*, and the *Ilias Latina* in the thirteenth century. When the last became unpopular with users, it was replaced by Claudian's *Rape of Proserpina*, and the resulting Classical and late Roman group of six was sometimes known as the *sex auctores*.[499] The collection adapted to the changing tastes of the fourteenth century, as Classical and late Roman texts gave way to more recent Christian works. The updated collection of eight, now sometimes

---

[495] BN 7537A, for example, contains part of Donatus, an anonymous work *De doctrina rudium*, and a Latin dictionary.

[496] Among the many manuscripts to contain both the *Distichs* and Eugenius are P^α, P^y, and H.

[497] The text group is also sometimes known as the *Liber Catonis*. Since the *Distichs* by themselves are occasionally known by this name, I use *Liber Catonianus* for the group in order to avoid confusion.

[498] According to Baldzuhn 2007–2009, 105–106, earlier educational manuscripts of the *Liber Catonianus* are found in England and France; but from the fourteenth century, as text-based learning spreads, German editions appear.

[499] While Statius dates to perhaps roughly the same time as the author of the *Distichs*, Avianus and Claudian were writers of the fifth century, Maximianus of the sixth, and Theodulus of perhaps the ninth or tenth. On the dating of Theodulus, see Green 1980, 114; for an introduction and translation, see Cook 2003. A good example of this version of the *Liber Catonianus* is Codex Vaticanus Barberinus Lat. VIII.41 (Bb), an excellent example of the *traditio Barberina*.

known as the *auctores octo morales*, still contained the *Distichs* and Theodulus, which were now joined by the Ovidian *Facetus* (on which see more below), *De contemptu mundi*, Matthew of Vendome's *Tobias*, Alan of Lille's *Liber parabolarum*, Gualterus Anglicus' *Fabulae Aesopi*, and the *Floretus*.[500] While according to some this new version may have been less popular in the classroom, with the manuscripts often going to libraries rather than into the hands of teachers,[501] nevertheless, it remained well known: there are approximately sixty extant manuscripts of the *Liber Catonianus*, and medieval writers were influenced by it, including Chaucer.[502] Less well known is a parallel reader for the Anglo-Saxon curriculum that comprised the *Distichs*, Juvencus' *libri Evangeliorum quattor*, Prudentius' *Psychomachia*, Prosper's *Epigrammata*, Sedulius' *Carmen Paschale*, Alcimus Avitus' *Poema de Mosaicae historiae gestis*, and Arator's *Historia Apostolica*, all Christian texts of the fourth to sixth centuries.[503]

Both readers demonstrate that the *Distichs* could be included in collections of both pagan and Christian texts, and their broad acceptability helped to guarantee their continued popularity.[504] Indeed between 1470 and 1500, 180 editions

---

[500] On all three stages in the *Liber Catonianus*' evolution, see Clogan 1982, McKenzie 2008, 235, and Baldzuhn 2007–2009, 90–100. See also the early work of Boas 1914, especially pp. 37–39. There is a recent English translation of the *Auctores octo* with very brief introduction to each text by Pepin 1999, and some of the texts are also translated in Thomson and Perraud 1990. Ovid's *Remedia amoris* is sometimes added. On Alan of Lille's *Liber parabolarum*, see Hunt 2005. On the *De contemptu mundi*, see Taylor 2004. The *Floretus* is a work of Christian dogma. Gualterus Anglicus rendered Aesop's *Fables* into distichs. On the inclusion and exclusion in the Renaissance of the Theodulus, see Schindel 1983, 451.
[501] Baldzuhn 2007–2009, 103.
[502] On Chaucer's use of the *Liber Catonianus* and the *Distichs* respectively, see Pratt 1947, and Hazelton 1956, xxiii–xxxvii, and Connolly (forthcoming). According to Clogan 1982, 206, the importance of the *Liber* lies in the fact that it "was designed and used for more than mere language training. The pedagogic techniques as found in the selection and commentaries on the *Sex Auctores*, representing five literary genres [practical ethics, eclogue, fable, elegy, epic], show the combination of grammar and morality, the study of the *artes* as a study of ethics, and the integration of the *ethica* in the *Septennium* of the liberal arts in the thirteenth and fourteenth centuries."
[503] On this collection, see Lapidge 1996, 3.
[504] Another common companion of the *Distichs* is Serenus Sammonicus, the second/third-century CE author of *De medicina praecepta*, a collection of popular remedies written in hexameter. The *Distichs*, Prosper, and Serenus Sammonicus, among others, are found in manuscripts K, Q, and BN 2773. An edition of Serenus Sammonicus is available in Baehrens 1881; on this author, see Champlin 1981. Despite Ovid's reputation as a sometimes racy poet, the repeated inclusion of his *Remedia amoris* with the *Distichs* is not surprising: the style is easy, and the poem is didactic and (at first sight) serious. It is found along with *Ars amatoria* 3 and works by

of the *Distichs* appeared.⁵⁰⁵ Educators and teachers favored the *Distichs* as a text well-suited to contemporary teaching techniques that taught valuable moral lessons; with the advent of printed books, publishers also favored the *Distichs* as a ready source of revenue. Caxton had already printed his *Dictes and Sayinges of the Philosophers* and *Moral Proverbs of Christine de Pisan* when he turned to the *Distichs*, producing his *Book callyd Cathon* in 1483. It was the popularity of the first text, which he would reprint in two further editions, that may have then turned his attention to the *Distichs*.⁵⁰⁶

Erasmus also produced editions of the *Distichs*. In his editions of 1514 and 1528, the *Distichs* appear with the *Liber Senecae*; in a posthumous volume of 1547, another edition of the *Distichs* appears alone.⁵⁰⁷ Comprising a text and commentary, his editions were so popular that they were even used in Spain after condemnation of his work in the Counter-Reformation (i.e., roughly the 1540s through the 1640s), and were the most widely used in Europe for two centuries. It is to Erasmus that we owe the title *Disticha Catonis*, since he recognized the collection's couplets as its distinctive feature. Editions by Scaliger (who ascribed the collection to "Dionysius Cato") and Scriverius followed, in 1598 and 1635 respectively.⁵⁰⁸

---

other authors in BN 7575; in BN 8246 with the *Tobias*, Aesop, and Macer (this is probably Floridus Macer, to whom was attributed Odo de Meung's *De viribus herbarum*; Aemilius Macer's work is no longer extant); in BN 8460 with Theodulus, *De contemptu mundi*, Aesop, and the *Tobias* again; and in BN 8246A.

505 The figures are from Hermannsson 1958, xxvi, who refers to the list in Nève 1926, 77–118, of fifteenth-century editions and translations of the *Distichs* into various languages. The numbers of manuscripts and printed books containing editions and translations of the *Distichs* may be understated because of incomplete catalogues and the fact that scholastic material is not always included in inventories, according to Munk Olsen 1991, 61.

506 *The Dictes and Sayinges of the Philosophers* was first published in 1477 and was the first dated, printed book in England. It is an English translation of Guillaume de Thionville's French rendering of the Latin version of the eleventh-century Arabic *Mukhtar al-hikam wa mahasin al-kalim* by Abū al-Wafā' Mubashshir ibn Fātik. *The Moral Proverbs of Christine de Pisan* was printed in 1478. Caxton's edition of the *Distichs* may not be the earliest in print: the British Library owns the one existing leaf of an Italian edition, possibly dating to 1480. See British Library 1980, 297. A German edition of the *Parvus Cato* (i.e., just the *Epistula* and *Breves Sententiae*), however, pre-dates them both: it dates to 1475. See British Library 1980, 300.

507 Erasmus' interest in paraenetic texts and proverbs, especially those of ancient origin, is also reflected in his composition of *Adagia*.

508 Scaliger's Latin text of the *Distichs* was accompanied by the *Sententiae* of Publilius Syrus, the *Proverbia Senecae*, Planudis' Greek rendering of the *Distichs*, and other sayings also in Greek. Scriverius' edition comprised the *Distichs*, a brief *expositio* on the *Distichs* by Erasmus,

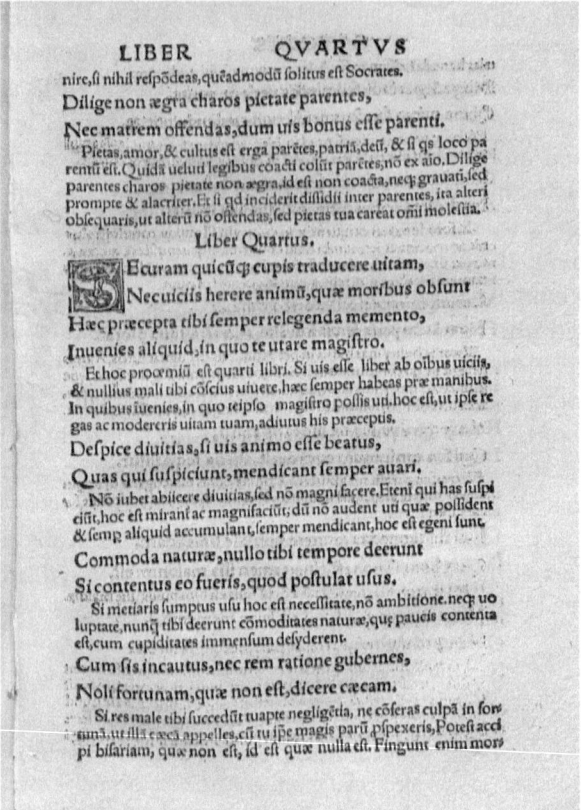

Fig. 3: Erasmus' commentary on *DC* 3.24. Bayerische Staatsbibliothek München, 4 L.impr.c.n.mss. 108, fol. 14r, urn:nbn:de:bvb:12-bsb00011397-1. *Catonis p[rae]cepta moralia: recognita atq[ue] interpretata ab Erasmo Roterodamo. Mimi Publiani. Septem sapientu[m] illustres sententi[a]e. Institutio homi[ni]s christiani uersib. hexametris. per Erasm. Roterodamum Isocratis Par[a]enesis ad Demonicum Rudolpho Agricola interprete, recognita per Martinum Dropium*, printed 1515. Image courtesy of Bayerische Staatsbibliothek, München.

While Erasmus' volumes answered the need for a classroom-friendly edition suited to teachers, Arntzenius' editions of 1735 and 1754 were a more scholarly enterprise. In these first full scholarly editions (titled *Dionysii Catonis Disticha de Moribus*), which ran to more than 700 pages, the text was followed by copi-

---

Planudis' Greek translation, Scaliger's Syrus in Greek, and a *dissertatio* on the *Distichs* by Marcus Zverius Boxhorn; he later produced a revised edition.

ous notes, scholia, and metaphrases from Scaliger, Erasmus, Planudes, and others, and by three *dissertationes* or essays.

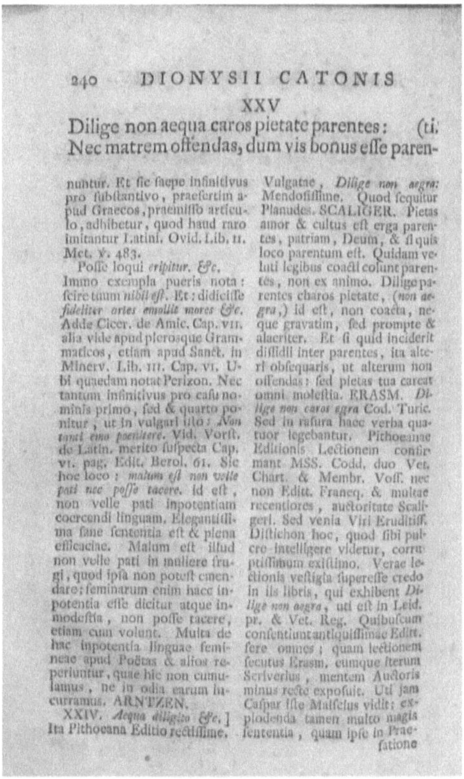

240 DIONYSII CATONIS

XXV

Dilige non aequa caros pietate parentes: (ti.
Nec matrem offendas, dum vis bonus eſſe paren-

nuntur. Et ſic ſaepe infinitivus pro ſubſtantivo, praeſertim apud Graecos, praemiſſo articulo, adhibetur, quod haud raro imitantur Latini. Ovid. Lib. II. Met. ✠. 483.

Poſſe loqui *eripitur*. *&c.* Immo exempla pueris nota: ſcire tuum *nihil eſt*. Et: didiciſſe *fideliter artes emollit mores &c.* Adde Cicer. de Amic. Cap. VII. alia vide apud pleroſque Grammaticos, etiam apud Sanct. in Minerv. Lib. III. Cap. VI. Ubi quaedam notat Perizon. Nec tantum infinitivus pro caſu nominis primo, ſed & quarto ponitur, ut in vulgari illo: *Non tanti emo poenitere*. Vid. Vorſt. de Latin. merito ſuſpecta Cap. VI. pag. Edit. Berol. 61. Sic hoc loco: *malum eſt non velle pati nec poſſe tacere*. Id eſt, non velle pati inpotentiam coercendi linguam. Elegantiſſima ſane ſententia eſt & plena efficaciae. Malum eſt illud non velle pati in muliere frugi, quod ipſa non poteſt emendare; feminarum enim haec inpotentia eſſe dicitur atque inmodeſtia, non poſſe tacere, etiam cum volunt. Multa de hac inpotentia linguae femineae apud Poëtas & alios reperiuntur, quae hic non cumulamus, ne in odia earum incurramus. ARNTZEN.

XXIV. *Aequa diligito &c.*] Ita Pithoeana Editio rectiſſime. Vulgatae, *Dilige non aegra:* Mendoſiſſime. Quod ſequitur Planudes. SCALIGER. Pietas amor & cultus eſt erga parentes, patriam, Deum, & ſi quis loco parentum eſt. Quidam veluti legibus coacti colunt parentes, non ex animo. Dilige parentes charos pietate, (*non aegra*,) id eſt, non coacta, neque gravatim, ſed prompte & alacriter. Et ſi quid inciderit diſſidii inter parentes, ita alteri obſequaris, ut alterum non offendas: ſed pietas tua careat omni moleſtia. ERASM. *Dilige non caros egra* Cod. Turic. Sed in raſura haec verba quatuor legebantur. Pithoeanae Editionis Lectionem confirmant MSS. Codd. duo Vet. Chart. & Membr. Voſſ. nec non Editt. Franeq. & multae recentiores, auctoritate Scaligeri. Sed venia Viri Eruditiſſ. Diſtichon hoc, quod ſibi pulcre intelligere videtur, corruptiſſimum exiſtimo. Verae lectionis veſtigia ſupereſſe credo in iis libris, qui exhibent *Dilige non aegra*, uti eſt in Leid. pr. & Vet. Reg. Quibuſcum conſentiunt antiquiſſimae Editt. fere omnes; quam lectionem ſecutus Eraſm. eumque iterum Scriverius, mentem Auctoris minus recte expoſuit. Uti jam Caſpar iſte Malſcius vidit: explodenda tamen multo magis ſententia, quam ipſe in Praefatione

Fig. 4: Select text and commentary on *DC* 3.24[25] from Arntzenius' edition. General Collection. Beinecke Rare Book and Manuscript Library, Yale University, Gnc36 735B, p. 240. *Dionysii Catonis Disticha de moribus ad filium. Cum notis integris Scaligeri, Barthii, Daumii; scholiis atque animadversionibus selectis Erasmi, Opitii, Wachii; et metaphrasi graeca Planudis et Scaligeri. Quibus accedunt Boxhornii dissertatio, et Henrici Cannegieteri rescripta Boxhornio de Catone; nec non Joan. Hild. Withofii dissertationes binae de distichorum auctore et vera illorum lectione. Recensuit, suasque adnotationes addidit Otto Arntzenius*, published 1754. Image courtesy of Beinecke Rare Book and Manuscript Library, Yale University.

While Arntzenius' text superseded that of Erasmus, his editions were probably less accessible. Hauthal's edition of 1869, however, was "cheap and commodious," and ran to only 118 pages of text, while still including an introductory textual history, notes, and an apparatus criticus.[509]

Hauthal's book, however, was an anachronism: there was no longer demand for inexpensive scholarly editions of the *Distichs*, since they had disappeared from school curricula.[510] When Baehrens edited the text, he included it in his 1881 Teubner of *Poetae Latini Minores*. The *Distichs* no longer merited their own volume, even though Baehrens' edition was an important one: it was the first to take into account the newly discovered codex Veronensis 163 (known as A), whose text belongs to *traditio* Φ.[511] The Duffs' edition for the Loeb Classical Library followed in 1934 and remains to date the most accessible printed text in school and university libraries. Boas' 1952 work is the most recent and best of the scholarly editions, and for him, the *Distichs* did deserve their own volume.[512] His edition too is a product of its own time: an expensive, highly specialized work for an audience of scholars, not teachers and pupils.[513] It is now out of print.[514]

Commentaries

When the *Distichs* were so popular that they were taught in every Latin classroom, teachers wanted not only texts, but also commentaries to save them time on preparation, supplement their knowledge, and provide authoritative help. Today canny academics and teachers develop their successful courses into lucrative textbooks with accompanying teacher's companions; earlier scholars and teachers too recognized the utility and appeal of including notes with texts of the *Distichs*. It is the inclusion of these notes that makes the *Distichs* in medi-

---

[509] Ellis 1871, 321. By "commodious," he presumably means handy (according to a now-outdated definition). Brunken 1987, 552, has a record of an 1838 translation titled *Gebete, Lieder und Gedichte. Angehängt ist eine Übersetzung der Sittensprüche Cato's*, published under the pseudonym F. F. Franke, which he attributes to Hauthal.
[510] Ellis 1871, 321, notes in his review that the *Distichs* is "a book now little known."
[511] On *traditio* Φ, see chapter 1.
[512] The edition was published posthumously: Boas died just three months before its planned date of completion. Johannes Botschuyver completed it from Boas' copious working papers (Boas 1952, v).
[513] The volume, which was published in the Netherlands, cost $10.75 or £4.4s in 1952. Today's equivalents are very roughly $85 or £60.
[514] Balbo 2021 reproduces the text of Boas, making it once more accessible, though the brief space available to him precluded inclusion of an apparatus criticus.

eval and early modern manuscripts and books look so different from modern editions.

Commentaries have a long pedigree. They are most likely the offshoot of scholia, of which the earliest known examples are those on Homer, dating to the fourth or fifth century BCE. Over time, scholia written in the margins of texts became so extensive that they were gathered together into commentaries, which accompanied the text.[515] Ancient commentaries seem to have had (deliberately) limited audiences. For example, Donatus' commentary on Vergil's *Aeneid* was the work of a *grammaticus* (teacher of boys aged eleven and older) aimed at inexperienced *grammatici*, while Servius' commentary on the same text (which draws heavily on Donatus) was aimed at pupils (as well as teachers, presumably). The latter, with its focus on language and greater attention to syntax and figures of speech than simple glosses, seems to have been pitched to the pupils of the *grammaticus*.[516] As we will see, commentaries on the *Distichs*, which were aimed at teachers rather than their pupils, are more flexible, offering material for teaching to a wide range of ages.

Manuscripts of the *Distichs* could contain commentaries, in addition to glosses.[517] Earlier manuscripts contained a few marginal comments, but later on, introductions were added to the commentaries, which begin to resemble Servius' prescription: "In the exposition of writers these things should be borne in mind: the life of the poet, the title of the work, the attributes of the poem, the purpose of the writer, the number of books, the order of the books, and an explication."[518] Over time, this supplementary material became so substantial that it was hard to place around the text and so was consolidated into the forms most familiar to us: the "footnote" commentary (with comments at the bottom

---

[515] Wilson 1967 and Zetzel 1975 explore the history of ancient collections of scholia; Dickey 2007, 3–17, provides an indispensable introduction to the Greek tradition of commentaries. The term commentary (*commentarius*) was already in use by the early seventh century: Isidore refers to it at *Etymologiae* 6.8.5. Copeland 2012 surveys the medieval history of the commentary, noting the variations of terminology and definitions.

[516] Kaster 1997, 161 and 169–170.

[517] On the commentaries and glosses on the *Distichs*, see especially Hazelton 1957. For a list of manuscripts that contain glosses, see Hazelton 1956, lxvi–lxvii. On the layout of manuscripts of the *Liber Catonianus*, which contained the *Distichs* and was arranged to accommodate glosses and commentaries, see Baldzuhn 2007–2009, 106–119.

[518] Serv. *Aen.* 1.pr.: *In exponendis auctoribus haec consideranda sunt: poetae vita, titulus operis, qualitas carminis, scribentis intentio, numerus librorum, ordo librorum, explanatio.* Such introductions would have helped teachers: according to Hazelton 1956, xiv, in the late medieval period, the teacher's lectio was preceded by a general discussion of the authorship of the text, its educational purpose, and its place in the curriculum.

of the text page) or the "endnote" commentary (which follows on from the end of the text). The most important commentaries on the *Disticks* illustrate these developments.

The first of our extant commentaries is that of Remigius of Auxerre, a ninth-century *grammaticus*, though only fragments survive.[519] Author of the *Regulae puerorum*, a series of glosses on Donatus' grammar, Remigius was perhaps drawn to the *Disticks* because they followed Donatus in standard curricula; with his work on Donatus and the *Disticks*, Remigius dominated the market in commentaries on early school texts, though others followed in the ninth century with their own glosses and commentaries, suggesting that the market was large.[520] Like Servius, Remigius begins by tackling the "who, what, where, with what aids, why, how, when" (*quis, quid, ubi, quibus auxiliis, cur, quomodo, quando*) of the *Disticks*—as he enjoins his readers to do with any text—and states (our earliest source to do so) that neither of the famous Catos is the author. In the marginal commentary that follows, Remigius ignores for the most part style and any difficult syntax (not that there is much of this in the *Disticks*),[521] and instead attends to basic syntax and morphology (such as syncopated forms), stylistic devices, etymology, orthography (including archaic forms), and unusual words, as well as providing paraphrases and explanations.[522] The resulting commentary is basic, but Remigius livens it up with anecdotes, *sententiae*, and proverbs, especially those of Solomon.[523]

Though the commentary is ascribed to Remigius, he was not the sole author of what is transmitted; rather it is a collaborative work. First, it draws largely (so Remigius admits) from the lecture notes of his teacher, Heiric of Auxerre.[524]

---

[519] The commentary survives in sixteen manuscripts, which are listed in Alcamesi 2007, 148. Parts of the commentary have been published by Mancini 1902 and Manitius 1913. Alcamesi 2007, who concentrates on the manuscripts' variant readings for the commentary, provides the most accessible introduction to the various formats in which Remigius' work was presented.

[520] On Remigius' competitors, see Alcamesi 2007, 149. Remigius states in his commentary: *intentio istius auctoris est reprehendere mores hominum, qui tunc temporis credebant se posse per inanem gloriam pervenire*; while pedagogy may have encouraged Remigius in his own work on the *Disticks*, his own reputation and renown may have played a role.

[521] Ruhe 1968, 16–32, notes the commentary's lack of sophistication.

[522] The unusual words include *blaesos* in *DC* 3.4, *loquax* in *DC* 3.19, and *libellum repudii* in *DC* 3.12, which Remigius explains as a *carta dimissoria* (see Mancini 1902, 185–190 and 372–373).

[523] Mancini 1902, 369–372, who uses the term "ravvivita" (p. 369).

[524] Alcamesi 2007, 147, who goes so far as to call the commentary "a collection of lecture notes." Heiric was the author of a florilegium and collection of proverbs and maxims, which he took in turn from the lectures of his teachers (on which see Talbot 1956, 12). The work of these

Then, in addition, a small number of English manuscripts transmit Anglo-Saxon glosses along with Remigius (and thus reveal how, at that time, glosses and commentaries were treated as works to be supplemented and personalized by others).[525] One manuscript even contains letters that were written above individual words in the text to indicate the order in which they are to be read and were probably added by the schoolteacher owner or reader of the manuscript.[526] Finally, some of the glosses are in fact variant readings and probably the work of scribes.[527] Remigius' commentary was repeatedly reformatted to suit users' tastes: in some manuscripts, the glosses are mostly interlinear and the comments marginal, while in others the glosses are moved to the margins; in yet others the glosses and comments are presented consecutively without the text.[528] The broad scope of Remigius' commentary and its potential for reformatting explain the lack of competition for five centuries and its inclusion in some of the Erasmus/Scaliger editions.[529] The simplicity of Remigius' commentary suited medieval teachers interested in getting across to their pupils the basic messages of the *Distichs*. Yet with Humanism's new curricula, a renewed interest in the Latin language, and the revival of high-level scholarship, the need grew for more sophisticated classroom aids.[530]

---

three generations of scholars in the field of paraenetic literature is testament to its fundamental importance in medieval education and literary culture.
525 Alcamesi 2007, especially 168.
526 Alcamesi 2007, 161–162.
527 See Alcamesi 2007, 164. This fact reveals that scribes were drawing from multiple texts of the *Distichs*.
528 See Hazelton 1956, xvii, and Alcamesi 2007, 148.
529 Other collections of glosses were produced during this period, including the *Glossulae Catoni*, which were repeatedly printed through the sixteenth century, as well as several traditions of glosses that appeared in Anglo-Saxon manuscripts of the tenth and eleventh centuries. On these, see Lapidge 1982 and 1996, 460–465. On the later incorporation of Remigius' commentary into later editions, see Ruggerini 1988, 250–251. Glosses on Cato were circulating independently of the text in tenth-century England, according to a list of books contained in a manuscript of the time; see Leach 1915, 95.
530 Commentaries of the intervening period include the commentaries in Bodley Canonici Latin Classical MS 72 and Lincoln Cathedral MS 132, which are discussed in Hazelton 1956, and those of Gisalbertus de Bergamo, Philippus de Bergamo, and Robertus de Euremodio (on whom see Boas 1930–1940). Later, Scaliger's edition (see above) would contain commentary of varying sorts by a veritable who's who of the Reformation scholarly world, including Marcus Zuerius Boxhorn, Caspar Barth, Christian Daumius, Martin Opitz, Gilbertus Wachius, and Johann Hildebrand Withof. For details on these and other commentaries, see Manitius 1923, 714, Hunt 1994, and *Gesamtkatalog* (GK) 1925, cols. 6298–6317.

Erasmus' commentary reflects the new spirit of the time: he is concerned with the correctness of the text (though his methods and rigor do not match today's expectations) and with the ancient context of the maxims. Gone are the laborious commentaries that moralize and refer to Christian teachings: Erasmus' new-style commentary quotes ancient authorities and interprets the collection from an ancient standpoint.[531] Erasmus is ambivalent about the *Distichs*. On the one hand, his commentary was (whether he liked it or not) one of his most-read works, and he believed that the text's pure Latinity reflected its pure morality, which for him justified its use in Humanist education.[532] Yet on the other, he had to defend his decision to produce the commentary: even his own publisher, Guillaume Budé, condemned the *Distichs* as a triviality.[533] When Erasmus himself described them as mere trifles (*minutas nugas*), he was probably applying a term that others used. But he justified his work on it as taking little time (*dieculam*), while contributing to education: "I will not shrink from tasks even more despicable than my so much despised Petty Cato, provided I can see that they help to promote liberal studies" (*Non refugiam etiam illo con-*

---

[531] On the content and purpose of Erasmus' commentary, see Hazelton 1957, 171, and Perraud 1988, 87–91, referring to *Correspondence* 4: 106. In the preface to his 1514 edition, Erasmus himself pointed out differences, saying of his predecessors de Euremodio and de Bergamo, "Of these men, the one orates without any wit at all, a man more childish than childhood itself, while the other philosophizes though entirely without skill" (*quorum alter insulsissime rhetoricatur, homo ipsa infantior infantia, alter ineptissime philosophatur*).
[532] Perraud 1988, 84–85.
[533] The letter from Budé to Erasmus is number 403. The translation, presented here for convenience, is in Mynors & Thomson 1974, vol. 3, pp. 279–280:

> I could wish that you were yourself as well satisfied as I am with these grand and noble subjects; for now I want to speak to you seriously. To be perfectly frank, I often exclaim with astonishment when I see you misusing such eloquence and such intellectual gifts on the trivialities in which you sometimes give your mind a rest, as if the right course were not to leave ordinary and unimportant topics to men with minds of similar caliber. But you devote the same attention to subjects of the first rank and the third, and even lower, and could justly be criticized on two counts: first, that you step in and deprive lesser men of moderate attainments of their chance to shine, and second, that you waste your own divine fire on things unworthy of it; besides which you reduce the value men set on distinction of both language and thought—something like what the ancients used to call 'lèse-majesté.'

temptissimo Catunculo contemptiora, modo sensero ad provehenda bona studia conducere).[534]

Erasmus' commentary is masterful in its brevity. For example, on *DC* 3.24, he explains:

> *Pietas, amor, & cultus est erga parentes, patriam, Deum, & siquis loco parentum est: quidem veluti legibus coacti colunt parentes non ex animo. Dilige parentes charos pietate non aegra, id est, non coacte neque gravatim, sed prompte & alacriter. Et si quid inciderit diffidii inter parentes, ita alteri obsequaris, ut alterum non offendas, sed pietas tua careat omni molestia.*

> There is piety, love, and reverence towards parents, one's country, God, and anyone who stands in the role of parents: certain people honor their parents, as if compelled by law, not from their hearts. 'Love your dear parents with a piety not feeble,' that is, not under duress and not as a burden, but spontaneously and enthusiastically. And if there should be any mistrust between parents, show respect to the one without giving offense to the other, though your piety should be not at all troublesome.

Erasmus takes *parentes* as standing not only for one's mother and father, but also guardian, country, and God. Traditionalist Christians could feel comfortable with the reference to God, while Humanists appreciated the historically sensitive reference to the *patria*.

Many publishing houses across much of Europe produced their own version of Erasmus' text and commentary, accompanied by texts of Pseudo-Ausonius, the *Liber Senecae*, the *Dicta Septem Sapientum*, and sayings of prominent Christians, among others, again with Erasmus' commentaries. Yet the title pages of

---

534 The quotation and claim that the *Distichs* work took little time come from Erasmus, letter 421. In letter 480, Erasmus acknowledges the *Distichs* as a relatively unimportant work. Yet of the *Distichs* and similarly insignificant texts, he writes,

> *In quibus et minus video nugacitatis et aliquanto plus fructus quam in magnificis illis, ut ipsis videtur, argumentis. Denique qui unum hoc spectat, non ut sese ostentet sed ut prosit, huic non perinde refert in quam splendidis versetur atque in quam utilibus. Non refugiam etiam illo contemptissimo Catunculo contemptiora, modo sensero ad provehenda bona studia conducere.*

> I see in them less frivolity and somewhat more profit than in those themes which the professional philosophers find so pre-eminent. Finally, the man whose sole object is not to advertise himself but to help other people, asks not so much Is it grand, my chosen field? as Is it useful? I will not shrink from tasks even more despicable than my so much despised Petty Cato, provided I can see that they help to promote liberal studies.

The translation is from Mynors & Thomson 1974, vol. 3, pp. 480–481.

these volumes advertise prominently the text of the *Distichs* and the fact that the accompanying commentary was by Erasmus, confirming that readers were most interested in the *Distichs* and wanted commentary by a distinguished authority; the addition of the other texts produced a user-friendly packet of Humanist educational materials.[535]

The move to print and the continued popularity of Erasmus' commentary signal another shift in commentaries on the *Distichs*: they now seem directed more at pupils than at teachers. A comparison between a manuscript page containing Remigius' commentary and a printed page containing Erasmus' illustrates the shift. Remigius' commentary overwhelms: with the text centered in the page, the commentary fills any remaining space—above lines, in margins, and not always next to the relevant maxims. To make room for all the glosses, explanations, and citations, the script is small and full of abbreviations. Of course, with a little practice it becomes easier to navigate through the page, but the format is better suited to a teacher than to a student. Erasmus' comments, however, appear beneath the relevant maxim; they lack citations and contain fewer (and easier) abbreviations, and so guide the reader more easily through the text.[536] This book was appropriate for both schoolchildren and adult learners, as well as teachers, in a classroom that now privileged reading and writing over listening and remembering.

Erasmus favored brief commentary, and indeed this format is found in most of his editions. But publishers apparently knew of markets for variations on the format. Some potential readers wanted more help for their students, and so a 1547 edition supplements Erasmus with the glosses, comments, and French translations of educator Mathurin Cordier (also discussed below). The discussion of *DC* 3.24 now reads:

> Cole parentes non ut coactus, sed ex animo. Et si quid inciderit inter eos dissidii, ita alteri obsequaris, ut alterum non offendas, sed pietas tua careat omni molestia. dilige, ama, reverare, cole, porte reverence pietate non aegra non gravatim: animo non coacto, voluntate non ficta, du bon cueur [sic], non fainctement, parentes utrumque parentem, a ton pere et la mere charos quibus es charus, vel qui te charum habent, qui t'ayment cherement nec et non offendas adferas incommodum, minus sis obediens, & ne offence point. matrem ta mere dum quando vis studes esse bonus obedire parenti patri, quant tu veulx te monstrer obeyssant a ton pere, hoc est, non obsis uni, dum alteri favebis, sed aeque unum atque alterum dilige.

---

535 On the appearance of glosses in the *Liber Catonianus*, which reflect the educational use of the collection in fourteenth and fifteenth-century England, see Hunt 1991, 66–79.

536 The 1515 edition can be viewed at http://daten.digitale-sammlungen.de/~db/0001/bsb 00013360/image_27, accessed 5/18/2022.

Honor your parents not as if compelled, but from the heart. And if some disagreement should occur between them, show obedience to the one without giving offense to the other, but let your piety be completely untroublesome. 'Esteem': love, respect, honor, *show respect*; 'with a piety not feeble': not unwillingly: not with a heart compelled, not with insincere willingness, of good heart, *not feebly*; 'parents': either parent, to your father and mother; 'dear': to whom you are dear or those who hold you dear, *who love you dearly*; 'and don't offend': inflict discomfort, be less obedient, *and do not offend*. 'Mother': *your mother*; 'when': at the time; 'you want': you are keen; 'to be good' obey; 'to your parent': to your father, *when you want to demonstrate obedience to your father*, that is, don't be obstructive to one, when you support the other, but love one and the other equally.

There were also readers who wanted translations into other languages, and so we find Richard Taverner's English and Planudes' Greek, with and without Erasmus' commentary. Introductory essays seem also to have been popular. Some customers wanted Erasmus' text, but not his commentary, preferring to use someone else's or read just a translation, while others wanted his text and comments, but only those on the *Breves Sententiae*.[537] In short, publishers put out whatever combination of text, commentary and translation might sell. And

---

[537] Another commentary blends Latin paraphrase with explanation and renders the result in verse. The fifteenth-century *Cathoniana confectio* of Alonso de Cartagena contains a commentary written in goliardic meter—a curious choice for a man of the cloth—that divides the text into twelve chapters. A text, discussion, and translation are available in Taylor 2004, who comments that the gloom of the *De contemptu mundi* that accompanies the commentary seems to have infected Cartagena's take on the maxims (xii-xiii). The commentary on *DC* 3.24, with Taylor's translation, reads as follows:

> Patrem matrem dilige regulas uibentes.
> Male servant plurimi eos offendentes
> set tu semper imitans plene diligentes
> dilige non egra caros pietate parentes.
> Amor iste senciat nichil detrimenti
> nam quid prodest alterum tantum diligenti
> Ne sit ergo sócio vinculo nescienti?
> Non matrem ofendas dum vis bônus esse parenti.

Love your father and mothers who obey the rules; most people keep them [parents] ill, offending them; but you, always imitating the most loving, love your dear parents with healthy piety. This love thinks no harm for what does it benefit one who loves another so much that he is not an unthinking bind to his companion? Do not offend your mother if you want to be good to your parent.

they did sell: between 1515 and 1859, over 160 appeared.[538] In 1506, bookshops in Barcelona together had 63 copies of the *Distichs* for sale, and in 1538 one bookshop was offering multiple copies of at least three different versions of the text.[539] While some may have sniffed at Erasmus' decision to work with the *Distichs*, he, along with some publishers, undestood the recognition to be gained and money to be made from serving the readers of one of the most popular Latin texts in Europe.

So far, I have considered the educational and financial motivations for producing commentaries, but spiritual motivations were also at play. The fact that the *Distichs* are not a Christian text could have undermined its popularity among educators; its suitability to changing pedagogical techniques, however, secured its position in curricula. While there were a few attempts to Christianize the text, commentaries and glosses were the more common media through which the maxims were aligned with Christian teaching.[540] One thirteenth-century commentary put the *Distichs* in a Christian context by connecting the mother and father of *DC* 3.24 with the Church and God, respectively. Yet the collection is, of course, pagan.[541] Aside from Christian interpretations, we also find commentators attempting to connect each book with its own virtue.[542]

---

538 A list of the editions, many of which are available electronically, is easily accessible at through WorldCat: http://www.worldcat.org/search?q=erasmus+catonis&fq=&se=yr&sd=asc&dblist=638&qt=first_page, accessed 5/18/2022.

539 Civil 1996, 257.

540 On the issue of Christianization, see especially Hazelton 1957. According to Hazelton (p. 161, n. 20), Baehrens and others believed that *DC* 2.2a (*An di sint caelumque regant, ne quaere doceri*) was the maxim's original first line, while *DC* 2.2.1 (*Mitte archana dei caelumque inquirere quid sit*) was an interpolation. From careful consideration of the ages of the various *traditiones* and manuscripts, Boas 1952, 98, however, believes that *DC* 2.2a is a scribe's summary of 2.2.1. The Christian line is therefore an interpolation of the original "pagan" version.

541 Following the construal, the commentator notes, "For it is written, 'Honor your father and mother so that you may be longer upon the earth'," (*Scriptum est enim: 'Honora patrem et matrem ut sis lengevus super terram'*), which is Exodus 20.12. A little later he adds, "According to certain men, the maxim is speaking about the father in a spiritual sense thus: 'Do not offend your mother,' that is, the Holy Church, 'when you want to be good to your father,' that is, to God the Father" (*Secundum quosdam, de patrem spirituali legitur sic: Non offendas matrem, id est sanctam ecclesiam, dum vis bonus esse patrem, id est deo patri.*). Hazelton 1957, 169, supplies the Biblical reference. He also points out that the quoted verses come from the *Cato Novus* 3.25, on which see below.

542 Hazelton 1957, 167, n. 41: "All of the thirteenth- and fourteenth-century commentaries I have examined contain in the prefatory remarks a statement that the book deals with the *quattuor virtutes cardinales* or *principales*."

We should not imagine that every medieval reader read the *Distichs* through the prism of Christianity. Granted, children were given Christian interpretations, such as that just quoted. But the maxims themselves were unchanged, and they and their Roman predecessors appealed to many of the same instincts. Indeed, even maxims such as *DC* 1.26 and 3.3 ("If someone talks like a friend, but isn't one at heart, / You do the same: then your deceit will deceive his" and "When brought to court as witness, though your shame has never yet been compromised, / As far as you can, hide the wrongdoing of a friend", respectively), which we might hesitate to present to children, remained part of the medieval and early modern text. That there was tolerance or even support for them is explained by Hazelton's comments that "the Middle Ages were populated largely by the bustling sons of the pagan Cato."[543] Hazelton imagines the *Distichs* appealing to medieval merchants—and, I would add, their children. These readers, who were more comfortable in the commercial world than the spiritual, probably appreciated the controversial maxims, as well as the Christian commentary. After all, later parodies, which I discuss in the next chapter, would poke fun at the maxims themselves, not Christian commentaries.[544]

The commentary of Erasmus is one of the last major contributions to explicating the *Distichs*. Since the eighteenth century, the *Distichs* have lost their educational role and become a minor curiosity, and the simplicity or purity (depending on one's inclination towards the text) of their language and unsophisticated content do not lend themselves to modern philological commentary, whose purpose is to help the reader (sometimes a student, more often a scholar) better appreciate the literary qualities, content, and cultural context of a work.[545]

---

[543] Hazelton 1957, 171–172.
[544] Hazelton 1957, 172. He also points out that: "In studying Cato [the young] were established in a tradition; for preserved in the *Distichs* and in the *glossulae* that interpreted them are the ideas, values, sentiments, and attitudes that flowed out of antiquity into the Christian medieval world" (p. 173).
[545] Though Balbo 2021 includes brief and partial notes on the maxims, supplying variously discussion of themes, connections to other maxims in the collections, and *exempla* and *fontes* on the model of and often drawing from Boas 1952.

7 Translations and Transformations

Every edition and commentary mentioned in the previous chapter (with the exception of the few comments of Cordier) was written in Latin. Latin was the language of research and instruction in universities for centuries and an important language of diplomacy and administration. Yet repeated attempts had to be made to keep Latin as the language of teaching and conversation in schools, a fact that points to a long and gradual decline in its influence, as it gave way to vernacular languages in more and more areas of life.[546] In the fifteenth century, children were already losing their facility with Latin: a couple of manuscripts of the time contain texts of the *Distichs* along with *expositiones* in German, which seem to be translations of Latin paraphrases of the maxims that were presumably intended to aid comprehension. In the classroom, translations of the maxims themselves were not used; instead, use of the vernacular was restricted to explanations and paraphrases that elucidated meaning or syntax.[547] Though cribs were avoided (for the same reasons that many Latin teachers today disapprove of facing translations), translations did exist. In education, at least, the primacy of Latin held on, as these vernacular aids (perhaps counterintuitively) attest.[548] But in the sixteenth and seventeenth centuries, the situation changed. The Humanist movement brought not only an interest in the vernacular languages for their own sake, but also an effort to provide education to artisans and people in commerce.[549] A multitude of translators—and their publishers—stepped forward to help, and with their translations helped to bolster the *Distichs* in a world that was increasingly forsaking Latin.

The number of translations of the *Distichs* is immense. In a recent study of the role of the *Distichs* in education, an annotated list of German translations from the 1200s to the 1600s fills fully seventy-three pages.[550] Given the availabil-

---

[546] On the history of Latin in schools, see Grubmüller 1983, 382–383.
[547] On the German manuscripts, see Grubmüller 1983, 384. On the avoidance of translations and use of the vernacular languages to explain grammar, see Grubmüller 1983, 387–390.
[548] Grubmüller 1983, 381–384, notes that some translations (not of the *Distichs*) catered to "Bemühungen um Popularisierung von Fachwissen ohne institutionellen Kontakt mit Schule und Universität" (p. 381). On vernacular aids reflecting Latin's primacy, see also Grubmüller 1983, 391.
[549] Grubmüller 1983, 392.
[550] Baldzuhn 2009, 922–995.

ity of this detailed list and several others, and because to reproduce them would be lengthy and redundant, the survey that follows is brief.[551]

Translations

Medieval

Pre-modern translations of the *Distichs* (and of other texts too) may seem odd to us. We are accustomed to "overt" translations: those that offer themselves as aids to understanding a text in its original language and thus aim to transfer its form, syntax, and expressions to another language. "Covert" translations, however, which are presented as self-standing texts and the products of their language's culture, have historically been the norm.[552] The divergences between covert translations and their sources reveal the cultural conceptions that informed them, such as Christianity, in contrast to the *Distichs*'s paganism.[553] So *urbanus* ("urbane, sophisticated") in *DC* 3.19 becomes "hovelich" (literally

---

[551] There are lists, some of which are annotated, in Brunner 1968, British Library 1980, and Gesamtkatalog 1925. There are also language-specific surveys. For German (which is especially well-served), see Zarncke 1852, Kesting 1978, Harmening 1970, Brunken 1987, 549–552, and Haag 2005. For Dutch, see Beets 1885. For Italian, see Roos 1984, 232–244. For French, see Stengel 1886 and Ulrich 1895, 1904a, 1904b, and 1904c (Stengel and Ulrich's texts are not the best, but they are readily available), Ruhe 1968, and Schulze-Busacker 1989. For English, there is a useful list of early editions and translations into English in Brüggemann 1797, s.v. "Dionysius Cato"; Early English Books Online contains many translations. On Spanish translations, see Pietsch 1902, Infantes 1997, Alvar and Lucía Megías 2002, 245–249, Bizzarri 2002, and Gago Jover 2003.
[552] The terms come from House 1997, 29–30.
[553] Haag 2005, 148ff. So, for example, *DC* 1.4, "Do not you tear yourself down—fight back! / No one should be at odds with himself" (*Sperne repugnando tibi tu contrarius esse: / Conveniet nulli, qui secum dissidet ipse*), is gently Christianized in the early fourteenth-century German translation found in Zwettl, Klosterbibliothek, Codex 357, fol. 89ra–98vb:

Dv salt in deheiner zit
wieder dich selben haben strit,
wand wizze got es missezimt,
Swer wider sich selben zoren nimt.

Haag 2005, 149, translates into modern German: "Du sollst zu keiner Zeit mit dir selbst in Widerstreit sein, denn es ist—weiß Gott!—unangemessen, wenn jemand gegen sich selbst zornig wird" ("You should at no time be in conflict with yourself, for it is—God knows!—inappropriate when a person becomes angry with himself").

"courtly") in a fourteenth-century German translation,[554] and Venus in *DC* 4.10 (*Cum te detineat Veneris damnosa voluptas...* "When Passion's harmful pleasure grips you...") is made abstract in Elie of Winchester's twelfth-century French: "Si tu ne te puez garder chastement..." (literally, "If you cannot preserve yourself modestly..."). Covert translations also deviate from their source's syntax and morphology, meter, and especially their length.[555] A survey of the translations of one maxim, which are collected in the Appendix, reveals that earlier translations frequently have four lines, sometimes even six, for the Latin's two.[556]

Our earliest known and extant translation of the *Distichs* forms the bulk of a tenth-century compilation of wisdom in Anglo-Saxon prose.[557] As befits a self-standing collection, the translation style of the Old English *Dicts of Cato* is covert, inspired by the Latin, rather than bound by it: the result is a series of variations, Anglo-Saxon in language and outlook, on Latin themes.[558] *DC* 2.1, for example, is rendered:

> *Si potes, ignotis etiam prodesse memento;*
> *Utilius regno est meritis adquirere amicos.*

> If you can, remember to help strangers:
> Attracting friends by kindness is more beneficial than power.

> Help æigðer gea cuðen gea uncuðen, þær þu muge;
> uncuð hware hwa oðres beðurfe.

> Help both known and unknown, where you may;
> (it) is uncertain where one will have need of another.[559]

---

554 Haag 2005, 149. The source is again Zwettl, Klosterbibliothek, Codex 357, fol. 89ra–98vb.
555 See Haag 2005, 150, on syntactical and metrical differences.
556 Of course, some covert translations are more covert than others. According to Morawski 1923, ix, who is describing early and therefore covert translations, "On peut classer les *translations* en trois groupes: les exercices s'écoliers, généralement dépourvus de valeur littéraire; les essais de vulgarisation qui ne s'astreignent pas à une fidélité rigoureuse, quoi qu'ils suivent encore d'assez près le texte latin; enfin, les adaptations et imitations qui s'éloignent beaucoup de l'original et nous transposent dans la société du moyen âge." (The reference comes from Ruhe 1968, 233.)
557 The translation is tenth century, but appears in manuscripts dating one or two centuries later. It contains eighty-six maxims drawn from the *Distichs*, Alcuin, and Anglo-Saxon collections. The editions in Brunner 1965 and Cox 1972 use slightly different orthographical conventions.
558 According to Brunner 1968, 113, "The translator has adapted the Latin to the exigencies of Anglo-Saxon society and often reinterprets the Latin distich, adding his own original moral or even misinterpreting the Latin."
559 *Dicts* 24. The translation is from Brunner 1965.

The first line of the Anglo-Saxon corresponds to the Latin first line; the second, however, is the author's own justification. Gone is the notion of putting friends before power: the Anglo-Saxon warns that help may be needed from anyone.[560] This was not a translation to be read alongside the Latin or to be used as an aid to understanding it, and indeed some maxims were rendered in paraphrases that even changed the sentiment of the original.[561] In Iceland too, where quotations from the *Distichs* are found as early as the twelfth century in grammars and sagas, a popular translation called the *Hugsvinnsmál* (*The Speech of the Wise One*) was read in its own right. This thirteenth-century translation—or, better, paraphrase—resembles a native Eddic poem and uses the traditional Old Norse didactic meter, the ljóðaháttr; it also mixes the Roman sentiments of the *Distichs* with Christian elements and even notions from Old Norse wisdom.[562] Both the Anglo-Saxon and Icelandic translators seem to have been familiar with Remigius' commentary, reminding us of the remarkable spread across cultures of a small number of early glosses and commentaries.[563]

---

560 Brunner 1965, 153: "The Anglo-Saxon gives a very general paraphrase of the first line of the Latin and then adds his own idea as to the motivation, one rather different and more selfish than that in the Latin. The Anglo-Saxon is on a more primitive level where virtue is inspired by showing it as a definite material asset rather than by saying that it has its own reward." Cox 1972, 36–38, explains that the divergences from the Latin original may derive in part from the translator's use of a text accompanied by Latin paraphrases and glosses.
561 See for example the rendering of *DC* 1.16 (*Multorum cum facta senex et dicta recenses, / Fac tibi succurrant, iuvenis quae feceris ipse*; "When as an old man you criticize what others say and do, / Remember what you did in youth") in *Dicts* 29: "When you see a younger, less wise and less wealthy person than yourself, think then how often one overcomes something, after having previously been overcome by it. As the old proverb says, 'now it is the young man's opportunity, now another's.'" The translation is from Cavill 1999, 65.
562 The *Distichs* were included in Icelandic curricula early: they were quoted in two grammars of the twelfth century, and the earliest text, from the fourteenth century, is already accompanied with glosses. See Ruggerini 1988, 221. They were quoted in the thirteenth-century *Riddarasögur* and *Katerine saga* (see Ruggerini 1988, 224 and 234). Forty-two manuscripts of the *Hugsvinnsmál* survive (though most of these date considerably later). For the text and notes, see Gering 1907, Hermannsson 1958, 63–83, and Tuvestrand 1977. Generally on the translation, see Evans 1993. Gering's numbering system remains useful. See also Hermannsson 1958 on the context of a barely existent educational system and the incomplete spread of Christianity even two centuries after its arrival. On the interrelationship between the *Hugsvinnsmál* and the *Distichs*, see especially Larrington 1993, 108–117, and McKinnell 2014, 59–75.
563 According to Cox 1972, 36 ff., and Ruggerini 1988, the Anglo-Saxon and Icelandic translators knew Remigius. Some scholars have suggested that the *Distichs* were an influence on the *Hávamál*, another early Icelandic poem, though Larrington 1993, 97–108, has convincingly overturned that notion.

The Anglo-Saxon renderings, while loose, are still in couplets. Their Anglo-Norman successors hew closer to the sense of the Latin, but abandon its form, a practice we see followed across the proto-Romance languages. For example, three Anglo-Norman translations of the twelfth century—by Everard le moine (who may be Everard of Kirkham), Elie of Winchester, and an unknown author— each translate the couplets of the *Distichs* into six-line verses that follow different rhyming patterns.[564]

The geographical limits of Norman culture in France probably explain why the Anglo-Norman translations exerted no influence on translations from the mainland; the dialectical differences that characterize the history of the French language also played a role: contemporary translations from Lorraine and Provence differ from each other in expression and vocabulary and are markedly different from the Anglo-Norman trio.[565] The existence of these early translations in multiple dialects attests to the spread of the *Distichs* across France and to the widespread need in classrooms for translations that could supplement texts, glosses, and commentaries.[566]

Adam de Suel's translation of the mid-thirteenth century deviates from the model of linguistically isolated translations: it was one of the most popular in the medieval period, despite the greater diversity of the translation market, and it was also one of the most influential. It was also well-timed: by the end of the thirteenth century, the *Distichs* had become more firmly entrenched in school curricula, and demand for translations had grown. De Suel renders the *Distichs* in pairs of brief rhyming couplets, producing a translation whose length roughly equals that of the Latin. His vocabulary and syntax are simple, also like his

---

[564] Brunner 1968, 114, believes Everard le moine to be Everard of Kirkham; on his translation, see Ginguené 1971 and, for a full text, Lincy 1846, 359–375. For the text of Elie of Winchester's translation, see Stengel 1886. The translation was the model for later versions in Middle English, and the fact that it appears earlier without the Latin text may point to its occasional availability as a stand-alone aid. On its influence on later Middle English translations, see Wright 1846, 123–129, Goldberg 1883, Stengel 1886, and Brunner 1968, 124. Hunt 1994 has a text and discussion of the anonymous translation. A contemporary collection inspired by the *Distichs* is the Anglo-Saxon *Durham Proverbs*, on which see Kessler 2008, chap. 5, and Arngart 1956.

[565] On the separateness of the Anglo-Norman translations, see Ruhe 1968, 233. Similarities in contemporary translations may derive from contemporary modes of translation: at certain times Latin words tend to be translated with particular words in the target language, according to Kesting 1975, 171.

[566] On the Old Lorrain prose translation, see Ulrich 1895, who also supplies a text; on the Old Provençal translation, Meyer's fragments (1896) were quickly superseded by the fuller text of Tobler 1897. Meyer 1896, 101, points out that the form of hexasyllabic rhyming couplets is often found in medieval Provençal didactic poetry.

source, and while his work is a paraphrase rather than a close translation, it communicates well the general message of each maxim. The judicious balance between covert and overt translation and the simplicity of his translation appealed to a wide audience, both in France and beyond. Respect for de Suel's work was such that translations from his work seem to have been as acceptable to educators in other languages as translations directly from the Latin. The market for translations of the *Distichs* (sometimes packaged with texts, commentary, etc.) was apparently so lucrative that copyists, and later print publishers, recognized the benefit of using de Suel's name to sell their product.

Adaptations of de Suel's translation came in various forms. Early manuscripts preserve it in a number of French dialects; a re-worked version appeared in 1300 under the name of Macé de Troies, without reference to de Suel; a copyist of a later French translation even inserted lines from de Suel as a supplement.[567] Such was its ubiquity that later copies regularly omitted de Suel's name, though the fact that he rendered some of the *Breves Sententiae* with French sayings may have contributed to a feeling that the translation was not his unique artistic property.[568] Perhaps more remarkable is that it influenced other translations so quickly: already Jean de Paris' translation of ca. 1260 drew heavily on it.[569]

Elsewhere on the Continent, our earliest Italian translations are educational, but they are the work of pupils, not educators. The first, written in Old Venetian prose and dating to 1258, is more paraphrase than translation. It may be school exercise, since the translation of *DC* 3.24, for example, is divided into small chunks over six lines.[570] Another Old Venetian translation is also divided

---

[567] There is an edition of the translation in Ulrich 1904c, who also discusses the use of various dialects. On Macé de Troies' reworking, see Meyer 1886.

[568] On the popularity of the translation and lack of attribution to de Suel, see Ruhe 1968, 148 and 165–172. Ruhe supplies examples of *breves sententiae* rendered with French sayings (pp. 161–165).

[569] Ulrich 1904c supplies a text of the translation by Jean de Paris (also known as Jean du Chastelet). Of the second French translation, in MS Darmstadt 2640, Hunt 1980 has a discussion; the translations of individual maxims in this translation are sometimes accompanied by a brief paraphrase. The earliest Dutch version (1283) is a translation from Italian; charmingly, it addresses not only a son, but also a daughter. On this translation, see Beets 1885, 23 and 53. On a 1480 Dutch translation from the French, see most recently Buuren, Lie, and Orbán 1998.

[570] There is a brief discussion and text of this translation in Tobler 1883. There is further discussion in Brunner 1968, 121, who suggests that it is a school exercise, and in Roos 1984, 232–233.

into small chunks, this time of no more than four words, and the Latin text that accompanies it is split into corresponding words and phrases.[571]

Our earliest Spanish translation was not an educational aid: it translates only some of the maxims (and these are not presented in order), and its author announces in a preface that his recreation of the ancient text is "un vademecum de cortesía cristianizada" ("a vademecum of Christianized etiquette").[572] The various versions of the German thirteenth-century so-called Rumpfübersetzung (literally a partial translation) also appear to be stand-alone texts.[573] These presented renderings of about one hundred maxims arranged thematically in pairs of rhyming couplets, and with some versions including native German *sententiae*, the result was a German-language wisdom collection that appears to have circulated among a secular audience.[574]

Planudes' translation into Greek is the longest-published. Written in the late thirteenth or early fourteenth century, it was frequently included in editions of the *Distichs* from the fifteenth century, including those of Scaliger in the sixteenth century and even Arntzenius in the eighteenth. Its popularity stems from its language: for readers in the East, this was the first translation of the *Distichs* and the only one available in the medieval period, and it aided them in learning Latin; for their Western counterparts, Planudes' Classicizing translation enabled a text that taught them Latin also to teach them Greek. Its frequent inclusion with texts, glosses, and comments broadened its appeal, especially as the teaching of Greek became more popular. The fact that it alone of all the translations was rendered in discrete hexameter couplets reflects the depth of Planudes' Classical education and explains its popularity for educators, especially Humanists.[575]

---

[571] On this translation, see also Tobler 1883, who notes (p. 4) that the Latin text is sometimes interspersed with brief explanatory additions in Latin and is sometimes changed, with the translation reflecting the change.

[572] On this thirteenth-century anonymous translation, see the discussions in Pietsch 1902, 19–31, Alvar and Lucía Megías 2002, 245–247, and Bizzarri 2002, 288, who puts this translation in the context of courtesy poems. A number of early Spanish translations are presented and discussed in Pérez Gómez 1964.

[573] The eleventh-century translation of Notker Labeo, now lost, pre-dates these. According to Brunner 1968, 102, it was probably a prose translation. A group of unrelated translations that are "oberdeutsch" and "niederdeutsch" follow, on which see Ruhe 1968, 233.

[574] For the texts, see Zarncke 1852. The references are *R-Hei²* (= Heidelberg, Universitätsbibliothek, Cod. pal. germ. 341, 71va-75rb) and *R-Gen* (= Genf-Cologny, Bibliotheca Bodmeriana, Cod. Bodmer 72, 34vb-38rb). On the audience, see Baldzuhn 2007–2009, 139.

[575] On Planudes' translation, see especially Boas 1931 and most recently Ortoleva 1992. Interestingly, Planudes seems to imply that he views the *Epistula* and *Breves Sententiae* as later

The late medieval period witnessed an explosion in the number of translations of the *Distichs* thanks to the expansion of formal education and the persistence of regional dialects. The stand-alone German Rumpfübersetzung gave way to a slew of related Gesamtübersetzungen (complete translations), as well as other unrelated translations, that appeared over the fourteenth and fifteenth centuries. Most were accompanied by the Latin, and these educational dual language editions later appeared in print. Those without a text remained only in manuscripts: the work of subsequently adding the Latin (and possibly comments too) seems to have made them less desirable to print publishers.[576]

The lack of development among translations into French in the fourteenth and fifteenth centuries demonstrates that de Suel's work had satisfied the needs of the French educational community. There are only two other well-known translations of this period: the first, by Jean Lefèvre, is heavily dependent on de Suel and also on de Paris, but it reorders the maxims by theme and cannily repackages them as a work of courtly advice. The adjustments served Lefèvre well, as his translation survives in more than thirty manuscripts. The second, which purports to be the work of a Jehan Akeyman, is in turn simply a heavily plagiarized version of Lefèvre.[577]

Translations of the *Distichs* into Spanish during this period, however, abound, and reflect several important contemporary trends in translation. In addition to translations for the classroom, that by Martín García Payazuelo,

---

additions. See also Opelt 1986, 181–191, who notes that while the translation is Christianizing, it is nevertheless influenced by Homer, Hesiod, and Classical Greek writers. Evidence for the translation's circulation around the Eastern Mediterranean comes from manuscripts found at Athens, Ioannina (now in the Vatican), and Athos (Opelt 1986, 184–185); for its circulation in the West, there are numerous manuscripts of the translation, sometimes included with Latin texts and commentaries (Opelt 1986, 182–184).

576 There are three strands among the Gesamtübersetzungen; the earliest translation from each of these appears in the Appendix. For discussion of the development of the Gesamtübersetzungen, see Harmening 1970, 347–348, and Haag 2005, 147–154. The other unrelated translations include the "niederrheinischer (mittelfränkischer) Cato," of which Graffunder 1897, 11–34, has a text and discussion; Stephen von Dorpat's translation, on which see Graffunder 1899, 13–33; the "Zwielichter Cato" (or "Rheinfraenkischer Cato"); the "Neusohler Cato," for which see Zatočil 1935, 85–102; the "Amorbacher Cato," a translation for a monastery library rather than the classroom, on which see Harmening 1970, 360–368; the "St. Galler Cato," a prose paraphrase, on which see Kesting 1975, 167–172.

577 On Jean Lefèvre's translation, "*Chaton fu preux chevalier et saige home*," see Reynhout 1986 and Ulrich 1904b. The author is not the fifteenth-century chronicler and authority on chivalry, but an earlier lesser-known translator. On the second translation, see Ruhe 1968, 229–230.

Bishop of Barcelona, was for an audience of university and Church scholars, an example of sophisticated and ambitious translation; Gonzalo García de Santa María's rough paraphrase, by contrast, would have appealed to learned readers who had no Latin, a wide audience eager for less sophisticated translations.[578] While many editors, commentators, and translators recommend the *Distichs* for edification of the young, García de Santa María turned to the *Distichs* for his own comfort as he isolated himself from the plague that ravaged Spain in 1493–94 and then used his translation to share the work with his fellow Castilians.[579] The offer of enlightenment and comfort in the *Distichs* was taken up by many: a large number of inexpensive print editions followed that catered to a wide audience.[580]

In Italy, where manuscript translations of the fourteenth and fifteenth centuries also aimed at educating children and the ignorant, incunabula and the earliest print editions bear witness to the co-existence of covert and increasingly overt translations.[581] We have a translation of the *Distichs* (along with Donatus), dating between 1492 and 1499, which comprises a Latin text, with each couplet followed first by an Italian translation and then by a re-ordering of the Latin into an Italianate word order. The result is a translation that is concerned with both the rudiments of grammar and explanation of the text. This is the first literal translation aimed at increasing the reader's lexical, morphological, and

---

578 Preceding these translations were a fourteenth-century anonymous prose translation into Catalan, on which see Bonsenyor 1889, and another Catalan anonymous prose translation of 1462, on which see Bofarull y Mascaró 1857, 303–310. For the translation of Martín García Payazuelo, there is a partial text in Pietsch 1902, 12–18, a facsimile text in Clavería 1989, and a discussion in Bizzarri 2002, 271–275. For an edition of García de Santa María, see Pérez Gómez 1964. On the purpose and audience of these translations, see Taylor 1999, 79, and Bizzarri 2002, 279. There is no known connection between these early Spanish translations, according to Alvar and Lucía Megías 2002, 247.
579 Martins 1968, 104–105.
580 On print editions, see Alvar and Lucía Megías 2002, 245.
581 The nobleman Catenaccio Catenacci d'Anagni targeted his translation of the early 1300s at the ignorant. On this translation, see especially Paradisi 2005. A popular translation from later in the century accompanied by a commentary, by the grammarian Bonvesin de la Riva, was aimed at the classroom. Although he omitted some maxims and incorporated others, parts of his translation and commentary appeared with Erasmus' edition of the text. For a text of the translation, see Contini 1941, 323–360; for discussions, see Biadene 1927, Bona 1979, and Roos 1984, 234–237. Several anonymous prose translations appeared in fourteenth-century Tuscany, on which see Vannucci 1829, Teoli 1872, Fontana 1979 (especially his appendix), and Roos 1984, 238–241.

syntactical understanding of the source language, though it was probably still written for teachers rather than students.[582]

The mass of continental European translations was a rich source for translators and publishers in England. In the fourteenth century, several Middle English renderings of Everard's Anglo-Norman translation appeared in manuscripts, sometimes along with the Latin text and Everard's own version.[583] One of Caxton's printings of the *Distichs* was accompanied by a prose translation that was based on a French translation, perhaps Everard's.[584] Printing would increase exponentially the production of aids to the *Distichs* and make it an even more international effort. The *Distichs* were among the earliest texts printed by Caxton: his 1477 printing, which contained a translation by Benedict Burgh, was only his tenth of any text. Caxton's decision to print it early and then follow with three further printings within ten years attests to its importance for him, as he explains in his last printing of 1483: "And as in my Jugement it is the beste book for to be taught to yonge children in schole/and also to peple of euery age it is ful conuenient yf it be wel understanden." His inclusion of Burgh's verse translation in the first three printings and a prose rendering in the last was perhaps a response to teachers' different needs. Caxton includes commentary, but places it after the text and translation, as had happened in only a few manuscripts. The ease of this new placement for printers may also have resulted in the expansion of commentary: Caxton's, for example, includes lengthy comparanda from contemporary stories and sayings. His commentary seems well suited for children: for example, his comments on *DC* 1.2 (*Plus vigila semper nec somno deditus esto; / nam diuturna quies vitiis alimenta ministrat*: Be mentally awake, do not sleep too much; / Idleness long-term leads to bad behavior") include an entertaining story, along with a reference to Christianity:[585]

---

582 See the Gesamtkatalog (vol. 7, col. 674) and Roos 1984, 241–242. Late fifteenth-century Italy produced at least ten translations, including a prose translation together with a paraphrase that was published in 1478, then twice in 1487, in 1490, and also in 1493 or 1494.

583 For texts of these translations, see Morris 1878, 1668–1673, Furnivall 1901, 553–609, Förster 1906, and Horrall 1981.

584 Everard's and the prose translation are similar, but a related French translation may be the more direct source. See Ruhe 1968, 234. On translations into English from this period through the seventeenth century, see generally Verbeke 2013.

585 The transcription from Caxton's 1484 printing was produced by the Early English Books Online Text Creation Partnership.

Thou oughtest to watche in good werkys and flee slouthfulnesse / whiche is moder and nourice of alle synnes / For by ouerlonge reste and ociosyte been gendred or goten pryncypally thre grete synnes / that is to wete auaryce lecherye and ouermoche talkyng / We reden in one hystorye of grece / of a man whyche founde a nother man alle naked wythin a deserte or wode / the whyche man fledde assone as he sawe hym come / But he ranne soo longe after hym that at the laste he ouertoke hym / And thenne whan that thys naked man sawe that he myght nomore flee / he abode styll / and the other demaunded of hym why he dyd renne so longe before hym / The whiche answerd to hym / that in his londe was a kynge whiche had a toure ful of golde and syluer the whiche toure the kyng made to be kepte meruaylously / For hit was dedicted in suche manere / that as longe as he that kepte hit watched that none myght not entre in to hit for to robbe the sayd tresour / but as sone as he slepte euery man myght entre in to hit and robbe what he wold / But for to eschewe the [h]ungers and parellis of the sayd toure to the ende that he myght not lese his tresoure / he gaue euery nyght to hym that wold watche hit a precious stone whiche had suche properte & vertu that who sommeuer had hit in his hande he myght not slepe But assone as the stone fyl from his hande / he forthwyth began to slepe / Thenne the sayd kyng dyd doo make a crye vpon payne to lese the heed / that he whiche shold kepe hys toure / shold not lete falle from his hand the sayd stone / to the ende that he shold not slepe and that he shold not lese hys tresoure / Thenne happed that on a nyght I was commytted for to kepe the sayd tresour and for to watche wythin the said toure / but I lete falle the sayd stone out of myn hande / and Incontynent I began toslepe / and whyle that I slepte the tresour of the sayd kyng was robbed / Wherfore feryng the punycion and sentence of the sayd kyng I am fledde and come in to thys deserte as thou seest / To speke morally by the same kynge is vnderstonden god the fader / whiche is kynge of kynges and lord of alle lordes / By the toure and tresoure thou oughtest to vnderstonde the humayn man in to the whyche god hath put a moche grete tresoure of alle gra[ce]s and vertues / By hym that kepte and watched the sa[y]d toure is to be vnderstonden the reason and wytte of the man / For whyle that reason watcheth in the man / It is Impossyble that the vyces and synnes entre wythin the toure / that is to wete in to the man / but assone as reason slepeth and wytte fayleth / the vyces and synnes entren in to the toure / That is to wete wythin the man and robben and putten to nought the tresoure of the kynge that is to wete the vertues of the man / Therfore he is put and condempned to be in the deserte vnto the tyme that he shal haue made satisfaccion / And therfore hit appereth clerely that euery man ought to watche in good werkes / By the precious stone is vnderstonden Ihesu cryste / whiche kepeth vs fro slepe of synne whan we haue in our memorye his blessyd passion.

Caxton uses his Greek story to help educators maintain their young students' focus during what might otherwise be a dull lesson. It is also a carefully chosen and successful illustration of *DC* 1.2, centered on the parallels between, respectively, the story's tower, treasure, and guard, and the maxim's reader, his virtues, and his reason. Caxton adds a moralizing Christianizing interpretation of both story and maxim, which will appeal to educators: the king of the story is God, who has put virtues in the reader, and the stone is Jesus, memory of whose suffering keeps the reader from the sinful sleep. The result is a text, translation, and commentary that make the *Distichs* acceptable and useful to educators and palatable to students.[586]

Early Modern Period

From the close of the fifteenth century through the end of the seventeenth, more translations appeared than before, and the print medium allowed printers to reprint editions, translations, and commentaries in seemingly inexhaustible combinations. Two important and related trends emerge during this period that impacted the production of translations: the increasing primacy of vernacular languages and the growing market of readers without Latin.[587] Erasmus may have professed embarrassment at working with the *Distichs*, but a few decades later Switzerland-based Mathurin Cordier, teacher of Calvin and another leading light in Reformation education, was willing to follow his lead—though he complained later that he would have liked not to work again with the *Distichs*, preferring Cicero's *Letters*. Cordier recognized the ubiquity and utility of the *Distichs*: he added to Erasmus' text a spare and more overt French translation that was written in single couplets (rather than the four- or five-line verses of his predecessors) and thus better emulated the original, and a commentary written in French, not Latin. Cordier's translation captured the spirit of the original for an audience with little or no Latin, and Caxton used it for his translation of the *Distichs*; a German retranslation was also made. Cordier's was a text for schools, and he, a teacher, helpfully explained the educational purpose of his work: it offered definitive readings and explanations to correct others' errors (which perhaps had spread in the haste to publish commentaries, etc.), reduced glosses because these were often out of context and therefore confusing, and added pertinent Gallic *sententiae* to reflect the growing importance of vernacular literature. Cordier suggests that one of the purposes of his work was to aid memorization of the text, and as we learn from the index to his 1588 edition, children knew the collection so well that they could recall maxims by their second lines

---

586 Brunner 1968, 112, argues that Caxton's commentary is a significant departure from manuscript precedent. I disagree with his claim that "He uses the *Distichs* as the bare skeleton which he pads with tales and homilies": the example of Caxton's commentary on *DC* 1.2 demonstrates that at least some of those tales and homilies are judiciously selected.
587 Other notable translations during this period include Sebastian Brant's of 1498; printings of this translation appear until 1575. Another is Abraham Moter's translation, which dates to 1535.

as well as their first: the index contains the opening words of both lines for every maxim.[588]

Martin Opitz's 1629 German translation marks an important moment. Like Cordier, he chose couplets, and while his is not a literal translation, it follows Cordier in its increased overtness. Opitz supplemented his translation with notes in Latin that drew heavily on Erasmus, Scaliger, and others and pointed out other ancient authorities for the maxims' sentiments, though he offered no help with understanding their Latin. In fact, the notes are something of an anomaly and were perhaps included to widen the translation's potential audience. Otherwise, his readers were those coming to the *Distichs* with no Latin and perhaps no intention of learning any. The *Distichs* were now a text not only for the literati, but also and increasingly for readers of any language: Opitz's translation was included in a collection of German poems, presenting the *Distichs* to a new group of readers as a literary text to be enjoyed in any language, rather than simply as a vehicle for acquiring Latin.[589]

New translations into English were produced roughly every three years during this period, and they are remarkable for their diversity:[590] translators wrote in rhyming couplets; one produced yet another retranslation of Cordier; one used an English translation to campaign for spelling reform; a couple translated

---

588 According to Bolgar 1973, 354, Cordier disapproved of the *Distichs* and set out to refute as well as explain their sentiments. He translated only those maxims with which he agreed; the rest he left in the Latin. The success of his work is reflected in the fact that it was being widely printed and disseminated across Europe: for example, it was printed multiple times in Ireland in the mid-eighteenth century; see O'Higgins 2017, 39. Johannes Fries, a schoolmaster in Zurich and author of a Latin-German dictionary, was inspired by Cordier's methods: he aimed to have pupils understand the meaning of a text in both Latin and the target language, and his equal regard for both languages prefigured the educational concerns of the rest of the century and that following. His 1551 edition contained a text, translation, and commentary of the *Distichs*, on which see Kettler 2002, 291–328, who uses the example of *DC* 4.30 to illustrate how Fries' book provided teachers and students with an easy-to-follow lesson plan (p. 309). See also Grubmüller 1983, 390f. Other French translations of the period included those of Estienne, Grosnet, and Habert; on the latter's influence on Pybrac and the tradition of writing on manners, see Buisson 1911. A near contemporary, Antonio de Nebrija, a key figure in the spread of Humanism and the study of grammar in Spain, produced an edition of the *Distichs*, along with the *De contemptu mundi* and Aesop. The text was that of Erasmus, while Nebrija added a few annotations of his own. On the French context for the increase in vernacular translations and, more generally, the growing interest in proverbial wisdom, see Zemon Davis 1975.
589 On the significance of this translation, see Brunker 1987, 556; for a text, see Schulz-Behrend 1990, 332–391.
590 According to Brüggemann 1797, s.v. "Dionysius Cato," twenty versions of the *Distichs* (including editions and commentaries) appeared between 1512 and 1771.

the *Distichs* more literally than ever to aid children's grammar, even using an interlinear format, while another embraced paraphrases, complaining that syntactical literalness came at the expense of expressing the maxims' true meaning.[591] Robert Burrant's translation is notable for presenting no Latin text, but simply a translation and also Erasmus' commentary into English. The diversity of these translations is the result of catering to a range of audiences (schoolchildren, a general adult audience, and, in the case of John Penkethman's translation, possibly also home decorators or weavers) and of holding different attitudes towards the original text and English: while some composed translations as aids for construing the original, others regarded English as worthy to express the maxims' sentiments, without the need for understanding the Latin.[592]

The *Distichs* had already reached the New World a century earlier, where the Spanish had been using it to educate inhabitants of what would become Mexico. The text made the westward journey again, this time taken by the British to their American colonies: Cotton Mather "conversed with Cato, Corderius,

---

591 Robert Burrant's translation of 1553 was in rhyming couplets; a retranslation of Cordier entitled 1584: *Cato Construed, or A familiar and easy interpretation upon Catos morall Verses* appeared in 1584; the campaigner for orthographic reform, William Bullokar, published his *Short Sentencez of the Wyz Cato in true Ortography, with grammar notz* in 1585; Brinsley (1612) and Hoole (1670) produced literal translations, the latter interlinear, while Richard Baker (1636) preferred multiple paraphrases: for example, for *DC* 1.33 he supplies ten versions.

592 John Penkethman in his 1623 *Handful of Honesty or Cato in English* included in appendices lists of maxims appropriate for decorating the hall or dining room, chamber, study or counting house, and shop or office. Given the fashion for incorporating *sententiae* into painted cloths, tapestries, mantelpieces, and other fixtures and furnishings, the *Distichs* would have been in the consciousness of many in early modern England both at school and in the home. On *sententiae* and other tags as formal and informal decoration, see Fleming 1999. The appearance of maxims from the *Distichs* in the fabric of homes would, in turn, have stimulated the market in translations for the Latin-less. Penkethman probably chose single couplets for his translation in the interest of concision: two lines of verse could be more easily fitted onto the mantelpiece than could a paragraph of prose or four or more verses. Penkethman suggested that the collection was authored by Valerius Cato, the only person I know of to do so.

For a good example of a teaching text, Brunner 1968, 103, quotes the full title of Bailey's eighteenth-century text published in London: "Cato's Distichs / De Moribus / with a / numerical Clavis / And Construing and Parsing Index. / The First shewing by Figures, answering / to each Word in every Line, in what Order the / Words ought to be looked out in the *Index*, to / be Construed into good Sense. The Second containing all the Words in/them digested into an Alphabetical Order, together with the *English* and a Grammatical Praxis on each word referring to the rules in Lilly's Grammar. To which is added, An English Translation of Erasmus' Commentaries on each Distich. / For the Use of Schools. / In a *method so Easy*, that Learners of the meanest attainment in the Latin Tongue may be enabled to Construe and Parse their Lessons with Ease to themselves, and without Trouble to the Teacher."

Terence, Tully [i.e., Cicero], Ovid, and Virgil" at the Boston Latin School around 1670.[593] Benjamin Franklin's translation of 1735, the first translation of the *Distichs*—and the first of any classical text—in North America, attests to the popularity of the work in schools. Franklin's rendering is mostly iambic and structured in rhyming couplets, a form that had become popular in English translations of the previous century.[594]

While Northern Europe and America saw increased interest in the content of the *Distichs*, whether in Latin or the new more literal translations, Southern Europe seems to have grown wary of the little text's power. In Spain, editions and translations moved further away from the original text, and by the nineteenth century, "Catos" had little to do with the *Distichs* beyond their title. Translators and transformers of the *Distichs* were now more interested in exploiting their ubiquity and popularity to support Catholicism than in passing on their pagan sentiments to children.[595] In Italy, the small size of the *Distichs* and their easy dissemination thanks to print helped to introduce them in a new more Christianized form to a wider audience. For example, Notturno Napoletano's 1555 translation, in terza rima, not couplets, offers an abridged and Christianized Cato in a small and very slim volume.[596]

---

593 The quotation comes from Mather's *Paterna*, in Bosco 1976, 7.
594 An edition of the *Distichs* that would have circulated was Ruddiman's *Rudiments of the Latin Tongue*, an introduction to Latin that contained the *Distichs*, the *Dicta Septem Sapientum*, William of Lille, Sulpitius, and other Christian texts. It was printed first in Edinburgh and then reprinted regularly there and elsewhere, including the United States, from 1714 for over 100 years (see Duff and Duff 1934, 588–589). The most recent reprinting was in 1970.
595 Among the better-known translators are Diego de Linares (1501), Siméon de la Pedraza (1517), Martín Godoy de Loaisa (1543), Ricardo de Mondejar (1629), Gabriel Rodríguez (1732), and León de Arroyal (1797). The Christianization of the *Distichs* helps to explain the spread of "Catos" despite their lack of connection to the original. Among works such as the *Caton cristiano para uso de las escuelas*, *Nuevo Caton cristiano*, and *Caton con ejemplos*, which were often ascribed to priests, even the didactic tone has disappeared. On these texts, see Pérez Gómez 1964, § VII.
596 For bibliography on Napoletano, a well-known poet, see Roos 1984, 242–243. In this Christianized translation, *archana dei* in *DC* 2.2 becomes "delle cose di figlio di Maria." Other Italian translations of this period include that of Cartelucio de Campania (on which see Brunner 1968, 121) and R. Don Pier Francesco Penazzi (1620) also in terza rima.

Modern Period

The history of translations of the *Distichs* in the nineteenth century and beyond is one of decline. With the reduced power of the Church, the increased importance of French and English as languages of diplomacy, science, and law, and the continuing democratization of education, Latin further lost its grip on education, and with the establishment of Caesar and Cicero as preferred elementary Latin texts, the *Distichs* were read by fewer and fewer children (let alone adults). For example, three new translations appeared in German in the nineteenth century, but the twentieth and twenty-first centuries have seen no new translations into that language.[597] In the Netherlands at the turn of the eighteenth century, we find an unusual translation that was designed to be sung to well-known tunes; thereafter, came just a couple of translations and paraphrases in the eighteenth and nineteenth centuries.[598] The twentieth century has seen only one Dutch translation, and this seems to be available only in the Netherlands.[599] Later French and Italian translations too are rarely available outside their countries: one nineteenth-century French translation is accessible now only in the Bibliothèque Nationale, while a couple of twentieth-century Italian translations are not even listed in the major library catalogues.[600] A new Italian translation will hopefully find a wider audience.[601] A translation into Hungarian was published in 2002, but is not widely available outside Hungary.[602] The *Distichs* have been better served in English: at least four translations appeared in the twentieth century, including in the Loeb Classical Library— though its relegation to the Minor Latin Poets volumes is testament to how far it has fallen in the estimation of educators.[603]

---

[597] The German translations are those of Pistorius, *Moralische Distichen*, 1816; Fleischner, *Distichorum de Moribus*, 1832; and Franke: *Gebete, Lieder und Gedichte*, 1838, pp. 237–260.

[598] On the translation for singers, see Boas 1924. From 1778 we have *Dionysii Catonis Disticha ad filium, In Belgicum sermonem conversa, Accedit Constructio Grammatica*—the latter is a paraphrase—and from 1835, *Dionisius Cato, Zedekundige Tweelingverzen voor zijnen zoon. In het Nederduitsch overgebracht*.

[599] Schockaert 1939.

[600] Bois produced a French translation in 1874. Copies of the Italian translations by Battaggia (1857) and Bauce (1906) cannot be easily found. Carlo Téoli's 1872 translation is a reprint of a thirteenth or fourteenth-century work.

[601] Balbo 2021.

[602] Nagyillés 2002. The review by Csaba 2003 offers a helpful summary of editions and translations of the *Distichs* produced in Hungary or available to Hungarian audiences.

[603] Chase 1922; Duff and Duff 1934, for the Loeb Classical Library; Thomson and Perraud 1990; Pepin 1999. A translation by James Marchand based on the text of Zatočil had been avail-

This survey of translations of the *Distichs* is unremarkable in a couple of important respects: first, developments in the nature of these translations parallel more general trends, a fact that makes them a helpful case study for exploring more closely the history of translation; second, the languages into which the *Distichs* have been translated—Italian, French, German, Spanish, English—are the most common target languages for renderings of Classical texts. Yet the number of translations is large, and they also appear in some unexpected languages: Greek (modern, as well as ancient), Hungarian, Old Czech, Bohemian, Croatian, Irish, Danish, Swedish, and Icelandic.[604]

The *Hólar Cato*, a seventeenth-century Icelandic schoolbook containing a translation of the *Distichs*, was the product of the theological school at Hólar, where a copy of the Latin had been held in the library as early as 1396. Its wider context was the emergence of the Icelandic school system in the previous century, in which all instruction was given in Latin. As an elementary school text, the *Distichs* played an important role: in 1537, it was mandated that all pupils read them. According to Hermannsson, "It is however, noteworthy, how little influence the Latin classics had upon Icelandic literature during the period ca. 1550–1800. Only a few passages and selections from various works were translated into Icelandic during this time. The only work rendered in full—as a textbook for the schools—was the *Catonis Disticha*." The *Hólar Cato* drew its text of the *Distichs* from Erasmus, which is testament to Iceland's educational connections with Europe; yet unlike most Icelandic textbooks, which were printed on the continent, this book was printed at home—presumably because so many copies were needed.[605]

---

able courtesy of James O'Donnell on his websites first at the University of Pennsylvania and then Georgetown University: http://www.faculty-georgetown.edu/jod/texts/cato.html (accessed 5/18/2022). A 2020 translation, *The Wisdom of Cato: Distichs of Cato in Latin Together with New English Translation*, published by Res Latinae, is available as an e-book exclusively from Amazon.

604 Aesop's *Fables*, another popular elementary Latin text for many centuries, were translated eleven times in England between 1540 and 1659, while the *Distichs* were translated nine times. Cordier states that he would have preferred Cicero's *Epistles* as a teaching text; yet there are only seven partial translations of the *Epistles* produced in England during that period; even Ovid's amatory poems, which were always popular, were translated only five times. The figures come from Cummings and Gillespie 2009. Details of translations into less common target languages are available in Brunner 1968, 122. On Marko Marulić's sixteenth-century Croatian translation, see Trogrančić 1953. Boas 1933 describes an early eighteenth-century Swedish publication of the *Distichs*, comprising a Latin text, Planudes' Greek, Opitz's German, and a Swedish rendering, a truly multi-lingual edition.

605 On this text and translation, see Hermannsson 1958; the quotation comes from p. xxv.

Transformations

The ubiquity of the *Distichs* until the eighteenth century encouraged educators and authors to produce their own reworkings in Latin. For example, Daniel of Beccles' *Cato Urbanus* (also known as the *Liber Urbani, Urbanus Magnus*, and sometimes—confusingly—the *Parvus Cato*), a 3000-line courtesy poem written around 1180, was clearly inspired by the *Distichs*, though it was transmitted separately. The author of the late fifteenth-century *Facetus* (sometimes called the *Cato Facetus, Parvus Cato, Liber Urbani* or *Supplementum Catonis*), set out to continue the *Dicta* by providing "pluseurs enseignemens de quoy Chatons fu negligens" ("multiple teachings about which Cato was negligent") and formalized his poem as a father's advice to his son, even instructing that, when speaking with others, the son should act *more Catonis* ("according to Cato's custom"). This work was sometimes found with the *Dicta*, as was the eleventh-century *Novus Cato*, which keeps the content of the individual maxims and prefaces of the *Distichs*, but reworks them into a continuous leonine hexameter poem. The *Cato Rhythmicus*, which is attested in only one manuscript, *Cato Secundus*, and *Cato Digestus* are further poetic reworkings.[606]

It is unsurprising that the *Distichs* were repeatedly reworked: pedagogical techniques that relied on recitation and paraphrasing led naturally to a large literature of imitation.[607] Moreover, works of advice, including those purportedly written by a parent to his child, were popular in medieval England and France

---

[606] Daniel of Beccles is named elsewhere as Daniel Ecclesiensis, presumably a mistake for Beccliensis. His poem of 3000 hexameter lines is discussed and partly translated in Frith and Treggiari 2007. Smyly 1939 provides a complete text; on the poem, see also Roussel 1994, 12–13. On the *Facetus*, the first quotation comes from Roussel 1994, 4; on the poem, see also Gillingham 2002, 271 and 279. There is another poem that also goes by the name *Facetus* and begins *Moribus et vita*, which seems to have been inspired principally by Ovid; on this poem, see Roussel 1994, 12. The instruction is found at *Facetus* 1. 102; the translation comes from Gillingham 2002, 275, n. 48 (who calls it the *Urbanus*). According to Schiendorfer 2000, 425, n. 12, the name *Supplementum Catonis* was also given to a spoof of the maxims. The *Novus Cato* is sometimes found along with the text of the *Distichs*, Remigius' commentary, and the *Glossulae Catonis*, and is set firmly in the tradition of re-workings of Latin texts, such as the *Novus-Aesop* and *Novus-Avianus*. On the poem, see Stammler et al. 1987, 1240, and Zarncke 1863, 31–48. On the *Cato Rhythmicus*, see Zarncke 1863, 49–73; on the *Cato Secundus*, see Boas 1930; on the *Cato Digestus*, see Boas 1932b. More generally on all of these reworkings, see Boas 1940 and Brunken 1987, 548.
[607] On education and the literature of imitation, see Paré, Brunet, and Tremblay 1933, 112. A Vienna manuscript presents the maxims, bulking out each original line with a new additional line, and follows them with paraphrases; see Mussafia 1865.

and later in Germany and Italy.⁶⁰⁸ For example, the Welsh *Catwg Ddoeth*, named after a native wisdom figure, seems also to have imitated the *Distichs*; the similarity of the name probably added authority to the new collection.

Giovanni Antonio Tagliente's *Libro maistrevole* (1524), a teaching manual of elementary Italian for adults, ends with a compendium of phrases useful in commercial life and a series of moralizing couplets.⁶⁰⁹ The rise of courtly literature, which aimed to help the reader become a *vir urbanus* and learn the manners of the table and more generally the court, also inspired new versions, and the *Distichs*, which had once taught morals were now reworked to teach manners; maxims that contradicted the new ethos were adapted.⁶¹⁰ Finally, the problem of paganism in the *Distichs*, which had given some educators pause, was solved with Christian reworkings, such as the Calvinist Theodore Beza's 1591 *Cato Censorius Christianus* and Mulcaster's *Cato Christianus* of seventeenth-century England.⁶¹¹

Some imitations gained their own following: the *Facetus* was translated into several languages, and Cervantes referred not only to the *Distichs*, but also to Michael Verino's imitation, titled variously *De puerorum moribus Disticha*, *Disticha moralia*, and *Liber distichorum*, which was a collection of brief essays grouped under headings, such as *Amor est causa timoris*, and accompanied by brief two-line hexameter couplets.⁶¹² Indeed, the association of wisdom with the *Disticha Catonis* and "Cato" was so strong that "Catón" was even used of political texts in Spanish that had few formal or material similarities, such as Alonso Rodríguez' *Catón Político Christiano* (1804).⁶¹³

The hours spent seated on wooden benches reading, remembering, and reciting the *Distichs* surely left their mark on children, as the allusions to and

---

608 On advice literature in France, see Mustanoja 1948, 29–78, and in Germany, see Kesting 1978, 1192, who notes the influence of the *Distichs* on Freidank and Konrad von Haslau, and Wells 1994. In England, the *Distichs* influenced a number of works, including the Anglo-Saxon *Fæder Lārcwidas*, the medieval *Proverbs of Alfred*, and Heywood's sixteenth-century *Dialogue of Proverbs*; on these works and others, see Habenicht 1963, 4–6.
609 According to Constantine 2008, 120, n. 22, "The sayings of 'Catwg Ddoeth' emerge from a complex process of muddled substitutions (not all, it must be said, attributable to Iolo) as the Iolo-ized version of the *Distichs Catonis*." On Tagliente's *Libro maistrevole*, see Grendler 1989, 158–159, and Jacobson Schutte 1986.
610 On courtly literature and the *Distichs*, see Hazelton 1957, 161. Generally on the rise of courtly literature, see Wells 1994, 302–307.
611 On Beza's *Cato*, see Green 2009, 157.
612 On the various translations of the *Facetus* into French and German, see Morawski 1923 and Schroeder 1911. The reference occurs in Cervantes, *Don Quixote* 2.3.7–8.
613 On the various Spanish works whose titles contain Catón, see Delgado 1990, 372–373.

reworkings of the text attest. The monotony of this style of learning, as well as the collection's relentless earnestness, drove some more imaginative readers to a different kind of reworking: parody.

Parodies appeared on the continent from at least the fifteenth century. Early examples include, in the sixteenth century, Prospero Acrimati's *Iocosum Carmen in Catonis praecepta* in Latin, while the French *Quedam dicta Catonis per antifrasin exposita* seems to have been based on Suel's translation rather than the Latin. This latter text contains light-hearted reworkings of the maxims and *Breves Sententiae* in rhyming couplets: so *DC* 1.12, *Rumores fuge, ne incipias novus auctor haberi, / Nam nulli tacuisse nocet, nocet esse locutum* ("Avoid rumors, so you are not thought the new source: / Keeping quiet brings no one harm; harm comes from speaking"), becomes "Et se tu ois nouvelles dire, / Va lo parmi la ville dire" ("And if you want to say something new, go tell it to the town") and *DC* 1.28, *Cum tibi sint nati nec opes, tunc artibus illos / Instrue, quo possint inopem defendere vitam* ("You have sons, but no means? Teach them a trade, / So they can avoid a life of want") becomes "Se Dieu te donne (plus) enfans avoir / Et tu n'ayes assez d'avoir, / Ne les dois duire et enseigner / De tolir, rober et embler" ("If God grants you to have a child (or children), and you don't have the means, you don't have to guide and teach them to seize, rob, and plunder").[614]

The German Dedekind's *Grobianus et Grobiana: sive, de morum simplicitate, libri tres*, a Latin poem in elegiacs of the mid-sixteenth century, appropriates the figure of St. Grobian, a well-known fictional patron saint of vulgarity, to teach men how to behave by indulging in bad manners; it was translated into English fourteeners and published in 1605 as *The Schoole of Slovenrie: Or, Cato turnd wrong side outward*. The result is a mocking transformation, rather than a close parody, that pokes fun at the *Distichs*'s broad concerns using absurd and pedestrian instructions. It also mocks the long-standing tradition of learning wisdom from the ancients, perhaps revealing that many children and adults found Greek and Roman texts unappealing educational material:

> Give place time-scouring 'Aristotle', vice-controuling Plato,
> Yeeld learned Tully, deepe Erasmus, and fault-finding Cato:

---

614 On Prospero Acrimati's *Iocosum Carmen in Catonis praecepta*, in Latin, see Boas 1927 and Bieler 1957, 235–236. There is a text and discussion of the French parody in Ruhe 1968, 236–244. *DC* 1.12 and 1.28 are found in vv. 36–37 and 70–74 of the French, respectively. Another parody, *La Devinette du Bénédicité*, was inspired by table sayings, proverbial wisdom, and moral treatises, as well as the *Distichs*; on this and other parodies and light-hearted reworkings, see Roy 1979.

> And you which by your tedious works, though to your mickle paine,
> Did teach behaviours perfect meanes, and manners to attaine.
> This Booke, which from a new found Schoole of late time did arise,
> Behaviours pure simplicitie within it doth comprise:
> Then young and olde that doe desire nurture and education,
> Peruse this Booke each day and houre with great deliberation.[615]

Another German parody cleverly draws from the *Breves Sententiae* and the maxims to create new instructions that mock the original texts' messages. For example, on the theme of money:

> *Sperne factum huiusmodi*
> *dixit Cato: rem custodi,*
> *dilige denarium.*
> *Nam qui sua sic consumit,*
> *aliena quando sumit,*
> *vertitur in odium.*[616]

> Reject doing things of this sort, said Cato: guard your property, love cash. For whoever uses up what he has in this way, when he uses someone else's, he is moved towards hatred.

But perhaps the most absurd parodic reworking is Henry Carey's drinking song, *Cato's Advice* (1740). The song draws from the earnest instructions of the *Distichs*, but perhaps also the general reputation of Cato Censorius for stern morals and upright living. The suggestion that "Cato" might advise some lightheartedness is not far-fetched, as *DC* 4.25 suggests, though drowning "care in an ocean of claret" cannot have been what the author of the *Distichs* had in mind.[617]

---

615 An example of the *Schoole of Slovrenrie*'s laughably pedantic instructions is:

> Being out of bed, let it suffice to clothe thee in thy shurt,
> To stay to put on all thy clothes with colde thou mightest thee hurt.

Another parody in the Grobian mold, the so-called "Cato-Parodie," which is ascribed to Hans Kemnater, has only a tenuous link with the *Distichs*, being addressed to a son. On this text, see Zarncke 1852, 143–153, and Kesting 1983, 1113–1114.

616 On this text, which may date to the fourteenth century, see Lehmann 1922, 82–83. The quoted lines draw from *Breves Sententiae* 13, *DC* 3.21 and *DC* 4.4.

617 There is an early precedent for Carey's song: *Carmina Burana* 221, a drinking song from the eleventh or twelfth century, also refers to "Cato" and the *Distichs*; *intelligite* in the second stanza is probably an allusion to the end of the *Epistula*.

> 'Cum animadverterem' dicit Cato.
> quis me redarguit de peccato?

What *Cato* advises, most certainly wise is,
Not always to labour, but sometimes to play,
To mingle sweet pleasure with search after treasure,
Indulging at night for the toils of the day:
And while the dull miser esteems himself wiser,
His bags to increase, while his health does decay,
Our souls we enlighten, our fancies we brighten,
And pass the long evenings in pleasure away.

All cheerful and hearty, we set aside party,
With some tender fair the bright bumper is crown'd;
Thus *Bacchus* invites us, and *Venus* delights us
While care in an ocean of claret is drown'd:
See, here's our physician, we know no ambition,
But where there's good wine and good company found;
Thus happy together, in spite of all weather,
'Tis sunshine and summer with us the year round.

---

laudem et honorem animus
nostro hospiti, cui bonus est animus.

Ergo, fratres carissimi, intelligite
et ad ora pocula porrigite!
et si aliquis inebrietur ex vobis,
declinet seorsum a nobis.

'As I observed...' says Cato,
who is going to convict me of sin?
We sing to the praise and honor
of our host, who has a good heart.

So my dearest brothers, be sensible
and raise your cups to your mouths!
Should any one of you become inebriated,
he should remove himself from our company.

The translation is from Traill 2018, 369–371. I owe the reference to Brunken 1987, 557.

Conclusion

In R.J. Palacio's best-selling book *Wonder*, Mr. Browne, a beloved middle-school teacher, presents to his students each month a precept that he hopes will encourage their social-emotional development. Palacio gathered together these precepts, along with others sent to her by readers, and reworked them into a spin-off book, *365 Days of Wonder: Mr. Browne's Book of Precepts*.[618]

Palacio's sources are "popular songs, great works of literature, inscriptions on Egyptian tombs, fortune cookies, characters who appeared in *Wonder*," and her own readers. Aside from three precepts culled from *Wonder* that Palacio herself had authored, the rest were composed by other individuals, though they were selected by her (and her family). Precepts included in the book range in time from the third-millennium BCE *Maxims of Ptahhotep* ("Teach him then the sayings of the past, so that he may become a good example for the children... No one is born wise") to the contemporary author Amy Tan ("If you can't change your fate, change your attitude"), as well as 100 original formulations by Palacio's young readers (e.g., "When it's dark, be the one who turns on the light" by Joseph, age 9, of Brooklyn, NY). Those readers of Palacio's first book are the target audience of *365 Days*: children aged 8–12, living in twenty-first century America. She has picked precepts that will be meaningful to them, and a few precepts make their temporal and geographical context clear: "Superheroes are made but heroes are born" and "Success does not come through grades, degrees or distinctions. It comes through experiences that expand your belief in what is possible" (by readers Antonio and Matea, respectively).[619]

The book opens with a preface written ostensibly by Mr. Browne, in which he explains that he was inspired by the usefulness of precepts in his own life to use them in turn to inspire his students. Presenting them with a precept each month, he had the children first discuss and then write about them. He chose precepts "with particular resonance for kids: kindness, strength of character, overcoming adversity, or simply doing good in the world." His purpose in "his"

---

[618] Palacio 2012 and 2014.
[619] An example of the importance of reading a precept in the context of its final audience, rather than that of its initial author, comes with this, from Archimedes: "Give me a firm place to stand, and I will move the earth." The original is δός μοί (φησι) ποῦ στῶ καὶ κινῶ τὴν γῆν, quoted in Pappus, *Synagoge* 8.19. Archimedes is asserting that, if he were given a place to stand, with the use of a simple lever, he could move even as heavy an object as the Earth. But in the twenty-first century context of *365 Days*, it no longer concerns mechanics, but rather has become an encouragement to realize one's own ability to effect social change.

book is simply that children will read one precept each day, and he hopes that they will come to "mean a lot" to them.

There follows a precept for each day, presented on a separate page (and occasionally spaced across two). January 1 offers "We carry within us the wonders we seek around us" (Sir Thomas Browne, a seventeenth-century polymath and debunker of mythology and erroneous science, and namesake of Mr. Browne), while January 2 brings "And above all, watch with glittering eyes the whole world around you because the greatest secrets are always hidden in the most unlikely places. Those who don't believe in magic will never find it" (Roald Dahl). Mr. Browne rounds out each month with reflections, addressed variously to children and parents, on the value of precepts (and also of kindness and wisdom): for example, at the end of January, noting that teachers and parents understand the social-emotional challenges of the middle-school years, he encourages children to accept their helpful gift of precepts.

Palacio has not referenced the *Distichs* or indeed any other paraenetic text in interviews about the book, despite being aware of some: she quotes from the *Maxims of Ptahhotep*. Yet her collection is remarkably similar to the *Distichs*—and some other paraenetic collections too—in certain key respects. The precepts range from high-brow (Lao Tzu's "He who knows others is clever, but he who knows himself is enlightened") to light-hearted and informal (Charles M. Schulz's "Life is like an ice-cream cone; you have to lick it one day at a time"), and though philosophers are included, the precepts' individual simplicity and collective miscellaneity are better suited to children than to scholars of systematic philosophy. Like the *Distichs*, this is not a serious philosophical collection. Moreover, like the *Distichs*, the precepts, regardless of their origin, are lexically and syntactically simple, and their messages are—on an initial reading, at least—easily understood. Binarism is also apparent in the structure of many of the precepts, as some of the examples above demonstrate. But unlike the *Distichs*, Palacio's collection is largely positive in tone. Indeed, one reviewer noted that "the cumulative effect of so many inspiring words can be deadening, like being trapped in a Hallmark card shop."[620] Taken one day at a time, however, that effect is lessened.

The book's calendar format helps a family to integrate it into their daily routine: every night at dinner, a member of the family might read aloud the precept of the day and begin discussion about it. The precepts are sufficiently brief—45 words at most—to hold in the head, though repeated close reference to the wording would help children with their understanding. There is no discernible

---

620 Review of "365 DAYS OF WONDER" 2014.

organizing principle, and the collection seems the better for it: a family will never know what it will read next, and the variety keeps the collection fresh and interesting (and masks the inevitable repetition of ideas that comes in a collection of 365 precepts). There is often more than one way to interpret a precept, or more than one scenario to which it may apply, and the more that family members talk about a precept, the more there may be to say: conversations may range far as a result. The precepts provide an excellent starting point for discussions about interpersonal relationships, a person's place in the world, and other big topics that might be lost amid the everyday tasks of school, work, and chores.

Palacio's collection has also become a teaching tool in schools: Penguin Random House (of which Knopf, her publisher, is an imprint) has compiled a webpage of resources, including planners and guides for teachers—the twenty-first century versions of commentaries and glosses—as well as classroom signs for students (in lieu of memorization).[621] There even is an official app that will present a person with a daily precept from *365 Days* on their mobile device, a sure indication that paraenetic collections can be adapted to different media. Educators have also created downloadable resources for colleagues to purchase, including comprehension questions and writing prompts.[622] Precepts continue to be marketable and lucrative.

In 2017 alone, three years after its publication, *365 Days* sold 125,062 copies.[623] While many of its purchasers may be fans of *Wonder* (the book and/or subsequent movie of the same title), others may be parents and teachers eager to feed their children advice in a kid-friendly digestible form. Indeed, an audience for such advice exists: collections of inspiring quotations and memorable precepts continue to be published, part of the thriving self-help and educational markets.[624] There is life in paraenesis yet.

---

621 https://wonderthebook.com/for-teachers, accessed 5/18/2022.
622 For example, https://www.teacherspayteachers.com/Browse/Search:365%20days%20of%20wonder#, accessed 5/18/2022.
623 https://www.publishersweekly.com/pw/by-topic/childrens/childrens-book-news/article/76168-facts-and-figures-2017-thriving-backlists-popular-tie-ins-and-more-children-s-bestsellers.html, accessed 5/18/2022.
624 Comparable titles include Michael Stutman and Kevin Conklin, *The Ultimate Book of Inspiring Quotes for Kids*; Katie Hurley, *A Year of Positive Thinking for Teens: Daily Motivation to Beat Stress, Inspire Happiness, and Achieve Your Goals*; M. Prefontaine, *The Best Smart Quotes Book: Wisdom That Can Change Your Life*; and Cyndie Spiegel, *A Year of Positive Thinking: Daily Inspiration, Wisdom, and Courage*.

Appendix: Selected Translations of *DC* 3.24

DC 3.24	Dilige non aegra caros pietate parentes.
	Nec matrem offendas, dum vis bonus esse parenti.
	Love your dear parents with equal devotion,
	And don't upset mother in trying to please father.
German	
Heidelberg, Universitätsbibliothek, Cod. pal. germ. 341, 71va–75rb (1300–1325)	Du solt mit allen sinnen
	dîne altvordern minnen;
	beswære niht die muoter dîn,
	wiltu dem vater liep sîn.
Zwettl, Stiftsbibliothek, Cod. Zwettl. 357, 89ra–98vb (early 14th C)	Dv solt mit allen sinnen
	Dine altvorderen minnen.
	Besvere niht diner muter mut,
	Ob du wilt sin dem vater gut.
Stuttgart, Württembergische Landesbibliothek, Cod. poet. et philol. 4° 50, 2r–76v (1462–4)	Vater vnd mûter alweg er,
	Das ist mein bot vnd ler;
	Wilt du dem vater lieb sein,
	So betrieb nit die mûter dein.
München, Bayerische Staatsbibliothek, Clm 7021, 114ra–120va (1400–1450)	Dv solt mit allen deinen sinnen
	dein lieb frevnt mit frevntschaft gewinnen
	Wetrub auch deiner mvter mut
	ob dv wilt sein deinem vater gut
	[The first two lines do not come from *DC* 3.24]

Neusohler Cato (mid 15th century)	Du salt dich mit mit fleisse vben, deyne eldern micht krenclichen lieben dir czorne auch nicht dy muter dein, wiltu dem vater beheigelich sein.
Wolfenbüttel, Herzog August Bibliothek, Cod. 535.16 Novi, 42r-50v, (1491–1500)	Mynne in gunsten alle gader Beyde moder ind vader! Dies du dyrne moder zorn, Du hais dyns vader hulde verlorn.
Stephan Dorpat: Danzig (Gdańsk), Biblioteka Gdańska - Polskiej Akademii Nauk, Ms. 2416, 2r-54r (late 14th C)	Nu hore, wat ik dy will leren: Vader vnde moder scaltu eren Mit ener leue, de stede si Vnde ok truwe al darbi. Wultu dyneme vadere gůd Wesen, se hebbe steden můd.
Zwielichter: Frankfurt/M., Stadt- und Universitätsbibliothek, Ms. germ. qu. 2, 10vb-15vb (1370/1380)	Liep vater vnd muter halt Mit grozzem flizze wan du salt Minne diner muter tragen Wiltu dem vater wol behagen.
Michelstaedter = Michelstadt, Nicolaus-Matz-Bibliothek, Cod. D 692/XV 3	Die liben vatter vnd mutter on wanck Hab liep mit liebin die da sy nit kranck Wen du wil dem vatter lip sin So betrub[gestr. p] nit die mutter din.
Sebastian Brant (1498)	Dyn eltern hab lieb vnd werd So wechst dir glück vnd heyl vff erd Erzürn ouch nyt die môter dyn So du dym vatter gôt wilt syn.

Abraham Moter (1535)	Ohn zwang und mit fröhlichem muth Die Eltern lieb und thu ihn gut Auch halt also dein Vater werth Das nicht die Mutter wird beschwerth.
Opitz (1629)	Schaw' auff damit du stets die Eltern gleiche liebest; Verhalt der Muter nicht was du dem Vater giebest.
Fleischner (1832)	Sei du mit gleicher Liebe den theueren Aeltern ergeben; Kränke die Mutter du nimmer, indem du den Vater verehrest.
Franke (1838)	Liebe dem Elternpaar mußt du ohn' Ärgerniß schenken: Und ja das Mutterherz aus Liebe zum Vater nicht kränken.
'Cato' (Basel: Martin Flach, um 1475)	Ein yeklich kind sich dar nach sent Als es die môtter hatt gewent Beschwer nit die môtter din Wiltu dinem vatter lieb sin.
Polish	
'Catonis disticha moralia' (Krakau: Hieronymus Vietor, 1535)	Práwie swe rodźice mituy Wszytkę gim łáskę vkázuy A práwa cnotę záchowas Jesli mátki nie rozgniewas. ¶ Dein eltern hab auch lieb vnd werd So wächst dir gluck vnd heyl auff erd. Erczurn auch nit die mütter dein So du deim vater güt wilt sein.

Dutch

Anon. 1283

Du salt met dinen sinne algader
Eeren moeder ende vader:
God seghet, diese belghen doet,
Dat hem te pinen werde(n) moet.

English

Middle English (date unknown) (Furnivall)

Ffader and moder loke þou loue
Wiþ parfyt herte wiþ-inne;
Look þat þou ne wraþþe hem nouȝt,
Heore benison to winne.

Sidney/Rawlinson (ca. 1400)

Loke þat þi frendis, dere sone, with þe
Be neuer loued with seke pite;
Ne ȝit þi moder neuer displese,
If þat þou þi frendis wil emplese.

Thi fader and moder, dere son, with the
Ne be feyntly loved with seek pyte;
Ne ȝet thi moder as fool displese,
ȝef tho hire lynage wyl wel enpese.

Burgh 1477 (pub'd by Caxton)

Goodes that ben geuen the of nature
They come to the of thy progenitours
Therfore my child with al thy force & cure
Loke thou loue hem: cherisshe at al hours
For they fostre yᵉ & kept in youth from shours
Thy moder my dere child yet in especial
Yet thou do wele neuer offende at al.

Appendix: Selected Translations of DC 3.24 — 197

Caxton 1484	Thou oughtest to loue thy fader & thy moder by good & trewe loue Withoute ony faynyng / for it is grete abusyon to angre his moder whan he wyl be good & be byloued of his fader.
Burrant 1553	Towarde thy father and mother let not thy loue be slender. Nor offende thy mother, if to thy father thou wilt be tender.
1584 anon.	Love thou, with an affection unconstrained, not by compulsion, but with a willyng mynd and harte, thy father and thy mother, whom thou ought to love dearely. That is to saie, to love willingly, and singulerly, and to have them in reverence, and offende not, thy mother willyng to favour thy father, that is to say, offend neither of them.
Bullokar 1585	Lọu' dềrly thy parentz, not with grụdg'ịng maner, whỵ̄lf̣t thụ wilt plæz father offend not thy mọther.
Brinsley 1612	Loue thy deere parents, not with a sicke [or constrained] pietie. Neither maiest thou offend [thy] mother, whilst thou wilt be good to thy father.
Penkethman 1623	Entirely loue thy Father and thy Mother, Neither, to please the one, displease the other.
Baker 1636	Love both thy Parents, in an equall measure: Displease not one, to doe the other, pleasure. Or thus, Love equally thy Father, and thy Mother: And doe not scratch the one; to claw the other.
Hoole 1659	Thy parents love, the one as well as th'other; To please thy Father, do not croß thy mother. OR Love thy dear parents with an unconstrained love; And offend not thy Mothers, whilst thou art willing to be dutiful to thy Father.

Franklin 1735	Equal Affection for both Parents bear; Nor flight the one the other to revere.
Chase 1922	For both dear parents equal love e'ever hold; Be not to father fond: to mother cold.
Duffs 1934	Love both your parents, one as much as other: To please your father never wound your mother.
Marchand	Love and do not bug your parents, dear in familial love, Nor offend your mother when you want to be nice to your father.
Pepin 1999	Love your dear parents with unrestrained affection; Do not offend your mother while you wish to be good to your father.
Res Latinae 2020	Love your dear parents not unequally and with care. Nor offend your mother, while you want to be good to your father.
French	
Everard (before 1145)	Aim tes chier parenz de quer parfit dedens ne mie malement; ne coruce ta mère, si vels plaire à ton père e servir à talent.
Elie of Winchester (12th C)	Aime tun [chier] parent, E si tul ueis dolent, Succur le bonement; Tun pere aies chier. Ta mere curucier, Ne uoilles suait[i]er.

Appendix: Selected Translations of DC 3.24 — **199**

Anonymous (12th C)	Tes parenz dais amer E mut tenir les cher En amur verrai; Ne curucez pas ta mere, Si tu vois devers tun per Ester de bone fai.
Old Provençal (12/13th C)	Se tu vols esser bos, amaras tos pairos. Qe se amas ta Maire, grat t'en sabra tos paire. Il no·t sabra ja grat, se fas ton pair' irat. Ama los e·lz te car, qe totz om o deu far. Qe eis Deus o comanda, Et es fezeltatz granda.
Jean de Paris (ca. 1260)	De Dieu se te vels aprochier, Tien ton pere et ta mere chier; Ne ne corrouce pas ta mere, Se bien vels estre de ton pere.
Adam de Suel (1250–1300)	Pere et mere aime sens feintise, Et se faire vues mon servise, Garde ne corrocier ta mere Par en gré servir a ton pere.
MS Darmstadt 2640 (13/14th C)	Aime d'one bone amur te pere et ta mere et se ne coroce nient te mere, se tu wes estre bien de ton pere.

Jean Lefèvre (ca. 1350)	Je te command a amer pere et mere; A nul des deux ne diz parole amere. Tu ne doiz pas vers ta mere groucier, Se tu ne veulz ton pere corroucier.
Mathurin Cordier (1551) or Estienne	A père & mere une vraye amour porte: N'offense l'un pour l'autre en quelque forte.

Spanish

Anonymous Catalan (14th C)	Ama coralment e no fenta ton pare e ta mare; no offendras la tua mare si vols fer plaer a ton pare.
Martín García Payazuelo (1467)	Padre et madre querer fijo mjo entu motiuo et deues ser su catiuo pues daron te el seyer guarda te de ofender fijo mjo atu madre si tu quieres atu padre todo sienpre conplazer.
Gonzalo García de Santa María (1493)	Amaras mucho tu padre y tu madre y guarda a tu madre de no offender si quieres quiça tu muy bueno ser al que te engendro y natural padre y ahunque mucho qualquier dellos ladre no los indignes mas con humildad sufre lo tu y con gran caridad porque en toda cosa la tu bondad quadre.

Appendix: Selected Translations of DC 3.24 — **201**

Anon. (16th C)	Primeramente piensa lo que has de hazer con tu padre ni co\<n\> tu madre no quieras contender alos que son buenos bien los deues querer y del bien que te hizieren acordado deues ser.
León de Arroyal (1797)	Ama con aficion tus padres caros, Y no ofendas ni agravies á tu madre Queriendo ser muy bueno con tu padre.
Italian	
Old Venetian (13th C?)	Ama Lo to caro padre ela toa care madre Cum no enferma amista; No ofendras atoa mare, [sic] Domentre qe tu uoi eser bon A to pare.
Bonvesin de la Riva (13th/14th C)	Tuo padre e toa madre ama cum grando feruore E fage uoluntariamente grando bene a grando honore E se to uol essere bono atuo padre e obediente Atoa madre tu ie di far grando honor maiormente.
Catenaccio (14th C)	Ama li toy parenti con tucto core et mente et fa' chi tu si' ad illi transattu boparente, ma puru patritu e mamata plu principalmente ama, servi et honora et sey bene obediente. Si lu tou patre e matre honori et servi, a Dio de placi e la soa lege observi.
Tuscan anon. (Fontana) (14th C)	Ama il tuo padre e lla tua madre, charamente e chon dolcie e diritta pietade, e nonn offendere la madre tua mentre che ttu vuoli essere buono a tuo padre, e non l'essere contrario.

Anon. (14th C)	Ama lo tuo padre e la tua madre, e non con inferma pietade; e non offendere la tua madre, quando tu vuoli essere buono al tuo padre.
Anon. (14th C)	Ama el padre e la madre tua con grande amore, e non offendere alla madre, se vuoi piacere al padre.
Anon. (14th C)	Ama i tuoi parenti ferventemente e non pigheramente; e non offendere tua madre tu, che vuogli essere tenuto buono.
Anon. (1493)	Dilige ama caros parentes li cari parenti. non aegra pietate non con inferma pietade. Nec offendas non offendere matrem tua matre. dum vis esse bonus domente che tu voi esser bono parenti a tuo patre. Figliolo mio te prego che tu debi amare lo tuo patre e tua matre con pura e sana pietade e con caritate e guarda bene non offendisse a niuno de loro se tu voi effere in gratia de dio e de la gente del mondo.
Teoli (1872)	Ama lo tuo padre e la tua madre, e non con inferma pietade; e non offendere la tua madre quando tu vuoli essere buono al tuo padre.
Balbo (2021)	Ama I tuoi genitori con eguale rispetto filiale e non offendere tua madre mentre vuoi esser buono con tuo padre.
Greek	
Planudes (13/14th C)	Μὴ ψυχρῇ στοργῇ σοὺς ἀμφαγάπαζε τοκῆας· Μητέρι μὴ πρόσκρουὶ, ἐθέλων ἀρέσαι γενετῆρι.

Works Cited

Aarts, J.G. 2005. "Coins, Money and Exchange in the Roman World. A Cultural-Economic Perspective." *Archaeological Dialogues* 12: 1–27.
Acker, Maureen, and Susan O'Leary. 1987. "Effects of Reprimands and Praise on Appropriate Behavior in the Classroom." *Journal of Abnormal Child Psychology* 15 (4): 549–557.
Adrados, Francisco Rodríguez. 2009. *Greek Wisdom Literature and the Middle Ages: The Lost Greek Models and their Arabic and Castilian Translations*. Bern; New York: Peter Lang.
Aguiló i Fuster, Marian. 1951. *Cançoner catalá recollit i ordenat: Edició fac-símil 1*. Ciutat de Mallorca: Alcover, Palma de Mallorca.
Alcamesi, Filippa. 2007. "Remigius's Commentary to the *Disticha Catonis* in Anglo-Saxon Manuscripts." In *Form and Content of Instruction in Anglo-Saxon England in the Light of Contemporary Manuscript Evidence: Papers Presented at the International Conference, Udine, 6–8 April 2006*, edited by Patrizia Lendinara, Loredana Lazzari, and Maria Amalia d'Aronco, 143–185. Turnhout: Brepols.
Alkire, Sabina, and Gisela Robles. 2017. "Multidimensional Poverty Index Summer 2017: Brief Methodological Note and Results." *OPHI Methodological Notes* 45.
Alster, Bendt. 1974. *The Instructions of Suruppak: A Sumerian Proverb Collection*. Copenhagen: Akademisk Forlag.
Alster, Bendt. 1997. *Proverbs of Ancient Sumer: The World's Earliest Proverb Collection*. Bethesda, MD: CDL Press.
Alvar, Carlos, and José Manuel Lucía Megías. 2002. *Diccionario filológico de literatura medieval española: textos y transmisión*. Madrid: Editorial Castalia.
Andreau, Jean. 1974. *Les affaires de Monsieur Jucundus*. Rome: École Française de Rome.
Andreau, Jean. 1999. *Banking and Business in the Roman World*. Cambridge; New York: Cambridge University Press.
Arewa, E. Ojo, and Alan Dundes. 1964. "Proverbs and the Ethnography of Speaking Folklore." *American Anthropologist* 66 (6): 70–85.
Arngart, Olof Sigfrid. 1952. "The Distichs of Cato and the Proverbs of Alfred," *Kungl. Humanistiska Vetenskapssamfundet i Lund. Årsberättelse* 1951–52: 95–118.
Arngart, Olof Sigfrid. 1956. *The Durham Proverbs: An Eleventh Century Collection of Anglo-Saxon Proverbs Edited from Durham Cathedral Ms.B.III.32*. Lund: C. W. K. Gleerup.
Astin, Alan E. 1978. *Cato the Censor*. Oxford; New York: Clarendon Press; Oxford University Press.
Baehrens, Emil. 1881. *Poetae Latini Minores*. Vol. III. Leipzig: B.G. Teubner.
Balbo, Andrea. 2021. "*Disticha Catonis*." in *Proverbi, sentenze e massime di sagezza in Grecia e a Roma*, edited by Emanuele Lelli, 710–727, 1714–1738. Florence; Milan: Bompiani.
Baldwin, Thomas Whitfield. 1944. *William Shakespeare's Small Latine & Lesse Greeke*. Vol. I. Urbana: University of Illinois Press.
Baldzuhn, Michael. 2007–9. *Schulbücher im Trivium des Mittelalters und der frühen Neuzeit: Die Verschriftlichung von Unterricht in der Text- und Überlieferungsgeschichte der "Fabulae" Avians und der deutschen "Disticha Catonis."* 2 vols. Berlin: W. de Gruyter.
Bang, Peter Fibiger. 2009. "The Ancient Economy and New Institutional Economics." *Journal of Roman Studies* 99: 194–206.
Bang, Peter Fibiger. 2011. *The Roman Bazaar: A Comparative Study of Trade and Markets in a Tributary Empire*. Cambridge: Cambridge University Press.

Barker, William, and Jean Chadwick. 1993. "Richard Mulcaster's Preface to Cato Christianus (1600): Text, Translation, and Commentary." *Humanistica Lovaniensia* 42: 323–367.

Barley, Nigel. 1972. "A Structural Approach to the Proverb and Maxim with Special Reference to the Anglo-Saxon Corpus." *Proverbium* 20: 737–768.

Barns, John. 1951. "A New Gnomologium: With Some Remarks on Gnomic Anthologies, II." *The Classical Quarterly* 1 (1/2): 1–19.

Bartolomé, Bernabé. 1993. "Las escuelas de gramática." In *Historia de la educación en España y América. [Vol. 2], La educación en la España moderna (siglos XVI-XVIII)*, edited by Buenaventura Delgado Criado, Quintín Aldea Vaquero, and María Fundación Santa, 194–216. Madrid: Morata.

Beets, Adriaan. 1885. "De 'Disticha Catonis' in het Middelnederlandsch." Groningen: J.B. Wolters.

Bernstein, Neil W. 2008. "Each Man's Father Served as his Teacher: Constructing Relatedness in Pliny's Letters." *Classical Antiquity* 27 (2): 203–230.

Bhattacharya, Ramkrishna. 2002. "Carvaka Fragments: A New Collection." *Journal of Indian Philosophy* 30 (6): 597–640.

Biadene, Leandro. 1927. "Un 'volgae' inedito di Bonvesin da la Riva." In *Miscellanea di studi critici in onore di Vincenzo Crescini*, edited by Antonio Viscardi, 1–32. Cividale: Fratelli Stagni.

Bieler, Ludwig. 1957. "Nachaugusteische nichtchristliche Dichter II. Von Hadrian bis zum Ausgang des Altertums." *Lustrum* 2: 207–293.

Bischoff, Bernard. 1981. *Mittelalterliche Studien: Ausgewahlte Aufsätze zur Schriftkunde und Literaturgeschiche. Band 3*. Stuttgart: Anton Hiersemann.

Bischoff, Bernhard. 1938. "Elementarunterricht und probationes pennae in der ersten Hälfte des Mittelalters." In *Classical and Mediaeval Studies in Honor of Edward Kennard Rand, Presented Upon the Completion of His Fortieth Year of Teaching*, edited by Leslie Webber Jones, 9–20. New York: Leslie Webber Jones.

Bischoff, Erich. 1890. *Prolegomena zu Dionysius Cato*. Erlangen: Friedrich-Alexander-Universität zu Erlangen.

Biville, Frédérique. 1999. "Les proverbes: nature et enjeux." In *Proverbes et sentences dans le monde romain: actes de la table-ronde du 26 novembre 1997*, edited by Frédérique Biville, 11–26. Lyon: Diffusion de Boccard.

Bizzarri, Hugo O. 2002. "Algunos aspectos de la difusión de los Disticha Catonis." *Medioevo romanzo* 26 (1): 127–148, 270–295.

Bloomer, W. Martin. 2011. *The School of Rome: Latin Studies and the Origins of Liberal Education*. Berkeley: University of California Press.

Bloomer, W. Martin. 2015. "The *Distichs* of Cato in Late Antique Spain." In *Culture and Literature in Late Antiquity. Continuities and Discontinuities*, edited by Paola Francesca Moretti, Roberta Ricci, and Chiara Torre, 345–363. Belgium: Brepols.

Bloomer, W. Martin. 2017. "Classical Literary Culture in North Africa." In *Augustine in Context*, edited by Tarmo Toom, 68–78. Cambridge; New York: Cambridge University Press.

Bloomer, W. Martin. Forthcoming. *Disticha Catonis. Catalogus translationum et commentariorum. Medieval and Renaissance Latin Translations and Commentaries. Annotated Lists and Guides*. Toronto: Pontifical Institute of Mediaeval Studies.

Boas, Marcus. 1914. "De Librorum Catonianorum historia atque compositione." *Mnemosyne* 42: 17–46.

Boas, Marcus. 1915. "De Parisina quadam sententiarum Catoniararum sylloga." *Mnemosyne* 43: 286–318.
Boas, Marcus. 1924. "C.A. Boomgaert, een vriend van Coornhert en Spieghel." *Tijdschrift voor Nederlandse taal- en letterkunde* 43: 40–54.
Boas, Marcus. 1927. "Een latijnsche metrische Cato-paraphrase met parodie in een onbekenden italiaanschen druk van 1539." *Het Boek* 16: 243–262.
Boas, Marcus. 1928. "Zur Orthographie der Veroneser Handschrift 163." *Philologische Wochenschrift* 48: 61–63.
Boas, Marcus. 1930. "Woher stammt der Name Dionysius Cato?" *Philologische Wochenschrift* 21: 649–656.
Boas, Marcus. 1930–40. "De Cato-Bewerking van Robertus de Euremodio." *Het Boek* 26: 49–68.
Boas, Marcus. 1931. "Planudes' Metaphrasis der sog. Disticha Catonis." *Byzantinische Zeitschrift* 31: 241–257.
Boas, Marcus. 1932a. "Cato und die Grabschrift der Allia Potestas." *Rheinisches Museum* 81: 178–186.
Boas, Marcus. 1932b. "Ein Catoflorilegium." *Historische Vierteljahrschrift* 27, no. 3: 601–609.
Boas, Marcus. 1933. "Nachträgliches zu den Titeln Dionysius Cato und Disticha Catonis." *Berliner philologische Wochenschrift* 53: 956–960.
Boas, Marcus. 1934. *Die Epistola Catonis. Verhandelingen der Koninklijke akademie van wetenschappen te Amsterdam. Afdeeling letterkund. Nieuwe reeks*, vol. XXXIII, no. 1. Amsterdam: Noord-Hollandsche Uitgevers-Maatschappij.
Boas, Marcus. 1937. *Alcuin und Cato*. Leiden: E.J. Brill.
Boas, Marcus. 1940. "De middeleeuwsche latijnsche complementa en Supplementa Catonis." *Neophilologus* 25, no. 1: 287–296.
Boas, Marcus. 1952. *Disticha Catonis recensuit et apparatu critico instruxit Marcus Boas*. Amsterdam: North-Holland Pub. Co.
Bodel, John P. 1994. *Graveyards and Groves: A Study of the Lex Lucerina*. Cambridge, Mass.: American Journal of Ancient History.
Bodel, John P. 2000. "Dealing with the Dead: Undertakers, Executioners and Potter's Fields in Ancient Rome." In *Death and Disease in the Ancient City*, edited by V. M. Hope and E. Marshall, 128–151. London; New York: Routledge.
Bofarull y Mascaró, Próspero. 1857. *Documentos literarios en antigua lengua catalana (siglos XIV y XV.) Publicados de real órden*. Barcelona: En la impr. del Archivo.
Bolgar, R. R. 1973. *The Classical Heritage and Its Beneficiaries*. Cambridge: Cambridge University Press.
Bona, Elena. 1979. "Un secondo manoscritto dei 'Disticha Catonis' di Bonvesin de la Riva." In *In Ricordo di Cesare Angelini: studi di letteratura e filologia*, edited by Cesare Angelini, Franco Alessio, and Angelo Stella, 34–45. Milan: Il saggiatore.
Bonaventure, Br. 1961. "The Teaching of Latin in Later Medieval England." *Mediaeval Studies* 23.
Bond, Sarah. 2016. *Trade and Taboo: Disreputable Professions in the Roman Mediterranean*. Ann Arbor, MI: University of Michigan Press.
Bonner, Stanley Frederick. 1977. *Education in Ancient Rome: From the Elder Cato to the Younger Pliny*. Berkeley: University of California Press.
Bons, Jeroen A. E. 1992. "Aetiologica." In *Historisches Wörterbuch der Rhetorik. Bd 1, A-Bib*, edited by Gert Ueding, Gregor Kalivoda, and Franz-Hubert Robling. Tübingen: Niemeyer.

Bonsenyor, Jahuda. 1889. *Llibre de paraules edits de savis e filosofs, los Proverbis de Salomo, lo llibre de Cato, fets estampar complets per primera vegada ab un pròlech y documents per en Gabriel Llabrés y Quintana*. Palma: Joan Colomor y Salas.

Bosco, Ronald A., ed. 1976. *Paterna: The Autobiography of Cotton Mather*. Delmar, NY: Scholars' Facs. & Reprints.

Bradley, Keith. 2016. "Publilius Syrus in Victoria." *Mouseion* 13 (3): 655–664.

Bradley, Keith. 2019. "Publilius Syrus and the Anxiety of Continuity." *Mouseion* 16 (S1): 65–90.

Breen, Katharine. 2010. *Imagining an English Reading Public, 1150–1400*. Cambridge: Cambridge University Press.

Breitenbach, Alfred. 2009. *Kommentar zu den Pseudo-Seneca-Epigrammen der Anthologia Vossiana*. Hildesheim: Weidmann.

British, Library. 1980. *The British Library General Catalogue of Printed Books to 1975. Vol. 56: Casti-Cazal*. London; Munich; New York; Paris: Bingley; Saur.

Brüggemann, Ludwig Wilhelm. 1797. *A View of the English Editions, Translations, and Illustrations of the Ancient Greek and Latin Authors, with Remarks*. Vol. 1. Stettin: J. S. Leich.

Brunhölzl, Franz. 1975. *Geschichte der lateinischen Literatur des Mittelalters, 1. Von Cassiodor bis zum Ausklang der karolingischen Erneuerung*. Munich: Fink.

Brunken, Otto. 1987. "Catho tzo Latyne vnde tzo Duytsche." In *Handbuch zur Kinder- und Jugendliteratur. Vom Beginn des Buchdrucks bis 1570*, edited by Theodor Brüggemann and Otto Brunken, 537–559, 1157–1160. Stuttgart: J. B. Metzler.

Brunner, Ingrid Arvide. 1965. "The Anglo-Saxon Translation of the Distichs of Cato: A Critical Edition." Ph.D. thesis, Columbia University.

Brunner, Ingrid Arvide. 1968. "On Some of the Vernacular Translations of Cato's Distichs." In *Helen Adolf Festschrift*, edited by Sheema Zeben Buehne, James L. Hodge, and Lucille B. Pinto, 99–125. New York: F. Ungar Pub. Co.

Brunt, Peter. 1965. "'Amicitia' in the Late Roman Republic." *Cambridge Classical Journal* 11: 1–20.

Brusendorff, Aage. 1929. "He Knew Nat Catoun for His Wit Was Rude." In *Studies in English Philology. A Miscellany in Honor of Frederick Klaeber*, edited by Kemp Malone and Martin B. Ruud, 320–39. Minneapolis: University of Minnesota Press.

Buisson, Ferdinand. 1911. "Civilité." In *Nouveau dictionnaire de pédagogie et d'instruction primaire*, edited by Ferdinand Buisson, 278–279. Paris: Hachette.

Buitenwerf, Rieuwerd. 2003. *Book III of the Sibylline Oracles and its Social Setting*. Leiden; Boston Brill.

Burkes, Shannon. 2002. "Wisdom and Apocalypticism in the Wisdom of Solomon." *Harvard Theological Review* 95 (1): 21–44.

Burnyeat, Myles. 1996. "Enthymeme: Aristotle on the Rationality of Rhetoric." In *Essays on Aristotle's Rhetoric*, edited by Amélie Oksenberg Rorty, 88–115. Berkeley, CA: University of California Press.

Burrow, J.A. 1990. "Reason's Horse." *The Yearbook of Langland Studies* 4 (1): 139–144.

Buuren, A.M.J. van, Orlanda Soei Han Lie, and A. P. Orbán. 1998. *Den duytschen Cathoen: naar de Antwerpse druk van Henrick Eckert van Homberch*. Hilversum (Nederlands): Verloren.

Byrne, Shannon N. 2004. "Martial's Fiction: Domitius Marsus and Maecenas." *Classical Quarterly* 54 (1): 255–265.

Calboli, Gualterio. 1999. "Sentences et proverbes dans la littérature et la rhétorique." In *Proverbes et sentences dans le monde romain: actes de la table-ronde du 26 novembre 1997*, edited by Frédérique Biville, 41–54. Lyon: Diffusion de Boccard.
Caldelli, Maria Letizia. 2001. "Amicus/-a nelle iscrizioni di Roma. L'apporto dell'epigrafia al chiarimento di un sentimento sociale." In *Aspects of Friendship in the Graeco-Roman World: Proceedings of a Conference Held at the Seminar für Alte Geschichte, Heidelberg, on 10–11 June, 2000*, edited by Michael Peachin, 21–30. Portsmouth, RI: Journal of Roman Archaeology.
Cantarella, Eva. 2003. "Fathers and Sons in Rome." *Classical World* 96 (3): 281–298.
Cannon, Christopher. 2016. *From Literacy to Literature: England, 1300–1400*. Oxford: Oxford University Press.
Carron, Delphine. 2009. "Présence de la figure de Caton le philosophe dans les proverbes et exemples médiévaux. Ses rapports avec les 'Disticha Catonis'," in *Tradition des proverbes et des exempla dans l'occident médiéval: Colloque Fribourgeois 2007 = Die Tradition der Sprichwörter und Exempla im Mittelalter: Freiburger Colloquium 2007*, edited by Hugo O. Bizzarri and Martin Rohde, 165–190. Berlin: De Gruyter.
Carusi, E., and W.M. Lindsay, eds. 1934. *Monumenti paleografici Veronesi*. Vol. 2. Rome: Biblioteca Apostólica Vaticana.
Casson, Lionel. 1965. "Harbour and River Boats of Ancient Rome." *Journal of Roman Studies* 55, no. 1/2: 31–39.
Cavill, Paul. 1998. "Maxims in The Battle of Maldon." *Neophilologus* 82 (4): 631–644.
Cavill, Paul. 1999. *Maxims in Old English Poetry*. Woodbridge; Rochester, NY: D.S. Brewer.
Champlin, Edward. 1981. "Serenus Sammonicus." *Harvard Studies in Classical Philology* 85: 189–212.
Chase, Wayland Johnson, ed. 1922. *The Distichs of Cato, a Famous Medieval Textbook Translated from the Latin*. Madison, WI: University of Wisconsin.
Chevallier, Raymond. 1997. "Perspectives de recherche sur les scènes de métiers (Gaule Cisalpine et Transalpine)." *Archeologia classica* 49: 47–63.
Christes, Johannes. 1979. "Reflexe erlebter Unfreiheit in den Sentenzen des Publilius Syrus und den Fabeln des Phaedrus: Zur Problematik ihrer Verifizierung." *Hermes* 107 (2): 199–220.
Cipolla, Carlo. 1880. "I codici veronesi dei Distici catoniani." *Rivista di filologia e di istruzione classica* 8: 517–536.
Civil, Pierre. 1996. "La formation morale de l'enfant au XVIe siècle à travers les Catones." In *La formation de l'enfant en Espagne aux XVIe et XVIIe siècles*, edited by Augustin Redondo, 253–271. Paris: Publications de la Sorbonne.
Clackson, James. 2011. "The Social Dialects of Latin." In *A Companion to the Latin Language*, edited by James Clackson, 505–526. Chichester, West Sussex; Malden, MA: Wiley-Blackwell.
Clavería, Carlos. 1989. "La traslación del muy excelente doctor Catón llamado, hecha por un egregio maestro, Martín García nombrado." *Cuadernos de Estudios Caspolinos* 15: 29–140.
Clifford, Richard J. 1999. "Proverbs as a Source for Wisdom of Solomon." In *Treasures of Wisdom: Studies in Ben Sira and the Book of Wisdom: Festschrift M. Gilbert*, edited by Núria Calduch-Benages and J. Vermeylen, 255–263. Leuven: Leuven University Press: Uitgeverij Peeters.

Clifford, Richard J. 2007. *Wisdom Literature in Mesopotamia and Israel*. Atlanta: Society of Biblical Literature.

Clogan, Paul Maurice. 1982. "Literary Genres in a Medieval Textbook." *Classica et Mediaevalia* n.s. 11: 199–209.

Coffee, Neil. 2017. *Gift and Gain: How Money Transformed Ancient Rome*. New York: Oxford University Press.

Cokayne, Karen. 2003. *Experiencing Old Age in Ancient Rome*. London: Routledge.

Colafrancesco, Pasqua, Matteo Massaro, and Maria Lisa Ricci. 1986. *Concordanze dei Carmina Latina epigraphica*. Bari: Edipuglia.

Connolly, Serena. 2004. "Women at the Edge: Gender and Ethnicity in Law at Dura-Europos." In *Gender and Diversity in Place: Proceedings of the Fourth Conference on Feminism and Classics*, edited by Marilyn Skinner. Diotima.

Connolly, Serena. 2010. "Lucan's *Pharsalia* in the *Disticha Catonis*." *Classica et Mediaevalia* 61: 193–202.

Connolly, Serena. 2011. "The Meter of the *Disticha Catonis*." *Classical Journal* 107 (3): 313–329.

Connolly, Serena. 2012. "Disticha Catonis Uticensis." *Classical Philology* 107 (2): 119–130.

Connolly, Serena. 2013a. "Binarism in the Disticha Catonis." *Mnemosyne* 66 (2): 228–246.

Connolly, Serena. 2013b. "Das älteste Distichazitat." *Latomus* 72: 122–127.

Connolly, Serena. Forthcoming. "Catoun, Caton (Dionysius Cato)." In *The Chaucer Encyclopedia*, edited by Richard Newhauser. Oxford: Wiley-Blackwell.

Constantine, Mary-Ann. 2008. "Welsh Literary History and the Making of 'the Myvyrian Archaiology of Wales'." In *Editing the Nation's Memory: Textual Scholarship and Nation-Building in Nineteenth-Century Europe*, edited by Dirk van Hulle and Joep Leerssen, 109–128. Amsterdam: Rodopi.

Conte, Gian Biagio. 1994. *Latin Literature: A History*. Baltimore, MD: The Johns Hopkins University Press.

Contini, Gianfranco, ed. 1941. *Le opere volgari di Bonvesin da la Riva. Vol. 1. Testi*. Rome: Presso la Società.

Cook, Patrick. 2003. "The *Ecloga Theoduli*." In *Medieval Literature for Children*, edited by Daniel T. Kline, 188–203. Florence: Taylor & Francis Group.

Copeland, Rita. 2012. "Gloss and Commentary." In *The Oxford Handbook of Medieval Latin Literature*, edited by Ralph J. Hexter and David Townsend, 171–191. Oxford; New York: Oxford University Press.

Cotton, Hannah. 1993. "The Guardianship of Jesus Son of Babatha: Roman and Local Law in the Province of Arabia." *Journal of Roman Studies* 83 (1993): 94–108.

Cox, R. S. 1972. "The Old English Dicts of Cato." *Anglia: Zeitschrift für englische Philologie* 90: 1–42.

Crane, Mary. 1986. "Intret Cato: Authority and Epigram in Sixteenth-Century England." *Harvard English Studies* 14: 158–186.

Crawford, Michael. 1971. "Le problème des liquidités dans l'Antiquité classique." *Annales. Histoire, Sciences Sociales* 26, no. 6: 1228–1233.

Cribiore, Raffaella. 2001. *Gymnastics of the Mind: Greek Education in Hellenistic and Roman Egypt*. Princeton, NJ: Princeton University Press.

Crook, John. 1967. *Law and Life of Rome*. London: Thames and Hudson.

Crook, John. 1986. "Women in Roman Succession." In *The Family in Ancient Rome: New Perspectives*, edited by Beryl Rawson, 58–82. London: Croom Helm.

Csaba, Németh. 2003. Review of Nagyillés, *Cato & Publilius (Latin mondások. Cato mondásai. Publilius Syrus szentenciái)*. *Jelenkor* 46: 542–547.
Cummings, Robert, and Stuart Gillespie. 2009. "Translations from Greek and Latin Classics 1550–1700: A Revised Bibliography." *Translation and Literature* 18 (1): 1–42.
Cuomo, Serafina. 2007. *Technology and Culture in Greek and Roman Antiquity*. Cambridge; New York: Cambridge University Press.
Dankoff, Robert. 1981. "Inner Asian Wisdom Traditions in the Pre-Mongol Period." *Journal of the American Oriental Society* 101 (1): 87–95.
Delgado, Buenaventura. 1990. "Un antiguo texto escolar: los 'Dísticos Morales' de Catón." In *Historia, literatura, pensamiento: estudios en homenaje a María Dolores Gómez Molleda*, edited by Mercedes Samaniego Boneu and Valentín del Arco López, 371–383. Salamanca: Universidad de Salamanca: Narcea.
Delhaye, Philippe. 1949. "L'enseignement de la philosophie morale au XIIe siècle." *Mediaeval Studies* 11: 77–99.
Deskis, Susan E. 1996. *Beowulf and the Medieval Proverb Tradition*. Tempe, AZ: Medieval & Renaissance Texts & Studies.
Díaz de Bustamente, José Manuel. 1999. "Regarding Some Latin Sources of the *Arcipreste de Talavera*: An Evaluation of their Incidence Upon the Establishment of a Critical Text." In *Latin and Vernacular in Renaissance Spain*, edited by Barry Taylor and Alejandro Coroleu, 13–24. Manchester: Manchester Spanish & Portuguese Studies.
Dickey, Eleanor. 1999. Review of George A. Kennedy, *The Latin Iliad: Introduction, Text, Translation, and Notes*. 1998. *Bryn Mawr Classical Review* 99.01.06.
Dickey, Eleanor. 2007. *Ancient Greek Scholarship: A Guide to Finding, Reading, and Understanding Scholia, Commentaries, Lexica, and Grammatical Treatises: From Their Beginnings to the Byzantine Period*. Oxford; New York: Oxford University Press.
DiGiulio, Scott J. 2020. "Gellius' Strategies of Reading (Gellius): Miscellany and the Active Reader in *Noctes Atticae* Book 2." *Classical Philology* 115 (2): 242–264.
Dixon, Suzanne. 1986. "Family Finances: Terentia and Tullia." In *The Family in Ancient Rome: New Perspectives*, edited by Beryl Rawson, 93–120. London: Croom Helm.
Dixon, Suzanne. 1992. *The Roman Family*. Baltimore, MD: The Johns Hopkins University Press.
Dixon, Suzanne. 1993. "The Meaning of Gift and Debt in the Roman Elite." *Echos du monde classique* 37, n.s. 12: 451–464.
Domach, Zachary M. 2013. "Tempered in the Christian Fire: Greek and Roman Wisdom Literature in Early Christian Teaching and Moral Traditions." M.A. thesis, Emory University.
Drogula, Fred. 2019. *Cato the Younger: Life and Death at the End of the Roman Republic*. Oxford; New York: Oxford University Press.
Duckworth, George E. 1969. *Vergil and Classical Hexameter Poetry: A Study in Metrical Variety*. Ann Arbor: University of Michigan Press.
Duemmler, Ernst Ludwig. 1881. *Monumenta Germaniae Historica. 5. Antiquitates. Poetae Latini medii aevi. Bd. 1. Poetae Latini aevi Carolini*. Berlin: Weidmann.
Duff, John Wight, and Arnold Mackay Duff. *Minor Latin Poets*. London; Cambridge, MA: Heinemann; Harvard University Press, 1934.
Düringsfeld, Ida von, and Otto von Reinsberg-Düringsfeld. 1872. *Sprichwörter der germanischen und romanischen Sprachen vergleichend*. Leipzig: H. Fries.
Dyck, Andrew R. 1996. *A Commentary on Cicero, De officiis*. Ann Arbor: University of Michigan Press, 1996.

Ebbeler, Jennifer. 2007. "Mixed Messages: The Play of Epistolary Codes in Two Late Antique Latin Correspondences." In *Ancient Letters: Classical and Late Antique Epistolography*, edited by Ruth Morello and A.D. Morrison, 301–24. Oxford; New York: Oxford University Press.

Elliott, Colin P. 2015. "The Crisis of A.D. 33: Past and Present." *Journal of Ancient History* 3 (2): 267–281.

Elliott, Colin P. 2020. *Economic Theory and the Roman Monetary Economy*. Cambridge: Cambridge University Press.

Ellis, R. 1871. "Review of *Catonis Philosophi Liber. Recensuit Ferdinandus Hauthal*." *The Academy* 2: 321–322.

Evans, D.A.H. 1993. "Hugsvinnsmál." In *Medieval Scandinavia: An Encyclopedia*, edited by Phillip Pulsiano and Kirsten Wolf, 306. New York: Garland.

Evans, Katherine G. 1997. "Friendship in Greek Documentary Papyri and Inscriptions: A Survey." In *Greco-Roman Perspectives on Friendship*, edited by John T. Fitzgerald, 181–202. Atlanta, Ga.: Scholars Press.

Evenepoel, Willy. 2006. "Seneca's Letters on Friendship: Notes on the Recent Scholarly Literature and Observations on Three Quaestiones." *L'Antiquité classique* 75: 177–193.

Fairclough, H. Rushton, ed. 1916. *Virgil, Eclogues, Georgics, Aeneid, Books 1–6*. London: Heinemann.

Falk, Doris V. 1967. "Proverbs and the Polonius Destiny." *Shakespeare Quarterly* 18 (1): 23–36.

Fantham, Elaine. 1972. *Comparative Studies in Republican Latin Imagery*. Toronto: University of Toronto Press.

Faral, Edmond. 1924. *Les arts poétiques du XIIe et du XIIIe siècle*. Paris: É. Champion.

Fehling, Detlev. 1985. *Die sieben Weisen und die frühgriechische Chronologie: eine traditionsgeschichtliche Studie*. Bern; New York: P. Lang.

Fink, Hanns-Peter. 1991. *Exercitia latina: vom Unterricht lippischer Junggrafen zur Zeit der Spätrenaissance*. Marburg: Jonas-Verlag.

Fink-Jensen, Morten. 2021. "Teaching and Educational Reforms in Denmark and Norway c. 1500–1750." In *Exploring Textbooks and Cultural Change in Nordic Education 1536–2020*, edited by Merethe Roos et al., 16–28. Leiden: Brill.

Fiore, Benjamin. 1986. *The Function of Personal Example in the Socratic and Pastoral Epistles*. Rome: Biblical Institute Press.

Fitzgerald, John T., ed. 1997. *Greco-Roman Perspectives on Friendship*. Atlanta, Ga.: Scholars Press.

Fitzgerald, William. 1996. "Labor and Laborer in Latin Poetry: The Case of the Moretum." *Arethusa* 29 (3): 389–418.

Fitzgerald, William. 2016. *Variety: The Life of a Roman Concept*. Chicago: University of Chicago Press.

Fitzpatrick, Matthew P. 2011. "Provincializing Rome: The Indian Ocean Trade Network and Roman Imperialism." *Journal of World History* 22 (1): 27–54.

Fleming, Juliet. 1999. "Graffiti, Grammatology, and the Age of Shakespeare." In *Renaissance Culture and the Everyday*, edited by Patricia Fumerton and Simon Hunt, 315–351. Philadelphia: University of Pennsylvania Press.

Flower, Harriet I. 1996. *Ancestor Masks and Aristocratic Power in Roman Culture*. Oxford New York: Clarendon Press; Oxford University Press.

Fontana, Laura. 1979. "Un inedito volgarizzamento toscano dei 'Disticha Catonis'." In *In ricordo di Cesare Angelini: studi di letteratura e filologia*, edited by Cesare Angelini, Franco Alessio, and Angelo Stella, 46–64. Milan: Il saggiatore.

Forbes, Clarence A. 1955. "Supplementary Paper: The Education and Training of Slaves in Antiquity." *Transactions and Proceedings of the American Philological Association* 86: 321–360.

Förster, Max. 1906. "Eine nordenglische Cato-Version." *Englische Studien* 36: 1–55.

Foster, John L. 1975. "Thought Couplets in Khety's 'Hymn to the Inundation'." *Journal of Near Eastern Studies* 34 (1): 1–27.

Foster, John L. 1977. *Thought Couplets and Clause Sequences in a Literary Text: The Maxims of Ptah-hotep*. Toronto: Society for the Study of Egyptian Antiquities.

Fox, Michael V. 2011. "Ancient Near Eastern Wisdom Literature (Didactic)." *Religion Compass* 5 (1): 1–11.

Frederiksen, M.W. 1966. "Caesar, Cicero and the Problem of Debt." *Journal of Roman Studies* 56: 128–141.

Freeman, Ann. 1998. *Monumenta Germaniae Historica. 2. Leges. 5. Concilia. 2, Suppl. 1. Opus Caroli regis contra synodum (Libri Carolini)*. Hannover: Hahnsche.

Frith, Anne Deed, and Susan Treggiari. 2007. *Daniel of Beccles: Urbanus Magnus, The Book of the Civilized Man*. Beccles, Suffolk: A. Deed Frith.

Fuhrmann, Christopher J. 2011. *Policing the Roman Empire: Soldiers, Administration, and Public Order*. Oxford: Oxford University Press.

Funghi, Maria Serena. 2003. *Aspetti di letteratura gnomica nel mondo antico*. Florence: L. S. Olschki.

Furnivall, Frederick James. 1901. *The Minor Poems of the Vernon Ms*. Vol. 2, London: K. Paul, Trench, Trübner & Co.

Gago Jover, Francisco. 2003. *Textos y concordancias de las versiones castellanas de la Disticha Catonis*. CD-ROM. New York: Hispanic Seminary of Medieval Studies.

Galloway, Andrew. 1987. "Two Notes on Langland's Cato: Piers Plowman B.I.88–91; IV.20–23." *English Language Notes* 25: 9–12.

Gammie, John G. 1990. "Paraenetic Literature: Toward the Morphology of a Secondary Genre." *Semeia* (50): 41–77.

Gardner, Jane. 1986. *Women in Roman Law & Society*. London: Croom Helm.

Garnsey, Peter, and Richard P. Saller. 1987. *The Roman Empire: Economy, Society, and Culture*. London: Duckworth.

Garrison, Daniel. 2004. *The Student's Catullus*. 3rd ed. Norman: University of Oklahoma Press.

Garthwaite, John. 1998. "Patronage and Poetic Immortality in Martial, Book 9." *Mnemosyne* 51 (2): 161.

Gazzaniga, Michael S., and George A. Miller. 1989. "The Recognition of Antonymy by a Language-Enriched Right Hemisphere." *Journal of Cognitive Neuroscience* 1 (2): 187–194.

Gehl, Paul. F. 1989. "Latin Readers in Fourteenth-Century Florence. Schoolkids and Their Books." *Scrittura e civiltà* 13: 387–440.

Gehl, Paul. F. 1993. *A Moral Art: Grammar, Society, and Culture in Trecento Florence*. Ithaca: Cornell University Press.

Gehl, Paul. F. 2008. *Humanism for Sale: Making and Marketing Schoolbooks in Italy, 1450–1650*. http://www.humanismforsale.org (accessed 5/18/2022).

Gerhard, Gustav Adolf. 1909. *Phoinix von Kolophon: Texte und Untersuchungen*. Leipzig; Berlin: B.G. Teubner.

Gering, Hugo, ed. 1907. *Hugsvinnsmál: ein altisländische Übersetzung der Disticha Catonis.* Kiel: Lipsius & Tischer.
Germann, Peter. 1910. *Die sogenannten Sententiae Varronis.* Paderborn: F. Schöningh.
Giancotti, Francesco. 1967. *Mimo e gnome. Studio su Decimo Laberio e Publilio Siro.* Messina; Florence: G. D'Anna.
Gibbs, Laura. 2002. *Aesop's Fables.* Oxford: Oxford University Press, 2002.
Gibson, Roy, and A. D. Morrison. 2007. "What is a Letter?" In *Ancient Letters: Classical and Late Antique Epistolography*, edited by Ruth Morello and A. D. Morrison, 1–16. Oxford; New York: Oxford University Press.
Gildersleeve, Basil Lanneau. 1895. *Latin Grammar.* 3rd ed. London: Macmillan & Co.
Gillingham, John. 2002. "From Civilitas to Civility: Codes of Manners in Medieval and Early Modern England." *Transactions of the Royal Historical Society* 12 (1): 267–289.
Ginguené, M. 1971. "Éverard ou Évrard, poète français." In *Histoire Littéraire de la France*, 67–70. Paris; Nendeln: Firmin Didot Kraus Reprint.
Glaser, Edward. 1954. "An Addition to the Cervantes Canon?" *Harvard Library Bulletin* 8: 88–96.
Glauche, Günter. 1972. "Die Rolle der Schulautoren im Unterricht von 800 bis 1100." In *La scuola nell'Occidente latino dell'alto Medioevo: 15–21 aprile 1971*, edited by Centro italiano di studi sull'alto Medioevo, 617–638. Spoleto: Presso la sede del Centro.
Goldberg, Max Otto. 1883. "Die catonischen Distichen während des Mittelalters in der englischen und französischen Literatur / 1. Der englische Cato." Ph.D. thesis. Universität Leipzig. Leipzig: Joachim et Jüstel.
Goodspeed, E.J. 1905. "Greek Documents in the Museum of the New York Historical Society." *Mélanges Nicole*: 181–183.
Görler, W. 1963. "Menandrou gnomai." Ph.D. thesis. Freie Universität Berlin. Berlin: Freie Universität Berlin.
Graffunder, Paul. 1897. *Cato's Distichen in niederrheinischer Übersetzung.* Berlin: Oldenbourg.
Graffunder, Paul. 1899. "Meister Stephans Mittelniederdeutscher Cato." *Jahrbuch des Vereins für niederdeutsche Sprachforschung* 25: 1–33.
Green, Ian M. 2009. *Humanism and Protestantism in Early Modern English Education.* Burlington, VT: Ashgate.
Green, R.P.H., 1980. *Seven Versions of Carolingian Pastoral.* Reading: Department of Classics, Reading University.
Green, Steven, ed. 2018. *Grattius: Hunting an Augustan Poet.* Oxford: Oxford University Press.
Greenough, J.B. 1900. *The Bucolics, Georgics, and Aeneid of Vergil.* Boston: Ginn and Co.
Gregory, C.A. 1982. *Gifts and Commodities.* London: Academic Press.
Grendler, Paul F. 1989. *Schooling in Renaissance Italy: Literacy and Learning, 1300–1600.* Baltimore, MD: The Johns Hopkins University Press.
Griffin, Miriam T. 2013. *Seneca on Society: A Guide to De beneficiis.* Oxford: Oxford University Press.
Griffin, Miriam T., and E.M. Atkins, eds. 1991. *Cicero, On Duties.* Cambridge: Cambridge University Press.
Grubmüller, Karl. 1983. "Der Lehrgang des Triviums und die Rolle der Volkssprache im späten Mittelalter." In *Studien zum städtischen Bildungswesen des späten Mittelalters und der frühen Neuzeit*, edited by Bernd Moeller et al., 371–397. Göttingen: Vandenhoeck & Ruprecht.

Grundmann, Herbert. 1958. "Litteratus-illitteratus: der Wandel einer Bildungsnorm vom Altertum zum Mittelalter." *Archiv für Kulturgeschichte* 40: 1–65.
Gwara, Scott, and David W. Porter, eds. 1997. *Anglo-Saxon Conversations: The Colloquies of Aelfric Bata*. Woodbridge; Rochester, NY: Boydell Press.
Haag, Guntram. 2002. "Illokution und Adressatenorientierung in der Zwettler Gesamtübersetzung und der Melker Rumpfbearbeitung der 'Disticha Catonis': funktionale und sprachliche Einflussfaktoren." *Arbeiten zur Mehrsprachigkeit = Working Papers in Multilingualism* 38: 1–25.
Haag, Guntram. 2005. "Kulturfilter in mittelalterlichen deutschen Übersetzungen der Disticha Catonis." *LiLi. Zeitschrift für Literaturwissenschaft und Linguistik* 35 (1): 146–156.
Habenicht, Rudolph E., ed. 1963. *John Heywood's A Dialogue of Proverbs*. Berkeley: University of California Press.
Hallik, Sibylle. 2007. *Sententia und Proverbium: Begriffsgeschichte und Texttheorie in Antike und Mittelalter*. Cologne: Böhlau.
Hamblenne, Pierre. 1973. "L'opinion romaine en 46–43 et les sentences 'politiques' de Publilius Syrus." In *Aufstieg und Niedergang der römischen Welt* 1.3, edited by Hildegard Temporini and Wolfgang Haase, 630–702. Berlin: W. de Gruyter.
Harmening, Dieter. 1970. "Neue Beiträge zum deutschen Cato." *Zeitschrift für deutsche Philologie* 89: 346–368.
Harris, William. 2006. "A Revisionist View of Roman Money." *Journal of Roman Studies* 96: 1–24.
Harrison, George W.M. 2001. "Martial on Sportula and the Saturnalia." *Mouseion* 1 (3): 295–312.
Hasluck, F. W. 1907. "Inscriptions from the Cyzicus District, 1906." *Journal of Hellenic Studies* 27: 61–67.
Hazelton, Richard. 1956. *Two Texts of the Disticha Catonis and its Commentary, With Special Reference to Chaucer, Langland and Gower*. New Brunswick, NJ: Rutgers University Press.
Hazelton, Richard. 1957. "The Christianization of "Cato". The Disticha Catonis in the Light of Late Mediaeval Commentaries." *Mediaeval Studies* 19: 157–173.
Heath, Jane M.F. 2020. *Clement of Alexandria and the Shaping of Christian Literary Practice: Miscellany and the Transformation of Greco-Roman Writing*. Cambridge; New York: Cambridge University Press.
Hellegouarc'h, Joseph. 1972. *Le vocabulaire latin des relations et des partis politiques sous la République*. 2nd ed. Paris: Les Belles lettres.
Hendrickson, G.L. 1917. "Horace and Valerius Cato. II." *Classical Philology* 12 (1): 77–92.
Hermannsson, Halldór. 1958. *The Hólar Cato: An Icelandic Schoolbook of the Seventeenth Century*. Ithaca, NY: Cornell University Press.
Herrmann, Léon. 1950. *Phèdre et ses fables*. Leiden: Brill.
Hervieux, Léopold, ed. 1899. *Les fabulistes latins depuis le siècle d'Auguste jusqu'à la fin du Moyen Âge*. Vol. 5. Paris: Firmin-Didot.
Holiday, Ryan. 2016. *The Daily Stoic: 366 Meditations on Wisdom, Perseverance, and the Art of Living*. New York: Portfolio/Penguin.
Hollander, David B. 2012. *Money in the Late Roman Republic*. Leiden; Boston: Brill.
Holleran, Claire. 2011. "The Street Life of Ancient Rome." In *Rome, Ostia, Pompeii: Movement and Space*, edited by Ray Laurence and David J. Newsome, 245–261. Oxford; New York: Oxford University Press.
Holton, Amanda. 2008. *The Sources of Chaucer's Poetics*. Aldershot; Burlington, VT: Ashgate.

Holzberg, Niklas. 2004. "Impersonating the Banished Philosopher: Pseudo-Seneca's 'Liber Epigrammaton'." *Harvard Studies in Classical Philology* 102: 423–444.

Hopkins, Keith. 1965. "Elite Mobility in the Roman Empire." *Past & Present* 32: 12–26.

Horden, Peregrine, and Nicholas Purcell. 2000. *The Corrupting Sea: A Study of Mediterranean History*. Oxford, U.K.; Malden, Mass: Blackwell.

Horrall, Sarah. 1981. "An Unknown Middle English Translation of the *Distichs* of Cato." *Anglia* 99: 25–37.

Horsfall, Nicholas. 1985. "CIL VI 37965 = CLE 1988 (Epitaph of Allia Potestas): A Commentary." *ZPE* 61: 251–272.

Horst, Pieter Willem van der, ed. 1978. *The Sentences of Pseudo-Phocylides*. Leiden: Brill.

House, Juliane. 1997. *Translation Quality Assessment: A Model Revisited*. Tübingen: Gunter Narr.

Howgego, Christopher. 1992. "The Supply and Use of Money in the Roman World 200 BC to AD 300." *Journal of Roman Studies* 82: 1–31.

Howlett, D.R. 1995. *The Celtic Latin Tradition of Biblical Style*. Blackrock, Co. Dublin: Four Courts Press.

Hunt, Tony. 1980. "The Old French Cato in Ms Darmstadt 2640." *Vox Romanica* 39: 44–63.

Hunt, Tony. 1991. *Teaching and Learning Latin in Thirteenth-Century England*. Cambridge: Brewer.

Hunt, Tony. 1994. *Le livre de Catun*. London: Anglo-Norman Text Society.

Hunt, Tony, ed. 2005. *Les paraboles Maistre Alain en françoys*. London: Modern Humanities Research Association.

Infantes, Víctor. 1997. "El Catón hispánico: versiones, ediciones y transmisiones." In *Actas del vi congreso internacional de la Asociación Hispánica de Literatura Medieval*, edited by José Manuel Lucía Megías, 839–846. Alcalá de Henares: Servicio de Publicaciones, Universidad de Alcalá.

Inwood, Brad. 2007. "The Importance of Form in the Letters of Seneca the Younger." In *Ancient Letters: Classical and Late Antique Epistolography*, edited by Ruth Morello and A.D. Morrison, 133–148. Oxford: Oxford University Press.

Inwood, Brad, ed. 2010. *Seneca, Selected Philosophical Letters*. New York: Oxford University Press.

Jacobs, John. 2020. *An Introduction to Silius Italicus and the Punica*. London: Bloomsbury.

Jacobson Schutte, Anne. 1986. "Teaching Adults to Read in Sixteenth-Century Venice: Giovanni Antonio Tagliente's Libro maistrevole." *The Sixteenth Century Journal* 17 (1): 3–16.

Jäkel, Siegfried, ed. 1964. *Menandri Sententiae; Comparatio Menandri et Philistionis*. Leipzig: Teubner.

James, M.R. 1908. *A Descriptive Catalogue of the Manuscripts in the Library of Gonville and Caius College*. Vol. 2. Cambridge: Cambridge University Press.

Johnson, Allan Chester. 1936. *Roman Egypt: To the Reign of Diocletian. An Economic Survey of Ancient Rome*, Vol. 2. Baltimore, MD: The Johns Hopkins University Press.

Johnson, William A. 2010. *Readers and Reading Culture in the High Roman Empire: A Study of Elite Communities*. Classical Culture and Society. New York: Oxford University Press.

Jones, David. 2006. *The Bankers of Puteoli: Finance, Trade and Industry in the Roman World*. Stroud: Tempus.

Joshel, Sandra R. 1992. *Work, Identity, and Legal Status at Rome: A Study of the Occupational Inscriptions*. Norman: University of Oklahoma Press.

Justice, Steven. 2015. *Adam Usk's Secret*. Philadelphia: University of Pennsylvania Press.

Kassis, Riad Aziz. 1999. *The Book of Proverbs and Arabic Proverbial Works*. Leiden; Boston: Brill.

Kaster, Robert A. 1997. *Guardians of Language: The Grammarian and Society in Late Antiquity*. Berkeley: University of California Press.

Kaster, Robert A. 2005. *Emotion, Restraint, and Community in Ancient Rome*. Oxford; New York: Oxford University Press.

Kay, Philip. 2014. *Rome's Economic Revolution*. Oxford; New York: Oxford University Press.

Kennedy, George A. 2007. *Aristotle on Rhetoric: A Theory of Civic Discourse*. 2nd ed. Oxford; New York: Oxford University Press.

Kessler, Rachel C. 2008. "Reading Gnomic Phenomena in Old English Literature." Ph.D. dissertation. University of Toronto. Toronto: University of Toronto.

Kesting, Peter. 1975. "Ein deutscher 'Cato' in Prosa. Cato und Cicero in der St. Galler Weltchronik." In *Würzburger Prosastudien II: Untersuchungen zur Literatur und Sprache des Mittelalters. Kurt Ruh zum 60. Geburtstag*, edited by Peter Kesting, 161–173. Munich: Fink.

Kesting, Peter. 1978. "Cato." In *Die deutsche Literatur des Mittelalters. Verfasserlexikon, Bd. 1. A - Colmarer*, edited by Wolfgang Stammle et al., 1192–1196. Berlin; New York: W. de Gruyter.

Kesting, Peter. 1983. "Kemnater, Hans." In *Die deutsche Literatur des Mittelalters. Verfasserlexikon, 4, Hildegard von Hürnheim-Koburger*, edited by Karl Langosch et al., 1112–1114. Berlin; New York: W. de Gruyter.

Kettler, Wilfried. 2002. *Trewlich ins Teütsch gebracht: Lateinisch-Deutsches Übersetzungsschrifttum im Umkreis des schweizerischen Humanismus*. Bern; New York: P. Lang.

Kitchen, Kenneth A. 1977. "Proverbs and Wisdom Books of the Ancient Near East: The Factual History of a Literary Form." *Tyndale Bulletin* 28 (1): 69–114.

Kitchen, Kenneth A. 1979. "The Basic Literary Forms and Formulations of Ancient Instructional Writings in Egypt and Western Asia." In *Studien zu altägyptischen Lebenslehren*, edited by Erik Hornung and Othmar Keel, 235–282. Freiburg; Göttingen: Universitätsverlag; Vandenhoeck & Ruprecht.

Kitchen, Kenneth A. 1998. "Biblical Instructional Wisdom: The Decisive Voice of the Ancient Near East." In *Boundaries of the Ancient Near Eastern World: A Tribute to Cyrus H. Gordon*, edited by Meir Lubetski, Claire Gottlieb, and Sharon R. Keller, 346–363. Sheffield: Sheffield Academic Press.

Kline, Anthony S. 2002. *Virgil—The Georgics*. Online. Poetry in Translation. https://www.poetryintranslation.com/klineasgeorgics.php (accessed 5/18/2022).

Knaake, Joachim Carl Friedrich, ed. 1883. *D. Martin Luthers Werke. Kritische Gesammtausgabe*. Weimar: H. Böhlaus.

Knapp, Charles. 1913. Review of *Die sogenannten Sententiae Varronis* by Peter Germann. *Classical Philology* 8 (3): 372–374.

Knapp, Robert C. 2011. *Invisible Romans: Prostitutes, Outlaws, Slaves, Gladiators, Ordinary Men and Women—The Romans that History Forgot*. London: Profile Books.

Konstan, David. 1996. "Friendship, Frankness, and Flattery." In *Friendship, Flattery, and Frankness of Speech: Studies on Friendship in the New Testament World*, edited by John T. Fitzgerald, 7–19. Leiden: Brill.

Konstan, David. 1997. *Friendship in the Classical World*. Cambridge; New York: Cambridge University Press.

Lambert, W.G. 1960. *Babylonian Wisdom Literature*. Oxford: Clarendon Press.
Langford Wilson, Harry. 1911. "Latin Inscriptions at the Johns Hopkins University. VI." *The American Journal of Philology* 32 (2): 166–187.
Langlands, Rebecca. 2018. *Exemplary Ethics in Ancient Rome*. Cambridge University Press.
Langslow, D.R. 2007. "The *Epistula* in Ancient Scientific and Technical Literature, with Special Reference to Medicine." In *Ancient Letters: Classical and Late Antique Epistolography*, edited by Ruth Morello and A. D. Morrison, 211–234. Oxford; New York: Oxford University Press.
Lapidge, Michael. 1982. "The Study of Latin Texts in Late Anglo-Saxon England: The Evidence of Latin Glosses." In *Latin and the Vernacular Languages in Early Medieval Britain. Papers Delivered to the Fifth Annual St. John's House Symposium, University of St. Andrews, 12 May 1979*, edited by Nicholas P. Brooks, 99–140. Leicester: Leicester University Press.
Lapidge, Michael. 1996. *Anglo-Latin Literature, 600–899*. London; Rio Grande, OH: Hambledon Press.
Lardinois, André. 1997. "Modern Paroemiology and the Use of Gnomai in Homer's Iliad." *Classical Philology* 92 (3): 213–234.
Lardinois, André. 2001. "The Wisdom and Wit of Many: The Orality of Greek Proverbial Expressions." In *Speaking Volumes: Orality and Literacy in the Greek and Roman World*, edited by Janet Watson, 93–107. Leiden: Brill.
Larrington, Carolyne. 1993. *A Store of Common Sense: Gnomic Theme and Style in Old Icelandic and Old English Wisdom Poetry*. Oxford: Clarendon Press.
Larsen, Mik Robert. 2015. "The Representation of Poverty in the Roman Empire." Ph.D. thesis. University of California, Los Angeles. Los Angeles: University of California, Los Angeles.
Lathrop, Thomas A., trans. 2005. *Miguel de Cervantes Saavedra, Don Quixote: Fourth-Centenary Translation*. Newark, Del.: Cervantes & Co.
Lazaridis, Nikolaos. 2007. *Wisdom in Loose Form: The Language of Egyptian and Greek Proverbs in Collections of the Hellenistic and Roman Periods*. Leiden; Boston: Brill.
Leach, Arthur Francis. 1911. *Educational Charters and Documents 598 to 1909*. Cambridge: Cambridge University Press.
Leach, Arthur Francis. 1915. *The Schools of Medieval England*. New York: B. Blom.
Lehmann, Paul. 1922. *Die Parodie im Mittelalter*. Munich: Drei Masken Verlag.
LeMoine Fannie, J. 1991. "Parental gifts: Father-Son Dedications and Dialogues in Roman Didactic Literature." *Illinois Classical Studies* XVI: 337–366.
Le Roux, Patrick. 1972. "Recherches sur les centurions de la Legio VII Gemina." *Mélanges de la Casa de Velázquez* 8: 89–159.
Lesne, Emile. 1938. *Histoire de la propriété ecclésiastique en France. Tome IV: les livres, "scriptoria" et bibliothèques du commencement du VIIIe à la fin du XIe siècle*. Lille: Facultés Catholiques.
Leutsch, Ernst von, and Friedrich Wilhelm Schneidewin, eds. 1839. *Corpus paroemiographorum praecorum*. Göttingen: Vandenhoeck and Ruprecht.
Lévi-Strauss, Claude. 1963. *Structural Anthropology*. New York: Basic Books.
Liapis, Vayos. 2002. *Menandrou Gnomai monostichoi: eisagoge, metaphrase, semeseioseis*. Athens: Stigme.
Liapis, Vayos. 2007. "How to Make a Monostichos: Strategies of Variation in the "Sententiae Menandri"." *Harvard Studies in Classical Philology* 103: 261–298.
Lichtheim, Miriam. 1973. *Ancient Egyptian Literature; A Book of Readings*. Berkeley: University of California Press.

Lichtheim, Miriam. 1983. *Late Egyptian Wisdom Literature in the International Context: A Study of Demotic Instructions*. Freiburg; Göttingen: Universitätsverlag; Vandenhoeck & Ruprecht.
Lindsay, Hugh. 2000. "Death-Pollution and Funerals in the City of Rome." In *Death and Disease in the Ancient City*, edited by Valerie M. Hope and Eireann Marshall, 152–173. London: Routledge.
Lindsay, W.M. 1923. "Collectanea Varia." *Palaeographia latina* 2: 5–55.
Löfstedt, Leena. 1966. *Les expressions du commandement et de la défense en latin et leur survie dans les langues romanes*. Helsinki, Société Néophilologique.
Lowe, Elias Avery. 1947. *Codices Latini antiquiores 4. Italy: Perugia—Verona*. Oxford: Clarendon Press.
Lutz, Cora E. 1957. "The Commentary of Remigius of Auxerre on Martianus Capella." *Mediaeval Studies* 19: 137–156.
MacCormack, Sabine. 2007. *On the Wings of Time: Rome, the Incas, Spain, and Peru*. Princeton: Princeton University Press.
MacMullen, Ramsay. 1974. *Roman Social Relations, 50 BC to AD 284*. New Haven: Yale University Press.
Malnati, T.P. 1987. "Juvenal and Martial on Social Mobility." *Classical Journal* 83 (2): 133–141.
Mancini, A. 1902. "Un commento ignoto di Remy d'Auxerre ai Disticha Catonis." *Rendiconti della Reale Accademia dei Lincei, Classe di scienze morali, storiche e filologiche* ser. 5, 11: 175–198; 369–382.
Manitius, Max. 1892. "Beiträge zur Geschichte römischer Dichter im Mittelalter." *Philologus* 51: 156–171.
Manitius, Max. 1913. "Remigiusscholien." *Münchener Museum für Philologie des Mittelalters und der Renaissance* 2: 79–113.
Manitius, Max. 1923. *Geschichte der lateinischen Literatur des Mittelalters. Zweiter Band: von der Mitte des zehnten Jahrhunderts bis zum Ausbruch des Kampfes zwischen Kirche und Staat*. Munich: C. H. Beck.
Manitius, Max. 1931. *Geschichte der lateinischen Literatur des Mittelalters. Dritter Band: vom Ausbruch des Kirchenstreites bis zum Ende des zwölften Jahrhunderts*. Munich: C. H. Beck.
Marchand, James. [N.D.] "Disticha Catonis." Online. http://faculty.georgetown.edu/jod/texts/distich.trans.html (accessed 5/18/2022).
Mariño Sánchez-Elvira, Rosa María, and Fernando García Romero, eds. 1999. *Proverbios griegos. Menandro Sentencias*. Madrid: Gredos.
Marrou, Henri Irénée. 1956. *A History of Education in Antiquity*. New York: Sheed and Ward.
Martin, Richard P. 1993. "The Seven Sages as Performers of Wisdom." In *Cultural Poetics in Archaic Greece: Cult, Performance, Politics*, edited by Carol Dougherty and Leslie Kurke, 108–128. Cambridge; New York: Cambridge University Press.
Martins, Mário. 1968. "Os 'Dísticos de Catão' na base da formação universitária." *Revista portuguesa de filosofia* 24: 103–113.
Massaro, Matteo. 2007. "Una coppia affiatata: CLE 959." In *Metric Inscriptions of the Roman Republic/Die metrischen Inschriften der römischen Republik*, edited by Peter Kruschwitz, 271–298. Berlin: Walter de Gruyter.
Matthaei, Louise E. 1907. "On the Classification of Roman Allies." *Classical Quarterly* 1 (2–3): 182–204.
Mayer, Roland. 1989. "Friendship in the Satirists." In *Satire and Society in Ancient Rome*, edited by S.H. Braund, 5–21. Exeter: University of Exeter.

McClure, Laura. 2003. "Subversive Laughter: The Sayings of Courtesans in Book 13 of Athenaeus' Deipnosophistae." *American Journal of Philology* 124 (2): 259–294.

McKenzie, Donald F. 2008. *Cambridge History of the Book in Britain. Vol. 2: 1100–1400*. Cambridge: Cambridge University Press.

McKinnell, John. 2014. "The Evolution of Hávamál." In *Essays on Eddic Poetry*, edited by John McKinnell, 59–95. Toronto: University of Toronto Press.

Mead, H. R. 1939. "Fifteenth-Century Schoolbooks." *Huntington Library Quarterly* 3 (1): 37–42.

Mettmann, Walter. 1960. "Spruchweisheit und Spruelídichtung in der spanischen und katalanischen Literatur des Mittelalters." *Zeitschrift für romanische Philologie* 76: 94–117.

Meyer, Paul. 1896. "Fragments d'une paraphrase provençale du Pseudo-Caton." *Romania* 25: 98–110.

Meyer, Wilhelm. 1886. "Franko-italienische Studien. III." *Zeitschrift für romanische Philologie* 10: 363–410.

Michel, Jacques. 1962. *Gratuité en droit romain*. Brussels: Université Libre de Bruxelles, l'Institut de Sociologie.

Milnor, Kristina. 2005. *Gender, Domesticity, and the Age of Augustus: Inventing Private Life*. Oxford; New York: Oxford University Press.

Milnor, Kristina. 2014. *Graffiti and the Literary Landscape in Roman Pompeii*. Oxford: Oxford University Press.

Mommsen, Theodor. 1887. *Römisches Staatsrecht*. Vol. 3. Leipzig: S. Hirzel, 1887.

Monroe, Paul, ed. 1911. *Cyclopedia of Education*. Vol. 2. New York: Macmillan.

Montefiore, C.G., and H.M.J. Loewe. 1974. *A Rabbinic Anthology*. Cambridge: Cambridge University Press.

Morawski, Jozef. 1923. *Le Facet en françoys. Édition critique des cinq des deux Facetus latins, avec introduction, notes et glossaire*. Poznan: Gebethner & Wolff.

Morgan, Teresa. 1998. *Literate Education in the Hellenistic and Roman Worlds*. Cambridge; New York: Cambridge University Press.

Morgan, Teresa. 2007. *Popular Morality in the Early Roman Empire*. Cambridge; New York: Cambridge University Press.

Morris, Richard, ed. 1878. *Cursor Mundi*. Vol. III, part 5. London: N. Trübner.

Morrison, A.D. 2007. "Didacticism and Epistolarity in Horace's Epistles 1." In *Ancient Letters: Classical and Late Antique Epistolography*, edited by Ruth Morello and A.D. Morrison, 107–132. Oxford: Oxford University Press.

Mrozek, Stanislaw. 1985. "Zum Kreditgeld in der frühen römischen Kaiserzeit." *Historia: Zeitschrift für Alte Geschichte* 34 (3): 310–323.

Müller-Reineke, Hendrik. 2006. "A Greek Miscellanist as a Libidinous Thessalian Witch? Pamphile in Apuleius' Metamorphoses 2-3." *Classical Quarterly* 56 (2): 648–652.

Munk Olsen, Birger. 1991. *I classici nel canone scolastico altomedievale*. Spoleto: Centro italiano di studi sull'alto Medioevo.

Murra, John V., Rolena Adorno, and Jorge Urioste, eds. 1987. *Felipe Guamán Poma de Ayala, Nueva crónica y buen gobierno*. Madrid: Historia 16.

Murray, J., and D. Wardle, eds. 2021. *Reading by Example: Valerius Maximus and the Historiography of Exempla*. Leiden; Boston: Brill.

Mussafia, A. 1865. "Zum Cato." *Germania* 10: 101–102.

Mustanoja, Tauno F. 1948. *The Good Wife Taught Her Daughter; the Good Wyfe Wold a Pylgremage; the Thewis of Gud Women*. Helsinki: Suomalaisen Kirjallisuuden Scuran.

Mynors, R.A.B., and D.F.S. Thomson, eds. 1974. *The Correspondence of Erasmus*. Toronto; Buffalo: University of Toronto Press.
Nagyillés, János, ed. 2002. *Cato & Publilius (Latin Mondások. Cato Mondásai. Publilius Syrus Szentenciái)*. Szeged: Lazi.
Nève, Joseph. 1926. *Catonis Disticha. Facsmilés, notes, liste des éditions du XVe siècle*. Liége: H. Vaillant-Carmanne.
Newlands, Carole E. 2011. *Statius: Silvae*. Cambridge: Cambridge University Press.
Nicols, John. 2001. "Hospitium and Political Friendship in the Late Republic." In *Aspects of Friendship in the Graeco-Roman World: Proceedings of a Conference Held at the Seminar für alte Geschichte, Heidelberg, on 10–11 June, 2000*, edited by Michael Peachin, 99–108. Portsmouth, RI: Journal of Roman Archaeology.
O'Higgins, L. 2017. *The Irish Classical Self: Poets and Poor Scholars in the Eighteenth and Nineteenth Centuries*. Oxford, New York: Oxford University Press.
Oikonomides, A.N. 1980. "The Commandments of Amenotes and Sansnos." *Serapis* 5: 43–50.
Ong, Walter J. 1982. *Orality and Literacy: The Technologizing of the Word*. London; New York: Routledge.
Opelt, Ilona. 1986. "Pseudo-Cato und Planudes." *Koinonia* 10: 175–191.
Opelt, Ilona. 1988. "Ein Baustein der Dichtungen Commodians: die Disticha Pseudo-Catonis." In *Paradeigmata poetica Christiana: Untersuchungen zur christlichen lateinischen Dichtung*, edited by Ilona Opelt, 138–147. Düsseldorf: Schwann.
Ortoleva, Vincentius, ed. 1992. *Disticha Catonis in graecum translata*. Rome: dell'Ateneo.
Osgood, Josiah. 2006. *Caesar's Legacy: Civil War and the Emergence of the Roman Empire*. Cambridge: Cambridge University Press.
Osorio Romero, Ignacio. 1980. *Floresta de gramática, poética y retórica en nueva España (1521–1767)*. Mexico: Universidad Nacional Autónoma de México.
Otto, A. 1890. *Die Sprichwörter und sprichwörtlichen Redensarten der Römer*. Leipzig: B.G. Teubner.
Palacio, R.J. 2012. *Wonder*. New York: Alfred A. Knopf.
Palacio, R.J. 2014. *365 Days of Wonder: Mr. Browne's Book of Precepts*. New York: Alfred A. Knopf.
Palao Vicente, Juan José. 2006. *Legio VII gemina (pia) felix: estudio de una legión romana*. Salamanca: Ediciones Universidad de Salamanca.
Panayotakis, Costas. 2010. *Decimus Laberius: The Fragments*. Cambridge; New York: Cambridge University Press.
Papi, Emanuele. 1994. "Un'attestazione del culto imperiale a Capena in un'epigrafe mal conosciuta." *Mélanges de l'École française de Rome. Antiquité* 106 (1): 139–166.
Paradisi, Paola. 2005. *I Disticha Catonis di Catenaccio da Anagni. Testo in volgare laziale (secc. XIII ex. - XIV in.)*. Utrecht: LOT.
Paré, Gérard Marie, Adrien Marie Brunet, and Pierre Tremblay. 1933. *La renaissance du XIIe siècle: les écoles et l'enseignement*. Paris: J. Vrin.
Parke, H.W. 1945. "The Use of Other than Hexameter Verse in Delphic Oracles." *Hermathena* 65: 58–66.
Peachin, Michael. ed. 2001. *Aspects of Friendship in the Graeco-Roman World: Proceedings of a Conference Held at the Seminar für alte Geschichte, Heidelberg, on 10–11 June, 2000*. Portsmouth, RI: Journal of Roman Archaeology.
Peachin, Michael. 2005. "Review: Economic 'Amicitia'." *Classical Review* 55 (1): 256–258.

Pepin, Ronald E. 1999. *An English Translation of Auctores octo, A Medieval Reader.* Lewiston, NY: Edwin Mellen Press.
Perdue, Leo G. 1981. "Paraenesis and the Epistle of James." *Zeitschrift für die Neutestamentliche Wissenschaft und die Kunde der älteren Kirche.* 72: 241–256.
Perdue, Leo G. 1990. "The Social Character of Paraenesis and Paraenetic Literature." *Semeia* 50: 23–27.
Perdue, Leo G. 2007. *Wisdom Literature: A Theological History.* Louisville: Westminster John Knox Press.
Perdue, Leo G. 2008. *The Sword and the Stylus: An Introduction to Wisdom in the Age of Empires.* Grand Rapids, MI: W.B. Eerdmans Pub. Co.
Pérez Gómez, Antonio, ed. 1964. *Gonzalo García de Santa María: el Catón en latín y en romance (1493/94).* Valencia: Artes Gráficos Soler.
Pernigotti, Carlo. 2008. *Menandri sententiae.* Florence: L.S. Olschki.
Perraud, Louis A. 1988. "A Document of Humanist Education: Erasmus' Commentary on the Disticha Catonis." *Journal of the Rocky Mountain Medieval and Renaissance Association* 8: 83–92.
Perry, Jonathan Scott. 2006. *The Roman Collegia: The Modern Evolution of an Ancient Concept.* Leiden; Boston: Brill.
Petrucci, Armando. 1995. *Writers and Readers in Medieval Italy: Studies in the History of Written Culture.* New Haven: Yale University Press.
Pfeiffer, R.H. 1955. *Ancient Near Eastern Texts Relating to the Old Testament*, edited by James B. Pritchard. Princeton: Princeton University Press.
Pfiffner, Linda, and Susan O'Leary. 1987. "The Efficacy of All-Positive Management as a Function of the Prior Use of Negative Consequences." *Journal of Applied Behavior Analysis* 20 (3): 265–271.
Pietsch, Karl. 1902. *Preliminary Notes on Two Old Spanish Versions of the Disticha Catonis.* Chicago: University of Chicago Press.
Pigliucci, Massimo. 2018. *How to Be a Stoic: Using Ancient Philosophy to Live a Modern Life.* [S.l.]: Basic Books.
Pleket, Henri Willy. 1983. "Epigrafiek: een vak?" *Hermeneus* 55 (3): 140–251.
Poinsotte, Jean Michel. 1996. "Commodien dit de Gaza." *Revue des études latines* 74: 270–281.
Poinsotte, Jean Michel, ed. 2009. *Commodien, Instructions.* Paris: Belles lettres.
Pompella, Giuseppe. 1997. *Menandro Sentenze.* Milan: Rizzoli.
Powell, J.G.F. 1990. *Cicero: Laelius, On Friendship & The Dream of Scipio: Laelius De Amicitia; Somnium Scipionis.* Warminster: Aris & Phillips.
Powell, J.G.F. 1995. *Cicero the Philosopher: Twelve Papers.* Oxford; New York: Clarendon Press.
Pradhan, Menno, and Martin Ravallion. 2000. "Measuring Poverty Using Qualitative Perceptions of Consumption Adequacy." *The Review of Economics and Statistics* 82 (3): 462–471.
Pratt, Robert A. 1947. "Chaucer's Claudian." *Speculum* 22 (3): 419–429.
Purcell, Nicholas. 1983. "The Apparitores: A Study in Social Mobility." *Papers of the British School at Rome* 51: 125–173.
Rauh, Nicholas K. 1993. *The Sacred Bonds of Commerce: Religion, Economy, and Trade Society at Hellenistic Roman Delos, 166–87 B.C.* Amsterdam: Gieben.

Ravallion, Martin. 2012. "Poor, or Just Feeling Poor? On Using Subjective Data in Measuring Poverty." *World Bank Policy Research Working Papers* no. WPS 5968. Online. https://openknowledge.worldbank.org/handle/10986/3254 World Bank.

Reichert, Heinrich G. 1956. *Urban und Human: Gedanken über lateinische Sprichwörter*. Hamburg: M. von Schröder.

[Anon.]. 2014. Review of "365 DAYS OF WONDER Mr. Browne's Book of Precepts." *Kirkus Reviews* 82 (16): 192.

Reynhout, Lucien. 1986. "Les manuscrits de Bruxelles des Disticha Catonis." *Archives et bibliothèques de Belgique* 57 (3–4): 462–486.

Riché, Pierre. 1962. "Recherches sur l'instruction des laïcs du IXe au XIIe siècle." *Cahiers de civilisation médiévale, X^e–XIIe siècles* 5 (2): 175–182.

Riese, Alexander. 1865. *M. Terenti Varronis Saturarum Menippearum reliquiae*. Leipzig: B. G. Teubner.

Risselada, Rodie. 1993. *Imperatives and Other Directive Expressions in Latin. A Study in the Pragmatics of a Dead Language*. Amsterdam: Gieben.

Robinson, Rodney Potter. 1923. "Valerius Cato." *Transactions of the American Philological Association* 54: 98–116.

Powell, J.G.F. 1939. *Manuscripts 27 (S. 29) and 107 (S. 129) of the Municipal Library of Autun, a Study of Spanish Half-Uncial and Early Visigothic Minuscule and Cursive Scripts*. New York: American Academy in Rome.

Römer, Willem Hendrik Philibert, and Günter Burkard. 1990. *Weisheitstexte*. Vol. 1. Gütersloh: Gütersloher Verlagshaus Gerd Mohn.

Roos, Paolo. 1984. *Sentenza e proverbio nell'antichita e i "Distici di Catone": il testo latino e i volgarizzamenti italiani*. Brescia: Morcelliana.

Rossi, Olga. 1924. "De M. Catonis dictis et apophthegmatis." *Athenaeum* 12 (3): 174–182.

Roueché, Charlotte, and Charlotte Tupman. 2011. "Sharing Ancient Wisdoms: Developing Structures for Charting Textual Transfer." Paper delivered to the Institute of Classical Studies Digital Seminar, King's College London, 17 June. Online. http://www.digitalclassicist.org/wip/wip2011-03cr.html (accessed 5/18/2022).

Roussel, Claude. 1994. "Le legs de la rose: modèles et préceptes de la sociabilité médiévale." In *Pour une histoire des traités de savoir vivre en Europe*, edited by Alain Montandon, 1–90. Clermont-Ferrand: Association des publications de la Faculté des lettres et sciences humaines de Clermont-Ferrand.

Roy, Bruno. 1979. "La devinette du bénédicité et les Distiques du Pseudo-Caton: observations sur la parodie médiévale." *Florilegium* 1: 195–221.

Rüdiger, Horst. 1966. "Göttin Gelegenheit. Gestaltwandel einer Allegorie." *Arcadia: Zeitschrift für Vergleichende Literaturwissenschaft* 2: 121–166.

Ruggerini, Maria Elena. 1988. "La ricezione dei *Disticha Catonis* nell'islanda medievale." In *Cultura classica e cultura germanica settentrionale: Atti del Convegno Internazionale di Studi, Università di Macerata, Facoltà di Lettere e Filosofia, Macerata*, edited by Pietro Janni, Diego Poli, and Carlo Santini, 221–277. Rome: Herder.

Ruhe, Ernstpeter. 1968. *Untersuchungen zu den altfranzösischen Übersetzungen der Disticha Catonis*. Munich: Max Hueber.

Russo, Joseph. 1997. "Prose Genres for the Performance of Traditional Wisdom in Ancient Greece: Proverb, Maxim, Apothegm." In *Poet, Public, and Performance in Ancient Greece*, edited by Lowell Edmunds and Robert W. Wallace, 49–64. Baltimore, MD: The Johns Hopkins University Press.

Saller, Richard P. 1982. *Personal Patronage under the Early Empire*. Cambridge; New York: Cambridge University Press.
Schanz, Martin von, ed. 1927. *Handbuch der Altertumswissenschaft, 8. Abt.: Geschichte der römischen Literatur bis zum Gesetzgebungswerk des Kaisers Justinian. Dritter Teil: Die zeit von Hadrian 117 bis zum Constantin 324*. Munich: Beck.
Scheidel, Walter. 2006. "Stratification, Deprivation and Quality of Life." In *Poverty in the Roman World*, edited by E.M. Atkins and Robin Osborne, 40–59. Cambridge: Cambridge University Press, 2006.
Schenkl, Karl. 1873. "Eine alte Handschrift der Disticha Catonis." *Zeitschrift für die deutschösterreichischen Gymnasien* 24: 485–499.
Schiendorfer, Max. 2000. "Ein vündelîn zu Heinrich Laufenbergs Liedercodex (Olim: Straßburg B 121) und zu seinem Wecklied Stand vf vnd sih ihesum vil rein." *Zeitschrift für deutsche Philologie* 119: 421–426.
Schindel, Ulrich. 1983. "Die 'Auctores' im Unterricht deutscher Stadtschulen im Spätmittelalter und in der frühen Neuzeit." In *Studien zum städtischen Bildungswesen des späten Mittelalters und der frühen Neuzeit*, edited by Bernd Moeller et al., 430–452. Göttingen: Vandenhoeck & Ruprecht.
Schockaert, R., ed. 1939. *Keus uit de koppelverzen van Dionysius Cato over de zeden*. Leuven: Nova et vetera.
Schöffel, Christian. 2002. *Martial, Buch 8: Einleitung, Text, Übersetzung, Kommentar*. Stuttgart: F. Steiner.
Schönberger, Otto ed. 1980. *M. Porci Catonis scripta quae manserunt omnia. Marcus Porcius Cato vom Landbau. Fragmente. Alle erhaltenen Schriften*. Darmstadt: Wissenschaftliche Buchgesellschaft.
Schroeder, Carl. 1911. "Deutsche Facetus." *Palaestra* 86: 14–28.
Schulz-Behrend, George, ed. 1990. *Martin Opitz. Gesammelte Werke. Kritische Ausgabe. T. 2. Bd. 4. Die Werke von Ende 1626 bis 1630*. Stuttgart: Hiersemann.
Schulze-Busacker, Elisabeth. 1989. "Des 'Disticha Catonis' en Espagne, Italie et France." In *Europhras 88: Phraséologie Contrastive; Actes du Colloque International, Klingenthal-Strasbourg, 12–16 Mai 1988*, edited by Gertrud Gréciano, 421–30. Strasbourg: Université des sciences humaines, Département d'études allemandes.
Sciarrino, Enrica. 2011. *Cato the Censor and the Beginnings of Latin Prose: From Poetic Translation to Elite Transcription*. Columbus: Ohio State University Press.
Searby, Denis Michael. 1998. *Aristotle in the Greek Gnomological Tradition*. Uppsala: Uppsala University Library.
Searby, Denis Michael. 2007. *The Corpus Parisinum*. 2 vols. Lewiston, N.Y.: Edwin Mellen Press.
Serralongue, J., Patrice Faure, and F. Bertrandy. 2004. "Un monument funéraire de prétorien récemment découvert à Annecy (Haute-Savoie)." *Zeitschrift für Papyrologie und Epigraphik* 146: 25–64.
Shippey, T.A. 1976. *Poems of Wisdom and Learning in Old English*. Cambridge: D. S. Brewer.
Shippey, T.A. 1994. "Miscomprehension and Re-Interpretation in Old and Early Middle English Proverb Collections." In *Text und Zeittiefe*, edited by Hildegard L.C. Tristram, 293–311. Tübingen: Narr.
Sick, David H. 1999. "Ummidia Quadratilla: Cagey Businesswoman or Lazy Pantomime Watcher?" *Classical Antiquity* 18 (2): 330–348.

Sidoli, Nathan. 2015. "Mathematics Education." In *A Companion to Ancient Education*, edited by W. Martin Bloomer, 387–400. Chichester: Wiley-Blackwell.
Simpson, William Kelly, ed. 2003. *The Literature of Ancient Egypt: An Anthology of Stories, Instructions, Stelae, Autobiographies, and Poetry*. New Haven; London: Yale University Press.
Sirks, Boudewijn. 2002. "Sailing in the Off-Season with Reduced Financial Risk." In *Speculum Iuris. Roman Law as a Reflection of Social and Economic Life in Antiquity*, edited by Jean-Jacques Aubert and Boudewijn Sirks, 134–150. Ann Arbor, MI: University of Michigan Press.
Skutsch, Otto. 1905. Pauly-Wissowa *Realencyclopaedia* V, s.v. "Dicta Catonis", col. 358-370.
Smyly, J. Gilbart. 1939. *Urbanus Magnus Danielis Becclesiensis*. Dublin; London: Hodges, Figgis & Co.; Longman, Green, & Co.
Sowards, Jesse K., ed. 1985. *Collected Works of Erasmus. 25: Literary and Educational Writings; 3, De Conscribendis Epistolis. Conficiendarum Epistolarum Formula. De Civilitate*. Toronto: University of Toronto Press.
Springer, Carl P.E. 2011. *Luther's Aesop*. Kirksville, MO: Truman State University Press.
Stammler, Wolfgang et al. 1987. *Die deutsche Literatur des Mittelalters: Verfasserlexikon 6*. Berlin; New York: W. de Gruyter.
Stechert, Eric. 1912. "De Catonis quae dicuntur Distichis." Ph.D. thesis. Universität Greifswald. Greifswald: Hartmann.
Stengel, E. 1886. "Elie's de Wincestre, eines Anonymous und Everarts Übertragungen der Disticha Catonis." *Ausgaben und Abhandlungen aus dem Gebiet der Romanischen Philologie* 47: 106–158.
Stewart, Roberta. 1995. "Catiline and the Crisis of 63–60 BC: The Italian Perspective." *Latomus* 54 (1): 62–78.
Stowers, Stanley Kent. 1989. *Letter Writing in Greco-Roman Antiquity*. Philadelphia: Westminster Press.
Talbot, Charles Hugh, ed. 1956. *Florilegium Morale Oxoniense. Ms. Bodl. 633. Pt. 2. Flores Auctorum*. Louvain; Lille: Nauwelaerts; Giard.
Taylor, Archer. 1934. "Problems in the Study of Proverbs." *Journal of American Folklore* 47, no. 183: 1–21.
Taylor, Archer. 1962. *The Proverb and an Index to "the Proverb."* Hatboro; Copenhagen: Folklore Associates; Rosenkilde and Bagger.
Taylor, Barry. 1999. "Michael Verinus and the *Distichs* of Cato in Spain: A Comparative Study in Reception." In *Latin and Vernacular in Renaissance Spain*, edited by Barry Taylor and Alejandro Coroleu, 72–82. Manchester: Manchester Spanish & Portuguese Studies.
Taylor, Barry, ed. 2004. *Alonso De Cartagena (?), Cathoniana Confectio: A Latin Gloss on the Disticha Catonis and the Contemptum Mundi*. Bristol: HiPLAM.
Taylor, Jon. 2005. "The Sumerian proverb collections." *Revue d'assyriologie et d'archéologie orientale* 99 (1): 13–38.
Téoli, Carlo [Salomone Eugenio Camerini]. 1872. *Gli ammaestramenti degli antichi raccolti e volgarizzati per Fra Bartolomeo da San Concordio*. Milan: M. Guigoni.
Teuffel, Wilhelm Sigismund. 1872. *Geschichte der römischen Literatur*. 2nd ed. Leipzig: B.G. Teubner.
Thomas, Antoine. 1886. "Les *Proverbes* de Guylem de Cervera." *Romania* 15: 25–108.
Thomson, Ian, and Louis A. Perraud. 1990. *Ten Latin Schooltexts of the Later Middle Ages: Translated Selections*. Lewiston, NY: Edward Mellen Press.

Tobler, Rudolf. 1883. *Die altvenezianische Übersetzung der Sprüche des Dionysius Cato*. Berlin: Verlag der Königlichen Akademie der Wissenschaften.
Tobler, Rudolf. 1897. *Die altprovenzalische Version der Disticha Catonis*. Berlin: E. Ebering.
Toner, Jerry P. 2009. *Popular Culture in Ancient Rome*. Cambridge; Malden, MA: Polity.
Traill, David. ed. 2018. *Carmina Burana*. Volume 2. Cambridge, MA; London: Harvard University Press.
Treggiari, Susan. 1991. *Roman Marriage: Iusti Coniuges from the Time of Cicero to the Time of Ulpian*. Oxford; New York: Clarendon Press; Oxford University Press.
Trigger, Bruce G. 2003. *Understanding Early Civilizations: A Comparative Study*. Cambridge; New York: Cambridge University Press.
Trogrančić, Franjo. 1953. *Storia della letteratura croata: dall'umanesimo alla rinascita nazionale (secolo XV-XIX)*. Rome: Editrice Studium.
Tsagalis, Christos. 2008. *Inscribing Sorrow: Fourth-century Attic Funerary Epigrams*. Berlin: W. de Gruyter.
Tuvestrand, Birgitta. 1977. *Hugsvinnsmál: handskrifter och kritisk text*. Lund: Carl Blom.
Ulrich, J. 1895. "Eine altlothringische Übersetzung des Dionysius Cato." *Zeitschrift für romanische Philologie* 19: 85–92.
Ulrich, J. 1904a. "Die Übersetzung der Distichen des Pseudo-Cato von Jean de Paris." *Romanische Forschungen* 15: 41–69.
Ulrich, J. 1904b. "Der Cato Jean Lefevre's." *Romanische Forschungen* 15: 70–106.
Ulrich, J. 1904c. "Der Cato des Adam de Suel." *Romanische Forschungen* 15: 107–140.
Van Sickle, J. 1980. "The Book-roll and Some Conventions of the Poetic Book." *Arethusa* 13: 5–42.
Vannucci, Michele, ed. 1829. *Libro di Cato, o tre volgarizzamenti del Libro di Catone de' costumi*. Milan: Stella.
Venturini, Teresa. 1929. *Ricerche paleografiche intorno all'Arcidiacono Pacifico di Verona*. Verona: La Tipografica Veronese.
Verbeke, Demmy. 2013. "Cato in England: Translating Latin Sayings for Moral and Linguistic Instruction." In *Renaissance Cultural Crossroads: Translation, Print and Culture in Britain, 1473–1640*, edited by Sara Barker and Brenda Hosington, 139–155. Leiden: Brill.
Verboven, Koenraad. 2002. *The Economy of Friends: Economic Aspects of Amicitia and Patronage in the Late Republic*. Brussels: Latomus.
Veyne, Paul. 2000. "La 'plèbe moyenne' sous le Haut-Empire romain." *Annales HSS* 6: 1169–1199.
von Reden, Sitta. 2002. "Money in the Ancient Economy: A Survey of Recent Research." *Klio* 84 (1): 141–174.
von Reden, Sitta. 2010. *Money in Classical Antiquity*. Cambridge; New York: Cambridge University Press.
von Reden, Sitta. 2012. "Money and Finance." In *The Cambridge Companion to the Roman Economy*, edited by Walter Scheidel, 266–286. Cambridge: Cambridge University Press.
Walker, Henry John. 2004. *Valerius Maximus, Memorable Deeds and Sayings: One Thousand Tales from Ancient Rome*. Indianapolis: Hackett.
Weaver, P.R.C. 1967. "Social Mobility in the Early Roman Empire: The Evidence of the Imperial Freedmen and Slaves." *Past & Present* 37: 3–20.
Weissenborn, Wilhelm, ed. 1875. *T. Livi ab urbe condita libri*. Berlin: Weidmann.
Wells, David. 1994. "Fatherly Advice: The Precepts of 'Gregorius', Marke, and Gurnemanz and the School Tradition of the 'Disticha Catonis'." *Frühmittelalterliche Studien* 28: 296–332.

West, M.L. 1973. *Textual Criticism and Editorial Technique Applicable to Greek and Latin Texts*. Stuttgart: B.G. Teubner.
West, M.L. 1978. "Phocylides." *Journal of Hellenic Studies* 98: 164–167.
Wheeler, Stephen M. 2015. *Accessus ad auctores: Medieval Introductions to the Authors (Codex Latinus Monacensis 19475)*. Medieval Institute Publications, Western Michigan University.
Whitlatch, Lisa. 2013. *The Hunt for Knowledge: Hunting in Latin Didactic Poets*. Ph.D. thesis, Rutgers, The State University of New Jersey. New Brunswick, NJ: Rutgers, The State University of New Jersey.
Williams, Craig. 2012. *Reading Roman Friendship*. Cambridge: Cambridge University Press.
Williams, P.J. 2000. Review of *The Book of Proverbs and Arabic Proverbial Works* by Riad Aziz Kassis. *Tyndale Bulletin* 51 (1): 151–154.
Williams, Ronald J. 1977. "Some Fragmentary Demotic Wisdom Texts." In *Studies in Honor of George R. Hughes: January 12, 1977*, edited by University of Chicago, Oriental Institute, 263–271. Chicago: Oriental Institute of the University of Chicago.
Wilson, N.G. 1967. "A Chapter in the History of Scholia." *Classical Quarterly* 17 (2): 244–256.
Wilson, Walter T. 1994. *The Mysteries of Righteousness: The Literary Composition and Genre of the Sentences of Pseudo-Phocylides*. Tübingen: J.C.B. Mohr.
Wilson, Walter T. 2022. *Ancient Wisdom. An Introduction to Sayings Collections*. Grand Rapids, MI: Eerdmans.
Woelfflin, Eduard. 1869. *Publilii Syri Sententiae*. Leipzig: B.G. Teubner.
Wolff, Catherine. 2015. *L'éducation dans le monde romain: du début de la République à la mort de Commode*. Paris: Picard.
Wolff, Étienne, ed. 2002. *Dracontius: Oeuvres: Tome IV: Poèmes profanes VI - X. Fragments*. Paris: Les Belles Lettres.
Wolkenhauer, J. 2014. *Senecas Schrift De beneficiis und der Wandel im römischen Benefizienwesen*. Göttingen: V&R unipress.
Woolf, Greg. 2006. "Writing Poverty in Rome." In *Poverty in the Roman World*, edited by E.M. Atkins and Robin Osborne, 83–99. Cambridge: Cambridge University Press, 2006.
Wright, Thomas. 1846. *Biographia Britannica Literaria: Or, Biography of Literary Characters of Great Britain and Ireland, Arranged in Chronological Order: Anglo-Norman Period*. London: J.W. Parker.
Young, Mary Vance, ed. 1901. *Les enseignements de Robert de Ho dits Enseignements Trebor*. Paris: Picard.
Zarncke, Friedrich. 1852. *Der deutsche Cato*. Leipzig: G. Wigand.
Zarncke, Friedrich. 1863. "Beiträge zur mittellateinischen Spruchpoesie." *Berichte über die Verhandlungen der Königlich-Sächsischen Gesellschaft der Wissenschaften zu Leipzig, philol.-hist. Classe* 15: 24–78.
Zatočil, Leopold, ed. 1935. *Der neusohler Cato*. Berlin: Hoffmann.
Zemon Davis, Natalie. 1975. "Proverbial Wisdom and Popular Errors." In *Society and Culture in Early Modern France: Eight Essays*, by Natalie Zemon Davis, 227–267. Stanford: Stanford University Press.
Zetzel, J.E.G. 1975. "On the History of Latin Scholia." *Harvard Studies in Classical Philology* 79: 335–354.

Index of Subjects

365 Days of Wonder: Mr. Browne's Book of Precepts (Palacio) 190–192

A

Abril, Simón 150
Accessus ad Auctores 145–146
accountant, Latin names for 110 n.358
accounting 110–111
Acrimati, Prospero 187
adjectives, Author's favorite 66
adverbs, Author's favorite 67
Aelfric Bata 143
Aesop 146–147, 149–150, 180 n.588, 184 n.604
Aesopus (actor) 115 n.377
Aimericus of Angoulême 144
Alan of Lille, *Liber Parabolarum* 154
Alcimus Avitus, *Poema de Mosaicae Historiae Gestis* 154
Alcuin xiv, 170 n.557
Alexander the Great 131
Allia Potestas 25 n.112
Alonso de Cartagena, *Cathoniana Confectio* 165 n.537
amare vs. *diligere* 79 n.253
amicitia, multivalence of 103
amicus 77 n.148, 87, 95
anthropology xxi
aphorisms
–binary structure 191
–in calendar form 190–192
–positive 191, 192 n.624
–use in schools 192
Aphthonius 55 n.198
apophthegmata, meaning of 15
apparatus criticus, readers' neglect of 3
Aramaic 48
Arator, *Historia Apostolica* 154
Archimedes 190 n.619
Aristotle
–*Protrepticus* 4 n.49
–*Rhetoric* xxii, 53–56, 61 n.217, 62 n.218, 63, 105
Armenian translations 49

Arntzenius 174
Arroyal, León de 201
ars vs. *ministerium* 123–124
Auctores Octo Morales 154
Augustine 108
Augustus, his divorce legislation 130 n.424
Ausonius 21 n.106
–Pseudo-Ausonius 163
avarice
–birth of 131 n.427
–reprehensible 133–134
Avianus 146–147, 153

B

Babrius 78, 81–82, 103
Bailey, Nathan 181 n.592
Baker, Richard 181 n.591, 197
Balbo, Andrea 183, 202
Baucis and Philemon 120
beneficium 84–85
benefits of friendship 88–94
Beza, Theodore xvi, 186
binarism 72–73
Boas, Marcus 3–4, 152, 158
Boio 45
Bonvesin de la Riva 176 n.581, 201
Book Callyd Cathon (Caxton) 155
Boston Latin School 182
Botschuyver, Hendrik 158 n.512
Brant, Sebastian 179 n.587, 194
Breves Sententiae (part of *Disticha*) 3, 5–7, 165, 173, 188
brevitas, as ideal 32
Brinsley, John 181 n.591, 197
Browne, Mr. (fictional character) 190–191
Browne, Sir Thomas 191
Brutus, Marcus Junius 93
Budé, Guillaume 162–165
budgets, household 110–111
Bullokar, William 181 n.591, 197
Burgh, Benedict 177, 196
Burrant, Robert 181, 197
Byzantine traditions 49

C

Caesar, Julius 183
—*apophthegmata* 41
Calvin, John 179
Carey, Henry 188–189
Carmina Burana xv, 188 n.617
carus 83–84
Cassius Dionysius Uticensis 22
Catenaccio Catenacci d'Anagni 176 n.581, 201
Cato as author
—Cato-type, generic author of the *Disticha* xv, 10–11, 22
——derived from *catus*, "wise man" 144–145
——'Dionysius Cato' 155–156
——not named in the corpus 21
—Cato Censorius (Cato the Elder) xv, 21, 145–146, 188
——as wisdom figure 42
——works, extant and lost 20
—Cato Uticensis (Cato the Younger) xv, 20–22, 23 n.106, 145–146
—Valerius Cato 20, 181 n.592
Cato Censorius Christianus (Beza) xvi, 186
Cato Christianus (Mulcaster) 186
Cato Digestus (anonymous work) 185
Cato Facetus (anonymous French work) 185
Cato Metricus 147 n.471
Cato Moralis 147 n.471
Cato Novus (epitome of the *Disticha*) 5 n.55
Cato-Parodie (Kemnater) 188 n. 615
Cato Parvus 147 n.471
Cato Rhythmicus (anonymous work) 185
Cato Urbanus (Daniel of Beccles) 185
Catón Político Christiano (Rodríguez) xv, 186
Cato's Advice (Carey) 188–189
Catoun (Chaucer's name for the *Disticha Catonis*) xiv
Catoun (horse-servant in *Piers Plowman*) xiv
Catwg Ddoeth xiv–xv, 186
Caxton, William 155, 177–179, 197

Cervantes xvi, 186
Charlemagne xiv
Chase, Wayland Johnson 183, 198
Chaucer, Geoffrey xiv–xv, 154
chreiai 15, 37
Christianity
—Christianized rewritings of the *Disticha* 156, 186
—influence of, on translations of the *Disticha* 169–171, 174, 182
—made acceptance of the *Disticha* problematic 156–157
—valued texts more as part of a tradition than works by particular authors 7
Christine de Pisan, *Moral Proverbs of* 155
Cicero 22, 37, 108, 183
—*De Amicitia* 78, 80, 82, 89, 92, 94, 98–100, 103–105
—*De Inventione* 82
—*De Officiis* 84–85, 92, 94, 104, 125, 137
—*Epistles* 84 n.275, 88 n.285, 90, 104, 109, 135 n.439, 179, 184 n.604
—*Tusculanae Disputationes* 134 n.436
—witticisms of 41–42
Cinna 132
classes, high and low, read the *Disticha* 104, 108–109
Claudian, *Rape of Proserpina* 153
coinage, invention of 131 n.427
Colloquia (Aelfric Bata) 143
Columbanus of Saint-Trod xiii–xiv
Commandments of Sansnos 44
commentaries on the *Disticha*
—briefer (Erasmus) *vs.* fuller 163–164
—earliest, fragmentary 160
—Erasmus 162–167
—footnote *vs.* endnote format 159–160
—moralizing *vs.* interpretative 162
—necessary parts of, according to Servius 159–160
—Remigius of Auxerre 160–161
—targeted at pupils *vs.* teachers 164
commerce, world of, absent from *Disticha* 66
Commodianus 29–31, 36
Comparatio Menandri et Philistionis 45 n.163

Index of Subjects — 229

Conrad of Hirsau 145–146
conservatism of paraenetic texts 52
contubernalis 77 n.148
Coptic translations 49
Cordier, Mathurin 151, 164–165, 179–180, 200
cosmic order, not a concern of the *Disticha Catonis* 52
Counsels of a Pessimist 43
Counsels of Wisdom 43
Counter-Reformation 155
couplet as feature of early paraenesis 45–46
credit, importance in Roman economy 137
Cynic philosophers 39

D
Dahl, Roald 191
Daniel Ecclesiensis 185 n.606
Daniel of Beccles 185
Dante 141, 148
dapsilis 93
Darius 131
De Contemptu Mundi 154, 165 n.537, 180 n.588
de Suel, Adam 172–173, 175, 187, 199
debt, personal 112–113, 135–136
–as servitude 127
Dedekind, Friedrich 187–188
Delphic Oracle 45
Demetrios of Phaleron 50
Demotic texts 44, 46
Dialogus super Auctores (Conrad of Hirsau) 145
dicta, meaning of 15
Dicta Septem Sapientum 6, 39 n.144, 50, 163
Dictes and Sayinges of the Philosophers 155
Dicts of Cato 170–171
Didascalicon (Hugh of St. Victor) 146–147
diligere vs. amare 79 n.253
Dio Chrysostom 119 n.383
Dionysus Cato, supposed author of the *Disticha* 22
Dirae/Lydia 20

Disticha Catonis passim
–audience xxv, 37–39, 167
–author 19–23
— –not Cato the Elder or Younger 19–20
— –singular xxiii, 8
— –writes as father to son xxiii
–composed in stages? 5–6
–constituent parts of 3, 6
–date xxiv–xxv, 41
— –evidence of meter for 32–35
–division into books 7–15
–earliest Roman unitary paraenetic text 46
–epilogue, last maxim 4.49 as 13–15
–first Latin text read in schools 141
–form of
— –consciously idiosyncratic xxiii
— –simple and regular 53
–little read and never quoted today xvii, 167
–manuscript, earliest 7, 16–17
–meter
— –as an aid in dating the corpus 32–35
— –of prefaces and maxims 10 n.68
— –summary of 33–35
–miscellany, not lacking organization 47–48
–mixed reputation of xvii
–multivalent xxv–xxvi
–neither systematic nor comprehensive xxv
–no single model 40
–only Latin text read in full in Iceland 1550-1800 184
–as oral text 54–55
–prefaces to books 8–15
–relation to Christian and Jewish thought 51
–relation to paraenetic tradition unclear 48
–Romanness of xx, xxii–xxvii, 52
–title, modern, assigned by Erasmus 155
–titles in the manuscripts 21
distichs *vs.* monostichs 46
divorce 129–130
doctors and friends as confidants 88–91
Domitius Afer 42

Don Quixote (Cervantes) 186 n.612
Donatus 146, 176
–commentary on the *Aeneid* 159
Dorpat, Stephen 194
Dracontius 45 n.163
drinking-houses, gymnasia, markets, not the best places to find friends 78, 81, 89–90, 94, 99
Dryden, John 141
Duffs (John Wright Duff and Arnold Mackay Duff) 3, 158, 183, 198
Durham Proverbs 172 n.564

E
Eberhard (Evrard) 144
economic language in discussion of friendship 79–81
editions and commentaries on the *Disticha Catonis*
–Early Modern 151–152
–Latin American 149
–Medieval 142–148
–Mexican 149
–Modern 152
–Remigius 141–142
–Renaissance 149–151
editions of the *Disticha Catonis*
–Arntzenius 157 fig.4
–Baehrens 158
–Erasmus 155–158, 156 fig.3
–Hauthal 157–158
–manuscript 153
–packaged with other improving texts 153
–Scaliger 155
–Scriverius 155
education, democratization of 183
Edward VI, king of England 149
Elie of Winchester 170, 172, 198
Enseignements de Robert de Ho 148 n.476
enthymemes 53
epigram *vs.* paraenesis 44 n.160
Epistula (first part of *Disticha*) 3–5, 143
Erasmus, Desiderius 141, 155, 162–167, 179–181, 184
–doubts about the value of his commentary on the *Disticha* 162–163
Estienne, Robert 180 n.588, 200
Eugenius of Toledo (Eugenius Toletanus) xiv, 153
Everard le moine 172, 177, 198
Everard of Kirkham 172
exempla 101–102

F
fables 101–102, 105–106
Facetus (anonymous French work) 185
Facetus (different, Ovidian work) 154, 185 n.606
financial advice, abstract *vs.* practical 108
first person in the *Disticha* 15
Fleischner, Johann 183 n.597, 195
florilegia 148
folklore studies xxi
Franke, F. F. 183 n.597, 195
Franklin, Benjamin xvi–xvii, 182, 198
Freidank (didactic poet) 144
friendship *vs.* bureaucratic systems 104
Fries, Johannes 180 n.588
Furius Bibaculus 41

G
García de Santa María, Gonzalo 176, 200
García Payazuelo, Martín 175–176, 200
Gellius, Aulus, *Noctes Atticae* 37, 48
Germanicus, *Aratea* 32–33
Glossulae Catoni 161 n.529
Glossulae Catonis 185 n.606
gnomai 15, 101–102, 106
–memorized in schools 37
gnomologia 38, 42
–Greco-Egyptian 41
grammaticus 159
gratia 83–84
Grobianus et Grobiana (Dedekind) 187–188
Gualterus Anglicus, *Fabulae Aesopi* 154
Guaman Poma de Ayala xvi, 149

H

handwriting, practiced by copying maxims 38
health and sickness 133
Heiric of Auxerre 160
Hellenistic paraenesis 49–50
Hellenistic texts 44, 46
Hesiod 174 n.575
–*Works and Days* 45
hexameter 45
Hólar Cato 184
Homer 45, 174 n.575
Hoole, Charles 152, 181 n.591, 197
Horace 110
Huggsvinnsmál (The Speech of the Wise One) 171
Hugh of St. Victor 146–147
humanism 148, 161, 164, 168
Hymn to Ninurta 43

I

Iceland, the *Disticha* in 171
Ilias Latina 153
illiteratus, used to mean ignorance of Latin 144–145
imperatives, future and present 57–60
Indian traditions 49
inscriptions
–funerary 106
–Hasluck no. 3 44
–quoting the *Disticha* 24–28, 31
Institutions of Shuruppak 43
instructions, grammar of 57–60
Instructions of Shuruppak 49 n.182
Iocosum Carmen in Catonis Praecepta (Acrimati) 187
Isocrates, *Ad Nicoclem* 4 n.49

J

Jean de Paris (= Jean du Chastelet) 173 n.569, 199
Jean le Bon of Lorraine xxii
Jesus 178
John of Salisbury 144
Juvenal 100–101
Juvencus, *Libri Evangeliorum Quattuor* 154

K

Kalila and Dimna xiv n.5
Kant, Immanuel 40
Kemnater, Hans 188 n. 615
knowledge, social stock of xxii

L

Labyrinthus (Evrard) 144 n.456
Langland, William xiv–xv
Lao Tzu 191
Latin, decline in importance of 183
Lefèvre, Jean 175, 200
Leonidas of Tarentum 45 n.165
letter-writing in ancient philosophy 4 n.49
Lévi-Strauss, Claude 72
Lex de repetundis 114 n.373
Lex Roscia theatralis 113 n.371
lexical density of the *Disticha* 67–68, 68 fig.2, 73 tab.1, 74 tab.2
Liber Catonianus (collection) 7, 153–154, 164 n.535
Liber Senecae 155, 163
Liber Urbani (anonymous French work) 185
Liber Urbani (Daniel of Beccles) 185
Libro Maistrevole (Tagliento) 186
literature of imitation 185–186
Livy 124
Loeb Classical Library xvii, 152, 158, 183
Lucan 10, 12
Lucian, *Anacharsis* 37–38
Luther, Martin 150
Lysippus xiii n.2

M

Macé de Troies 173
Macer 10, 12
Maecenas 42, 115
Magnus Cato (Maxims, without the *Epistula* and *Breves Sententiae)* 5, 147 n.471
Mago of Carthage 22
Manilius, *Astronomica* 32–33
manners *vs.* morals 186
manuscripts of the *Disticha* 16–19
–sudden increase in, in 10th-11th centuries 143–144

Marchand, James 183 n.603, 198
Marius 132
Martial 31–32, 78, 109, 111, 113, 121, 124 n.406, 134 n.436, 135
Mather, Cotton 181–182
Matthew of Vendome, *Tobias* 154
maxim, meaning of 15
Maximian, *Elegies* 153
Maxims (main part of *Disticha*) 7–15
 –as core of the collection 12
 –list of those not found in *traditio vulgata* 34 n.127
Maxims of Ptahhotep 190
maxims suitable for older people 54
meaning, up to three levels of, in proverbial language 70
Melanchthon, Philip 150–151
Melissus, C. 42
Menander *see Sententiae Menandri*
Mesopotamian proverbs 49
Metellus Celer, Q. Caecilius 88 n.285
Metellus Macedonicus, Q. Caecilius 129 n.423
metrical factors in composition 59–60
Mexico 181
mirror of princes 51
miscellanies and miscellaneity 7, 47–48
money
 –elite attitudes toward 111
 –right and wrong ways of earning 136–137
Montaigne 150
Moretum 120
Moter, Abraham 179 n.587, 195
Mulcaster, Richard 186
Multidimensional Poverty Index 120
munificus 85–86
munus 96

N
Napoletano, Notturno 182
Nebrija, Antonio de 180 n.588
negative tone of the *Disticha* 71
nomen, "reputation" 135
Notker Labeo 174 n.573
nouns, Author's favorite 65–66

O
obsequium 96
Occasion (mythological character) xiii
officiperdus, hapax legomenon 83 n.274
officium 83–85
old age, a time for spending - on friends 115–116
Olen the Hyperborean 45
opes vs. utilitas 116–117
Opitz, Martin 180, 184 n.604, 195
Oppius Secundus, Q. 24–26, 31, 36
Opportunity (mythological character) xiii
orality 55–56
original thought, not much found in the *Disticha* 28
over-analysis, dangers of xxvi
Ovid 10, 12, 22, 120
 –*Remedia Amoris* 154 n.500

P
Palacio, R.J. 190–192
Pamphila of Epidauros, *Historica Hypomnemata* 47–48
pantomimes 116 n.379
Pappus 190 n.619
papyri
 –Bouriant 38
 –Insinger 46
 –Oxyrhynchus 44, 46
paraenetic texts 41
 –organized thematically, by first letter, or randomly 46–47
parallel text of the *Disticha* 152
parity, helps friendship 95–97
parsimony, reprehensible 133–134
Parvus Cato (anonymous French work) 185
Parvus Cato (Daniel of Beccles) 185
Parvus Cato (Epistula and *Breves Sententiae,* without the *Maxims)* 5, 147 n.471
patria potestas 123
patronage, omitted from the *Disticha* 87–88
peculium 123
Pedro I, king of Portugal 144
Penkethman, John 181 n.592, 197

Pepin, Ronald E. 183, 198
Perraud, Louis A. 183
Petrarch 141
Petronius 39, 124–125, 128 n.419
Phaedrus 78, 117
Philemon and Baucis 120
philosophical *vs.* popular texts as evidence 104, 106–107
Phocylides 44
–Pseudo-Phocylides, *Sententiae* 44, 45 n.163
Phoinix of Colophon, *Sententiae* 44 n.160
Photius 47
Piers Plowman (Langland) xiv
Pistorius 183 n.597
plague 176
Planudes, Maximus 165, 174, 184 n.604, 202
Platter, Thomas 151
Plautus 129 n.422
Plebiscitum Claudianum 114 n.373
Pliny the Elder 20, 115 n.377, 124, 131 n.427
Pliny the Younger 20 n.95, 134 n.436
Plutarch 20, 78, 80, 83, 89, 92–93, 99, 102
Poetae Latini Minores 158
politics, absent from the *Disticha* 66, 72
Posidonius 117
"posing Cato" 151 n.492
poverty
–absolute and relative 119–121
–elite attitudes toward 119–121
–feigned 121
–not to be feared 127–131
primary and secondary meanings in proverbial language 70
print, move to 164
printing, vastly increased production of editions and commentaries 177
probatio pennae 142–143
problematic friends 96–101
prohibitions, grammar of 60–61
Prosper, *Epigrammata* 154
Proverbia Grecorum 142 n.447

proverbial language in the *Disticha* 68–71
proverbs, as a genre 101–102, 105–106
Proverbs, Biblical Book of 46 n.169, 51
Proverbs of Alfred xv
Prudentius, *Psychomachia* 154
Publilius Syrus *see* Syrus, Publilius
publishers, making money from the *Disticha* 165–166
Pyrrhus 132

Q
Quedam dicta Catonis per antifrasin exposita (anonymous) 187
Quintilian 39

R
Rape of Proserpina (Claudian) 153
Raymond de Beziers xiv
reading lists for Medieval schools 147–148
reception studies xvii
reciprocity, in friendship 77–88, 103–104, 106
Remigius of Auxerre 20–21, 22 n.103, 91, 141–142, 164
reputation, importance of 133–137
Rhetorica ad Herennium xvii, 54–55, 61 n.217, 62 n.218
Rodríguez, Alonso xv, 186
Roman borrowings from Greek xxiii–xxiv

S
sailing, dangers of 113–115
Sallust 136–137
saving and spending 109–117
Scaliger, Joseph Justus 155, 174, 180
scholia, Homeric 159
The Schoole of Slovenrie: Or, Cato turnd wrong side outward 187
schools
–monastic *vs.* lay 143
–use of the *Disticha* in 37–38, 141
Schulz, Charles M. 191
Scriverius 155
Sedulius, *Carmen Paschale* 154
self-interest, in friendship 86–87

self-referentiality 12
Senatus consultum Macedonianum 123 n.398
'Seneca', *Proverbia Senecae* 155
Seneca the Elder 41
Seneca the Younger 22, 26 n.115, 37, 42 n.150, 78, 80, 82–84, 89, 104, 108, 117
– *De Beneficiis* 84–85
– *De Tranquillitate Animi* 133
– *Epistulae Morales* 101, 112–115, 122, 131
sententiae 102
– popularity of in the late Republic 41
Sententiae Menandri 44 n.160, 49–50
Sententiae Septem Sapientum 28 n.116
Sententiae Sextii 49
Sententiae Varronis 42
Septuagint 42
Serenus Sammonicus 45 n.165
– *De Medicina Praecepta* 154 n.504
Sergius Orata, Gaius 115 n.377
Servius, commentary on the *Aeneid* 159
Shakespeare, William
– *All's Well that Ends Well* xiii
– *Hamlet* xvi
– *Much Ado about Nothing* xiii
– *Othello* xiii
Sharing Ancient Wisdoms (SAWS) project xxvi
Sibylline Oracles 44 n.161
Simon VII, Count of Lippe-Detmold 151
Simonides 125
slaves
– in the *Disticha* 66 n.230
– mentioned but not advised in the *Disticha* 38
social capital xxiv
social history, Roman xvii–xviii
social mobility 127–128
socius 77 n.148, 87, 95
sodalis 77 n.148
Solon 37–38
sportulae 124 n.406
statements of wisdom, grammar of 61–62
Statius, *Achilleid* 153
stemma codicum of the *Disticha* 18, 19 fig.1

Stobaeus 50
stylistic analysis, difficulties of 56 n.204
Sumerian Proverbs 49 n.182
Supplementum Catonis (anonymous French work) 185
Supplementum Catonis (spoof of the maxims) 185 n.606
Syriac translations 49
Syrus, Publilius 41, 44, 101, 103–105, 127

T
Tagliento, Giovanni Antonio 186
Taverner, Richard 165
teaching with reprimands vs. praise 71
Téoli, Carlo 183 n.600, 202
textual companions to editions 153
theft of property, dealing with 128–129
thematic groupings in some manuscripts 17–18
thematic similarities to other wisdom texts, not necessarily from borrowing 50–52
Theodulus, *Eclogues* 153–154
Theognidea 44, 45 n.163
Thomson, Ian 183
Tiro 41
trades and occupations 124–125
– worthy and unworthy, according to Cicero 125
traditio Barberina 16, 34
traditio vulgata 16, 19, 34
tradition and memory, not a concern of the *Disticha Catonis* 52
transformations and rewritings of the *Disticha Catonis* 185–189
– English 187–189
– German 188
– Italian 186
– parodies 187–189
– Welsh 186
translation
– balanced between covert and overt 173
– change from covert to overt 176
– covert 170
– overt vs. covert 169
translations of the *Disticha Catonis*
– American 181–182

–Anglo-Norman 172
–Anglo-Saxon 170–172
–Bohemian 184
–Catalan 176 n.578, 200
–classicizing, hexameter 174
–Croatian 184
–Danish 184
–dual-language (Latin and vernacular) 175
–Dutch 183, 196
–Early Modern 179–182
–English 165, 180–181, 183, 196–198
–fewer since the 19th century 183
–French 164–165, 179–180, 183, 198–200
–German 169 n.553, 180, 183, 193–195
–Gesamtübersetzungen (complete German) 175
–Greek 165, 174, 202
–Hungarian 183–184
–Icelandic 171, 184
–immense number of 168–169
–interlinear 181
–Irish 184
–Italian 183, 201–202
–lists of 169 n.551
–Mediaeval 169–184
–Modern 183–183
–Old Czech 184
–Old Lorrain 172 n.566
–Old Provençal 172 n.566, 199
–Old Venetian 173–174
–paraphrasing 181
–Polish 195
–Rumpfübersetzung (partial German) 174–175
–Spanish 174–176, 181, 200–201
–Swedish 184
transmission of the *Disticha* 16–19
Trebonius 41

U
universities, *Disticha* taught in 150
Urbanus Magnus (Daniel of Beccles) 185
utilitas vs. opes 116–117

V
Valentinian II, emperor 8, 36, 89, 105
Valerius Maximus 62 n.220, 78, 93, 102, 109, 115 n.377, 119–120, 131 n.427, 132
Varro 42
Venus 170
verbs, Author's favorite 64–65
Vergil 10, 12, 26
–*Aeneid* 32–33, 35
–*Georgics* 32–33, 126
Verino, Michael 186, xvi
vernacular literature, increasing importance of 179
verse texts, easier to memorize, preferred in Medieval schools 148
Vindicianus 8, 31, 36, 89, 105
virtues and vices, universal 51–52
vocabulary, commonplace 63

W
wealth
–evils of 133
–inherited 123, 135
–not to be coveted 129–132
–right and wrong ways of acquiring 136–137
wisdom
–timeless, in the *Disticha* 67
–universal xxi n.25, 51–52
wisdom figures as authors of paraenetic literature 42–43
wisdom literature xvii–xviii
–Akkadian 43 n.156
–best overview of 41 n.146
–Egyptian 43–44
–forms of, listed 40–41
–Mesopotamian 43
–modern work on xviii, xxi
–mostly in verse or elevated style 43
–normative grammar of 55
–paraenetic texts 41
–self-defining and self-affirming xxii
–Sumerian 43 n.156
–used in social situations xxii
Wisdom of Solomon (*Book of Wisdom*) 42
wives, and money 129–130
women

–and friendship   100–101
–mentioned but not advised in the
   Disticha   38
Wonder (Palacio)   190–192
wrong-doing to help a friend   91–92

Z
Zatočil, Leopold   183 n.603

Index Locorum

Anthologia Graeca
9.369 (Cyrillos) 44 n.160
16.275.7–10 (Posidippus) xiii n.2

Aphthonius
Progymnasmata
4 55 n.198

Aristotle
Rhetoric
1394a10–12 xxii
1394a21–25 15 n.79, 56 n.203,
 61 n.217
1394b1–3 62 n.218
1395a2–3 54
1395a6–7 63 n.221
1395b1–2 63 n.221
1395b18–33 54

Athenaeus
Deipnosophistae
577d–585f 39

Augustine
Confessions
2.3.5 108 n.353

Babrius
99 (= Perry 335 = Gibbs 50) 81–82
106 (= Perry 337 = Gibbs 19) 94 n.308

Carmina Burana
19 xv

Carmina Epigraphica (CE)
857 25 n.112, 27–28
1567 (= CIL 6.11252) 24–26
1988 (= CIL 6.37965) 25 n.112

Catullus
10.33–34 129 n.423

Cicero
Ad familiares
1.6 90
5.2 88 n.285
5.6 135 n.439
9.24.3 94 n.308
15.21.1–3 42 n.149
16.14.3 84 n.275
De amicitia
15 82
18 79 n.256
20 82 n.266
22 89
26–27 100
29 82 n.267
33 99
34 97
44 98
52–53 86 n.282
54 99
56 94
61 37 n.134, 92
63 99
69 97
71 98
76–77 99
95 80
De inventione
2.166 82
De officiis
1.48 84–85
1.150 125
2.87 111
3.43–44 37 n.134
3.43–46 92
3.84 86 n.282
In Verrem
I.4 136–137
Pro Caelio
36 129 n.423
Tusculanae disputationes
3.5 134 n.436

Cicero, Quintus (?)
Commentariolum petitionis
26, 29   103 n.339

Commodianus
Carmen apologeticum
15   29 n.117
67   29 n.117
Instructiones
1.32.1–2   29 n.117
1.35.15–16   29 n.117

Corpus Inscriptionum Latinorum (CIL)
6.11252 (= CE 1567)   24–26
6.37965 (= CE 1988)   25 n.112
11.600   28 n.116

Curtius Rufus
7.4.13   69 n.238

Cyrillos
Anthologia Graeca 9.369   44 n.160

De Remediis Fortuitorum
2.1   26 n.115

Demetrius
De elocutione 9   14 n.77

Dio Chrysostom
7.103–107   118 n.383

Disticha Catonis
'fifth book' (spurious) xiv n.5
Epistula   xiv n.5, 4–5, 15
1.1   8–9, 12, 22 n.106
1.2   177–179
1.3   62
1.4   169 n.553
1.6   116–117
1.9   98
1.10   62 n.220
1.11   72 n.245, 78–80
1.12   187
1.14   29 n.117, 68 n.235
1.16   5, 171 n.561
1.19   148 n.475
1.20   96–97
1.21   118–121
1.23   19 n.91, 97–98, 100
1.24   121–122
1.26   99–100, 167
1.27   68 n.236
1.28   122–125, 187
1.29   133–134
1.31   92 n.298
1.33   148 n.475
1.34   95–96
1.35   80–81
1.39   126–127
1.40   63 n.222, 93–94
2.Pref.   9–12
2.1   86–87, 170–171
2.2   25 n.112, 27–28, 166 n.540, 182 n.596
2.2a   166 n.540
2.3   24–26
2.5   115
2.6   53, 69 n.238, 70, 113–115
2.7   95
2.8   xxiii n.34, 136–137
2.9   8, 24, 89
2.10   96
2.17   110–111
2.19   134
2.22   24, 77, 88–90
2.22.2   8
2.26   xiii, 70 n.239
2.31   xiv n.6, 65 n.226
2.31a   7 n.63, 12
3.Pref.   11–13, 15
3.1   12
3.3   37, 91–93, 167
3.8   134–135
3.9   5, 85–86, 115–116
3.11   127–128
3.12   129–130
3.16   64 n.225
3.17   29–31
3.19   169–170
3.21   111–113, 188 n.616

3.24	141, 156 fig.3, 157 fig.4, 163–166, 165 n.537, 173, 193–202	**Horace** *Ars poetica* 325–332	110
		Epistulae	
4.Pref.	13	1.2.57	35
4.1	130–132	1.18.101	78 n.252
4.4	188 n.616	*Satirae*	
4.5	133	2.6	120
4.8	79 n.256		
4.10	26 n.113, 170	**Isidore**	
4.13	29 n.117, 90	*Etymologiae*	
4.15	87–88, 95	6.8.5	159 n.515
4.16	135		
4.17	xiv n.8, 29 n.117	**Juvenal**	
4.18	5	6	100
4.25	188		
4.28	90–91	**Livy**	
4.30	26 n.113	39.6.9	124
4.31	69 n.238		
4.33	69 n.238	**Lucian**	
4.35	128–129	*Anacharsis*	
4.36	77 n.248	21	37–38
4.36a	77 n.248		
4.39.2	25 n.112	**Macrobius**	
4.41	98–99	*Saturnalia*	
4.42	63 n.222, 83–85	2.1.12	42 n.149
4.47	100–101, 102 n.336, 106	**Martial**	
		2.51	135 n.437
4.49	xxiii n.35, 4–5, 12–15, 16 n.83, 31–32, 53, 56	3.7	124 n.406
		3.12–13	134 n.436
		4.15	113
		4.26	113
Eugenius of Toledo		4.51	135
Carmen 38	xiv n.5	5.81	113
		5.82	135 n.438
Euripides		6.5	113
Medea		7.92	113
294–295	54 n.196	8.19	121
		8.29	15 n.81, 31–32
Gellius, *Noctes Atticae*		9.14	94 n.308
1.3	37 n.134	9.50	32 n.121
1.6.2–3	129 n.423	11.32	121
1.17.1	129 n.423	14.216	69 n.237
11.2	20 n.94		
		Moretum	
		55–56	120

Ovid
Metamorphoses
8.611–724   120

Pappus
Synagoge
8.19   190

Papyri
P.Bad. 2.35.10   135 n.438
P.Bour. I   102 n.335
P.Flor. XXII (= P.Brookl.) 102 n.335
P.Insinger   46
P.Louvre 2414   43, 46 n.166
P.Oxy. 42.3004   42 n.152, 46
P.Oxy. 42.3004–6   44
P.Oxy. 50.3541   44

Pausanias
10.5.7–8   45 n.164

Petronius, *Satyrica*
38   124–125
46   124–125
55   39

Phaedrus, *Fabulae*
3.9.5–7 (= Perry 500 = Gibbs 94) 90 n.296
4.23 (= Perry 519 = Gibbs 412)   125
5.8 (= Perry 530 = Gibbs 536)   xiii n.3

Photius
Bibliotheca
cod. 175   47

Plautus
Aulularia
534–535   129
Casina
545   129 n.423

Pliny the Elder
Historia naturalis
18.108   124
29.16–23   77 n.247
33   115 n.377
33.48   131 n.427

Pliny the Younger
Epistulae
2.6.7   134 n.436
7.24   116 n.379

Plutarch
Moralia
49D-E   80
51B-C   83
53B   89
55A   89
94A   90 n.296, 99
94B   83
175E4   94 n.308
186C3   92
402D   45 n.164
531C   92 n.303
808A   92 n.303

Posidippus
Anthologia Graeca 16.275.7–10   xiii n.2

Publilius Syrus, see Syrus, Publilius

Quintilian
Institutio oratoria
6.3.5   42 n.149
6.3.42   42 n.149
8.5   39

Rhetorica ad Herrennium
4.17   62 n.218
4.17.24   xvii, 54–55, 61 n.217

Sallust
Catilina
9–13   112, 136–137

Seneca the Elder
Controversiae
7.3.8   41

Seneca the Younger
De beneficiis
2.21.2   84–85
3.9.1   85 n.280

3.18.1	84–85	**Syrus, Publilius**	
3.21.34	84–85	10	99
4.40	84 n.278	11	127
6.34.5	85 n.281	41	90
De tranquillitate animi		53	81
8.1	133	54	94
De vita beata		56	99
22.1	120	106	100
24.5	117	134	90
Epistulae morales		143	81
3.2	80	173	94
3.2–3	89	225	81
9.10	82–83	245	81
18.5–7	131	300	89
19	99 n.325, 114–115	522	98
19.10–11	94 n.308	549	94
19.11	85 n.281, 112	576	89
20.7–12	122	590	89
33.7	37 n.135	634	98
87.3	117		
87.5–6	113	**Valerius Maximus**	
87.18	131	3.4	132
94.9	38	3.5.2	132
99.8	26 n.115	4.3	132
115.16–17	128–129	4.4.pr.	119
119.7–9	131	4.7.1–7	93
		9.1	115 n.377
Servius		9.4.pr.	131 n.427
Aen.			
1.pr.	159 n.518	**Varro**	
		De agri cultura	
Suetonius		1.1.1	22 n.106
Augustus			
89.4	37 n.136	**Vergil**	
De grammaticis		*Aeneid*	
11	20 n.94	1.1	26
21	42 n.149	*Georgics*	
		3.318–320	126

www.ingramcontent.com/pod-product-compliance
Lightning Source LLC
Chambersburg PA
CBHW020225170426
43201CB00007B/326